Shojo Beat

BABY & Me

Vol. 8

Story & Art by Marimo Ragawa

BABY & ME

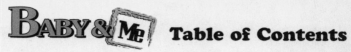

Table of Contents

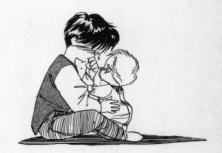

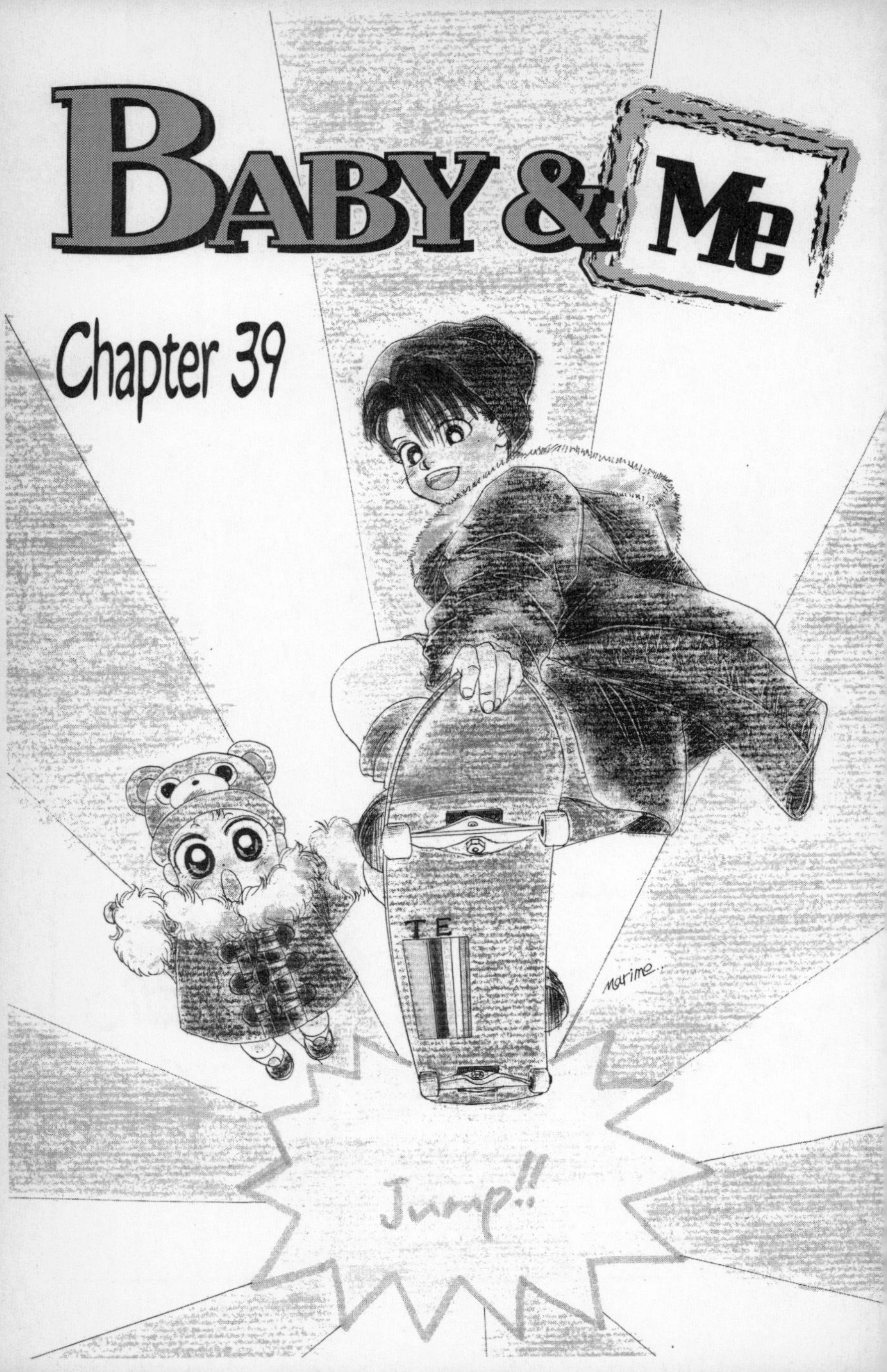
BABY & Me
Chapter 39
TE
marime.
Jump!!

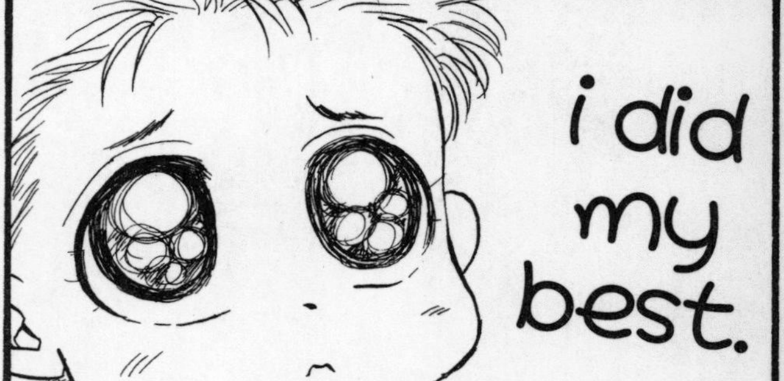
i did my best.

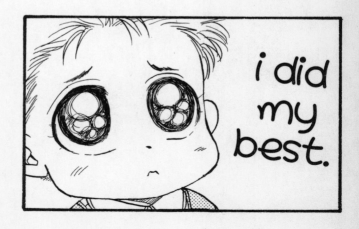

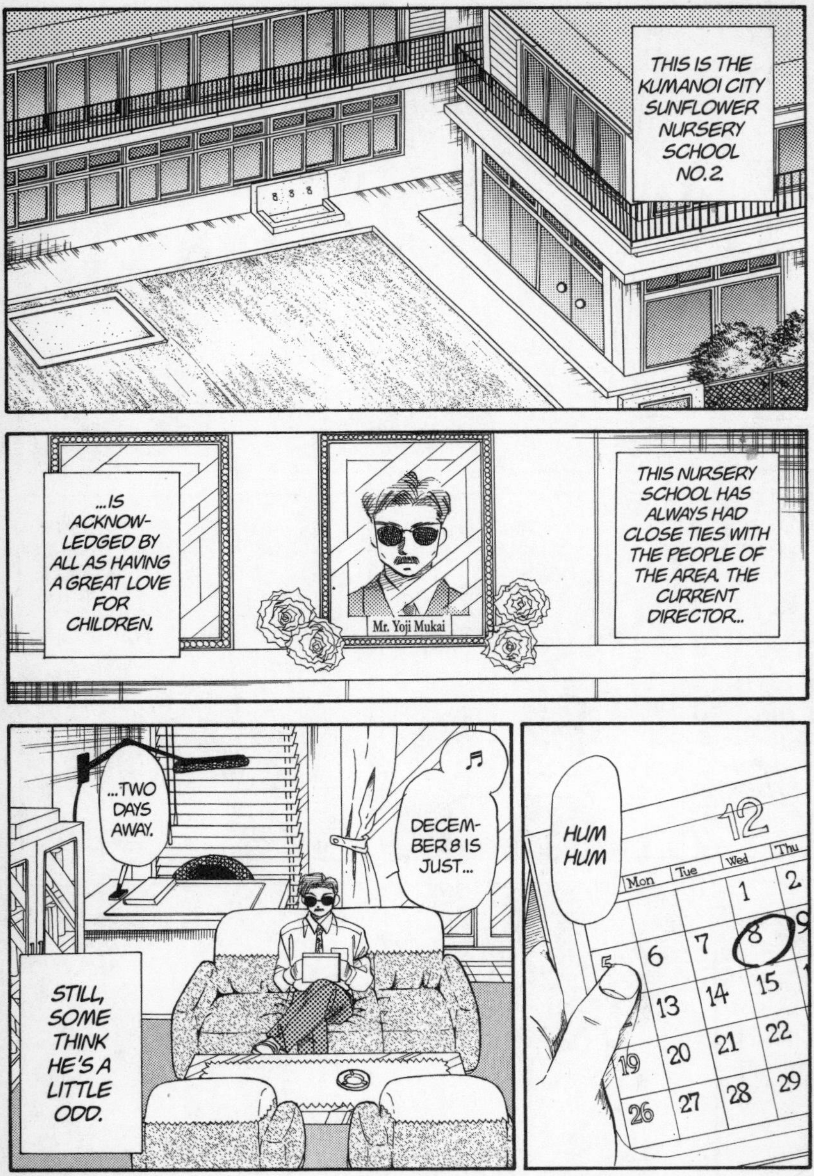
THIS IS THE KUMANOI CITY SUNFLOWER NURSERY SCHOOL NO.2.
THIS NURSERY SCHOOL HAS ALWAYS HAD CLOSE TIES WITH THE PEOPLE OF THE AREA. THE CURRENT DIRECTOR...
Mr. Yoji Mukai
...IS ACKNOW-LEDGED BY ALL AS HAVING A GREAT LOVE FOR CHILDREN.
HUM HUM
DECEM-BER 8 IS JUST...
...TWO DAYS AWAY.
STILL, SOME THINK HE'S A LITTLE ODD.

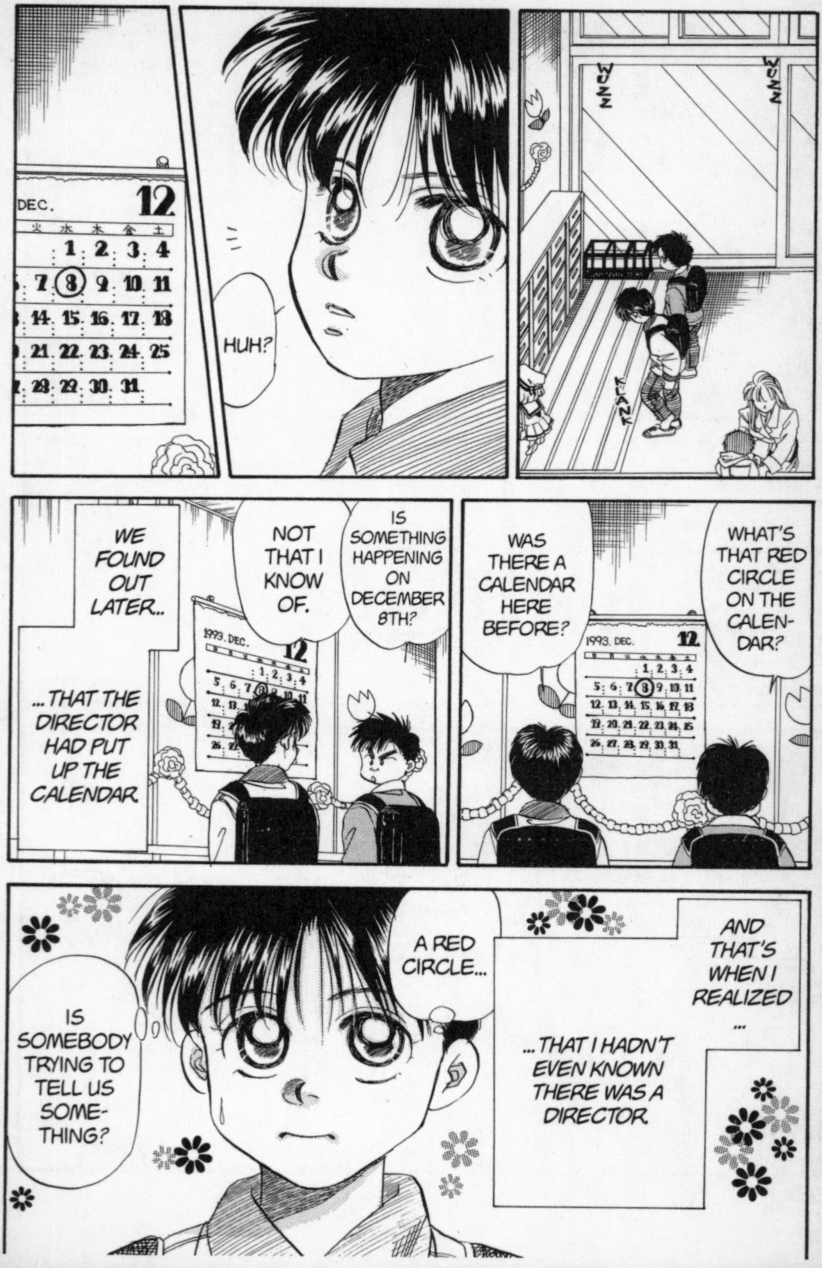
WUZZ
WUZZ
KLANK
HUH?
DEC.
12
WHAT'S THAT RED CIRCLE ON THE CALEN-DAR?
WAS THERE A CALENDAR HERE BEFORE?
IS SOMETHING HAPPENING ON DECEMBER 8TH?
NOT THAT I KNOW OF.
WE FOUND OUT LATER...
...THAT THE DIRECTOR HAD PUT UP THE CALENDAR.
AND THAT'S WHEN I REALIZED ...
...THAT I HADN'T EVEN KNOWN THERE WAS A DIRECTOR.
A RED CIRCLE...
IS SOMEBODY TRYING TO TELL US SOME-THING?

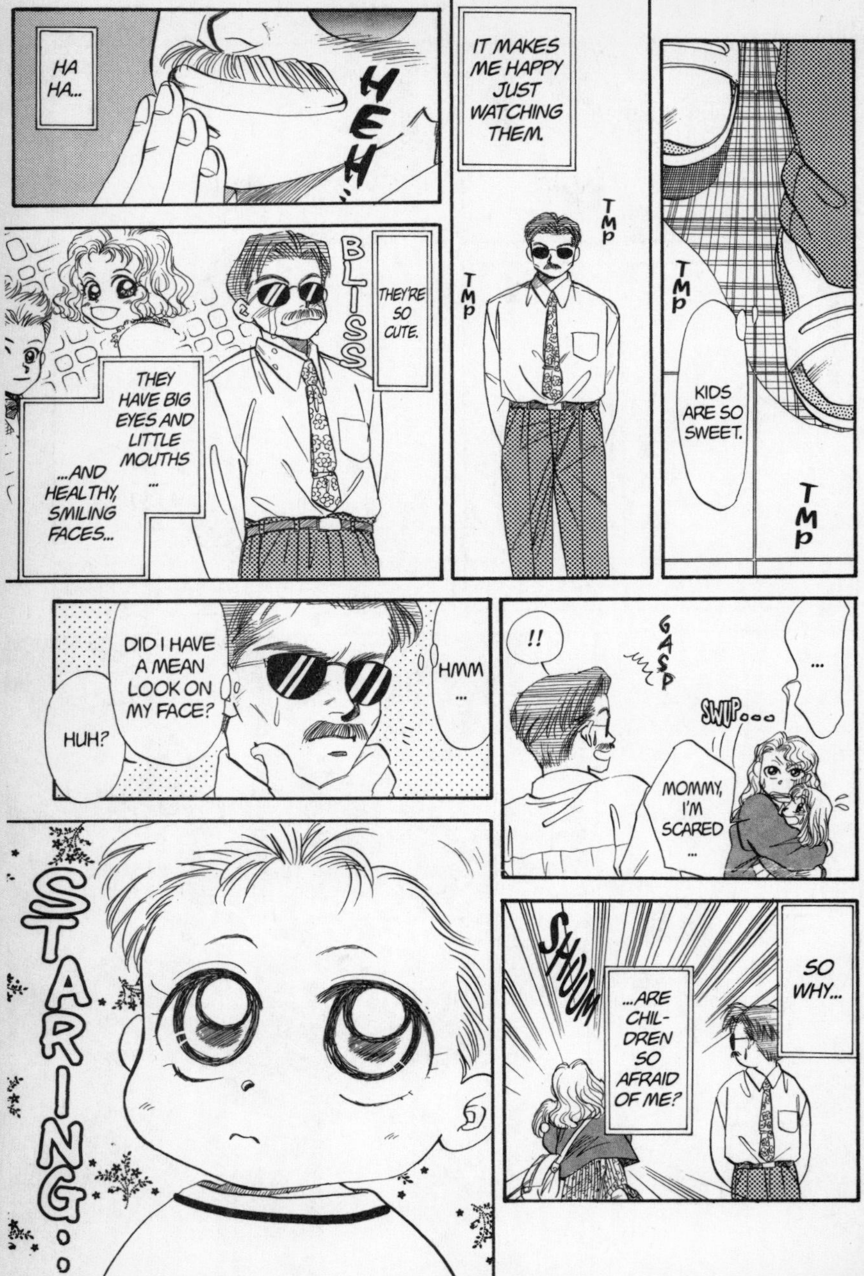

KIDS ARE SO SWEET.
TMP
TMP
IT MAKES ME HAPPY JUST WATCHING THEM.
TMP
TMP
HA HA...
HEH...
BLISS
THEY'RE SO CUTE.
THEY HAVE BIG EYES AND LITTLE MOUTHS...
...AND HEALTHY, SMILING FACES...
!!
GASP
...
SWUP...
MOMMY, I'M SCARED...
HMM...
DID I HAVE A MEAN LOOK ON MY FACE?
HUH?
SO WHY...
SHOOM
...ARE CHILDREN SO AFRAID OF ME?
STARING...

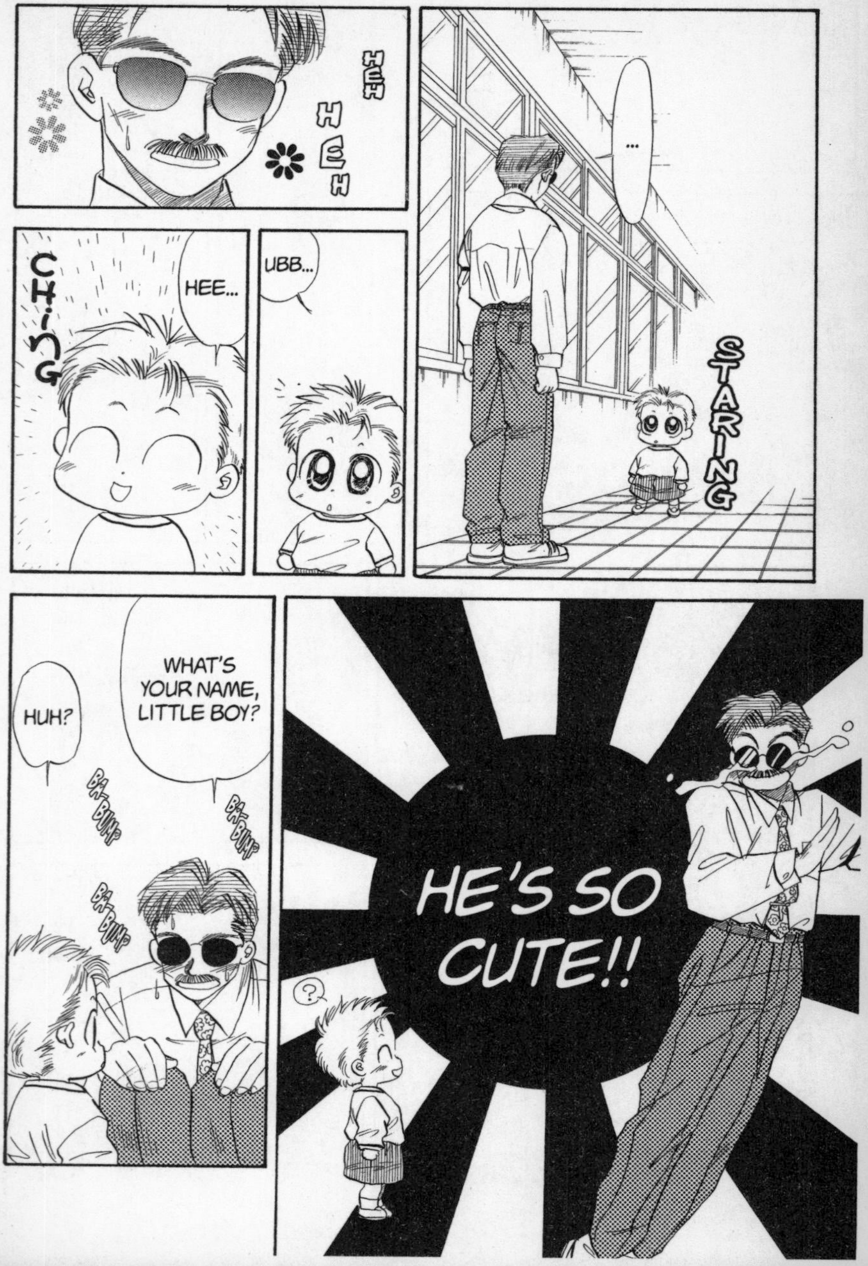
...
STARING
HEH HEH
UBB...
HEE...
CHING
HE'S SO CUTE!!
WHAT'S YOUR NAME, LITTLE BOY?
HUH?
BA-BUMP
BA-BUMP
BA-BUMP

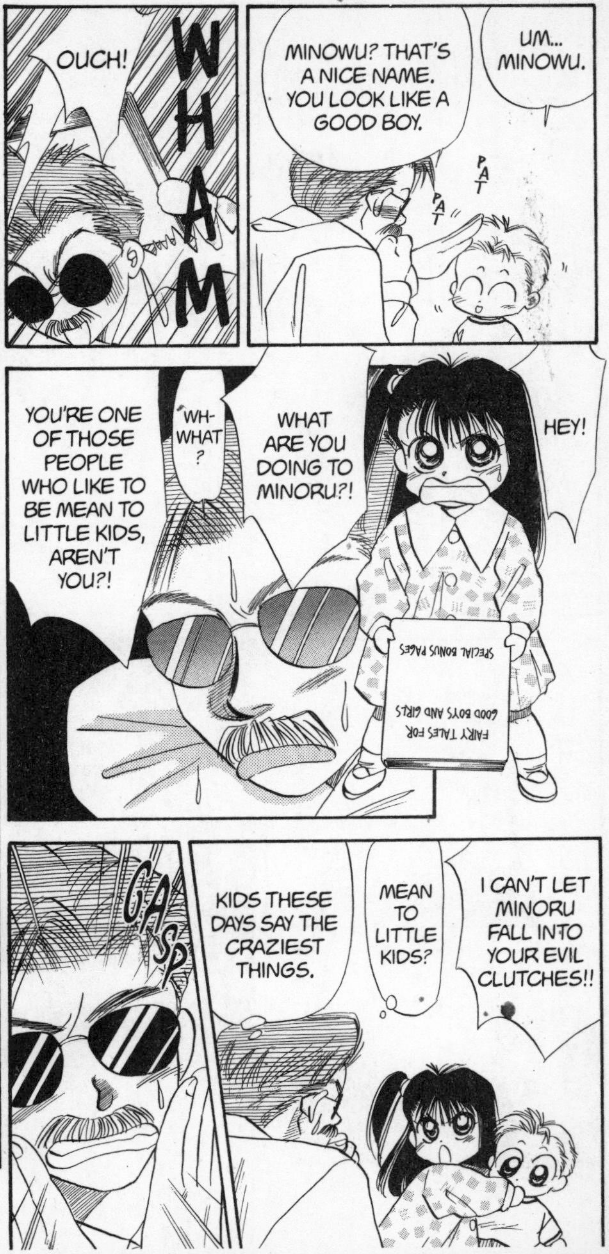
UM... MINOWU.
MINOWU? THAT'S A NICE NAME. YOU LOOK LIKE A GOOD BOY.
PAT PAT
WHAM
OUCH!
HEY!
WHAT ARE YOU DOING TO MINORU?!
WH-WHAT?
YOU'RE ONE OF THOSE PEOPLE WHO LIKE TO BE MEAN TO LITTLE KIDS, AREN'T YOU?!
FAIRY TALES FOR GOOD BOYS AND GIRLS
SPECIAL BONUS PAGES
I CAN'T LET MINORU FALL INTO YOUR EVIL CLUTCHES!!
MEAN TO LITTLE KIDS?
KIDS THESE DAYS SAY THE CRAZIEST THINGS.
GASP

Author's Note 1

Hello, Ragawa here. So, Baby and Me is already up to volume 8. Heh heh heh... (Ragawa grins.)

HUM DEE DUM

HUM DEE DUM

What an awful back view... 💧💧

In the story about Sachiko (the rabbit in volume 2), Sachiko drank milk, but that's because she was still a baby. Adult rabbits drink water. They eat raw vegetables, but not wet ones. Yoshizo really loves corn.

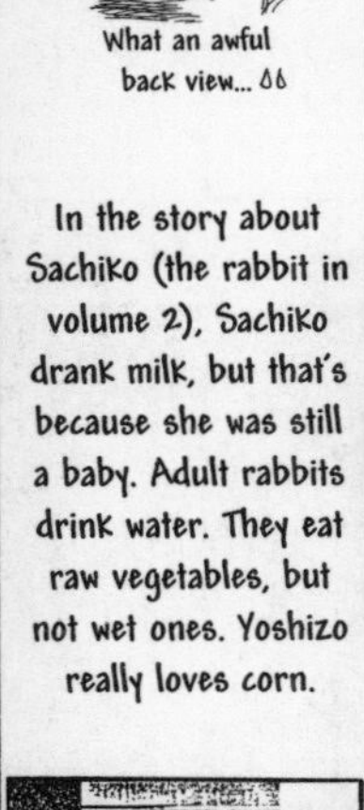
赤ちゃんと僕

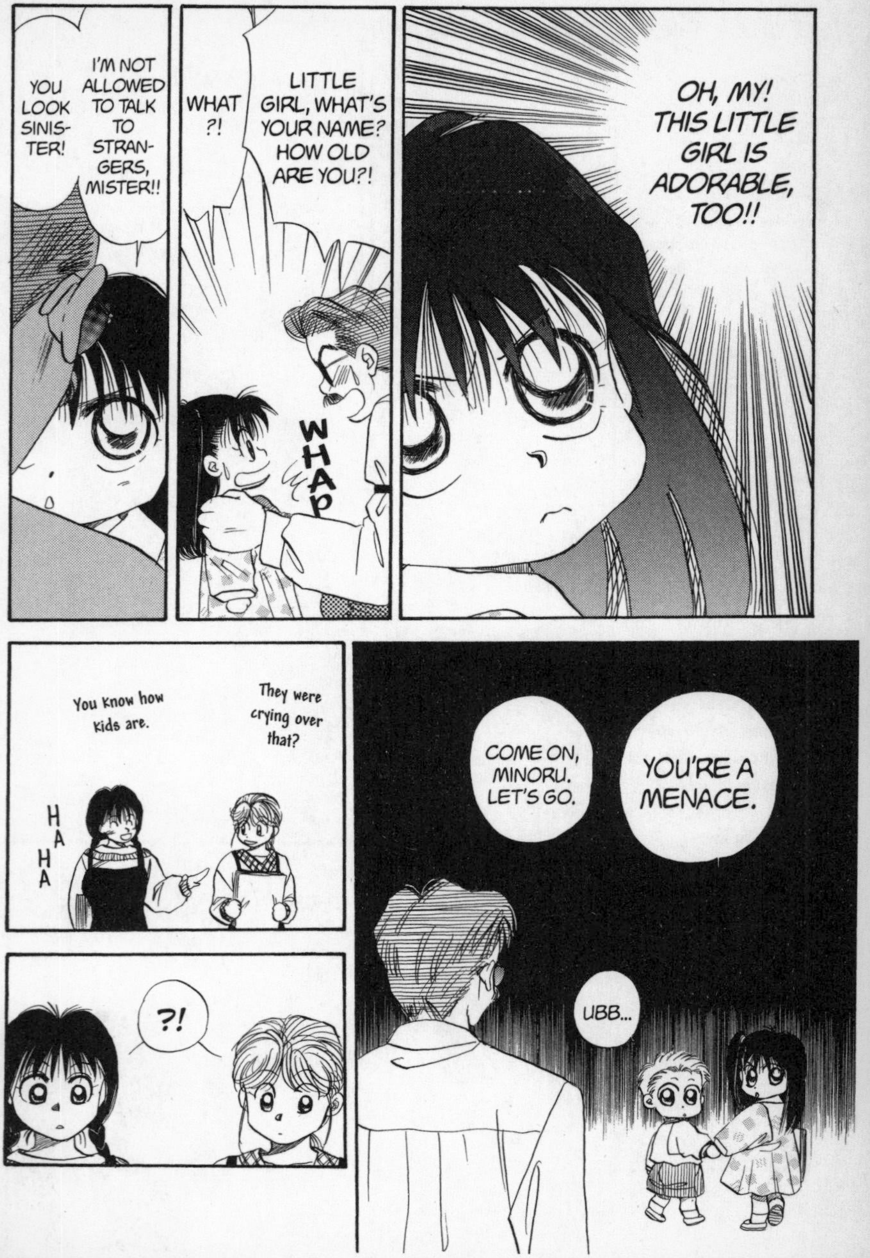
OH, MY! THIS LITTLE GIRL IS ADORABLE, TOO!!
LITTLE GIRL, WHAT'S YOUR NAME? HOW OLD ARE YOU?!
WHAT ?!
WHAP
I'M NOT ALLOWED TO TALK TO STRANGERS, MISTER!!
YOU LOOK SINISTER!
YOU'RE A MENACE.
COME ON, MINORU. LET'S GO.
UBB...
They were crying over that?
You know how kids are.
HA HA
?!

PANDA CLASS

YACK
YACK

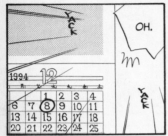

OH.

1994 12

	1	2	3	4
6	7	8	9	10	11
13	14	15	16	17	18
20	21	22	23	24	25

YACK

OH, HE STARTLED ME.

TWITCH

GLOOM...

A MENACE?

MR. MUKAI, COULD YOU PLEASE GO SOMEWHERE ELSE? YOU'LL SCARE THE CHILDREN.

ACTUALLY, I HEAR THEY DON'T GET ALONG.

THEY MUST BE VERY CLOSE IF THEY BOTH CHOSE THE SAME PROFESSION.

YACK
YACK

DID YOU KNOW THAT THE DIRECTOR OF SUNFLOWER NURSERY NO.1 IS MR. MUKAI'S OLDER BROTHER?

NO, I DIDN'T.

DECEMBER 8?! I WONDER WHAT HE'S TRYING TO TELL US.

LOOK. THE DIRECTOR'S PUT A CIRCLE ON THE CALENDARS IN ALL OF THE CLASSROOMS.

Hmph! That man...

TEACHER
TEACHER

OKAY!

LET'S GO HOME.

YACK
YACK

MI-NORU...

11

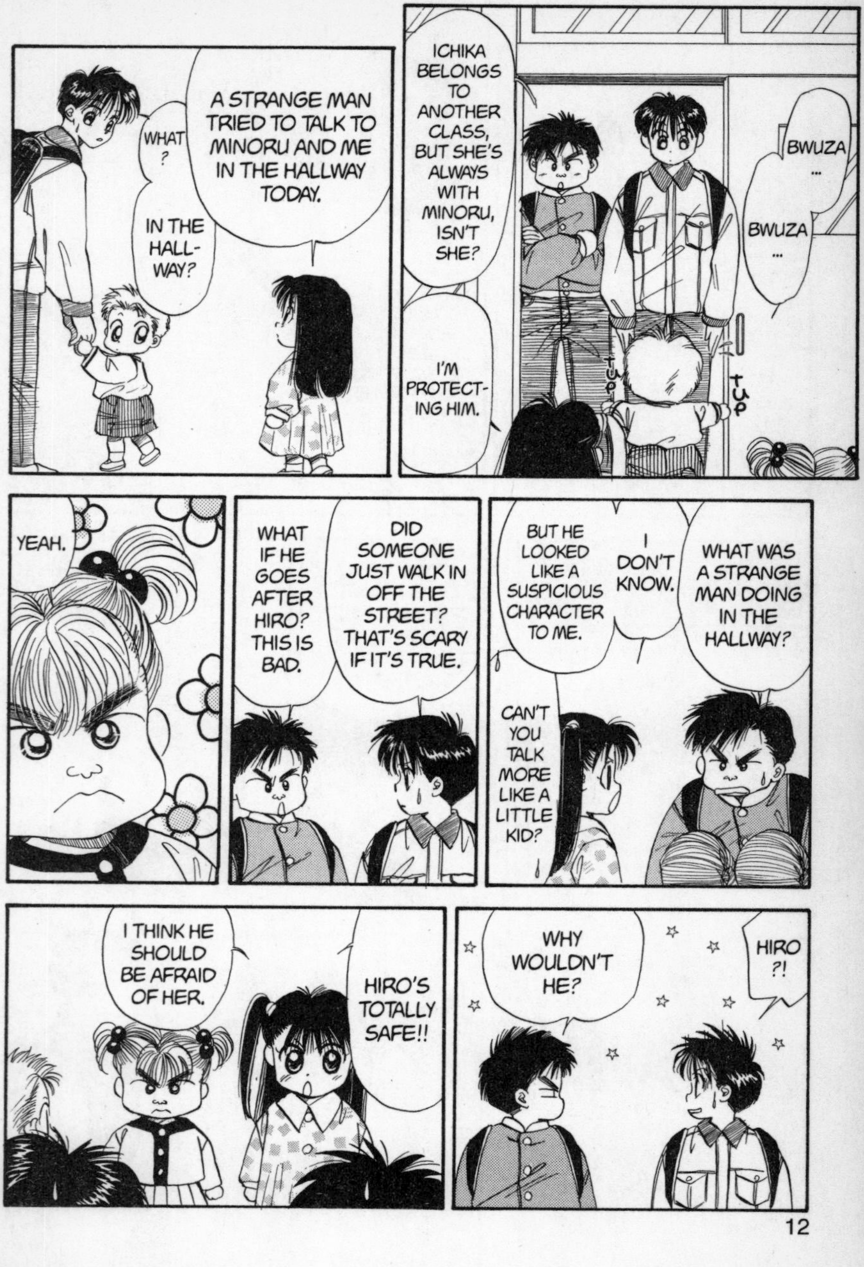
BWUZA ... BWUZA ...
ICHIKA BELONGS TO ANOTHER CLASS, BUT SHE'S ALWAYS WITH MINORU, ISN'T SHE?
I'M PROTECTING HIM.
TUP TUP
A STRANGE MAN TRIED TO TALK TO MINORU AND ME IN THE HALLWAY TODAY.
WHAT?
IN THE HALL-WAY?
WHAT WAS A STRANGE MAN DOING IN THE HALLWAY?
I DON'T KNOW.
BUT HE LOOKED LIKE A SUSPICIOUS CHARACTER TO ME.
CAN'T YOU TALK MORE LIKE A LITTLE KID?
DID SOMEONE JUST WALK IN OFF THE STREET? THAT'S SCARY IF IT'S TRUE.
WHAT IF HE GOES AFTER HIRO? THIS IS BAD.
YEAH.
HIRO ?!
WHY WOULDN'T HE?
HIRO'S TOTALLY SAFE!!
I THINK HE SHOULD BE AFRAID OF HER.

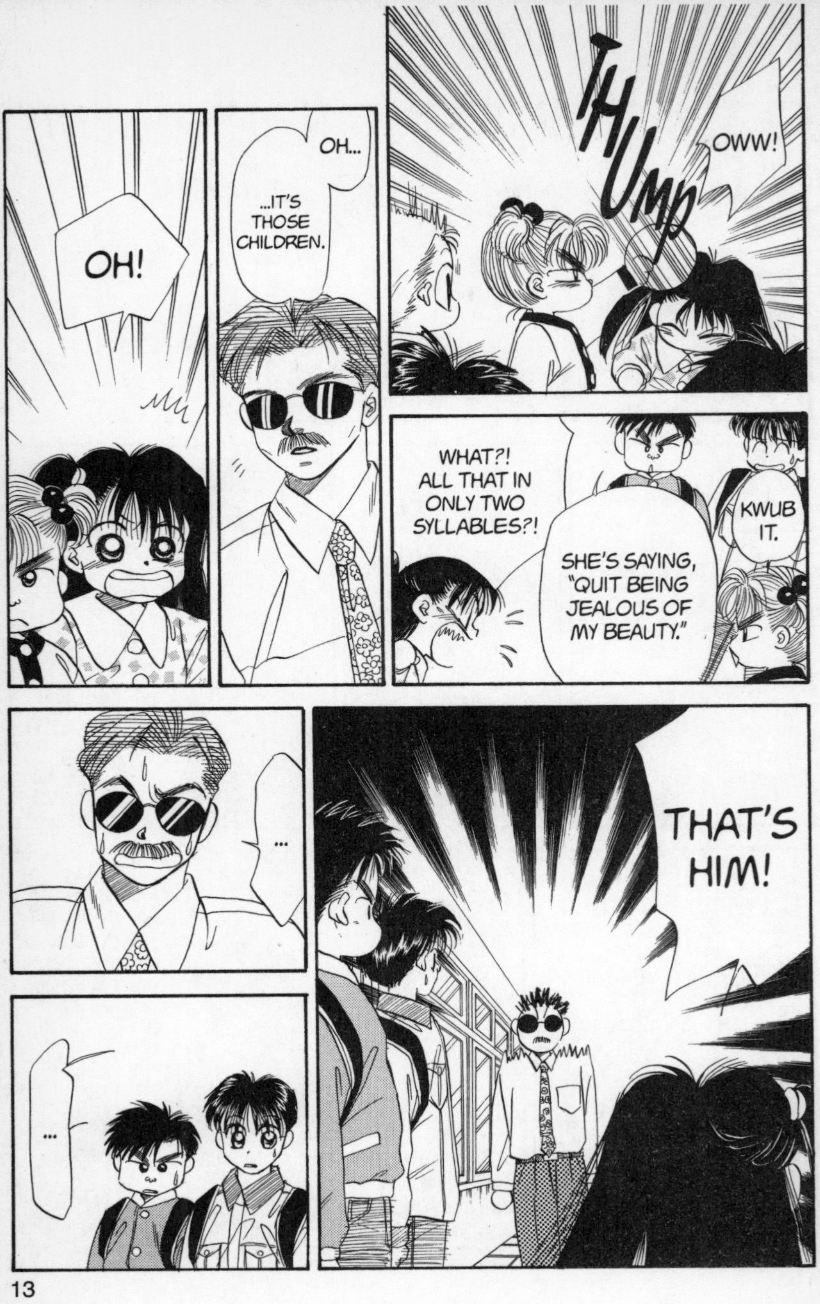
THUMP
OWW!
KWUB IT.
SHE'S SAYING, "QUIT BEING JEALOUS OF MY BEAUTY."
WHAT?! ALL THAT IN ONLY TWO SYLLABLES?!
OH...
...IT'S THOSE CHILDREN.
OH!
THAT'S HIM!
...
...

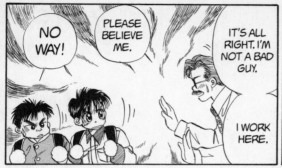

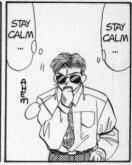

STAY CALM ...
STAY CALM ...
AHEM
IT'S ALL RIGHT. I'M NOT A BAD GUY.
I WORK HERE.
PLEASE BELIEVE ME.
NO WAY!
MINOWU, I DIDN'T HURT YOU, DID I?
HUH?
...
GUESS WHAT! GUESS WHAT! I WIKE DA BUBBA FIVE!
HUH?
WELL, ISN'T THAT NICE?
SEE? HE ACTS SO INNOCENT, BUT HE'S FINDING OUT WHAT MINORU LIKES.
HE IS A SUSPI-CIOUS CHARAC-TER.
HE VOLUNTEERED THAT INFORMATION!!
UM... YOU SAID YOU WORK HERE. ARE YOU A TEACHER?
HMM?

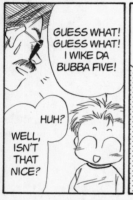

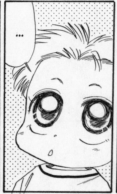

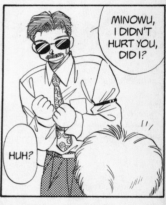

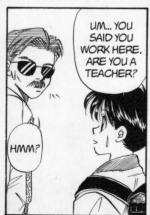

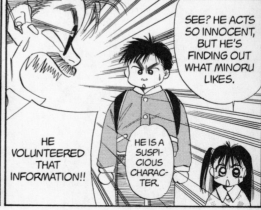

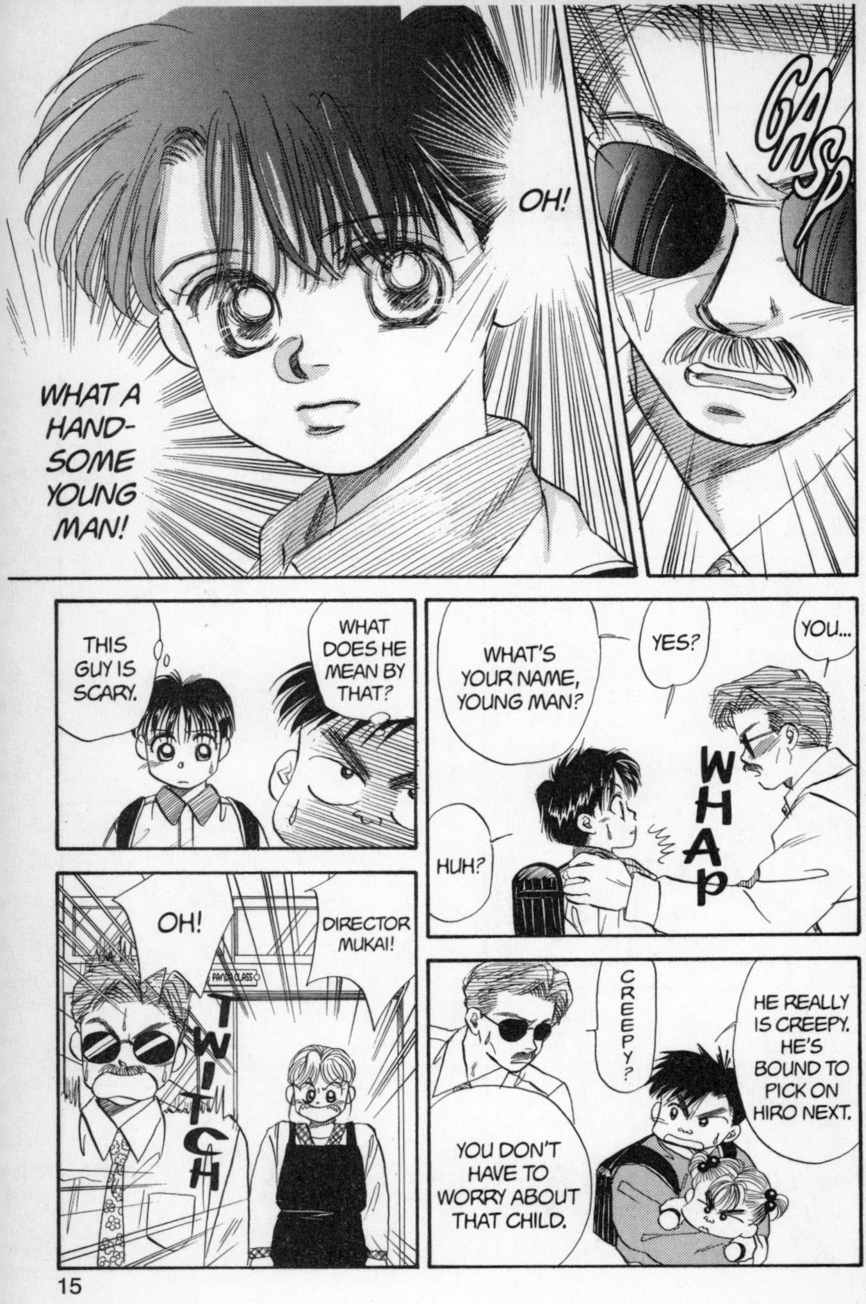
GASP
OH!
WHAT A HANDSOME YOUNG MAN!
YOU...
YES?
WHAT'S YOUR NAME, YOUNG MAN?
WHAP
HUH?
WHAT DOES HE MEAN BY THAT?
THIS GUY IS SCARY.
HE REALLY IS CREEPY. HE'S BOUND TO PICK ON HIRO NEXT.
CREEPY?
YOU DON'T HAVE TO WORRY ABOUT THAT CHILD.
DIRECTOR MUKAI!
OH!
PANDA CLASS
TWITCH

BUT I LOVE KIDS! REALLY, I DO!!

YOU PROBABLY SCARED TAKUYA HALF TO DEATH!!

WHY DO YOU ALWAYS HAVE TO LOOK SO SINISTER?

WAAH

WHY ARE YOU POKING ME?

PLEASE DON'T USE EXPRESSIONS THAT CAN BE MISUNDER-STOOD.

PLEASE STOP BARING YOUR FANGS AT THE CHILDREN.

I-I'M SORRY!!

YOU'RE NOT SUPPOSED TO PUT PERSONAL NOTATIONS ON ALL THE SCHOOL CALENDARS!!

GAAH

OUCH.

KRAK

DON'T ACT INNO-CENT.

OH, MS. KOBAYASHI ...

WHY DID YOU DO THAT?

SHE ACTS MORE DIGNIFIED THAN MR. MUKAI, SO PEOPLE TEND TO THINK SHE'S THE DIRECTOR.

SHE'S THE OLDEST TEACHER HERE.

OLD LADY ?

WHO'S THAT OLD LADY?

I've seen her here before.

...IS THIS ?!

WHAT ...

DECEMBER

SUNDAY	MONDAY	TUESDAY	WEDNESDAY	THURSDAY	FRIDAY	SATURDAY
		1	2	3	4	
5	6	7	8	9	10	11
12	13	14	15	16	17	18
19	20	21	22	23	24	25
26	27	28	29	30	31	

16

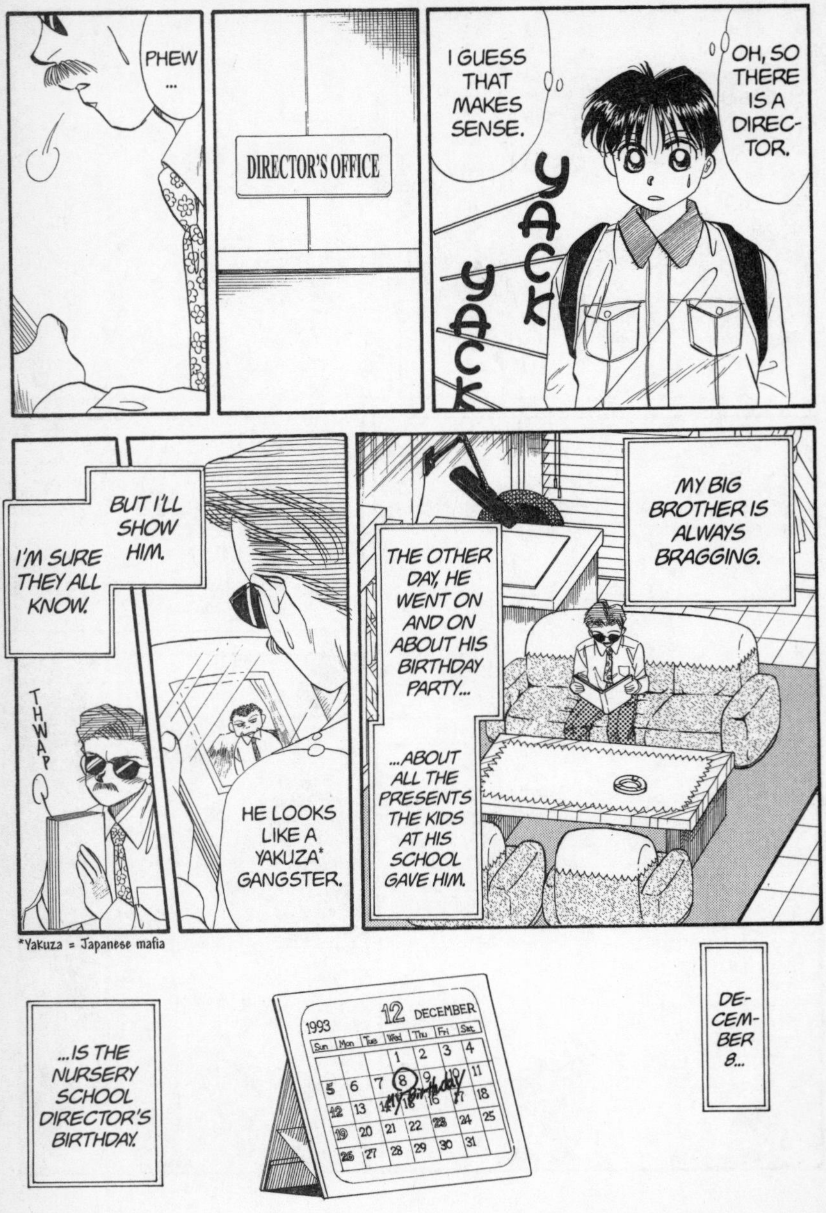
OH, SO THERE IS A DIREC-TOR.
I GUESS THAT MAKES SENSE.
YACK
YACK
DIRECTOR'S OFFICE
PHEW ...
MY BIG BROTHER IS ALWAYS BRAGGING.
THE OTHER DAY, HE WENT ON AND ON ABOUT HIS BIRTHDAY PARTY...
...ABOUT ALL THE PRESENTS THE KIDS AT HIS SCHOOL GAVE HIM.
HE LOOKS LIKE A YAKUZA* GANGSTER.
BUT I'LL SHOW HIM.
I'M SURE THEY ALL KNOW.
THWAP
DE-CEM-BER 8...
1993
12 DECEMBER
MY Birthday
...IS THE NURSERY SCHOOL DIRECTOR'S BIRTHDAY.

*Yakuza = Japanese mafia

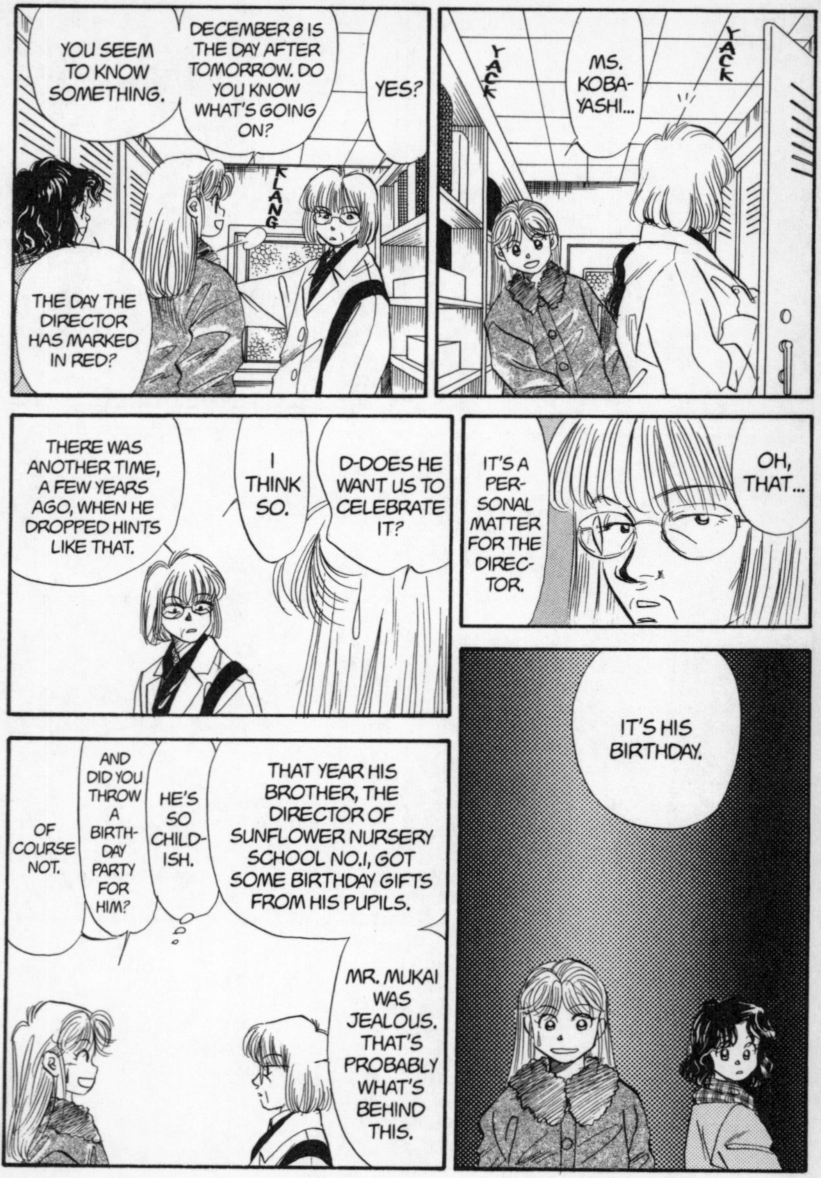
YACK
MS. KOBA-YASHI...
YACK
YES?
DECEMBER 8 IS THE DAY AFTER TOMORROW. DO YOU KNOW WHAT'S GOING ON?
YOU SEEM TO KNOW SOMETHING.
KLANG
THE DAY THE DIRECTOR HAS MARKED IN RED?
OH, THAT...
IT'S A PER-SONAL MATTER FOR THE DIREC-TOR.
D-DOES HE WANT US TO CELEBRATE IT?
I THINK SO.
THERE WAS ANOTHER TIME, A FEW YEARS AGO, WHEN HE DROPPED HINTS LIKE THAT.
IT'S HIS BIRTHDAY.
THAT YEAR HIS BROTHER, THE DIRECTOR OF SUNFLOWER NURSERY SCHOOL NO.1, GOT SOME BIRTHDAY GIFTS FROM HIS PUPILS.
HE'S SO CHILD-ISH.
AND DID YOU THROW A BIRTH-DAY PARTY FOR HIM?
OF COURSE NOT.
MR. MUKAI WAS JEALOUS. THAT'S PROBABLY WHAT'S BEHIND THIS.

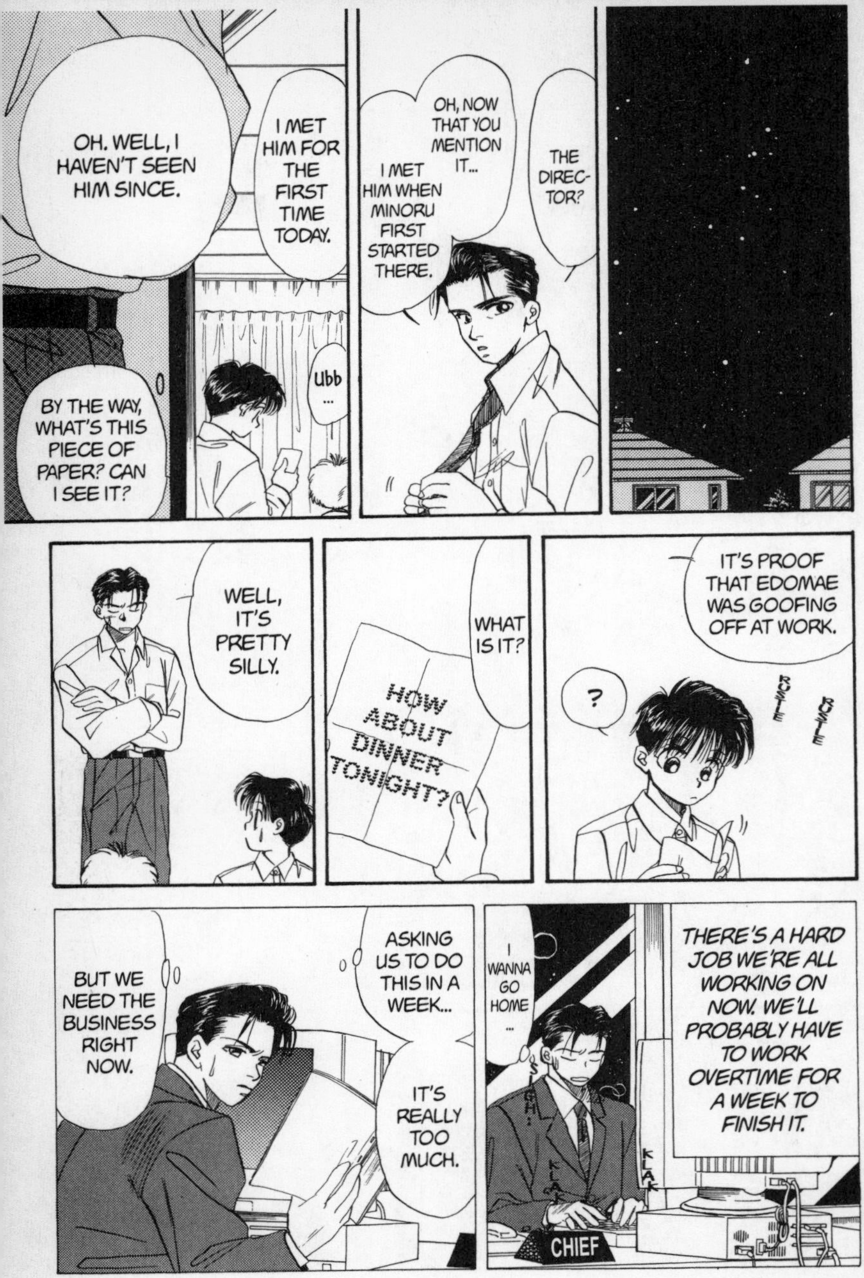
THE DIRECTOR?
OH, NOW THAT YOU MENTION IT...
I MET HIM WHEN MINORU FIRST STARTED THERE.
I MET HIM FOR THE FIRST TIME TODAY.
OH. WELL, I HAVEN'T SEEN HIM SINCE.
Ubb ...
BY THE WAY, WHAT'S THIS PIECE OF PAPER? CAN I SEE IT?
IT'S PROOF THAT EDOMAE WAS GOOFING OFF AT WORK.
RUSTLE
RUSTLE
?
WHAT IS IT?
HOW ABOUT DINNER TONIGHT?
WELL, IT'S PRETTY SILLY.
THERE'S A HARD JOB WE'RE ALL WORKING ON NOW. WE'LL PROBABLY HAVE TO WORK OVERTIME FOR A WEEK TO FINISH IT.
KLAK
I WANNA GO HOME ...
SIGH...
KLAK
CHIEF
ASKING US TO DO THIS IN A WEEK...
BUT WE NEED THE BUSINESS RIGHT NOW.
IT'S REALLY TOO MUCH.

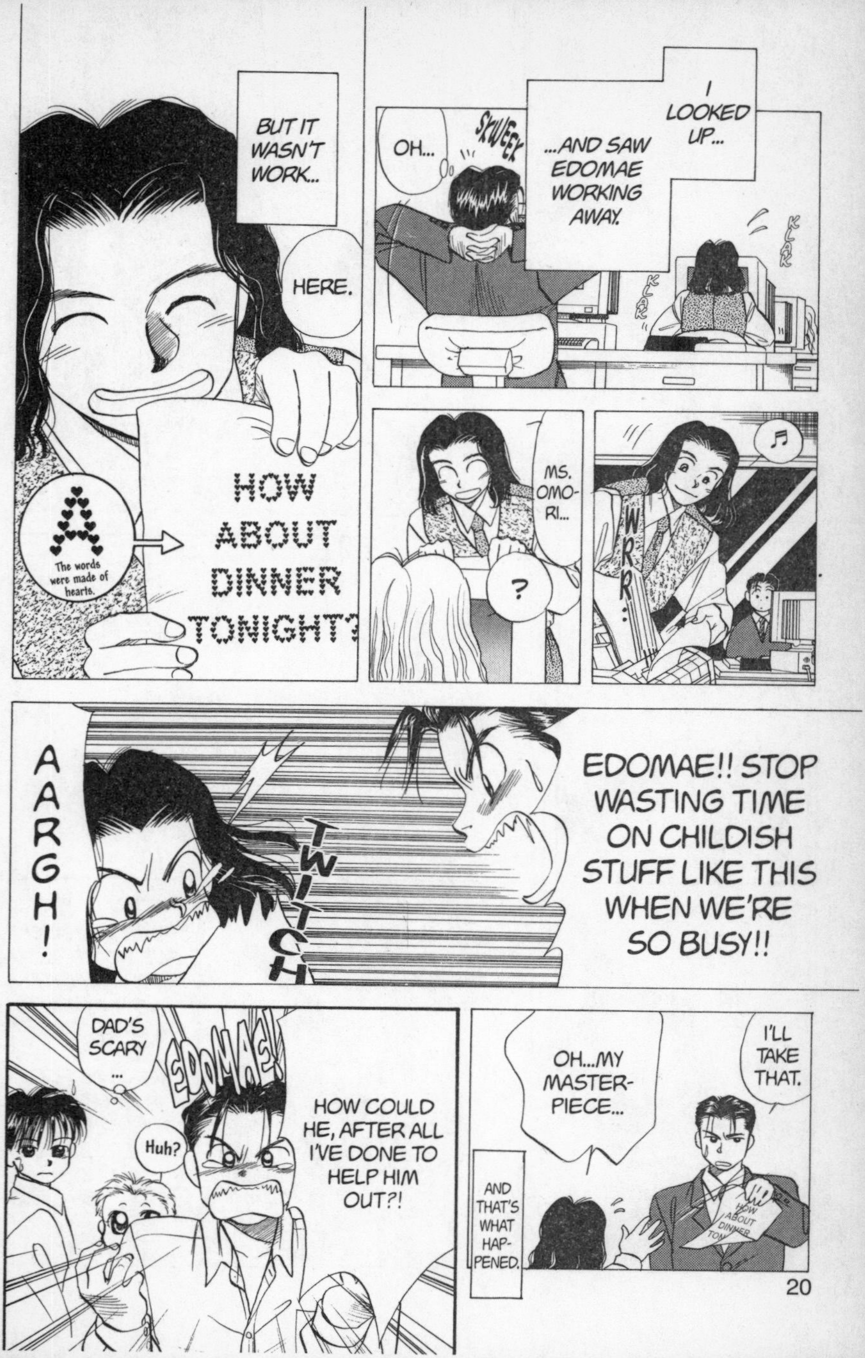
I LOOKED UP...
...AND SAW EDOMAE WORKING AWAY.
KLAK
KLAK
SKWEEK
OH...
♪
WRR
MS. OMORI...
?
BUT IT WASN'T WORK...
HERE.
HOW ABOUT DINNER TONIGHT?
The words were made of hearts.
EDOMAE!! STOP WASTING TIME ON CHILDISH STUFF LIKE THIS WHEN WE'RE SO BUSY!!
TWITCH
AARGH!
I'LL TAKE THAT.
OH...MY MASTERPIECE...
AND THAT'S WHAT HAPPENED.
HOW ABOUT DINNER TON
HOW COULD HE, AFTER ALL I'VE DONE TO HELP HIM OUT?!
EDOMAE!
DAD'S SCARY ...
Huh?

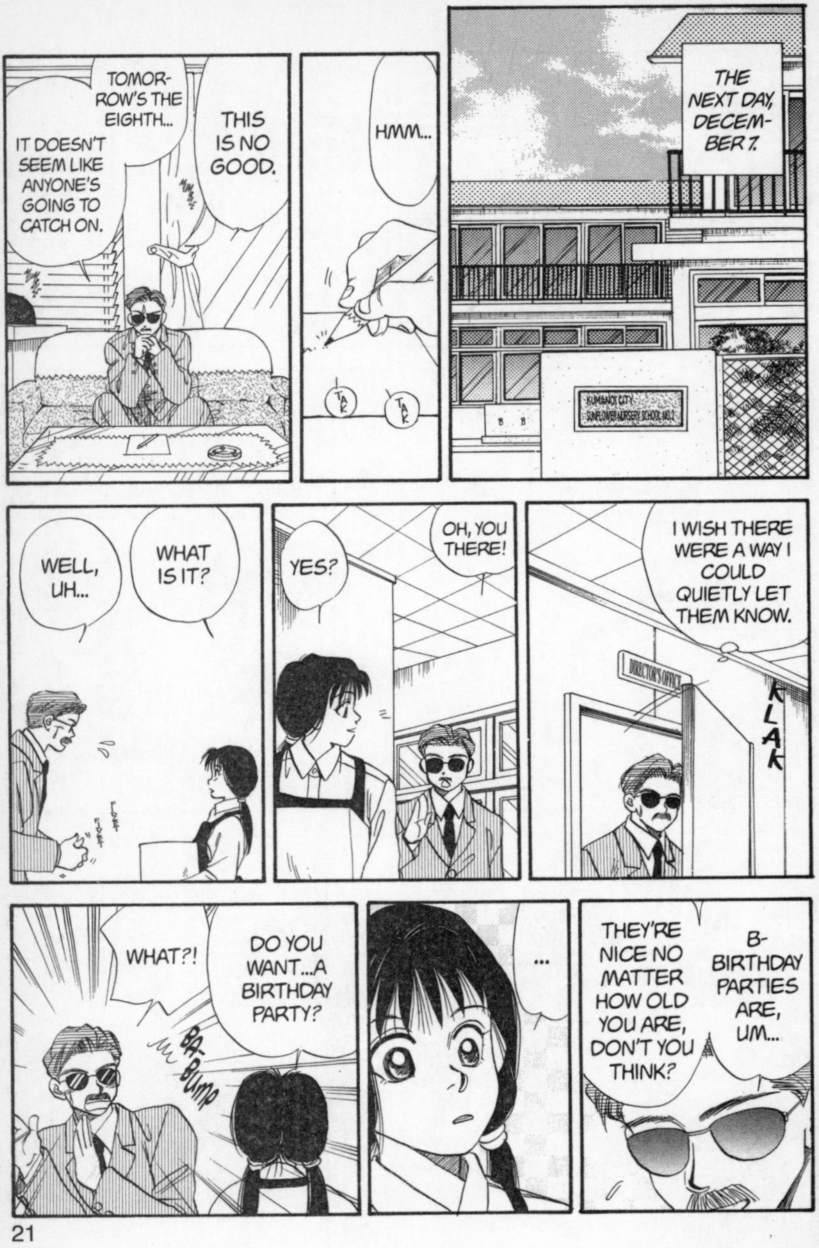
THE NEXT DAY, DECEMBER 7.
KUMANOI CITY SUNFLOWER NURSERY SCHOOL NO.2
HMM...
TAK
TAK
THIS IS NO GOOD.
TOMORROW'S THE EIGHTH...
IT DOESN'T SEEM LIKE ANYONE'S GOING TO CATCH ON.
I WISH THERE WERE A WAY I COULD QUIETLY LET THEM KNOW.
DIRECTOR'S OFFICE
KLAK
OH, YOU THERE!
YES?
WHAT IS IT?
WELL, UH...
FIDGET FIDGET
B-BIRTHDAY PARTIES ARE, UM...
THEY'RE NICE NO MATTER HOW OLD YOU ARE, DON'T YOU THINK?
...
DO YOU WANT...A BIRTHDAY PARTY?
WHAT?!
BA-BUMP

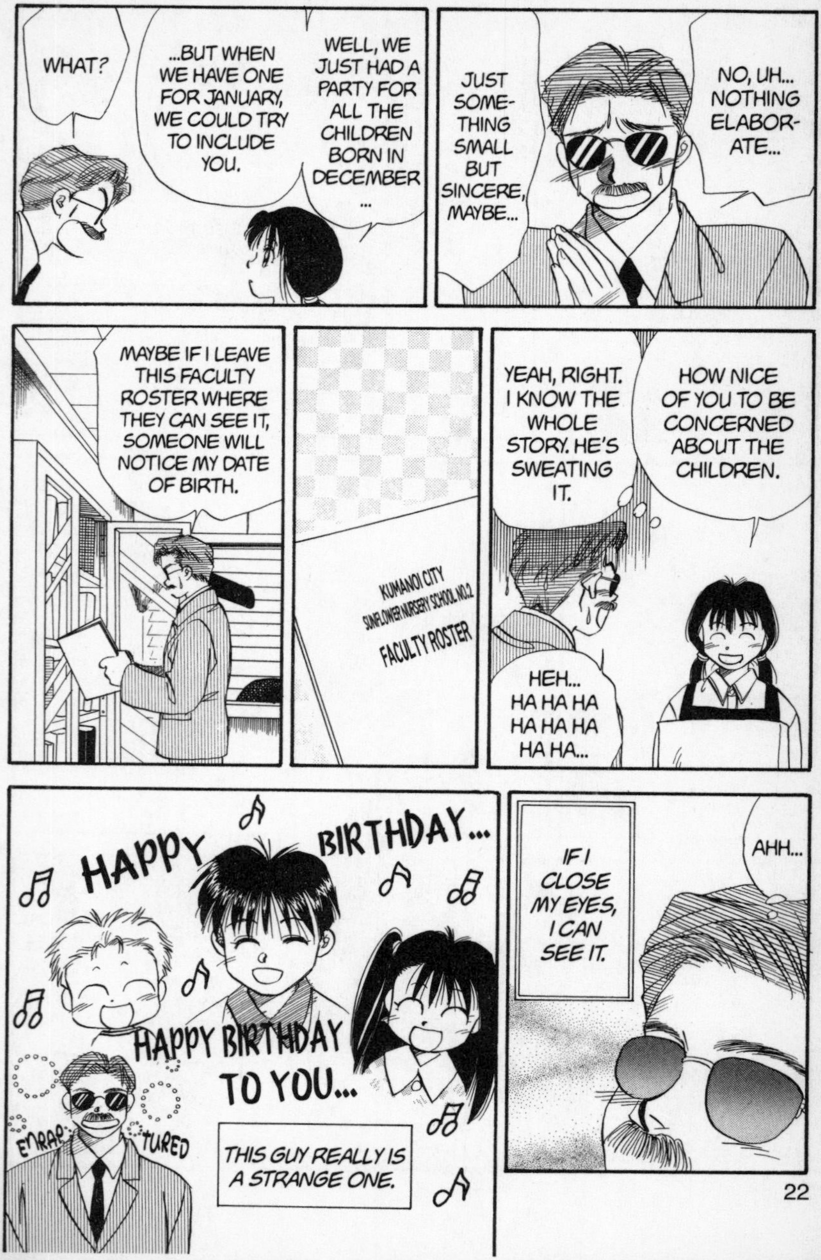
NO, UH... NOTHING ELABORATE...
JUST SOMETHING SMALL BUT SINCERE, MAYBE...
WELL, WE JUST HAD A PARTY FOR ALL THE CHILDREN BORN IN DECEMBER ...
...BUT WHEN WE HAVE ONE FOR JANUARY, WE COULD TRY TO INCLUDE YOU.
WHAT?
HOW NICE OF YOU TO BE CONCERNED ABOUT THE CHILDREN.
YEAH, RIGHT. I KNOW THE WHOLE STORY. HE'S SWEATING IT.
HEH... HA HA HA HA HA HA HA HA...
KUMANOI CITY SUNFLOWER NURSERY SCHOOL NO.2 FACULTY ROSTER
MAYBE IF I LEAVE THIS FACULTY ROSTER WHERE THEY CAN SEE IT, SOMEONE WILL NOTICE MY DATE OF BIRTH.
AHH...
IF I CLOSE MY EYES, I CAN SEE IT.
HAPPY BIRTHDAY...
HAPPY BIRTHDAY TO YOU...
ENRAPTURED
THIS GUY REALLY IS A STRANGE ONE.

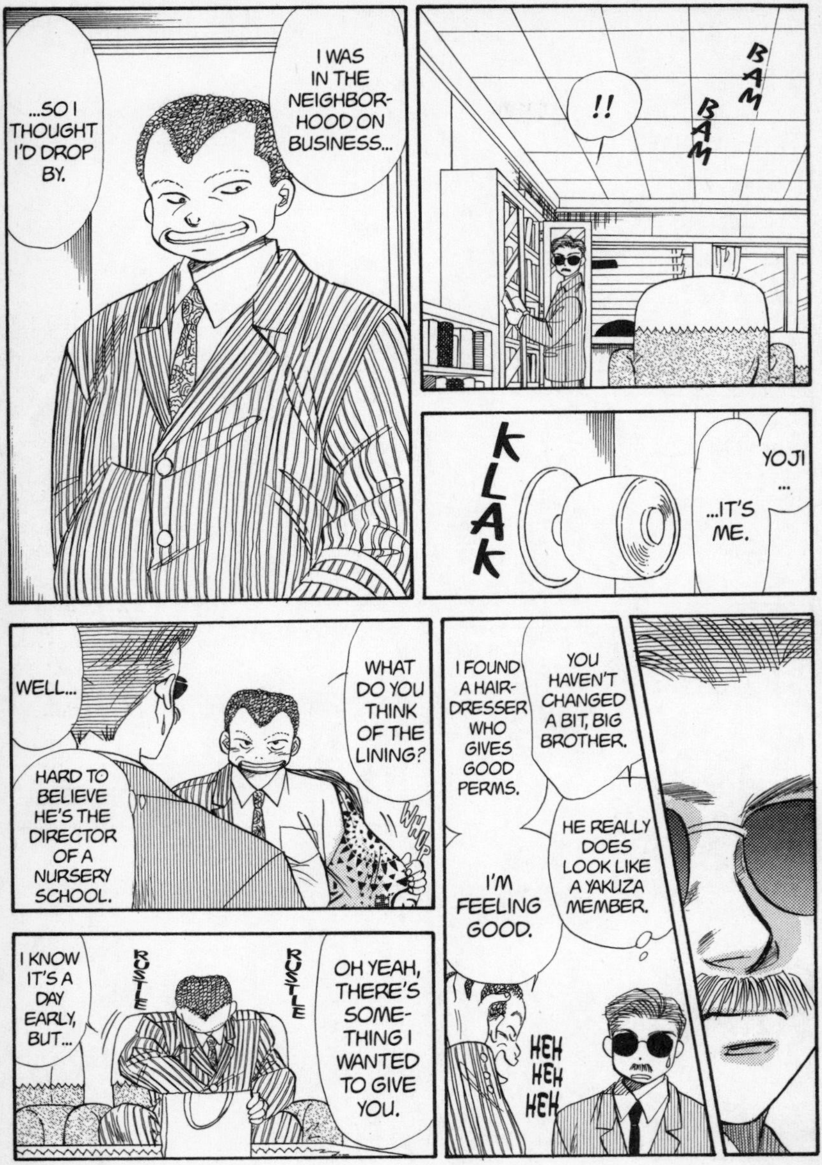
BAM
BAM
!!
YOJI...
...IT'S ME.
KLAK
I WAS IN THE NEIGHBOR-HOOD ON BUSINESS...
...SO I THOUGHT I'D DROP BY.
YOU HAVEN'T CHANGED A BIT, BIG BROTHER.
I FOUND A HAIR-DRESSER WHO GIVES GOOD PERMS.
HE REALLY DOES LOOK LIKE A YAKUZA MEMBER.
I'M FEELING GOOD.
HEH HEH HEH
WHAT DO YOU THINK OF THE LINING?
WELL...
WHIP
HARD TO BELIEVE HE'S THE DIRECTOR OF A NURSERY SCHOOL.
OH YEAH, THERE'S SOME-THING I WANTED TO GIVE YOU.
RUSTLE
RUSTLE
I KNOW IT'S A DAY EARLY, BUT...

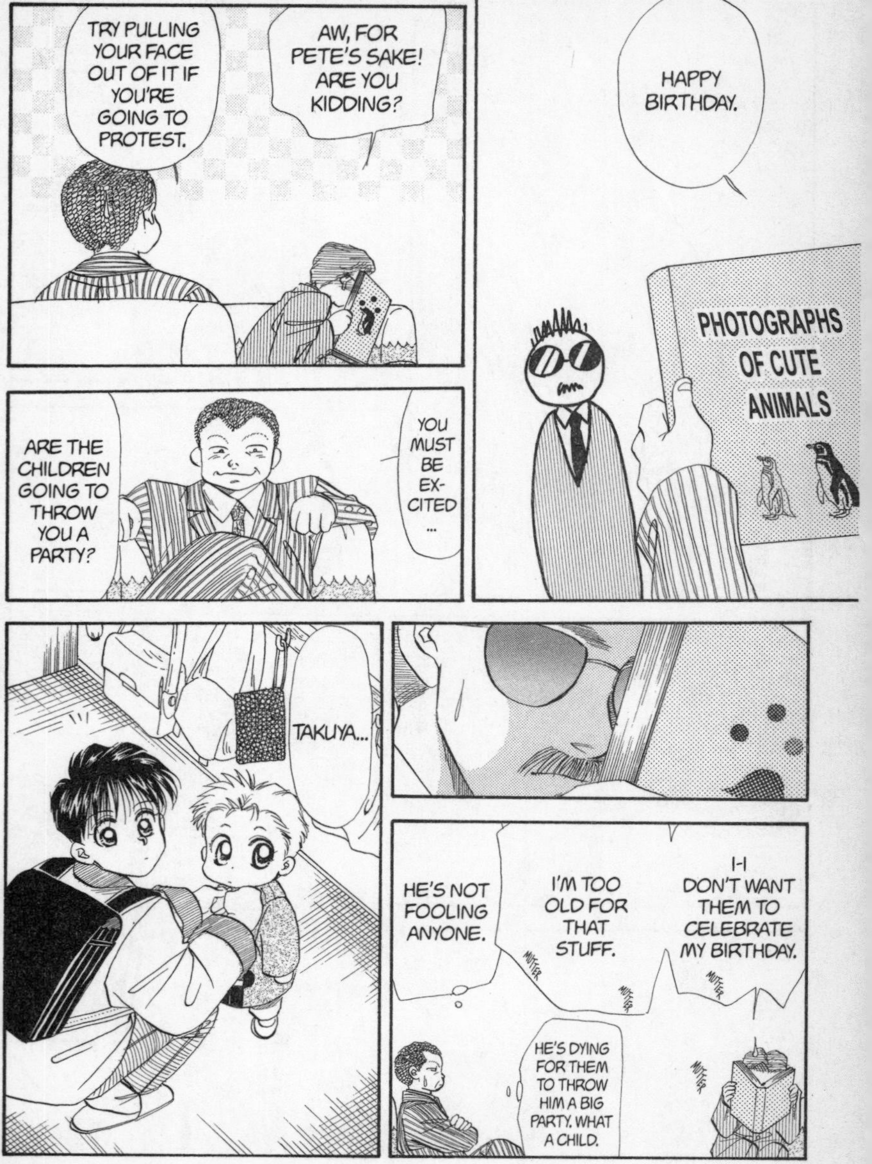
HAPPY BIRTHDAY.
PHOTOGRAPHS OF CUTE ANIMALS
AW, FOR PETE'S SAKE! ARE YOU KIDDING?
TRY PULLING YOUR FACE OUT OF IT IF YOU'RE GOING TO PROTEST.
YOU MUST BE EX-CITED ...
ARE THE CHILDREN GOING TO THROW YOU A PARTY?
I-I DON'T WANT THEM TO CELEBRATE MY BIRTHDAY.
MUTTER
I'M TOO OLD FOR THAT STUFF.
MUTTER
MUTTER
HE'S NOT FOOLING ANYONE.
MUTTER
HE'S DYING FOR THEM TO THROW HIM A BIG PARTY. WHAT A CHILD.
TAKUYA...

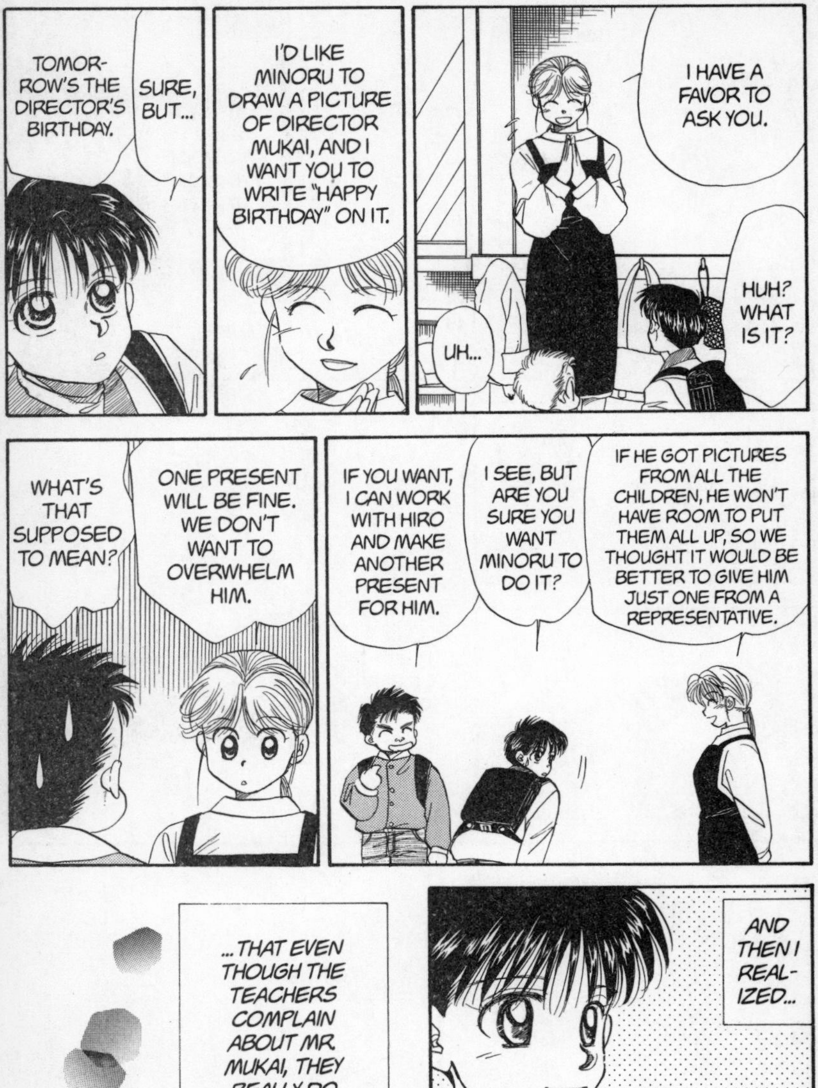
I HAVE A FAVOR TO ASK YOU.
HUH? WHAT IS IT?
UH...
I'D LIKE MINORU TO DRAW A PICTURE OF DIRECTOR MUKAI, AND I WANT YOU TO WRITE "HAPPY BIRTHDAY" ON IT.
SURE, BUT...
TOMOR-ROW'S THE DIRECTOR'S BIRTHDAY.
IF HE GOT PICTURES FROM ALL THE CHILDREN, HE WON'T HAVE ROOM TO PUT THEM ALL UP, SO WE THOUGHT IT WOULD BE BETTER TO GIVE HIM JUST ONE FROM A REPRESENTATIVE.
I SEE, BUT ARE YOU SURE YOU WANT MINORU TO DO IT?
IF YOU WANT, I CAN WORK WITH HIRO AND MAKE ANOTHER PRESENT FOR HIM.
ONE PRESENT WILL BE FINE. WE DON'T WANT TO OVERWHELM HIM.
WHAT'S THAT SUPPOSED TO MEAN?
AND THEN I REAL-IZED...
...THAT EVEN THOUGH THE TEACHERS COMPLAIN ABOUT MR. MUKAI, THEY REALLY DO LIKE HIM.

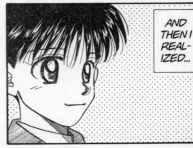

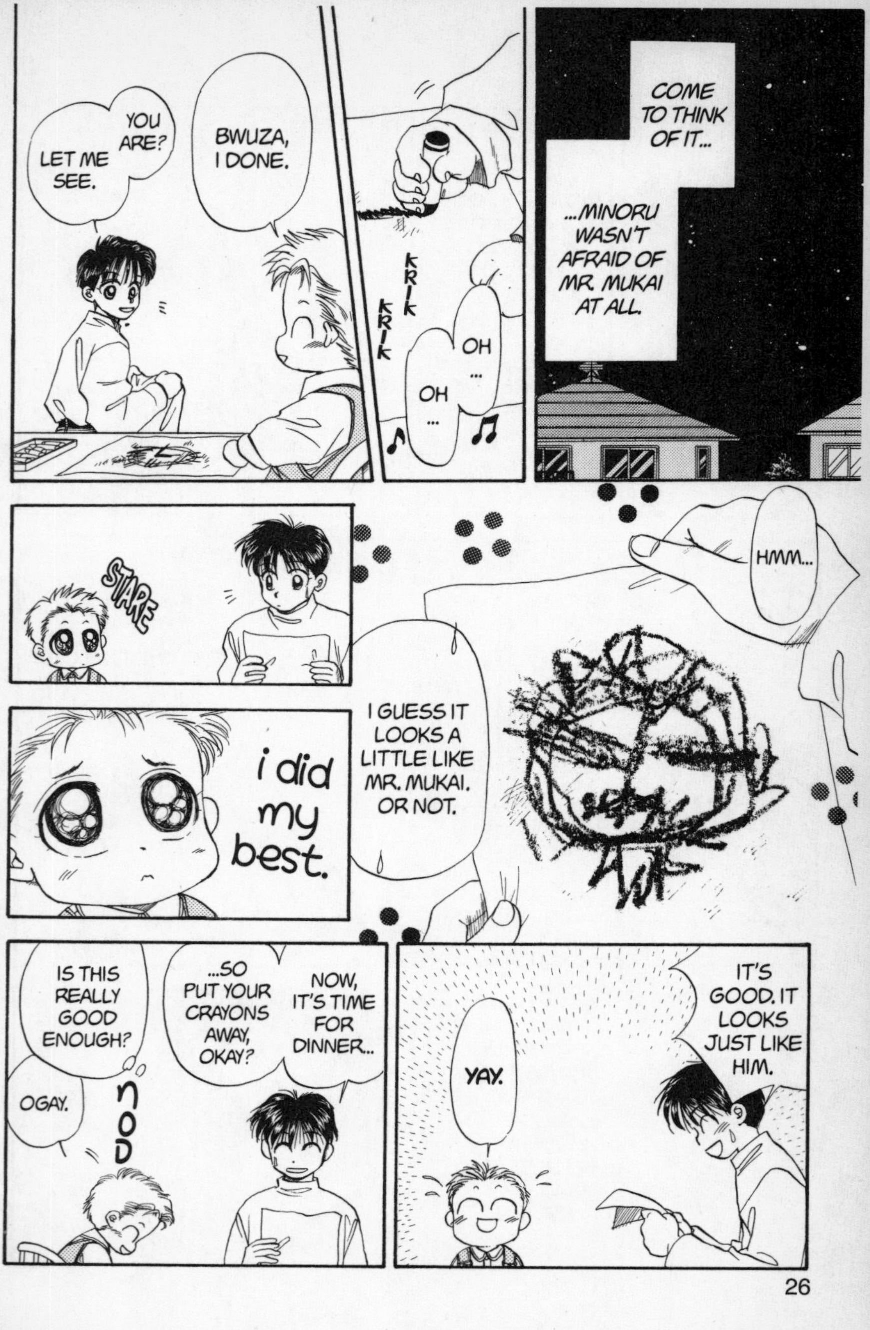
COME TO THINK OF IT...
...MINORU WASN'T AFRAID OF MR. MUKAI AT ALL.
KRIK KRIK
OH ...
OH ...
BWUZA, I DONE.
YOU ARE? LET ME SEE.
HMM...
I GUESS IT LOOKS A LITTLE LIKE MR. MUKAI. OR NOT.
STARE
i did my best.
IT'S GOOD. IT LOOKS JUST LIKE HIM.
YAY.
NOW, IT'S TIME FOR DINNER...
...SO PUT YOUR CRAYONS AWAY, OKAY?
IS THIS REALLY GOOD ENOUGH?
NOD
OGAY.

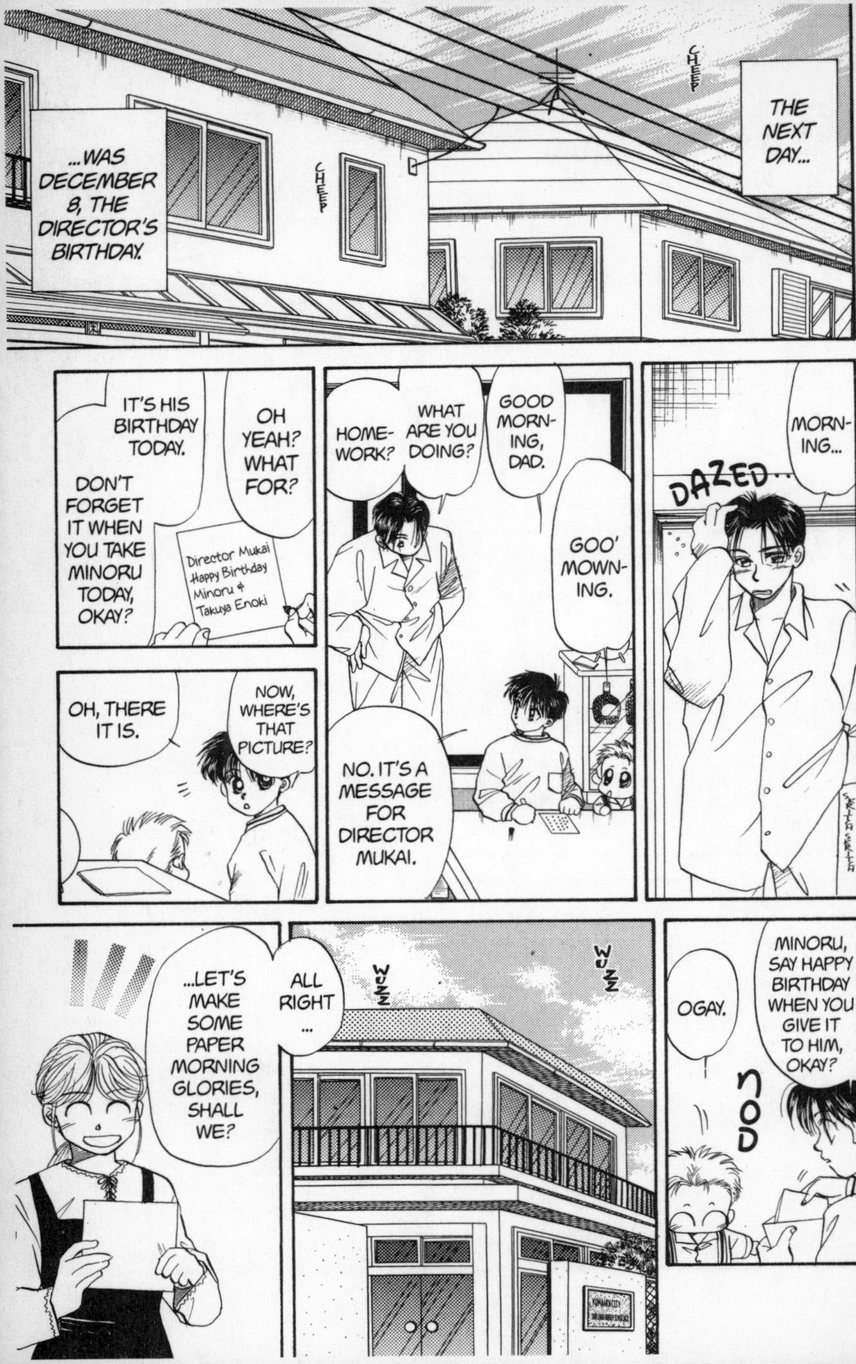
THE NEXT DAY...
CHEEP
CHEEP
...WAS DECEMBER 8, THE DIRECTOR'S BIRTHDAY.
MORNING...
DAZED...
SKRITCH SKRITCH
GOOD MORNING, DAD.
GOO' MOWNING.
WHAT ARE YOU DOING?
HOMEWORK?
NO. IT'S A MESSAGE FOR DIRECTOR MUKAI.
OH YEAH? WHAT FOR?
IT'S HIS BIRTHDAY TODAY.
DON'T FORGET IT WHEN YOU TAKE MINORU TODAY, OKAY?
Director Mukai Happy Birthday Minoru & Takuya Enoki
NOW, WHERE'S THAT PICTURE?
OH, THERE IT IS.
MINORU, SAY HAPPY BIRTHDAY WHEN YOU GIVE IT TO HIM, OKAY?
OGAY.
NOD
WUZZ
WUZZ
ALL RIGHT ...
...LET'S MAKE SOME PAPER MORNING GLORIES, SHALL WE?

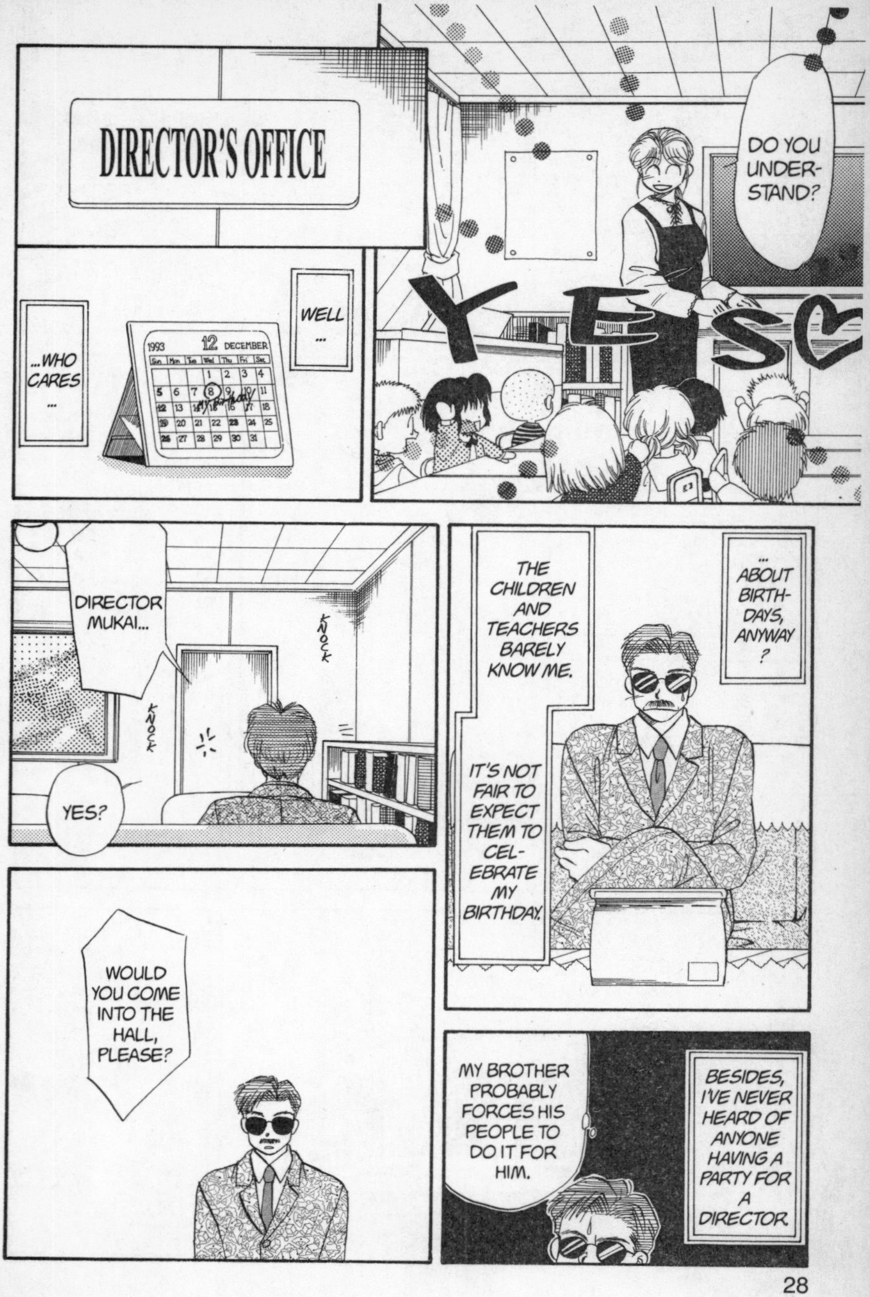
DO YOU UNDERSTAND?
YES♡
DIRECTOR'S OFFICE
WELL ...
...WHO CARES ...
1993 12 DECEMBER
MY BIRTHDAY!
... ABOUT BIRTHDAYS, ANYWAY ?
THE CHILDREN AND TEACHERS BARELY KNOW ME.
IT'S NOT FAIR TO EXPECT THEM TO CELEBRATE MY BIRTHDAY.
BESIDES, I'VE NEVER HEARD OF ANYONE HAVING A PARTY FOR A DIRECTOR.
MY BROTHER PROBABLY FORCES HIS PEOPLE TO DO IT FOR HIM.
DIRECTOR MUKAI...
KNOCK
KNOCK
YES?
WOULD YOU COME INTO THE HALL, PLEASE?

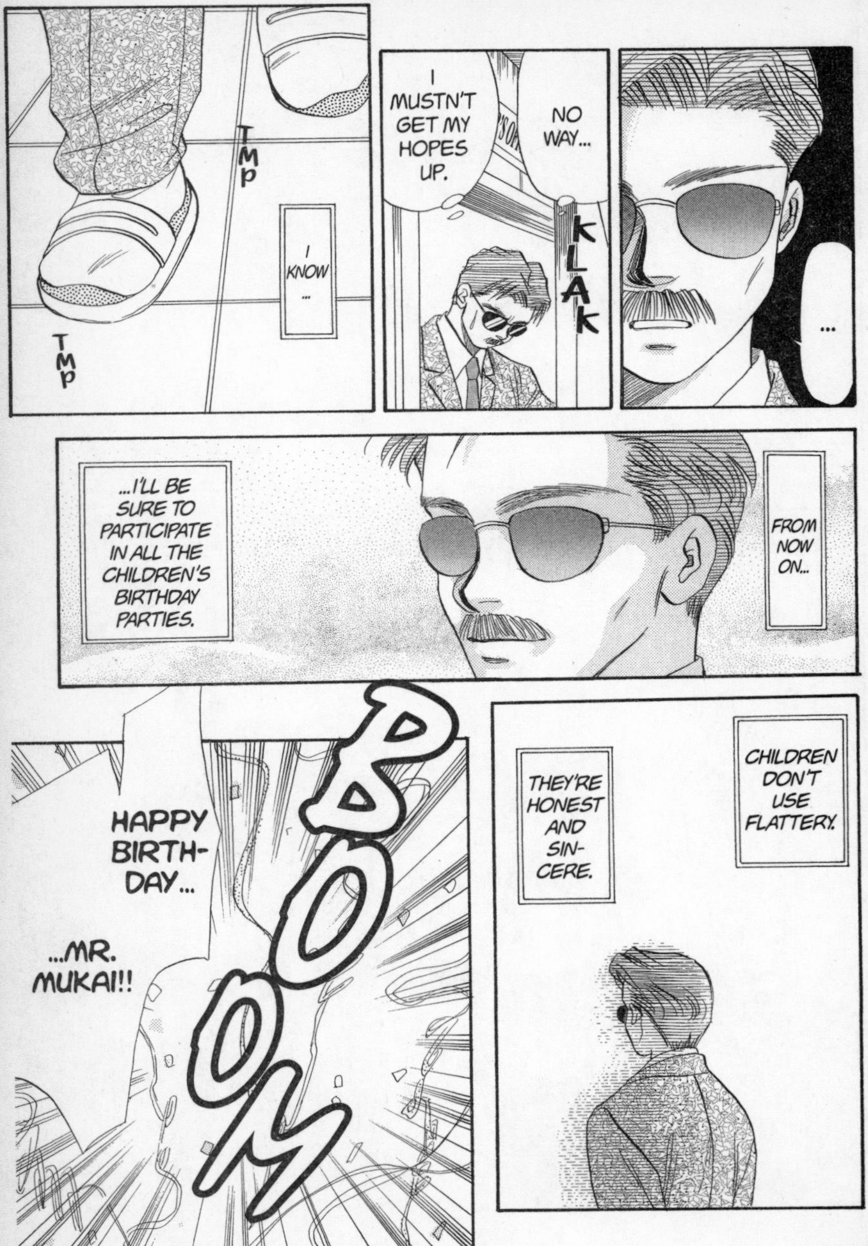

...
NO WAY...
I MUSTN'T GET MY HOPES UP.
KLAK
I KNOW ...
TMP
TMP
FROM NOW ON...
...I'LL BE SURE TO PARTICIPATE IN ALL THE CHILDREN'S BIRTHDAY PARTIES.
CHILDREN DON'T USE FLATTERY.
THEY'RE HONEST AND SIN-CERE.
BOOM
HAPPY BIRTH-DAY...
...MR. MUKAI!!

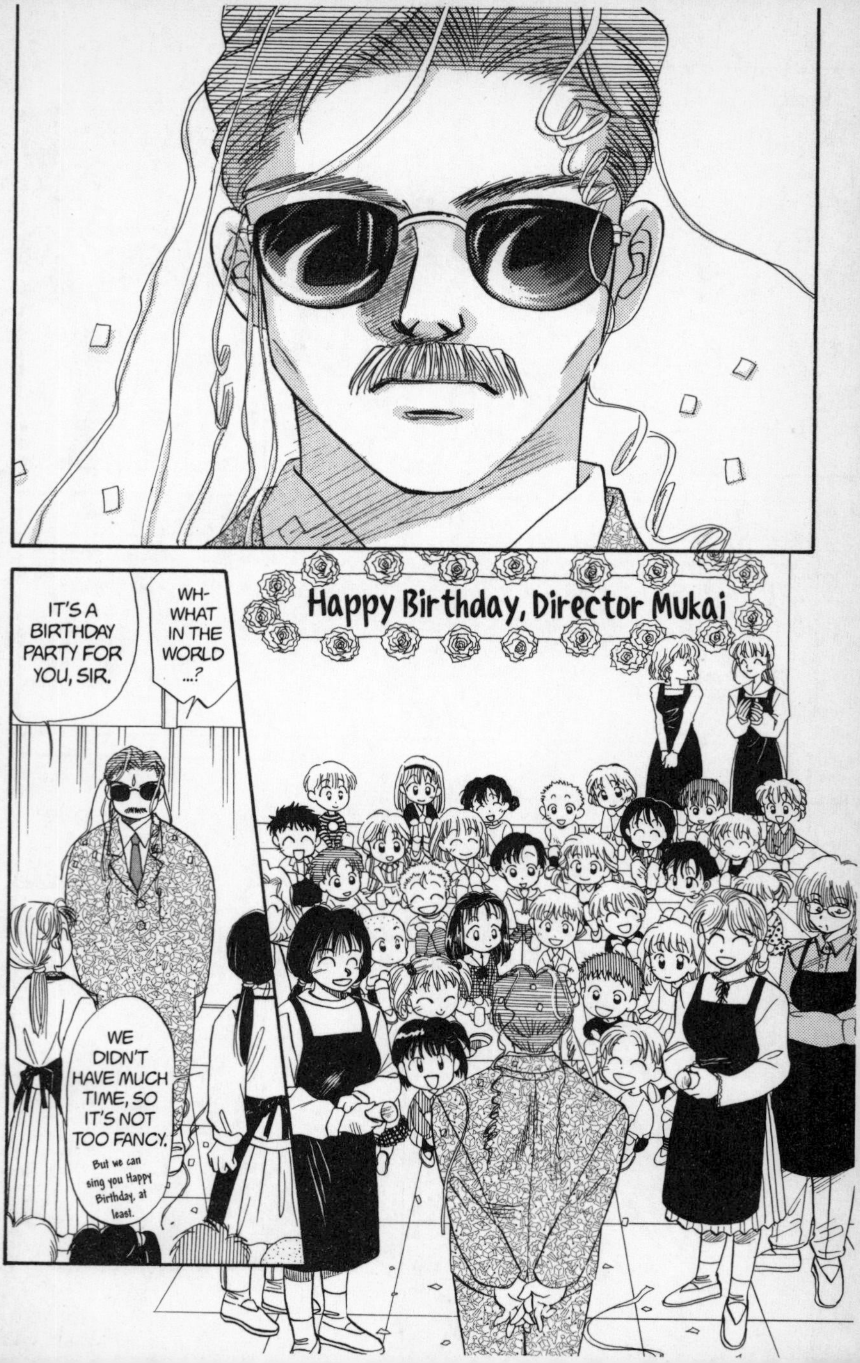
Happy Birthday, Director Mukai
WH-WHAT IN THE WORLD ...?
IT'S A BIRTHDAY PARTY FOR YOU, SIR.
WE DIDN'T HAVE MUCH TIME, SO IT'S NOT TOO FANCY.
But we can sing you Happy Birthday, at least.

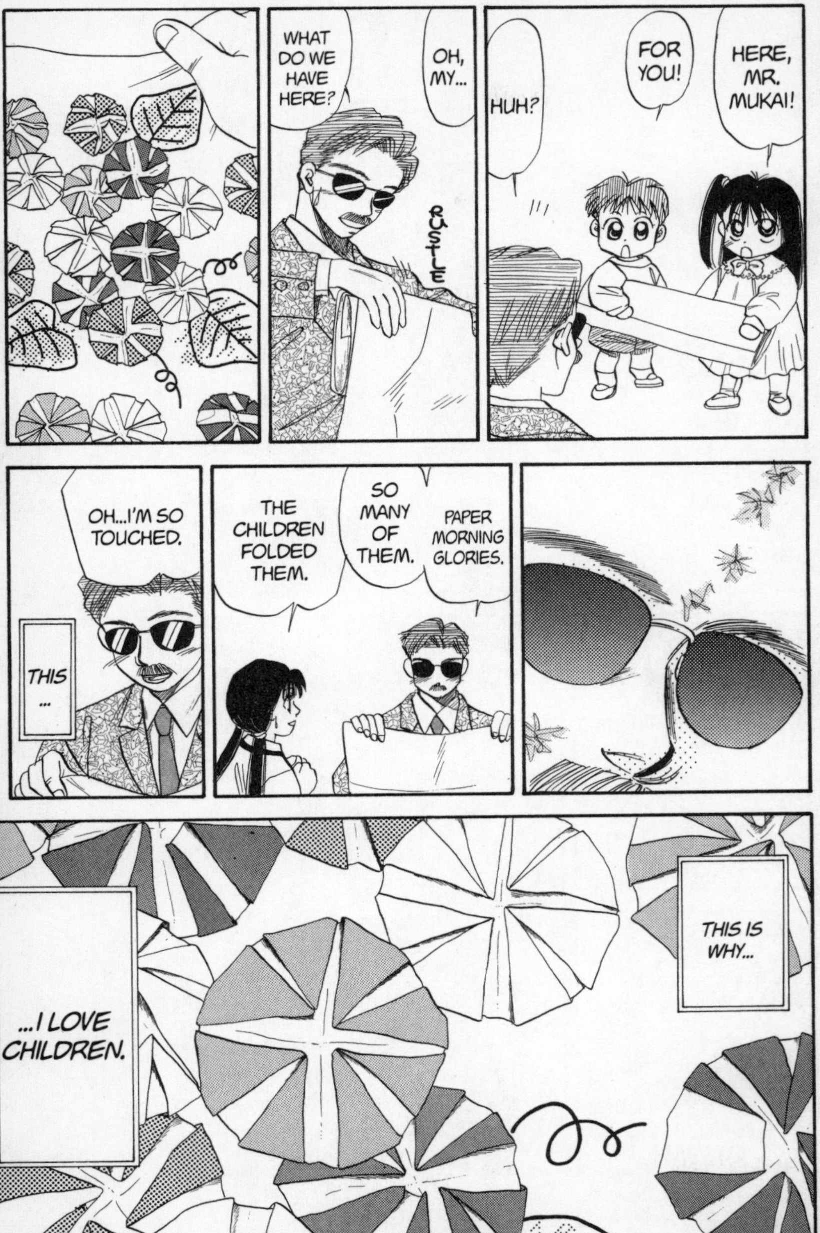
HERE, MR. MUKAI!
FOR YOU!
HUH?
OH, MY...
WHAT DO WE HAVE HERE?
RUSTLE
PAPER MORNING GLORIES.
SO MANY OF THEM.
THE CHILDREN FOLDED THEM.
OH...I'M SO TOUCHED.
THIS ...
THIS IS WHY...
...I LOVE CHILDREN.

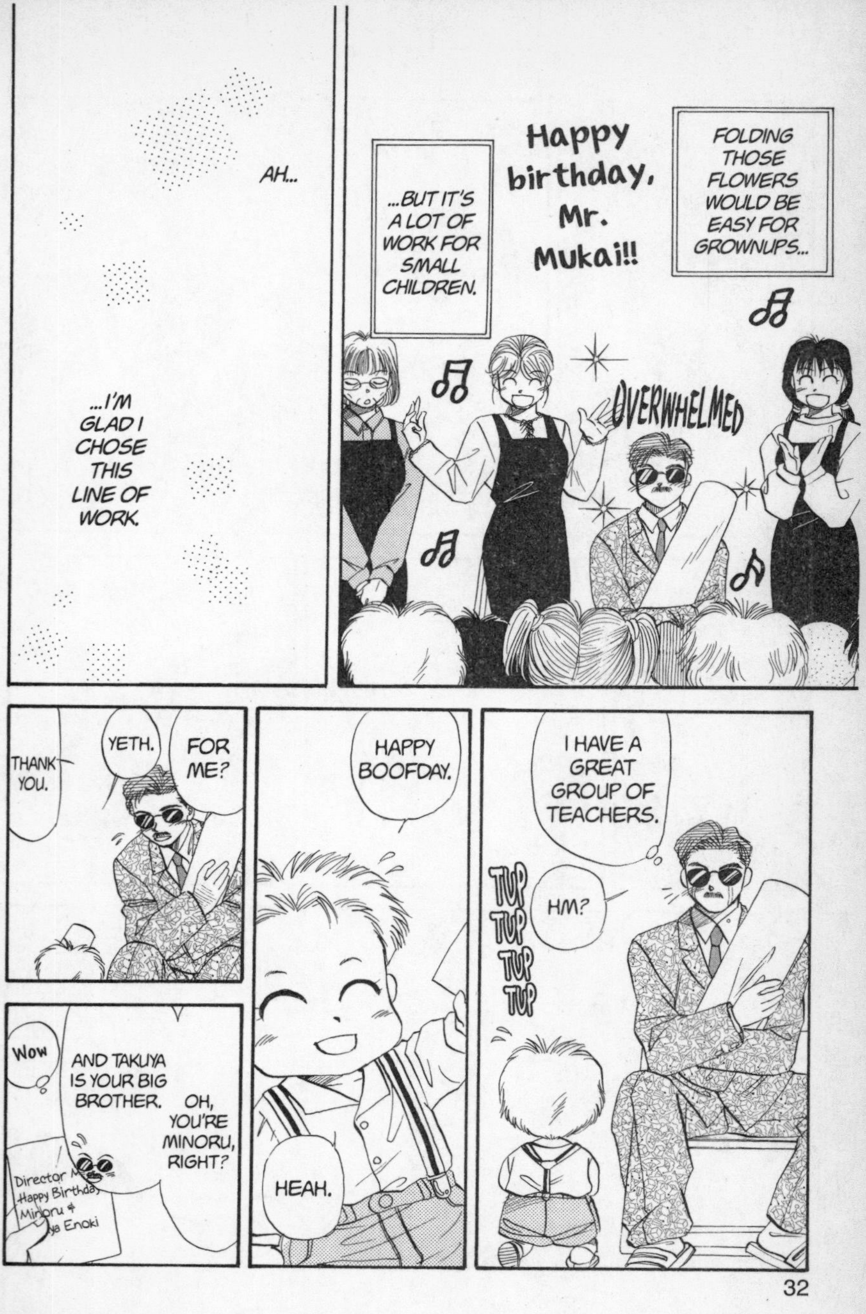
FOLDING THOSE FLOWERS WOULD BE EASY FOR GROWNUPS...
Happy birthday, Mr. Mukai!!
...BUT IT'S A LOT OF WORK FOR SMALL CHILDREN.
OVERWHELMED
AH...
...I'M GLAD I CHOSE THIS LINE OF WORK.
I HAVE A GREAT GROUP OF TEACHERS.
HM?
TUP TUP TUP TUP
HAPPY BOOFDAY.
HEAH.
FOR ME?
YETH.
THANK YOU.
OH, YOU'RE MINORU, RIGHT?
AND TAKUYA IS YOUR BIG BROTHER.
Wow
Director
Happy Birthday
Minoru &
Enoki

RUS TLE..

RUSTLE

RUSTLE

HEE HEE

WHAT COULD THIS BE?

ISN'T THAT NICE, MR. MUKAI?

RUSTLE

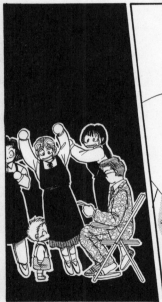

HOW ABOUT DINNER TONIGHT?

...I CHOSE THIS PROFESSION.

I'M SO GLAD...

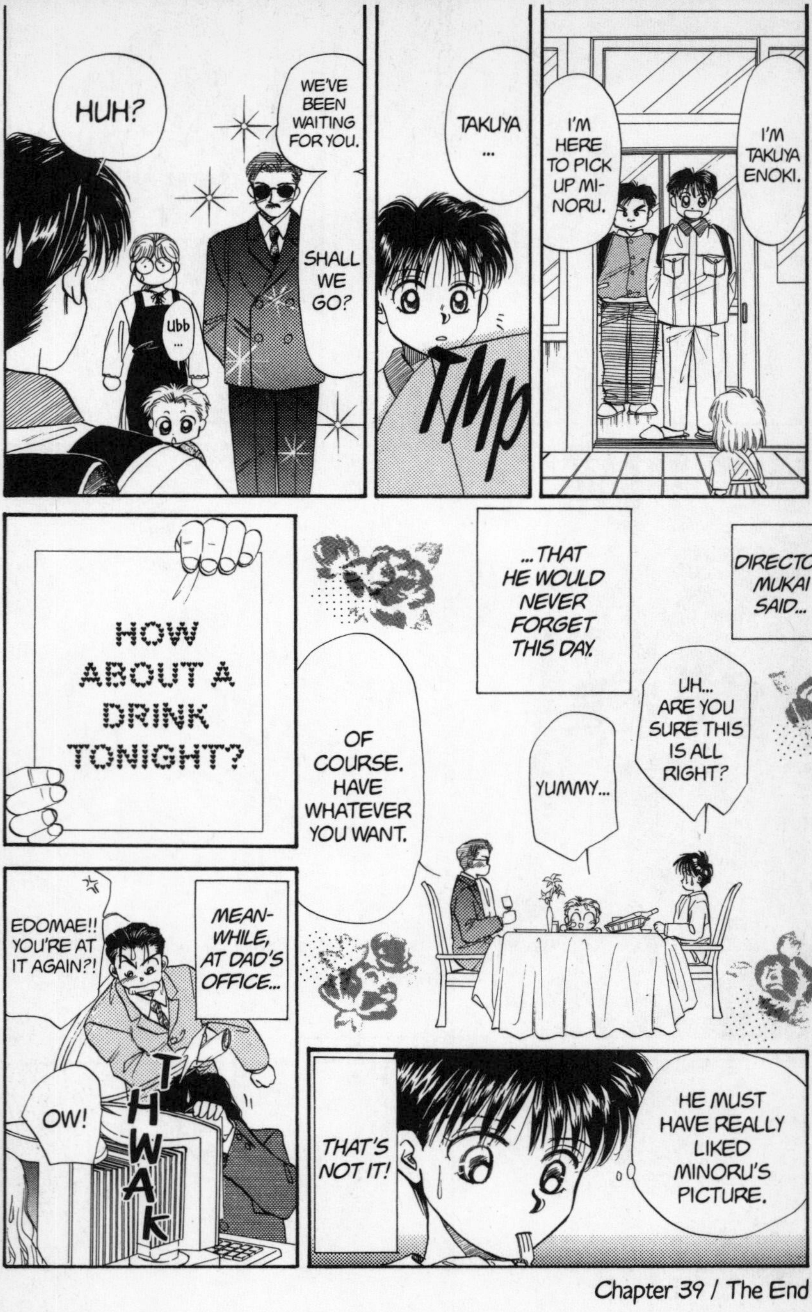
I'M TAKUYA ENOKI.
I'M HERE TO PICK UP MI-NORU.
TAKUYA ...
TMp
WE'VE BEEN WAITING FOR YOU.
HUH?
SHALL WE GO?
Ubb ...
DIRECTOR MUKAI SAID...
...THAT HE WOULD NEVER FORGET THIS DAY.
UH... ARE YOU SURE THIS IS ALL RIGHT?
YUMMY...
OF COURSE. HAVE WHATEVER YOU WANT.
HOW ABOUT A DRINK TONIGHT?
HE MUST HAVE REALLY LIKED MINORU'S PICTURE.
THAT'S NOT IT!
MEAN-WHILE, AT DAD'S OFFICE...
EDOMAE!! YOU'RE AT IT AGAIN?!
OW!
THWAK

Chapter 39 / The End

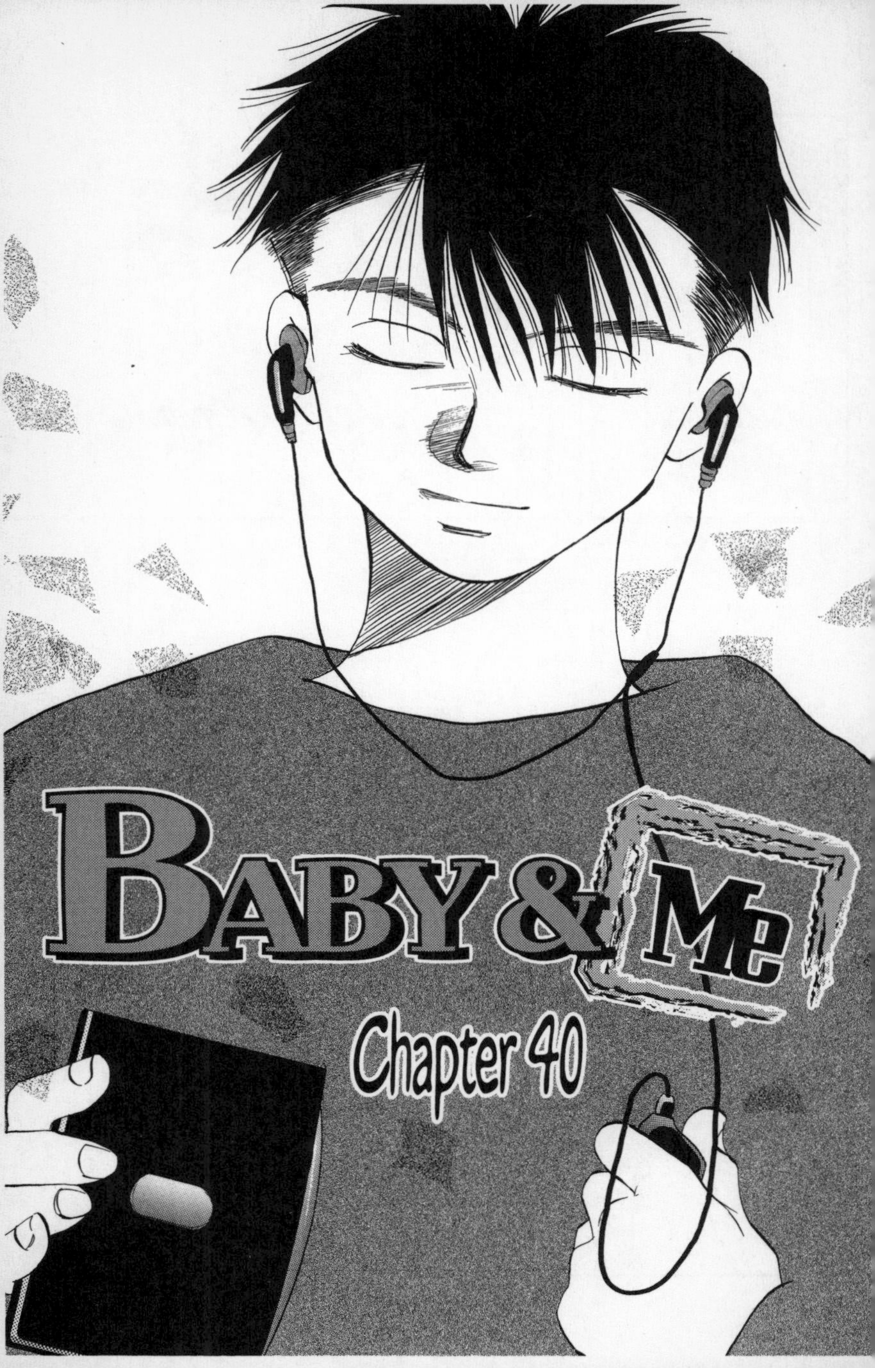
BABY & ME
Chapter 40

CHRISTMAS MUSIC FILLS THE STREETS...

Merry X'mas

THIS CHAPTER...

MARIMO PRODUCTIONS
12月 25

...AND THERE'S EXCITEMENT IN THE AIR.

302							
FUJII							
ISAO	EMIKO	AKEMI	TOMOYA	ASAKO	AKIHIRO	ICHIKA	MASAKI

...IS ABOUT THE FUJII FAMILY.

SANTA CWAUS IS COMING!

OH BOY! IT'S CHRISTMAS!

BA-BUMP...

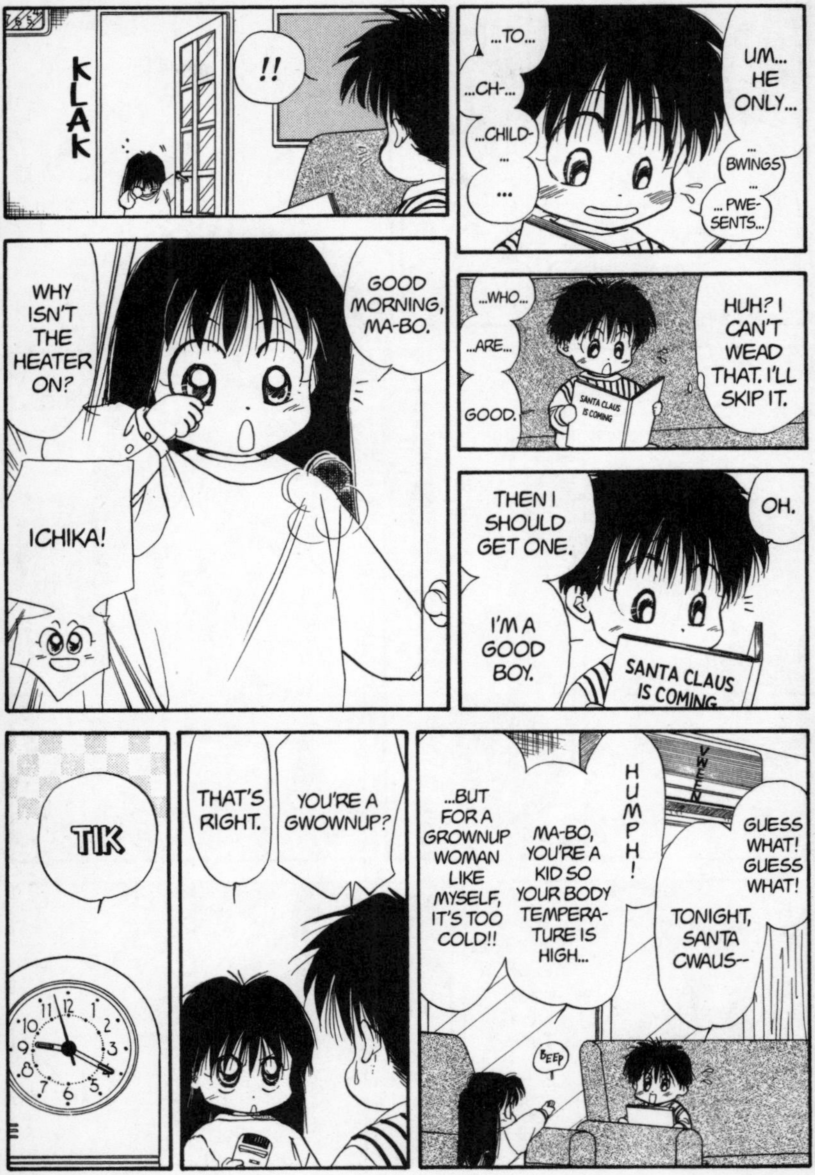
UM... HE ONLY...
... BWINGS ...
... PWE-SENTS...
...TO...
...CH-...
...CHILD- ...
...
KLAK
!!
HUH? I CAN'T WEAD THAT. I'LL SKIP IT.
...WHO...
...ARE...
GOOD.
SANTA CLAUS IS COMING
OH.
THEN I SHOULD GET ONE.
I'M A GOOD BOY.
SANTA CLAUS IS COMING
GOOD MORNING, MA-BO.
WHY ISN'T THE HEATER ON?
ICHIKA!
GUESS WHAT! GUESS WHAT!
TONIGHT, SANTA CWAUS--
VWEEN
HUMPH!
MA-BO, YOU'RE A KID SO YOUR BODY TEMPERA-TURE IS HIGH...
...BUT FOR A GROWNUP WOMAN LIKE MYSELF, IT'S TOO COLD!!
BEEP
YOU'RE A GWOWNUP?
THAT'S RIGHT.
TIK

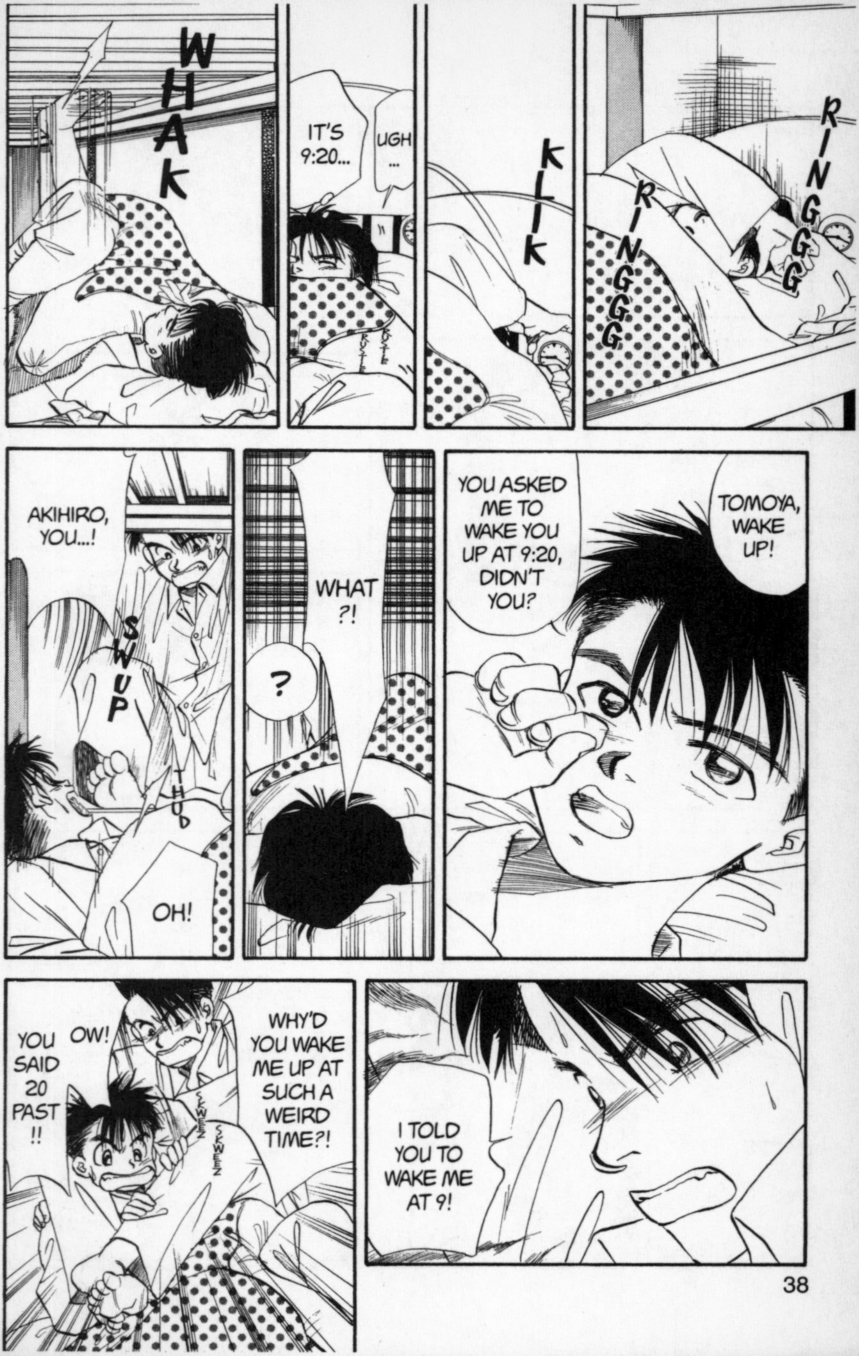
RINGGG
RINGGG
KLIK
UGH ...
IT'S 9:20...
RUSTLE
RUSTLE
WHAK
TOMOYA, WAKE UP!
YOU ASKED ME TO WAKE YOU UP AT 9:20, DIDN'T YOU?
WHAT ?!
?
AKIHIRO, YOU...!
SWUP
THUD
OH!
I TOLD YOU TO WAKE ME AT 9!
WHY'D YOU WAKE ME UP AT SUCH A WEIRD TIME?!
OW!
YOU SAID 20 PAST !!
SKWEEZ
SKWEEZ

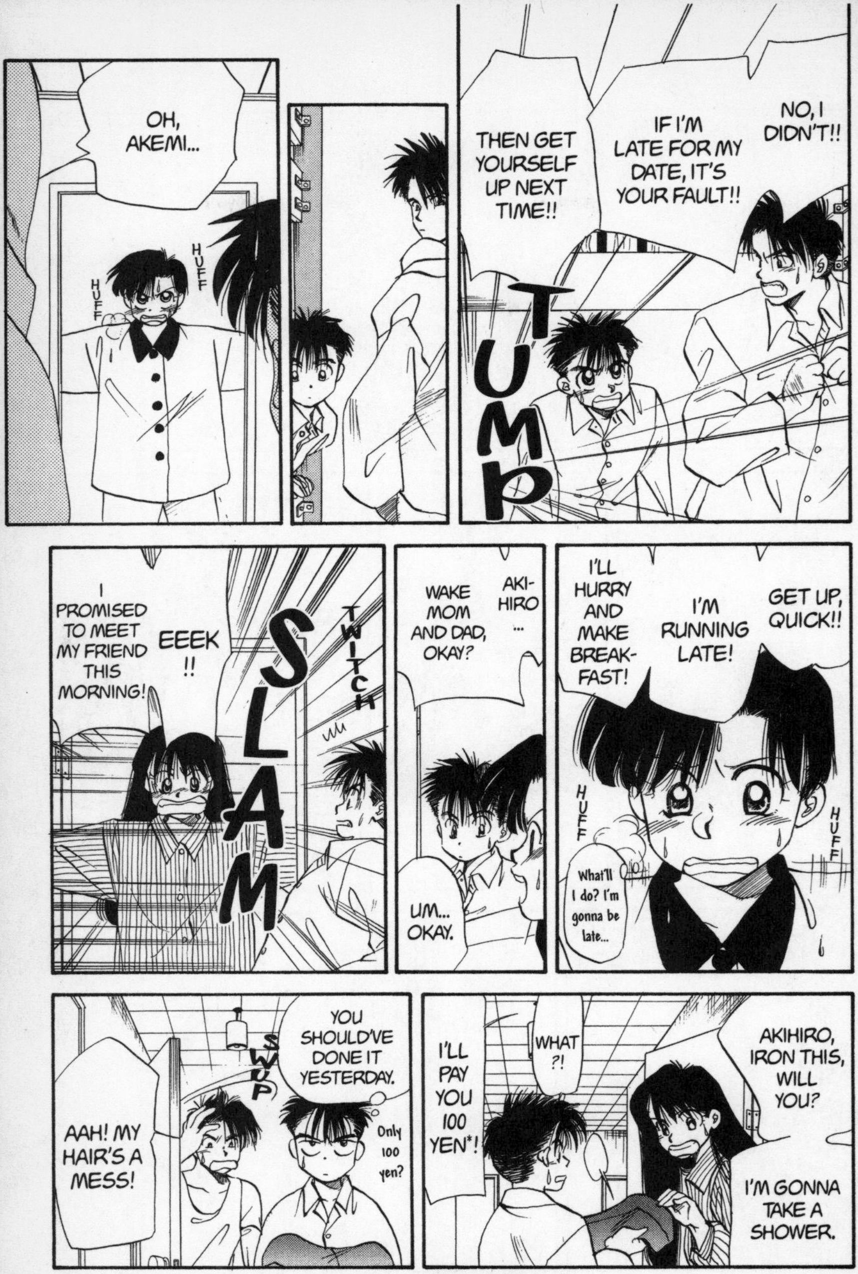
NO, I DIDN'T!!
IF I'M LATE FOR MY DATE, IT'S YOUR FAULT!!
THEN GET YOURSELF UP NEXT TIME!!
TUMP
OH, AKEMI...
HUFF HUFF
GET UP, QUICK!!
I'M RUNNING LATE!
I'LL HURRY AND MAKE BREAK-FAST!
HUFF
What'll I do? I'm gonna be late...
HUFF
AKI-HIRO ...
WAKE MOM AND DAD, OKAY?
UM... OKAY.
TWITCH
SLAM
EEEK !!
I PROMISED TO MEET MY FRIEND THIS MORNING!
AKIHIRO, IRON THIS, WILL YOU?
WHAT ?!
I'M GONNA TAKE A SHOWER.
I'LL PAY YOU 100 YEN*!
YOU SHOULD'VE DONE IT YESTERDAY.
SWUP
Only 100 yen?
AAH! MY HAIR'S A MESS!

*Approximately $0.80

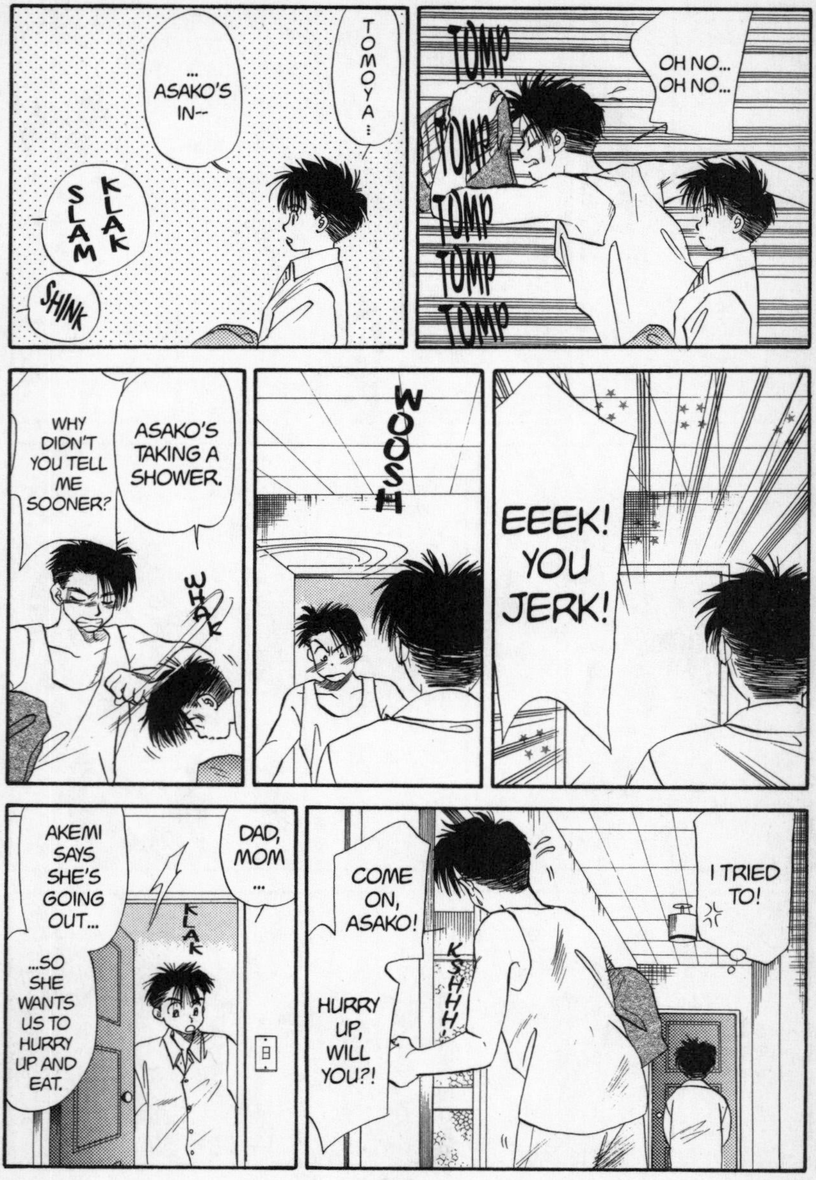
OH NO... OH NO...
TOMP TOMP TOMP TOMP TOMP TOMP
TOMOYA...
...ASAKO'S IN--
KLAK SLAM
SHINK
EEEK! YOU JERK!
WOOSH
ASAKO'S TAKING A SHOWER.
WHY DIDN'T YOU TELL ME SOONER?
WHAK
I TRIED TO!
COME ON, ASAKO!
KSHHH
HURRY UP, WILL YOU?!
DAD, MOM ...
AKEMI SAYS SHE'S GOING OUT...
KLAK
...SO SHE WANTS US TO HURRY UP AND EAT.

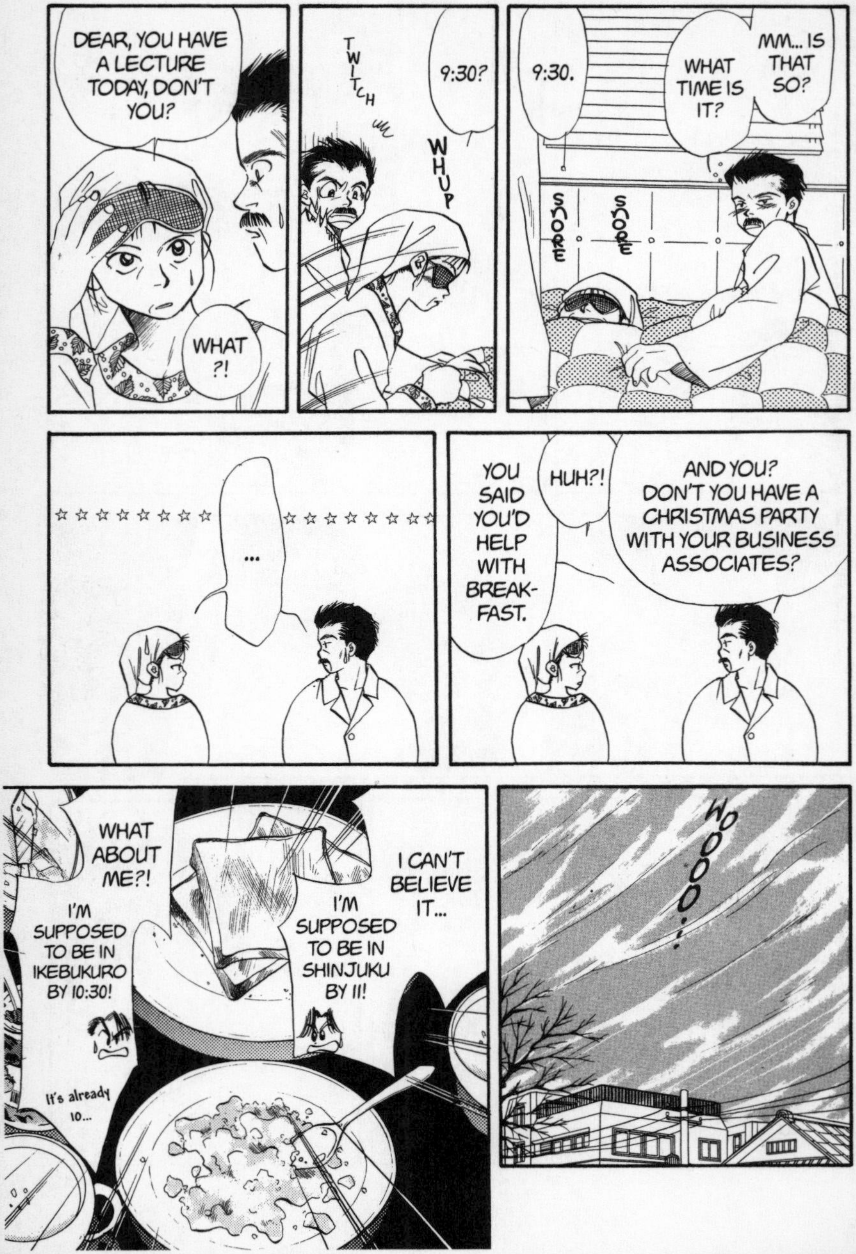
MM... IS THAT SO?
WHAT TIME IS IT?
9:30.
SNORE
SNORE
9:30?
TWITCH
WHUP
DEAR, YOU HAVE A LECTURE TODAY, DON'T YOU?
WHAT ?!
AND YOU? DON'T YOU HAVE A CHRISTMAS PARTY WITH YOUR BUSINESS ASSOCIATES?
HUH?!
YOU SAID YOU'D HELP WITH BREAK-FAST.
...
WOOOOO..!!
I CAN'T BELIEVE IT...
I'M SUPPOSED TO BE IN SHINJUKU BY 11!
WHAT ABOUT ME?!
I'M SUPPOSED TO BE IN IKEBUKURO BY 10:30!
It's already 10...

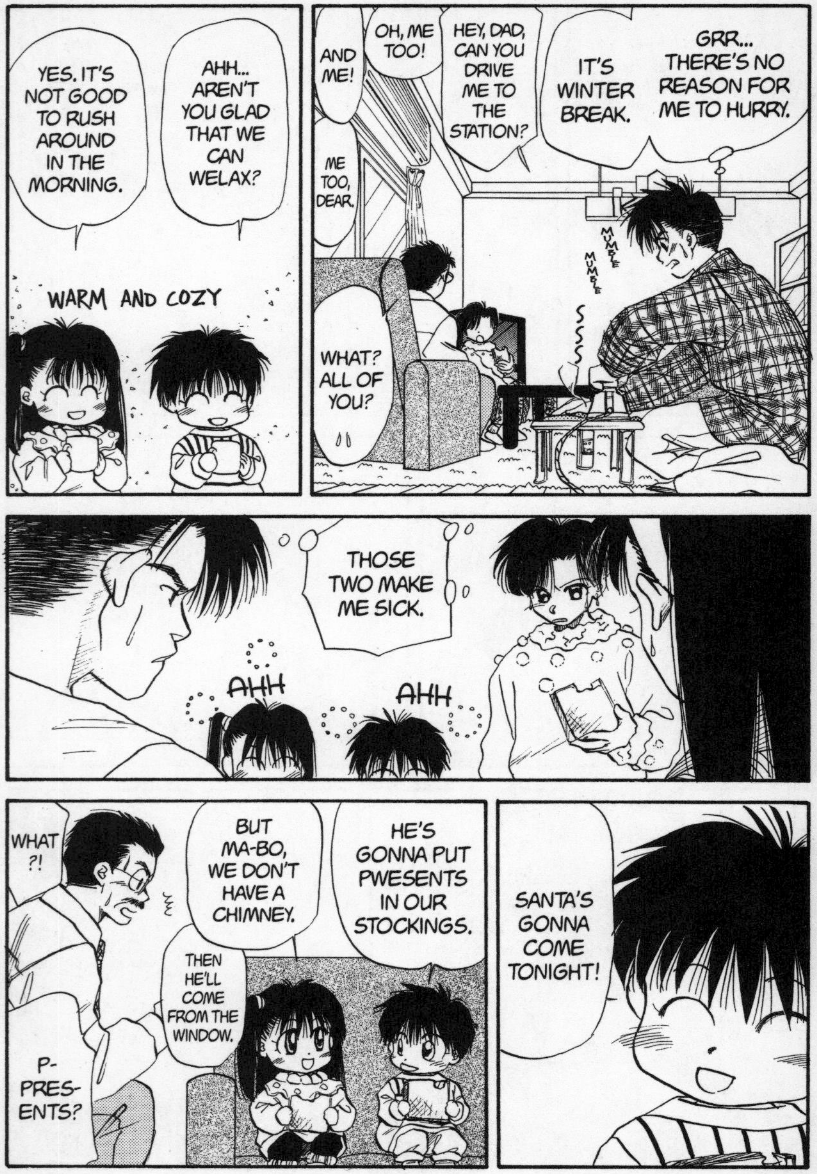
GRR... THERE'S NO REASON FOR ME TO HURRY.
IT'S WINTER BREAK.
MUMBLE MUMBLE
HEY, DAD, CAN YOU DRIVE ME TO THE STATION?
OH, ME TOO!
AND ME!
ME TOO, DEAR.
WHAT? ALL OF YOU?
AHH... AREN'T YOU GLAD THAT WE CAN WELAX?
YES. IT'S NOT GOOD TO RUSH AROUND IN THE MORNING.
WARM AND COZY
THOSE TWO MAKE ME SICK.
AHH
AHH
SANTA'S GONNA COME TONIGHT!
HE'S GONNA PUT PWESENTS IN OUR STOCKINGS.
BUT MA-BO, WE DON'T HAVE A CHIMNEY.
THEN HE'LL COME FROM THE WINDOW.
WHAT?!
P-PRESENTS?

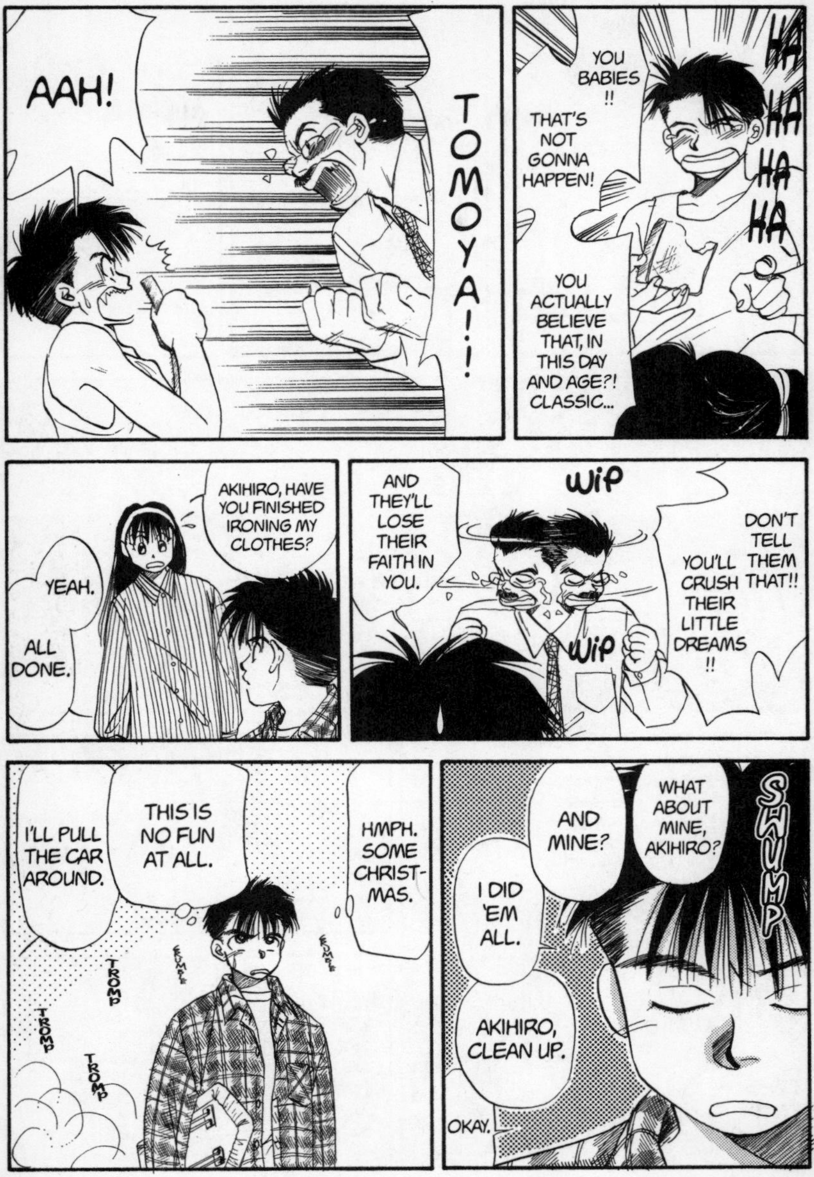
HA HA HA HA
YOU BABIES!!
THAT'S NOT GONNA HAPPEN!
YOU ACTUALLY BELIEVE THAT, IN THIS DAY AND AGE?! CLASSIC...
TOMOYA!!
AAH!
DON'T TELL THEM THAT!!
YOU'LL CRUSH THEIR LITTLE DREAMS!!
wip
AND THEY'LL LOSE THEIR FAITH IN YOU.
wip
AKIHIRO, HAVE YOU FINISHED IRONING MY CLOTHES?
YEAH.
ALL DONE.
SHUMP
WHAT ABOUT MINE, AKIHIRO?
AND MINE?
I DID 'EM ALL.
AKIHIRO, CLEAN UP.
OKAY.
HMPH. SOME CHRIST-MAS.
THIS IS NO FUN AT ALL.
I'LL PULL THE CAR AROUND.
TROMP
TROMP
TROMP

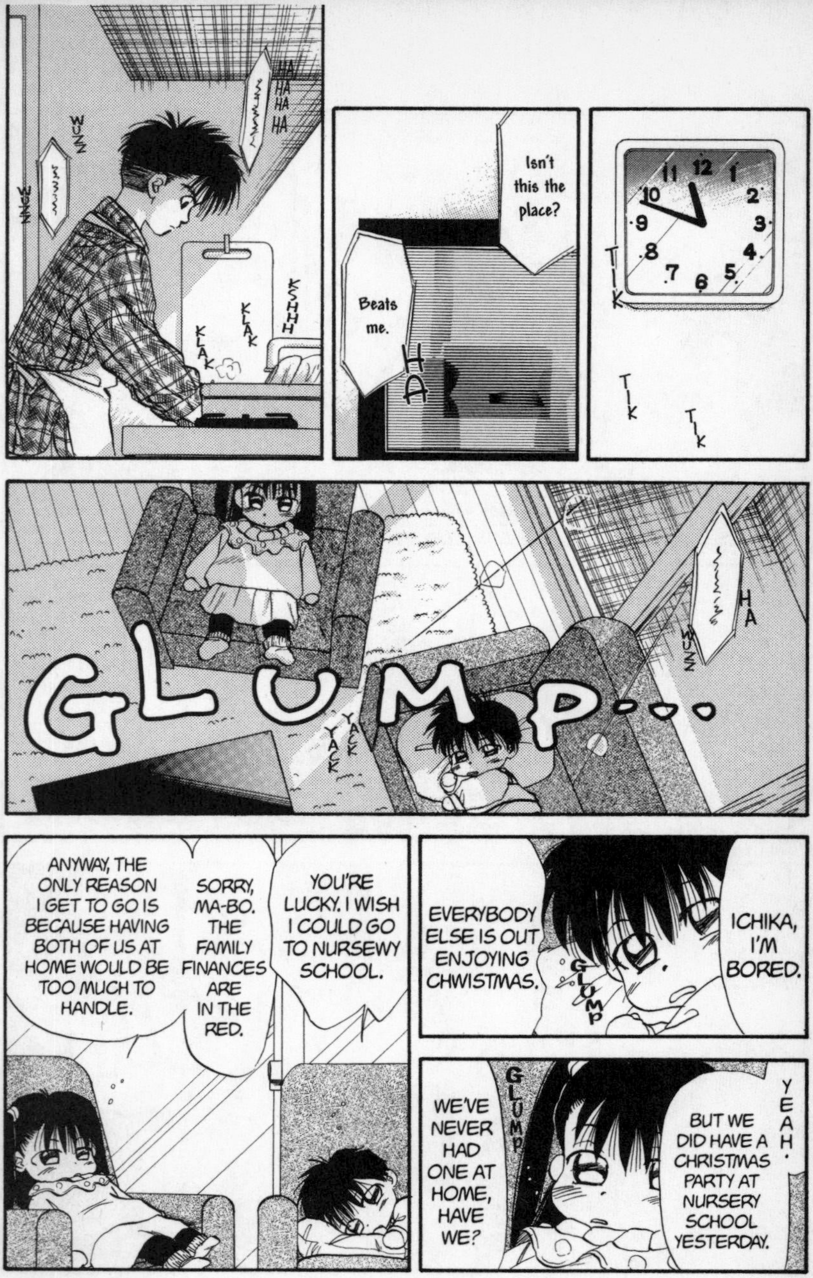
TIK
TIK
TIK
Isn't this the place?
Beats me.
HA
HA HA HA HA
WUZZ
WUZZ
KSHHH
KLAK
KLAK
HA
WUZZ
GLUMP...
YACK YACK
ICHIKA, I'M BORED.
EVERYBODY ELSE IS OUT ENJOYING CHWISTMAS.
GLUMP
YEAH.
BUT WE DID HAVE A CHRISTMAS PARTY AT NURSERY SCHOOL YESTERDAY.
WE'VE NEVER HAD ONE AT HOME, HAVE WE?
GLUMP
YOU'RE LUCKY. I WISH I COULD GO TO NURSEWY SCHOOL.
SORRY, MA-BO. THE FAMILY FINANCES ARE IN THE RED.
ANYWAY, THE ONLY REASON I GET TO GO IS BECAUSE HAVING BOTH OF US AT HOME WOULD BE TOO MUCH TO HANDLE.

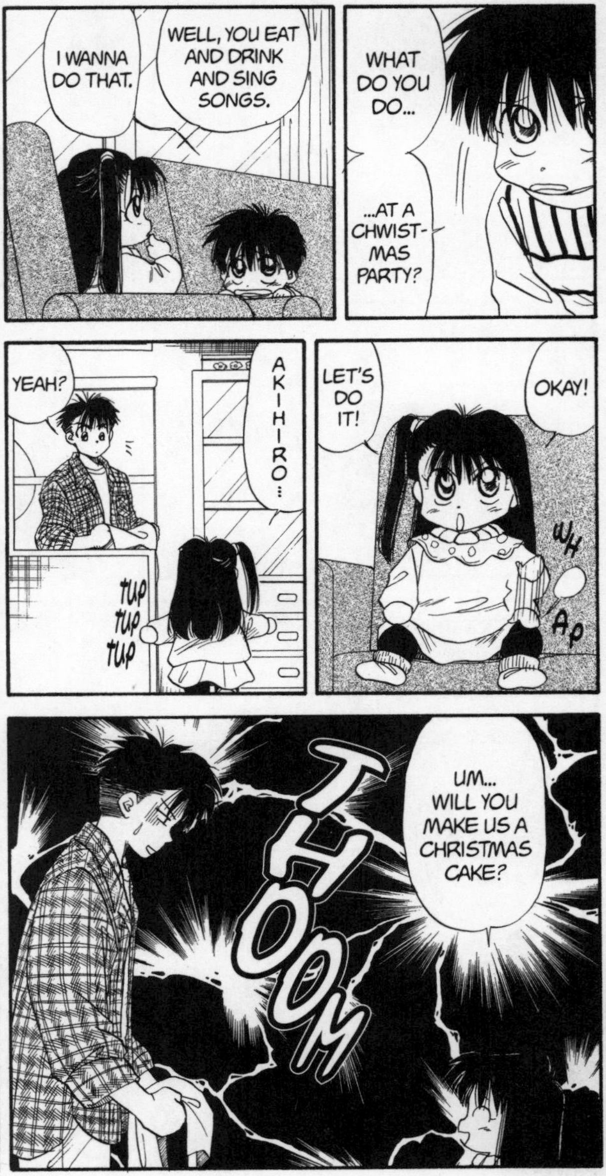
WHAT DO YOU DO...
...AT A CHWIST-MAS PARTY?
WELL, YOU EAT AND DRINK AND SING SONGS.
I WANNA DO THAT.
OKAY!
LET'S DO IT!
WH AP
AKIHIRO...
YEAH?
TUP TUP TUP
UM... WILL YOU MAKE US A CHRISTMAS CAKE?
THOOOM

Author's Note 2

The parents of my sister's fiancé, Devil Fujino, spoil Yoshizo almost beyond belief. Below is proof...

I might be right inside, so please open and close the door carefully.

Yoshizo

▲ Written by Devil's dad (a high school teacher). It was stuck to the door of his room.

MEMO

I have kidnapped Yoshizo. Pay me a ransom!! Ha ha ha...

▲ Written by Devil's mom. This was on the door to my workroom the day she took Yoshizo out without my permission.

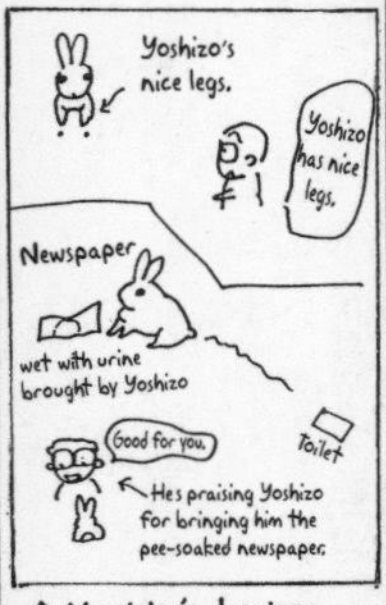
Yoshizo's nice legs.
Yoshizo has nice legs.
Newspaper
wet with urine brought by Yoshizo
Good for you.
Toilet
He's praising Yoshizo for bringing him the pee-soaked newspaper.

▲ My sister's drawings showing what Devil's dad had done.

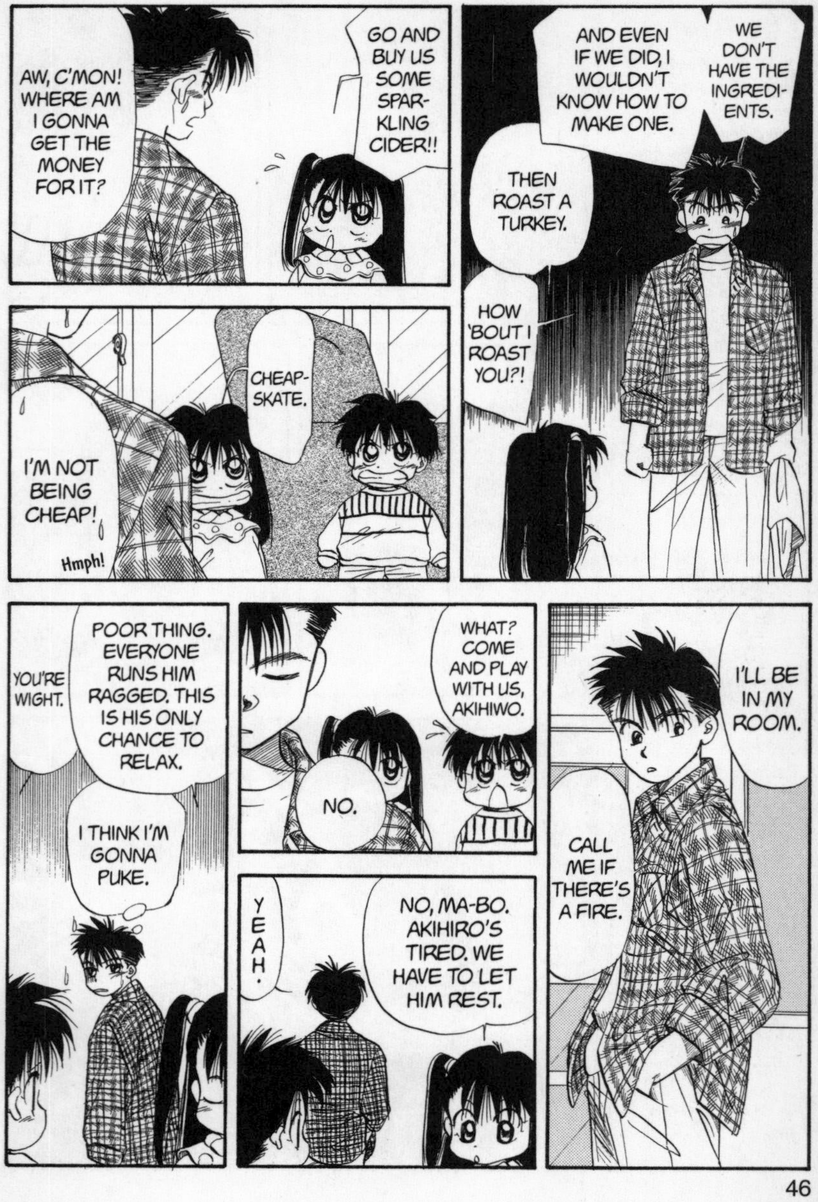
WE DON'T HAVE THE INGREDIENTS.
AND EVEN IF WE DID, I WOULDN'T KNOW HOW TO MAKE ONE.
THEN ROAST A TURKEY.
HOW 'BOUT I ROAST YOU?!
GO AND BUY US SOME SPARKLING CIDER!!
AW, C'MON! WHERE AM I GONNA GET THE MONEY FOR IT?
CHEAPSKATE.
I'M NOT BEING CHEAP!
Hmph!
I'LL BE IN MY ROOM.
CALL ME IF THERE'S A FIRE.
WHAT? COME AND PLAY WITH US, AKIHIWO.
NO.
NO, MA-BO. AKIHIRO'S TIRED. WE HAVE TO LET HIM REST.
YEAH.
POOR THING. EVERYONE RUNS HIM RAGGED. THIS IS HIS ONLY CHANCE TO RELAX.
YOU'RE WIGHT.
I THINK I'M GONNA PUKE.

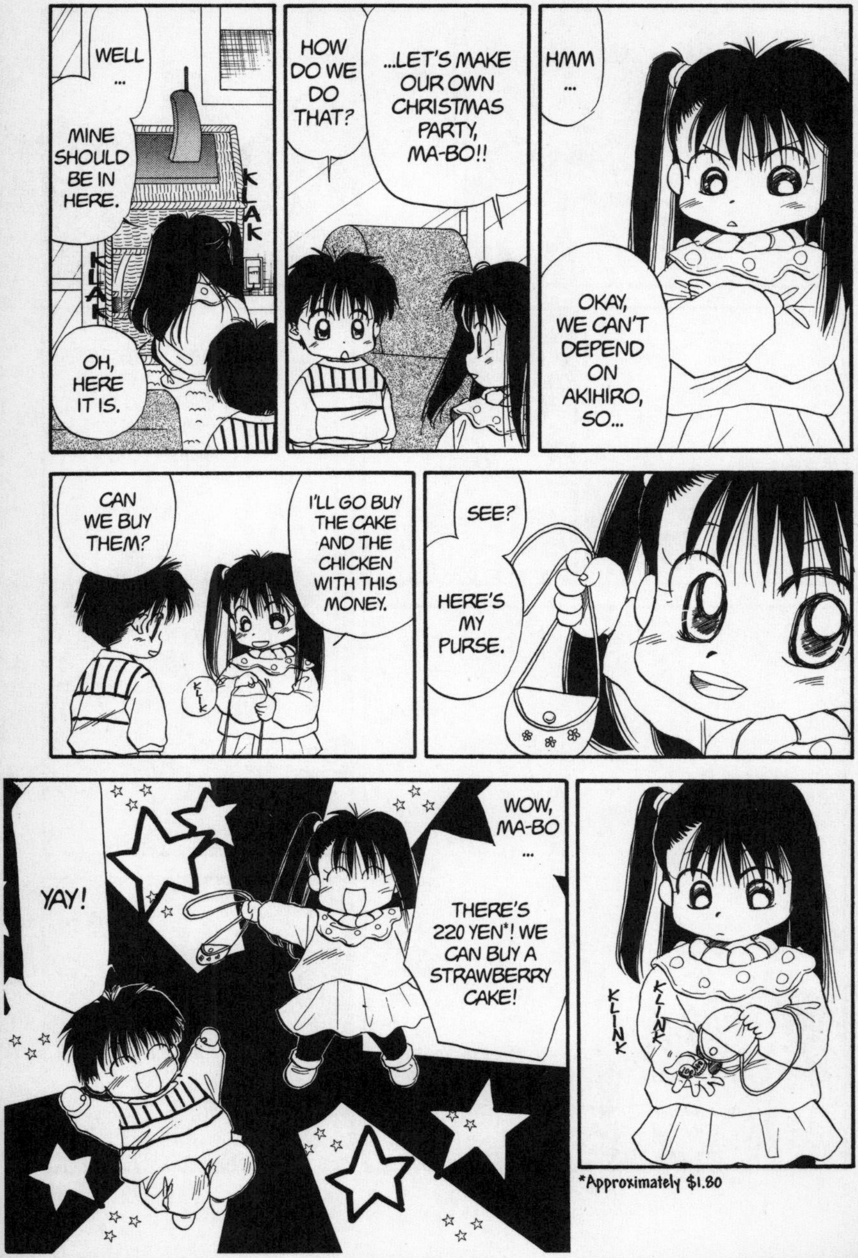
HMM ...
OKAY, WE CAN'T DEPEND ON AKIHIRO, SO...
...LET'S MAKE OUR OWN CHRISTMAS PARTY, MA-BO!!
HOW DO WE DO THAT?
WELL ...
MINE SHOULD BE IN HERE.
KLAK
KLAK
OH, HERE IT IS.
SEE?
HERE'S MY PURSE.
I'LL GO BUY THE CAKE AND THE CHICKEN WITH THIS MONEY.
CAN WE BUY THEM?
KLIK
KLINK
KLINK
WOW, MA-BO ...
THERE'S 220 YEN*! WE CAN BUY A STRAWBERRY CAKE!
YAY!

*Approximately $1.80

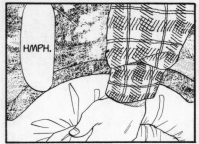

HMPH.

CHAK

OKAY.

MA-BO, BRING ALL THE MONEY YOU HAVE TOO.

WUSH

MA-BO... HE GETS UP BRIGHT AND EARLY, BUT HE NEVER PUTS HIS BEDDING AWAY.

KLAK

SHUP

UMPH

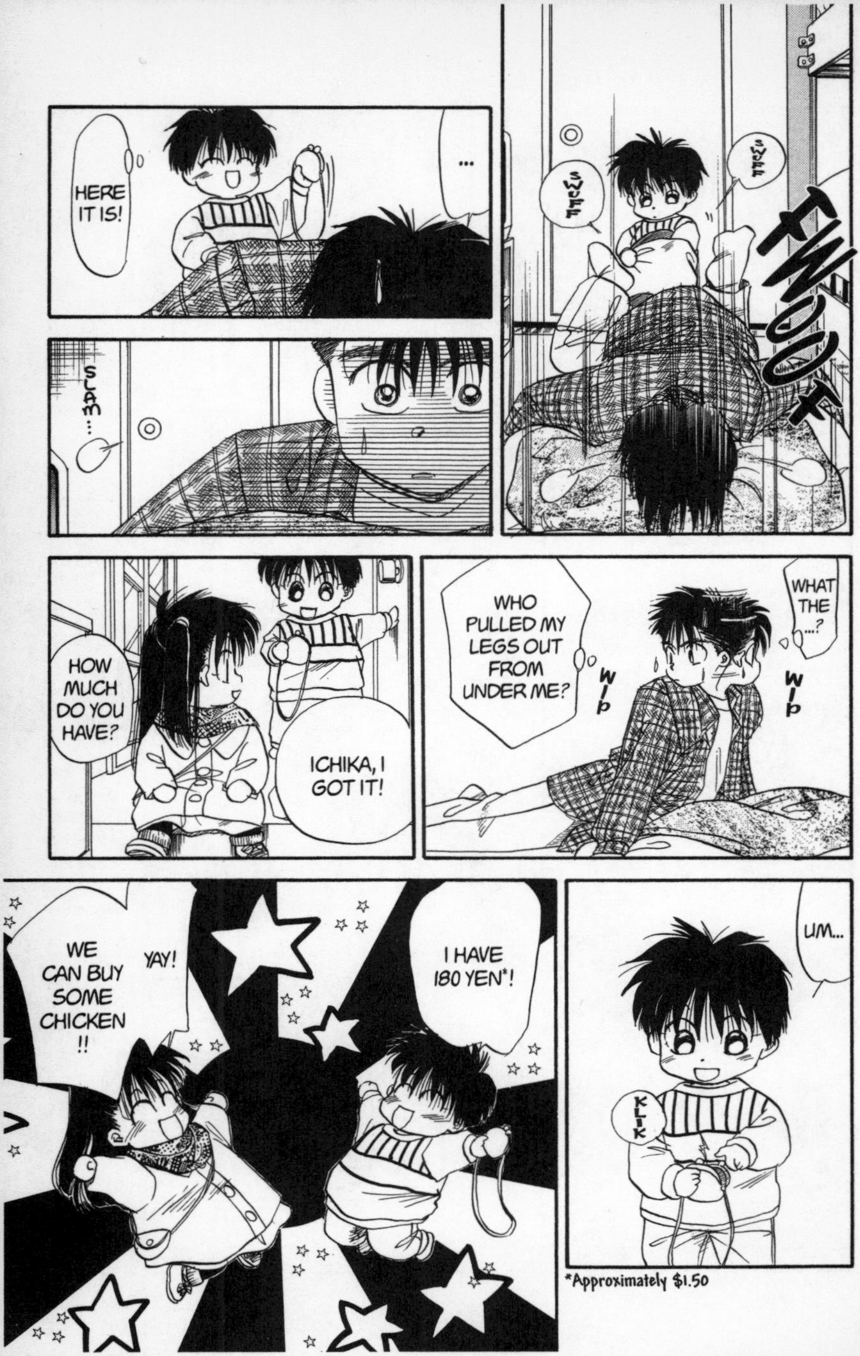
SWUFF
SWUFF
FWOOF
...
HERE IT IS!
SLAM...
WHAT THE ....?
WHO PULLED MY LEGS OUT FROM UNDER ME?
WIP
WIP
ICHIKA, I GOT IT!
HOW MUCH DO YOU HAVE?
UM...
KLIK
I HAVE 180 YEN*!
YAY!
WE CAN BUY SOME CHICKEN !!

*Approximately $1.50

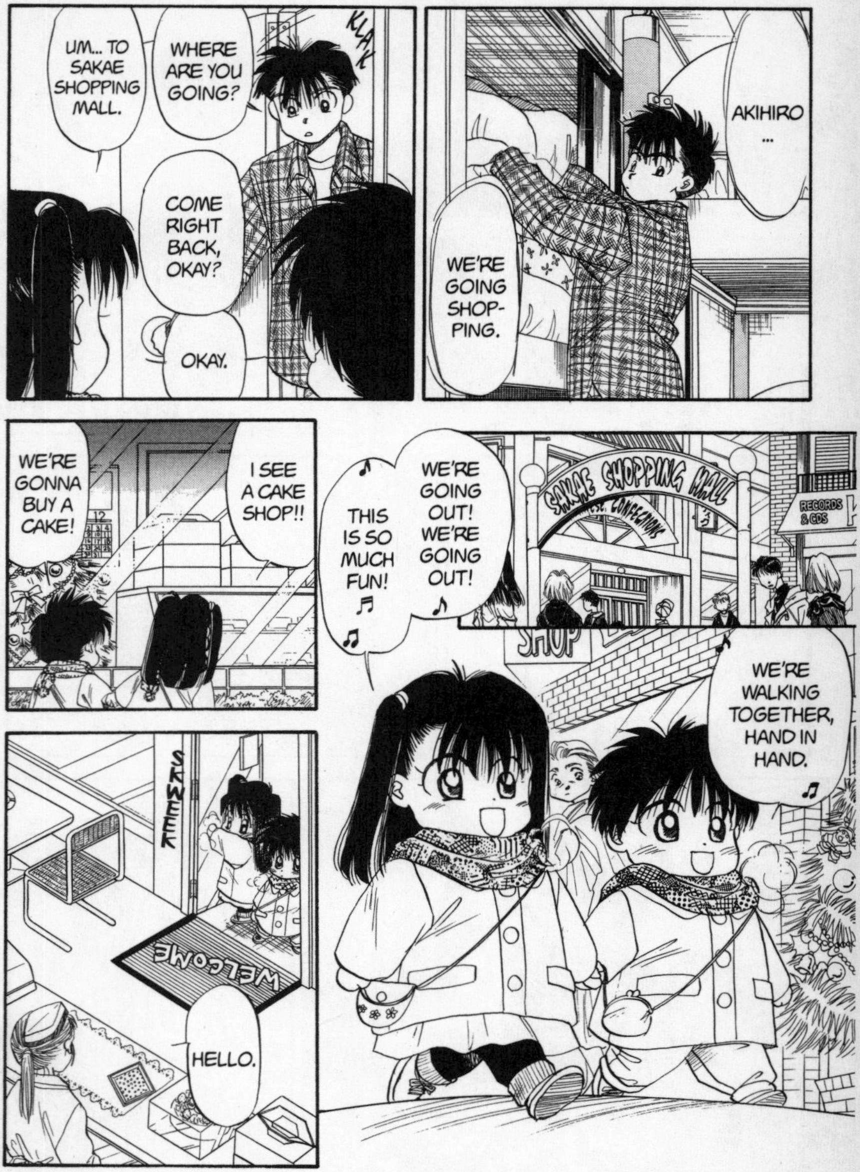
AKIHIRO ...
WE'RE GOING SHOPPING.
KLAK
WHERE ARE YOU GOING?
UM... TO SAKAE SHOPPING MALL.
COME RIGHT BACK, OKAY?
OKAY.
SAKAE SHOPPING MALL
RECORDS & CDS
WE'RE GOING OUT! WE'RE GOING OUT!
THIS IS SO MUCH FUN!
SHOP
WE'RE WALKING TOGETHER, HAND IN HAND.
I SEE A CAKE SHOP!!
WE'RE GONNA BUY A CAKE!
SKWEEK
WELCOME
HELLO.

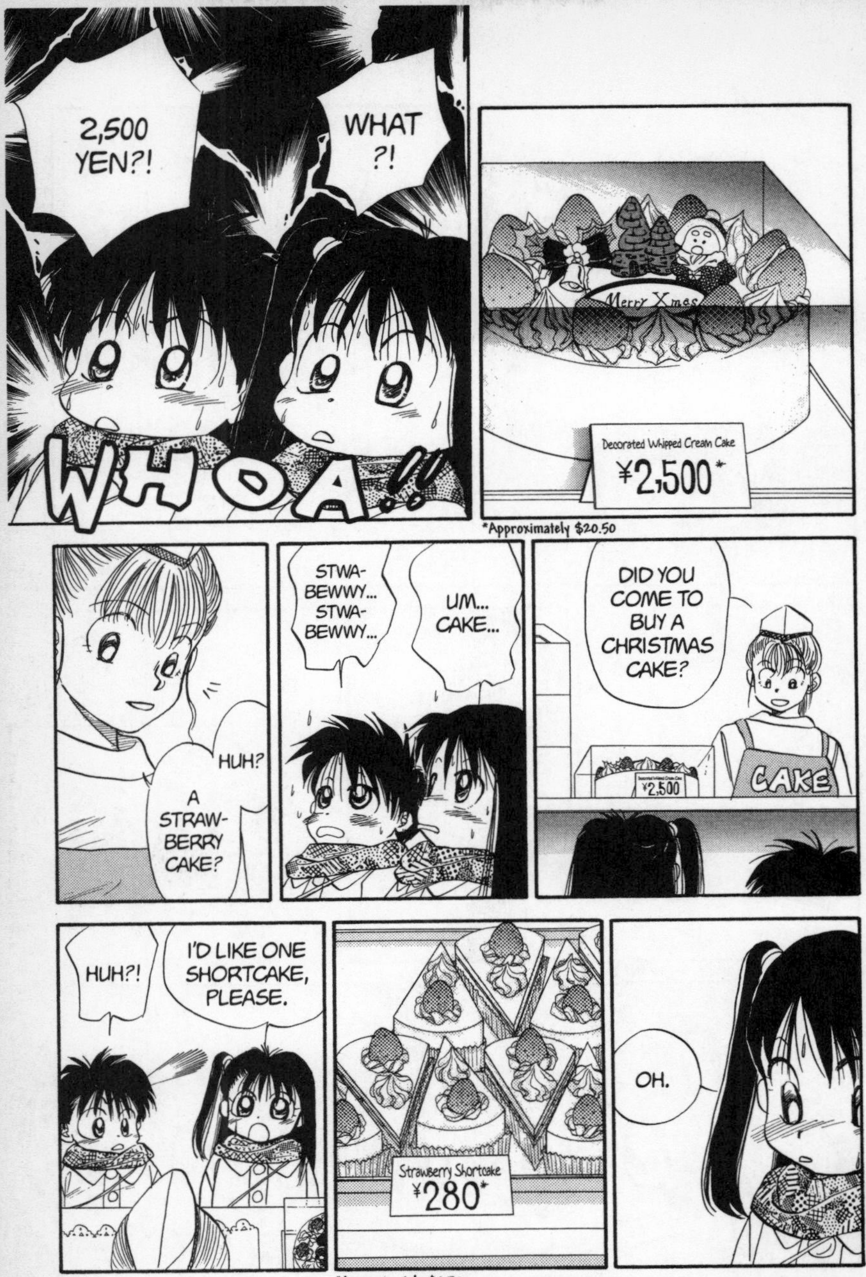
Decorated Whipped Cream Cake
¥2,500*
Merry Xmas
WHAT ?!
2,500 YEN?!
WHOA!!
DID YOU COME TO BUY A CHRISTMAS CAKE?
CAKE
UM... CAKE...
STWA-BEWWY... STWA-BEWWY...
HUH?
A STRAW-BERRY CAKE?
OH.
Strawberry Shortcake
¥280*
I'D LIKE ONE SHORTCAKE, PLEASE.
HUH?!

*Approximately $20.50

*Approximately $2.30

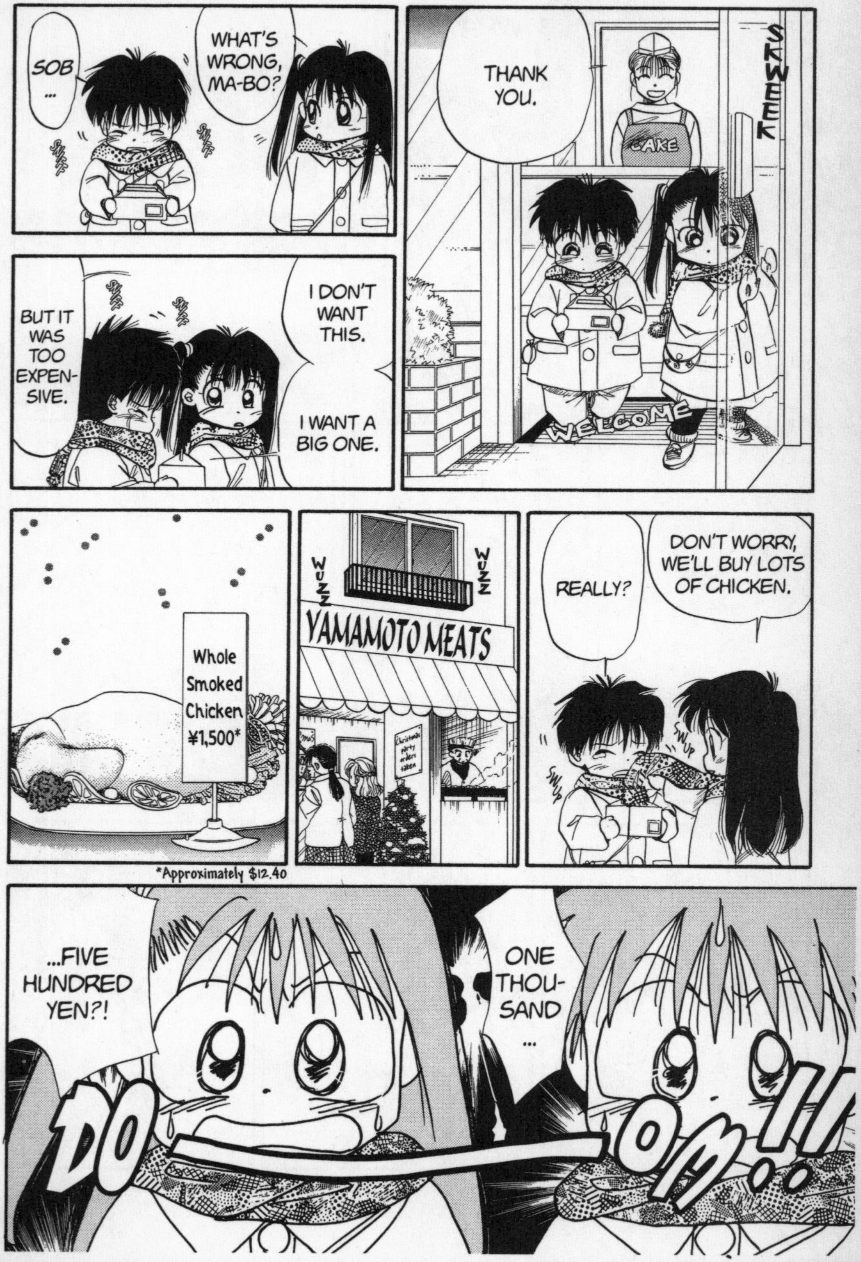
SKWEEK
THANK YOU.
CAKE
WELCOME
WHAT'S WRONG, MA-BO?
SOB ...
SNIFF
SNIFF
I DON'T WANT THIS.
I WANT A BIG ONE.
SNIFF
SNIFF
BUT IT WAS TOO EXPENSIVE.
DON'T WORRY, WE'LL BUY LOTS OF CHICKEN.
REALLY?
SWUP
SWUP
WUZZ
WUZZ
YAMAMOTO MEATS
Whole Smoked Chicken ¥1,500*
ONE THOUSAND ...
...FIVE HUNDRED YEN?!
DO-ON!!
*Approximately $12.40

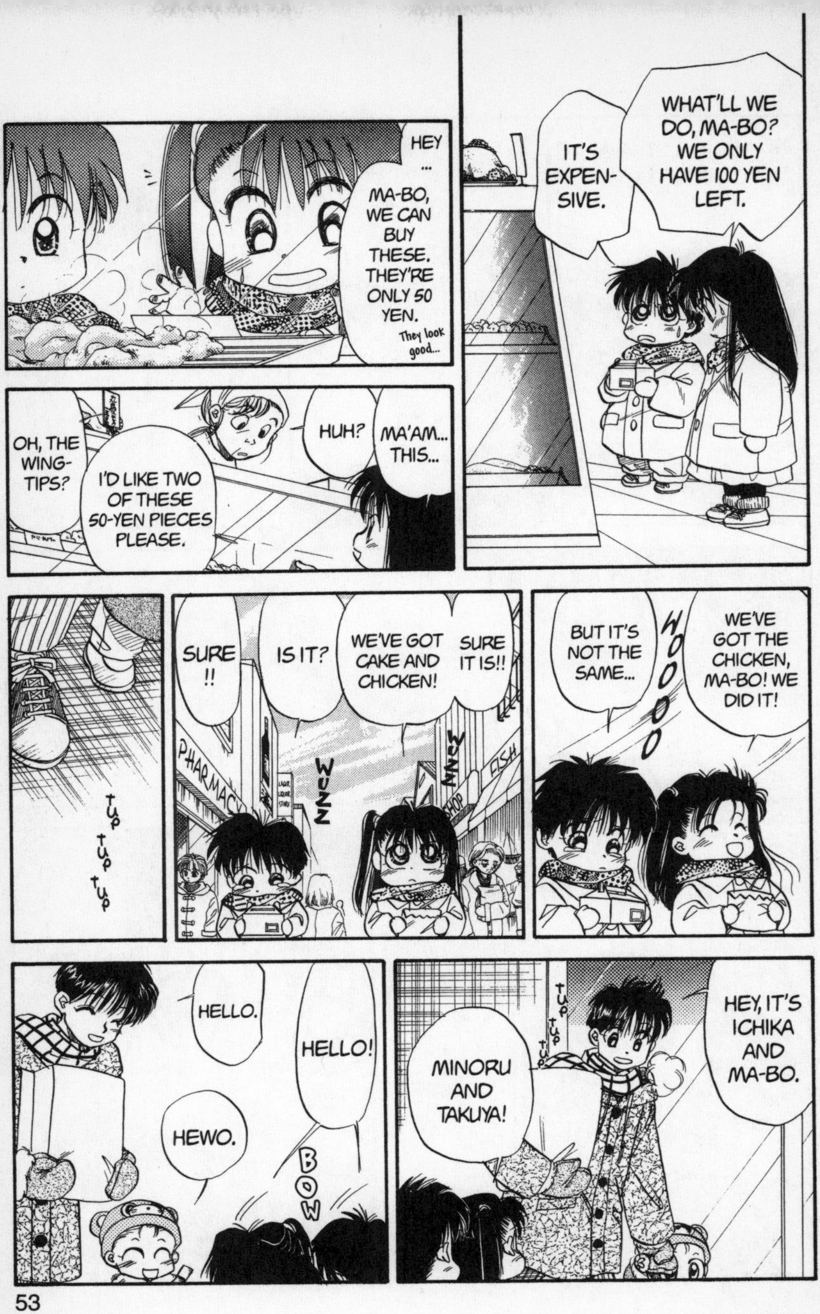
WHAT'LL WE DO, MA-BO? WE ONLY HAVE 100 YEN LEFT.
IT'S EXPENSIVE.
HEY ...
MA-BO, WE CAN BUY THESE. THEY'RE ONLY 50 YEN.
They look good...
MA'AM... THIS...
HUH?
OH, THE WING-TIPS?
I'D LIKE TWO OF THESE 50-YEN PIECES PLEASE.
WE'VE GOT THE CHICKEN, MA-BO! WE DID IT!
WOOOOOO
BUT IT'S NOT THE SAME...
SURE IT IS!!
FISH
SHOP
WE'VE GOT CAKE AND CHICKEN!
IS IT?
WUZZ
LIQUOR STORE
PHARMACY
SURE !!
TUP TUP TUP
HEY, IT'S ICHIKA AND MA-BO.
TUP TUP TUP
MINORU AND TAKUYA!
HELLO!
HELLO.
BOW
HEWO.

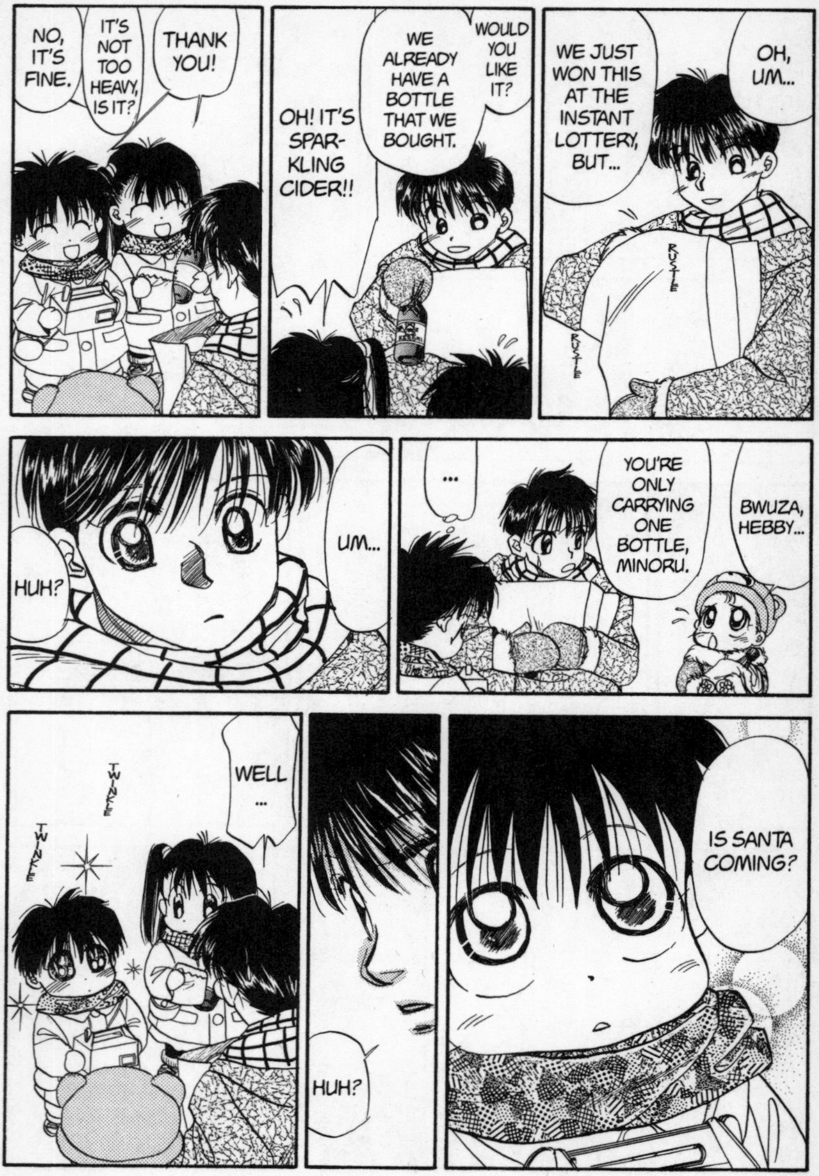
OH, UM...
WE JUST WON THIS AT THE INSTANT LOTTERY, BUT...
RUSTLE
RUSTLE
WOULD YOU LIKE IT?
WE ALREADY HAVE A BOTTLE THAT WE BOUGHT.
OH! IT'S SPAR-KLING CIDER!!
THANK YOU!
IT'S NOT TOO HEAVY, IS IT?
NO, IT'S FINE.
BWUZA, HEBBY...
YOU'RE ONLY CARRYING ONE BOTTLE, MINORU.
...
UM...
HUH?
IS SANTA COMING?
HUH?
WELL ...
TWINKLE
TWINKLE

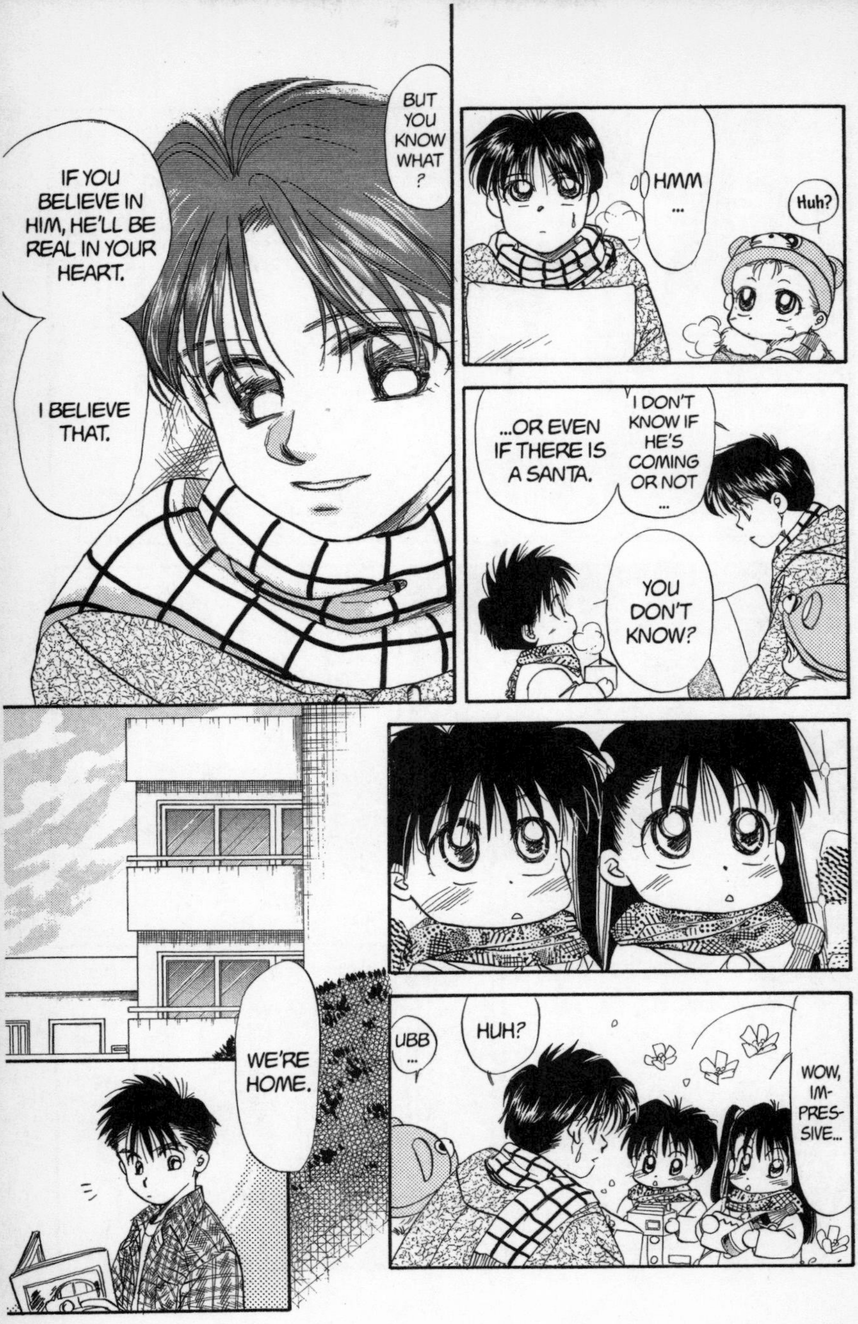
Huh?
HMM ...
I DON'T KNOW IF HE'S COMING OR NOT ...
...OR EVEN IF THERE IS A SANTA.
YOU DON'T KNOW?
BUT YOU KNOW WHAT?
IF YOU BELIEVE IN HIM, HE'LL BE REAL IN YOUR HEART.
I BELIEVE THAT.
WOW, IM-PRES-SIVE...
HUH?
UBB ...
WE'RE HOME.

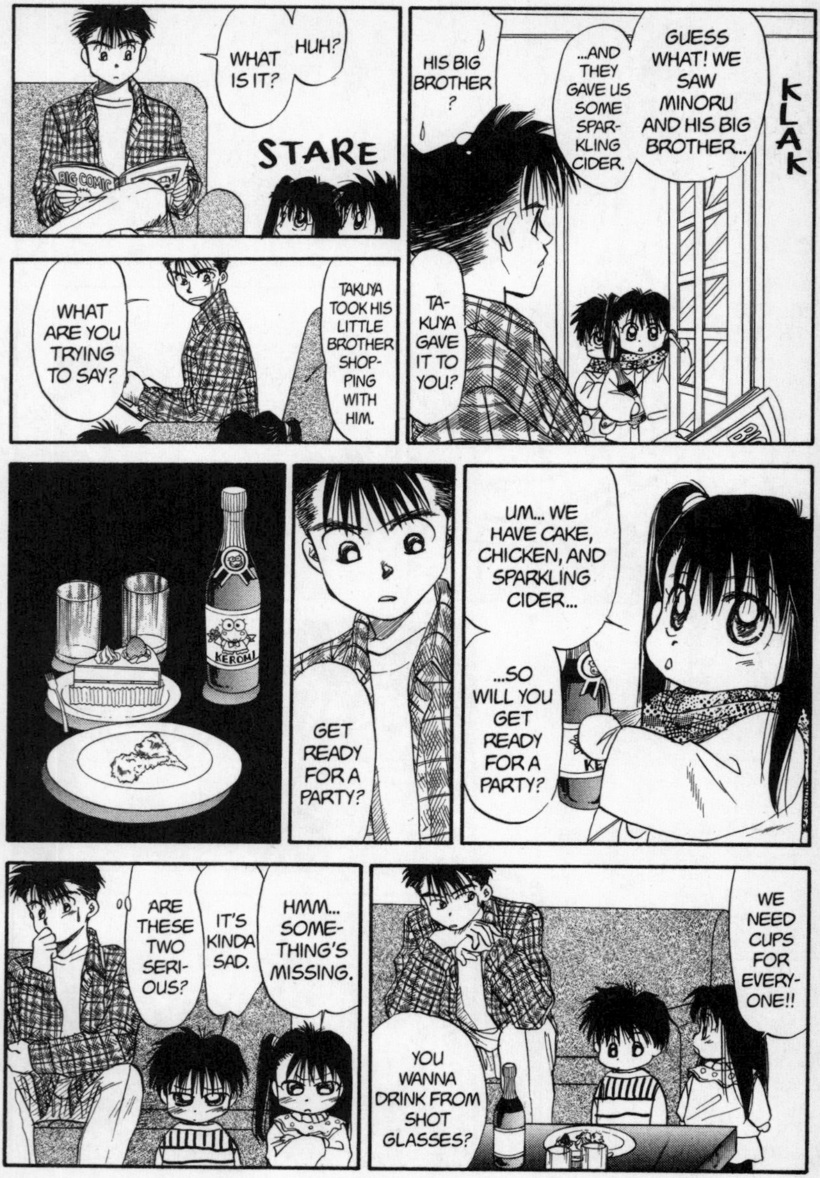
KLAK
GUESS WHAT! WE SAW MINORU AND HIS BIG BROTHER...
...AND THEY GAVE US SOME SPAR-KLING CIDER.
HIS BIG BROTHER?
TA-KUYA GAVE IT TO YOU?
HUH?
WHAT IS IT?
STARE
BIG COMIC
TAKUYA TOOK HIS LITTLE BROTHER SHOP-PING WITH HIM.
WHAT ARE YOU TRYING TO SAY?
UM... WE HAVE CAKE, CHICKEN, AND SPARKLING CIDER...
...SO WILL YOU GET READY FOR A PARTY?
GET READY FOR A PARTY?
KEROMI
WE NEED CUPS FOR EVERY-ONE!!
YOU WANNA DRINK FROM SHOT GLASSES?
HMM... SOME-THING'S MISSING.
IT'S KINDA SAD.
ARE THESE TWO SERI-OUS?

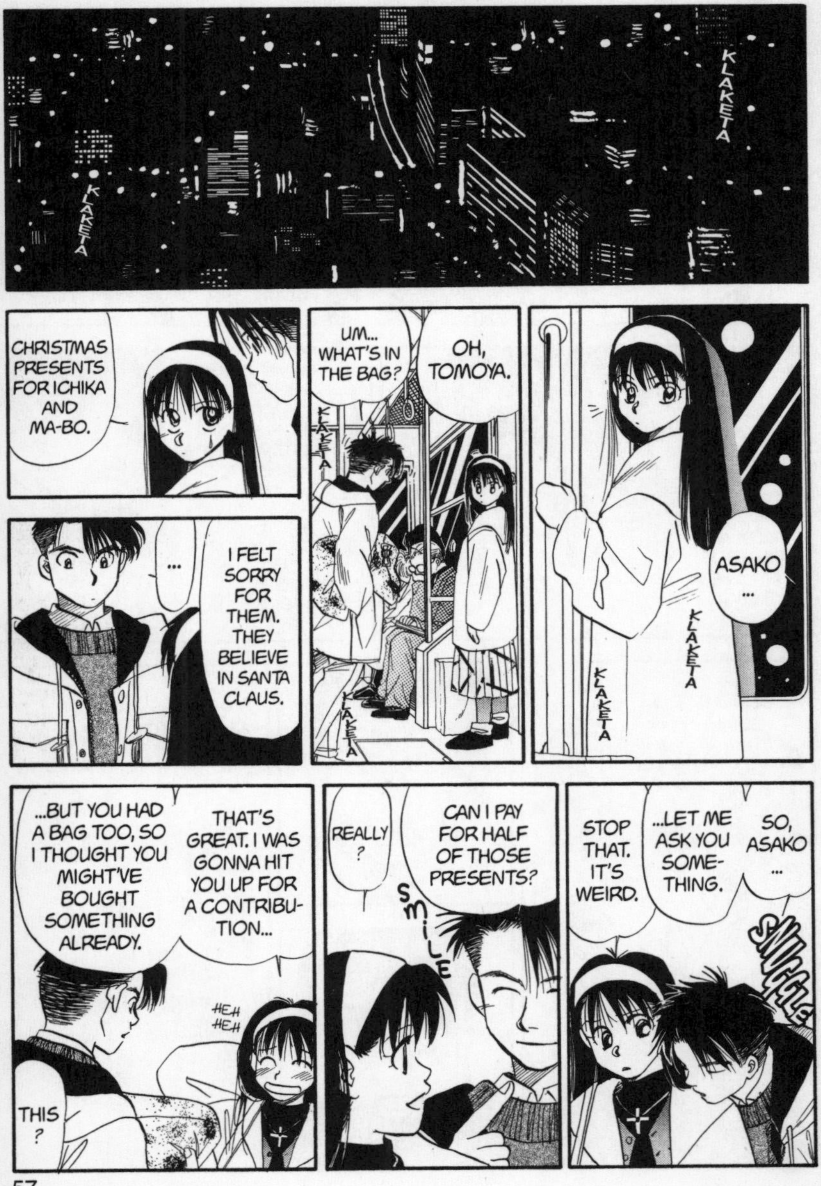
KLAKETA
KLAKETA
ASAKO ...
KLAKETA
KLAKETA
OH, TOMOYA.
UM... WHAT'S IN THE BAG?
KLAKETA
KLAKETA
CHRISTMAS PRESENTS FOR ICHIKA AND MA-BO.
I FELT SORRY FOR THEM. THEY BELIEVE IN SANTA CLAUS.
...
SO, ASAKO ...
...LET ME ASK YOU SOME-THING.
STOP THAT. IT'S WEIRD.
SNUGGLE
CAN I PAY FOR HALF OF THOSE PRESENTS?
REALLY ?
SMILE
THAT'S GREAT. I WAS GONNA HIT YOU UP FOR A CONTRIBU-TION...
...BUT YOU HAD A BAG TOO, SO I THOUGHT YOU MIGHT'VE BOUGHT SOMETHING ALREADY.
HEH HEH
THIS ?

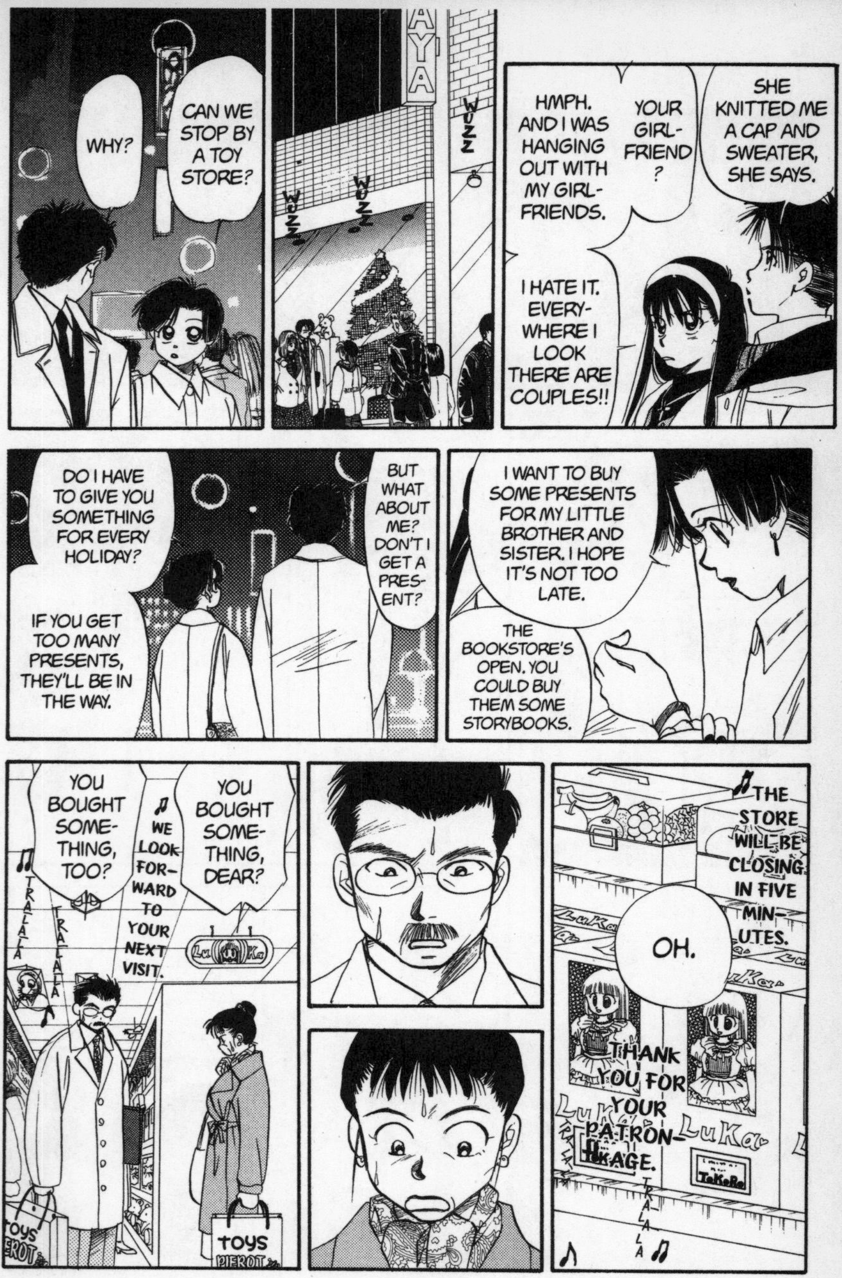
SHE KNITTED ME A CAP AND SWEATER, SHE SAYS.
YOUR GIRLFRIEND?
HMPH. AND I WAS HANGING OUT WITH MY GIRLFRIENDS.
I HATE IT. EVERYWHERE I LOOK THERE ARE COUPLES!!
AYA
WUZZ
WUZZ
WUZZ
CAN WE STOP BY A TOY STORE?
WHY?
I WANT TO BUY SOME PRESENTS FOR MY LITTLE BROTHER AND SISTER. I HOPE IT'S NOT TOO LATE.
THE BOOKSTORE'S OPEN. YOU COULD BUY THEM SOME STORYBOOKS.
BUT WHAT ABOUT ME? DON'T I GET A PRESENT?
DO I HAVE TO GIVE YOU SOMETHING FOR EVERY HOLIDAY?
IF YOU GET TOO MANY PRESENTS, THEY'LL BE IN THE WAY.
THE STORE WILL BE CLOSING IN FIVE MINUTES.
OH.
THANK YOU FOR YOUR PATRONAGE.
TRALALA
YOU BOUGHT SOMETHING, DEAR?
WE LOOK FORWARD TO YOUR NEXT VISIT.
YOU BOUGHT SOMETHING, TOO?
TRALALA
TRALALA
TOYS PIEROT

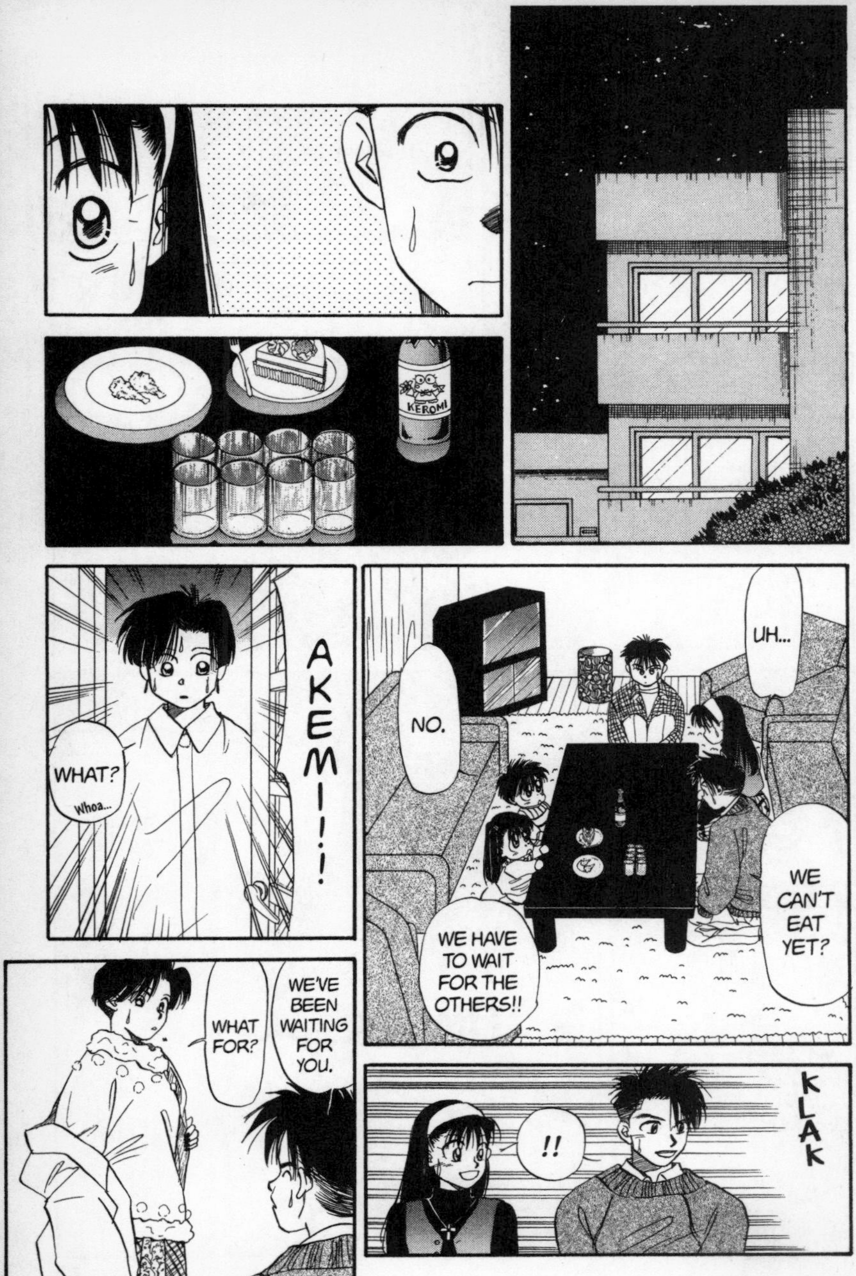
KEROMI
UH...
NO.
WE CAN'T EAT YET?
WE HAVE TO WAIT FOR THE OTHERS!!
AKEMI!!!
WHAT?
whoa...
KLAK
!!
WE'VE BEEN WAITING FOR YOU.
WHAT FOR?

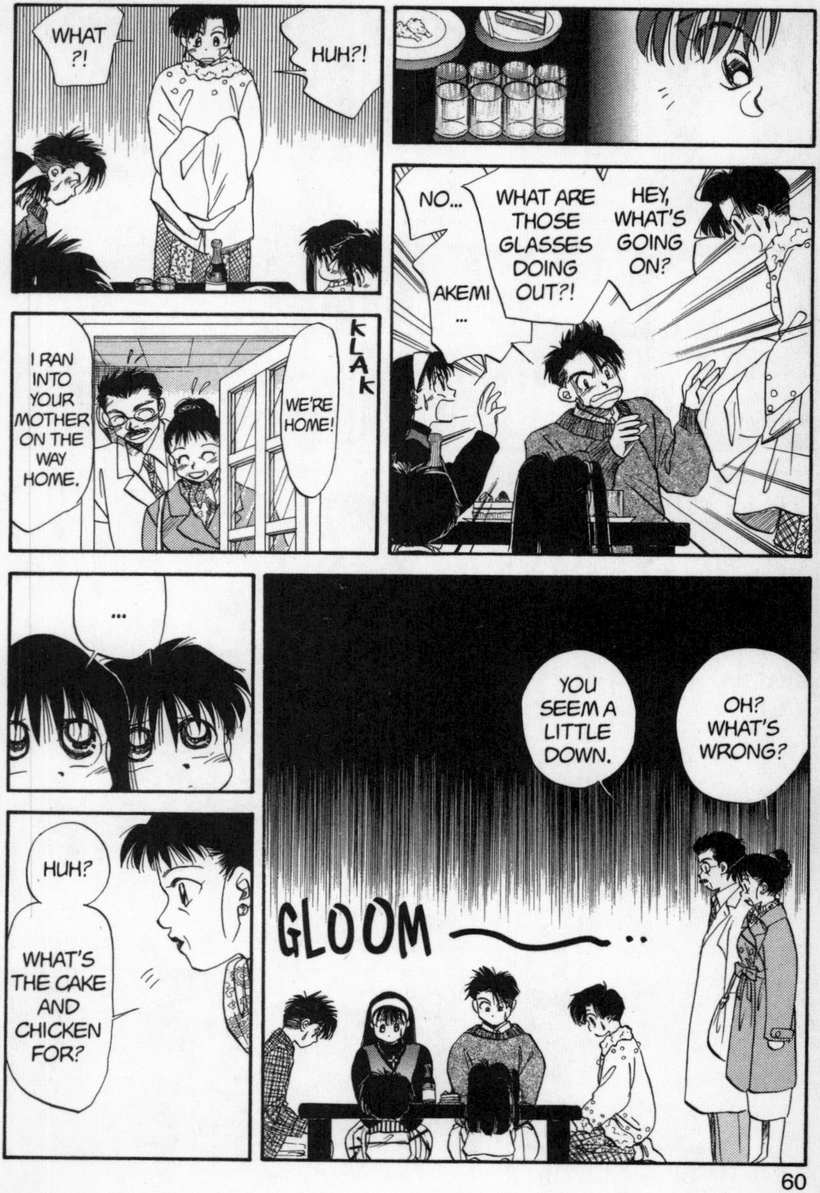
HUH?!
WHAT ?!
HEY, WHAT'S GOING ON?
WHAT ARE THOSE GLASSES DOING OUT?!
NO... AKEMI ...
KLAK
WE'RE HOME!
I RAN INTO YOUR MOTHER ON THE WAY HOME.
OH? WHAT'S WRONG?
YOU SEEM A LITTLE DOWN.
GLOOM
...
HUH?
WHAT'S THE CAKE AND CHICKEN FOR?

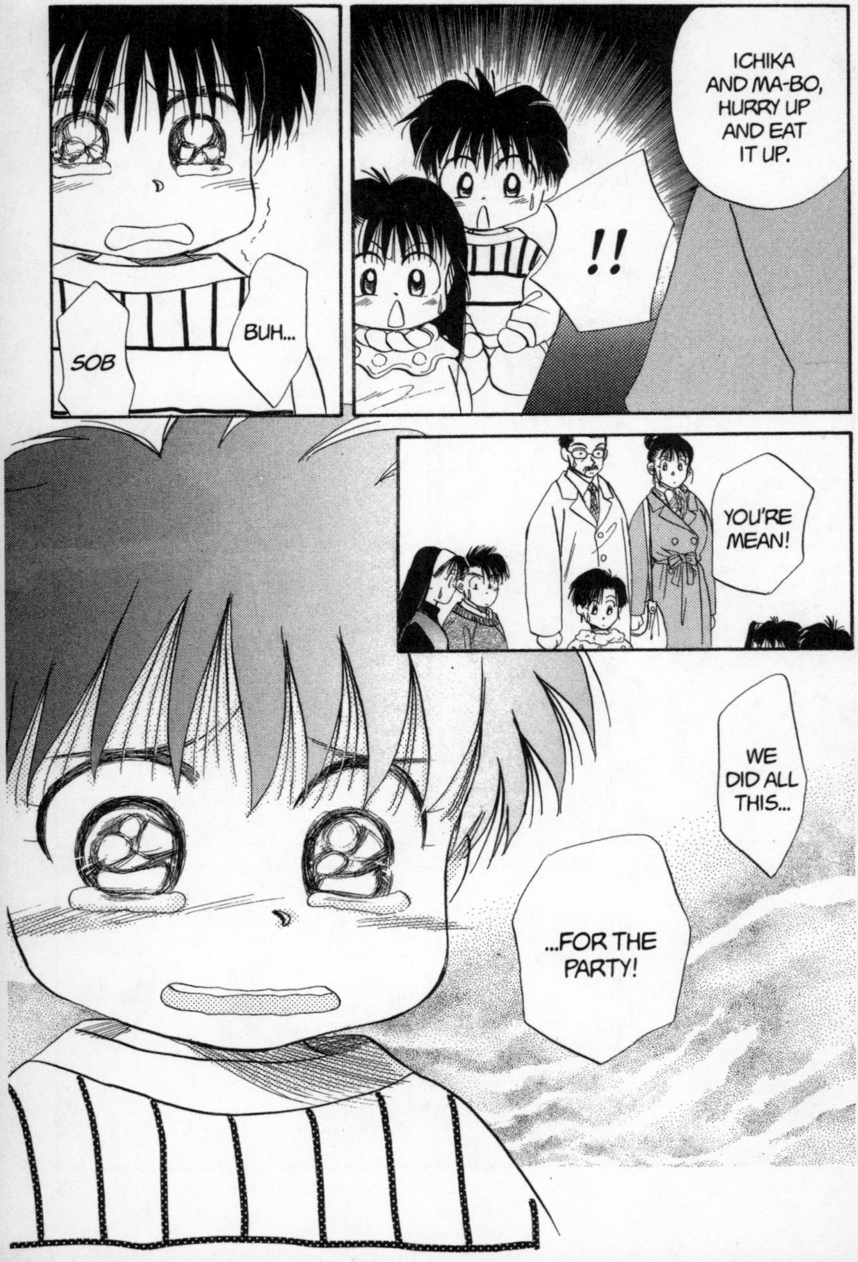
ICHIKA AND MA-BO, HURRY UP AND EAT IT UP.
!!
BUH...
SOB
YOU'RE MEAN!
WE DID ALL THIS...
...FOR THE PARTY!

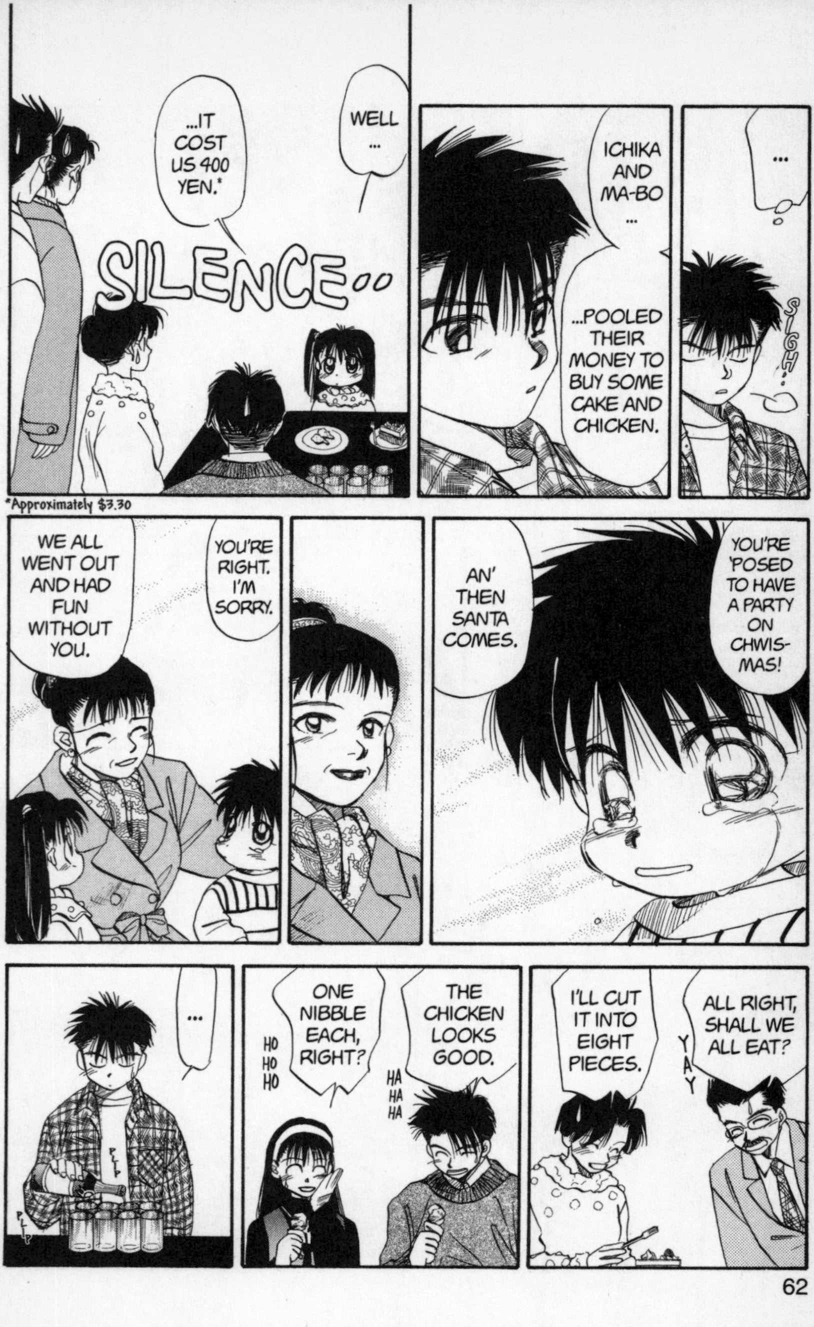
...
SIGH!
ICHIKA AND MA-BO ...
...POOLED THEIR MONEY TO BUY SOME CAKE AND CHICKEN.
WELL ...
...IT COST US 400 YEN.*
SILENCE...
YOU'RE 'POSED TO HAVE A PARTY ON CHWIS-MAS!
AN' THEN SANTA COMES.
YOU'RE RIGHT. I'M SORRY.
WE ALL WENT OUT AND HAD FUN WITHOUT YOU.
ALL RIGHT, SHALL WE ALL EAT?
YAY
I'LL CUT IT INTO EIGHT PIECES.
THE CHICKEN LOOKS GOOD.
HA HA HA
ONE NIBBLE EACH, RIGHT?
HO HO HO
...
PLIP
PLIP
*Approximately $3.30

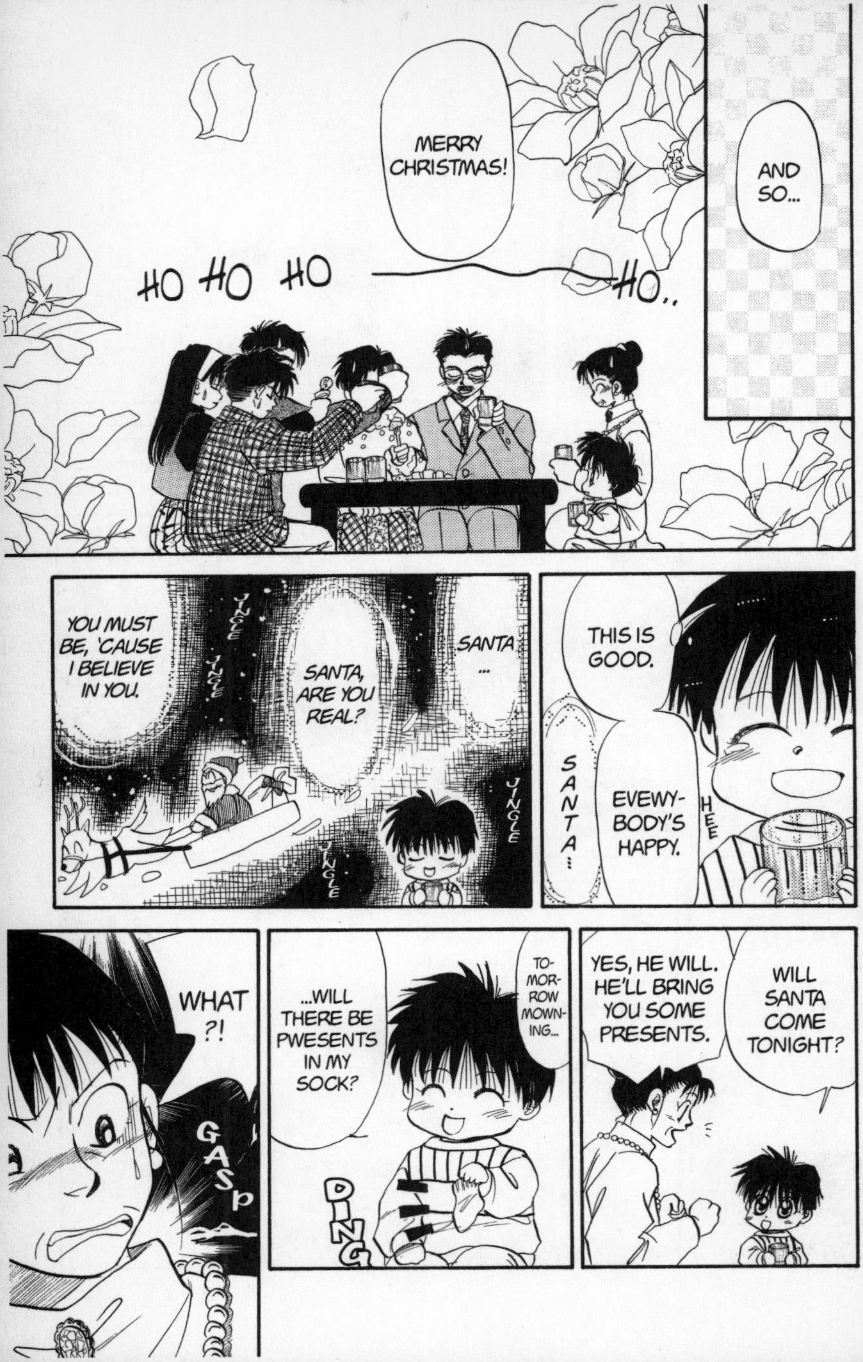
AND SO...
MERRY CHRISTMAS!
HO HO HO HO..
THIS IS GOOD.
EVEWY-BODY'S HAPPY.
HEE
SANTA...
JINGLE
SANTA ...
SANTA, ARE YOU REAL?
JINGLE
JINGLE
YOU MUST BE, 'CAUSE I BELIEVE IN YOU.
JINGLE
WILL SANTA COME TONIGHT?
YES, HE WILL. HE'LL BRING YOU SOME PRESENTS.
TO-MOR-ROW MOWN-ING...
...WILL THERE BE PWESENTS IN MY SOCK?
DING
WHAT ?!
GASp

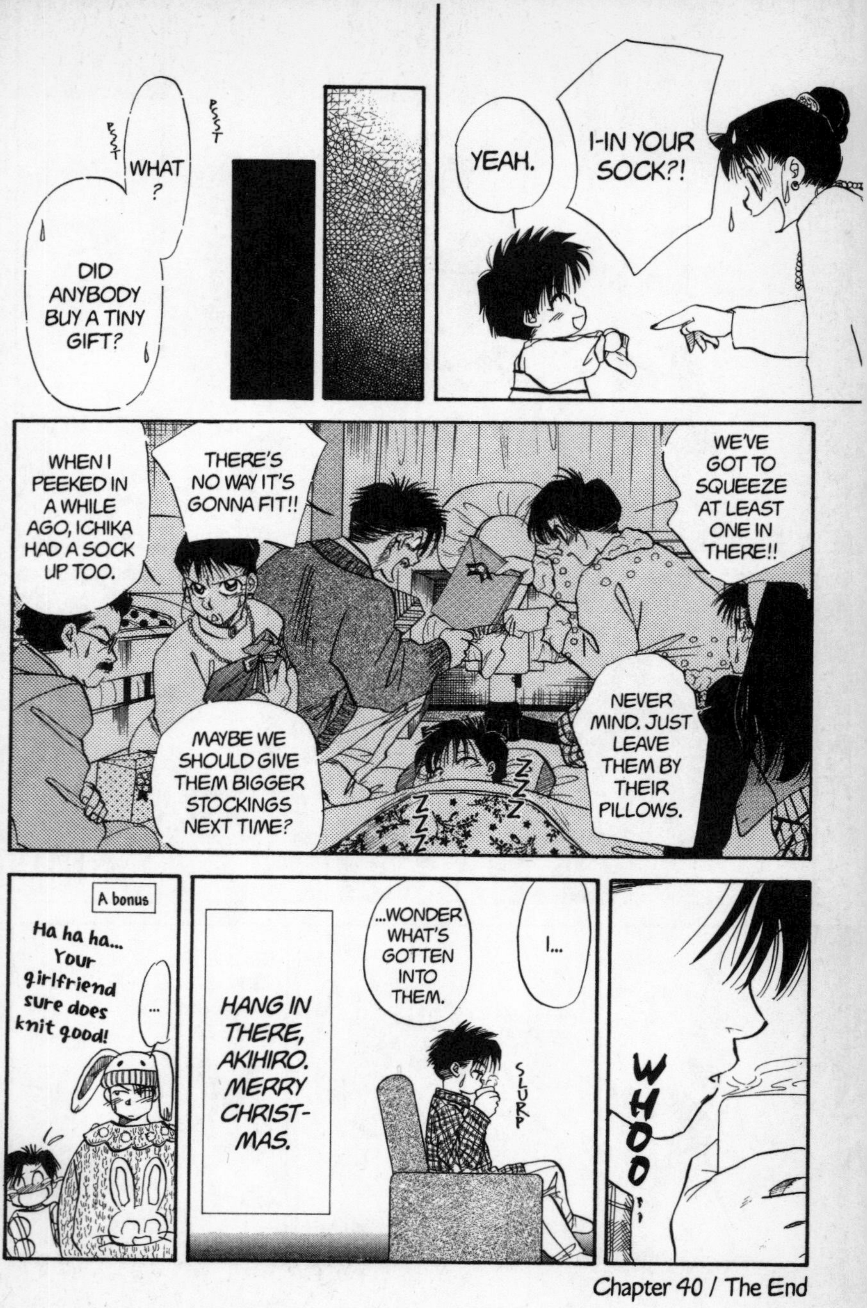
I-IN YOUR SOCK?!
YEAH.
PSST
PSST
WHAT?
DID ANYBODY BUY A TINY GIFT?
WE'VE GOT TO SQUEEZE AT LEAST ONE IN THERE!!
THERE'S NO WAY IT'S GONNA FIT!!
WHEN I PEEKED IN A WHILE AGO, ICHIKA HAD A SOCK UP TOO.
NEVER MIND. JUST LEAVE THEM BY THEIR PILLOWS.
ZZZ
ZZZ
MAYBE WE SHOULD GIVE THEM BIGGER STOCKINGS NEXT TIME?
WHOO
I...
...WONDER WHAT'S GOTTEN INTO THEM.
SLURP
HANG IN THERE, AKIHIRO. MERRY CHRIST-MAS.
A bonus
Ha ha ha... Your girlfriend sure does knit good!
...

Chapter 40 / The End

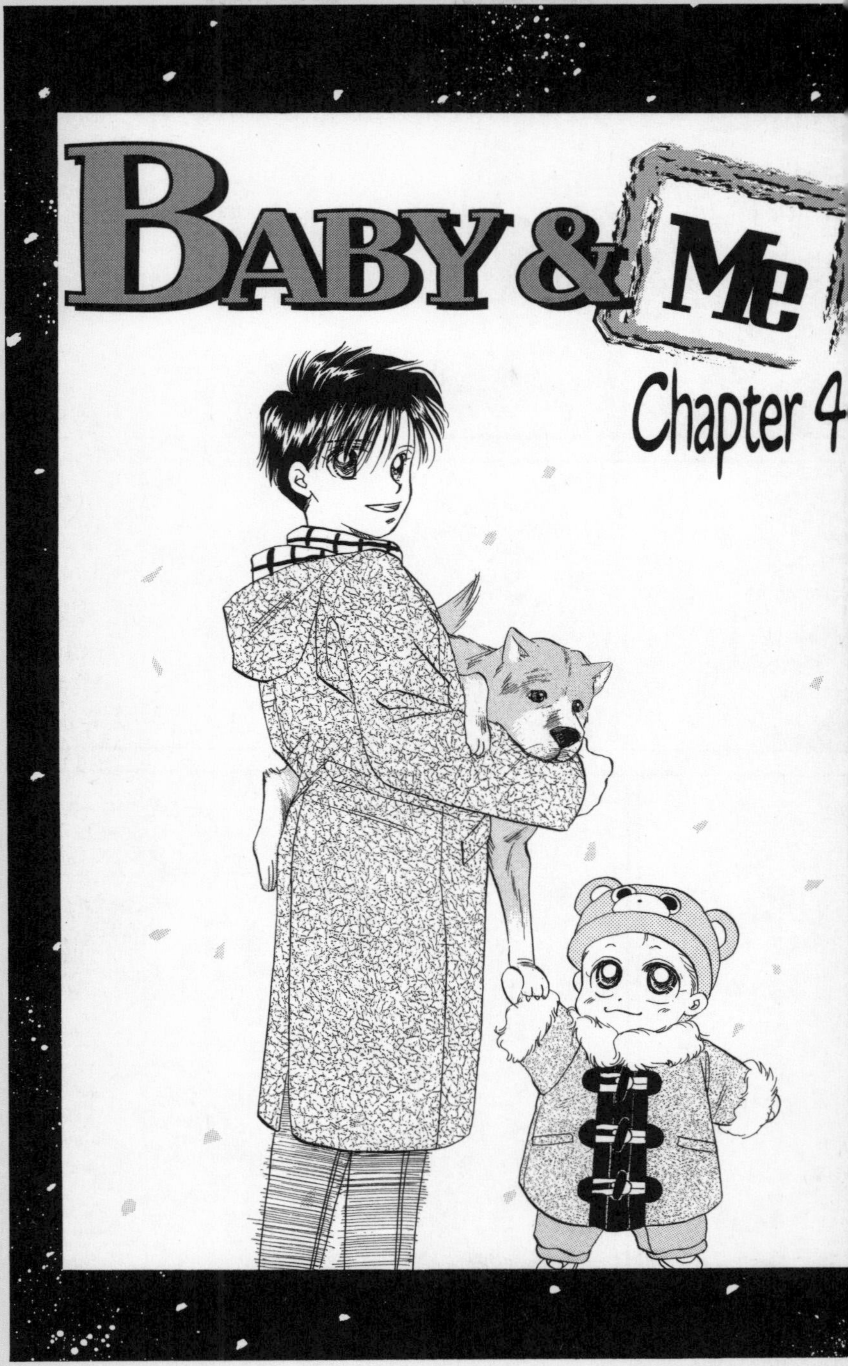
BABY & Me
Chapter 4

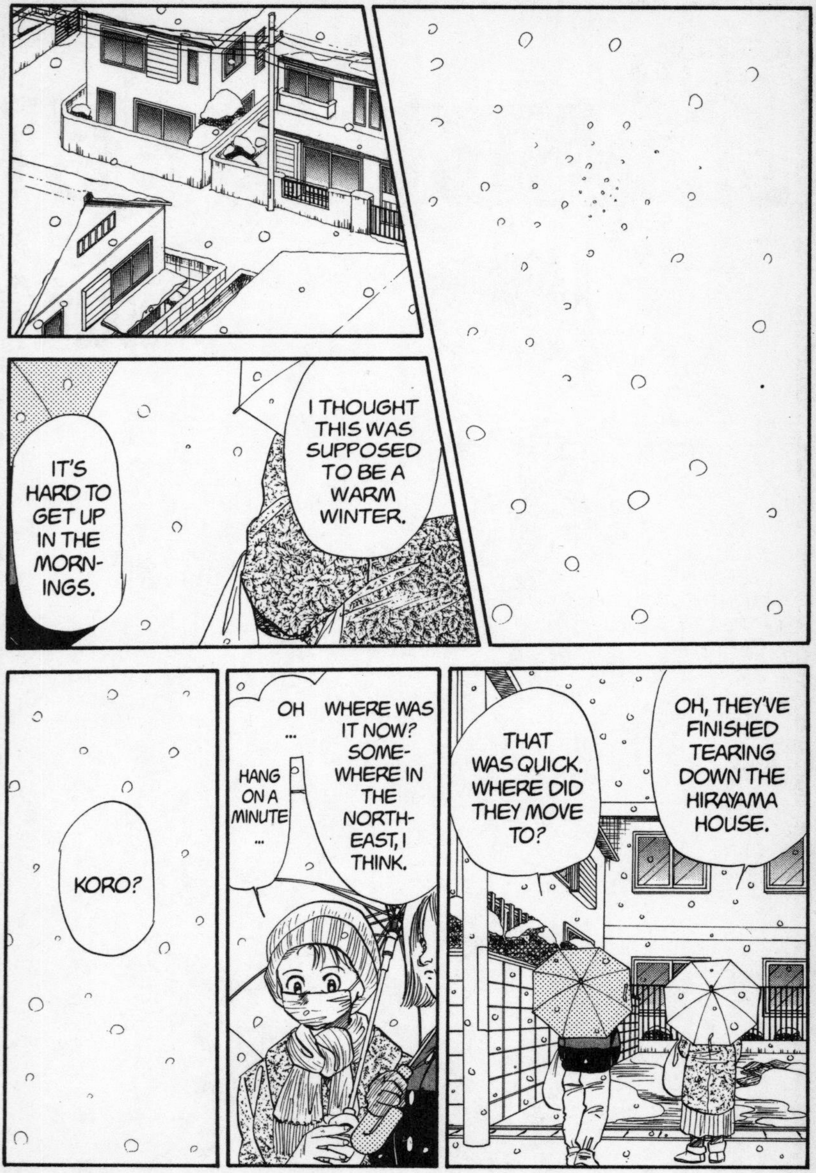
I THOUGHT THIS WAS SUPPOSED TO BE A WARM WINTER.
IT'S HARD TO GET UP IN THE MORNINGS.
OH, THEY'VE FINISHED TEARING DOWN THE HIRAYAMA HOUSE.
THAT WAS QUICK. WHERE DID THEY MOVE TO?
WHERE WAS IT NOW? SOMEWHERE IN THE NORTHEAST, I THINK.
OH ...
HANG ON A MINUTE ...
KORO?

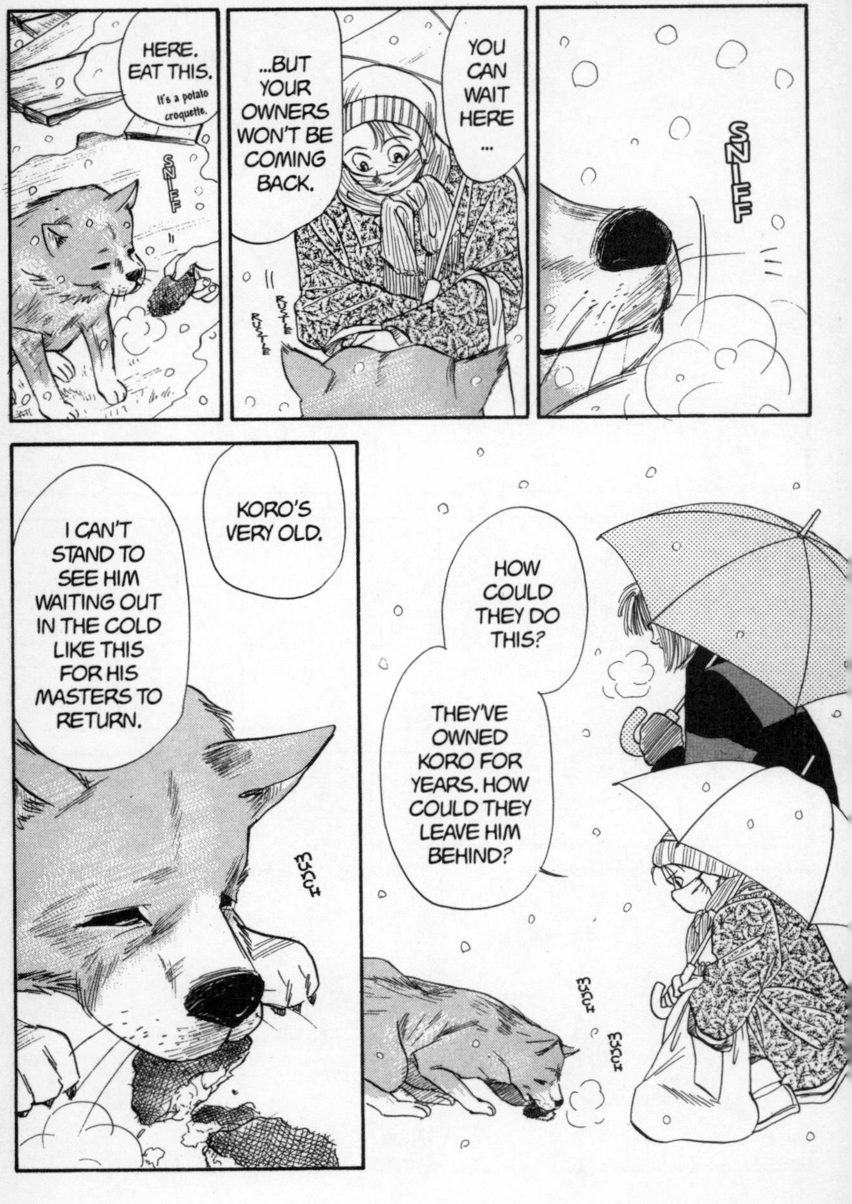

SNIFF
YOU CAN WAIT HERE ...
...BUT YOUR OWNERS WON'T BE COMING BACK.
RUSTLE RUSTLE
HERE. EAT THIS.
It's a potato croquette.
SNIFF
HOW COULD THEY DO THIS?
THEY'VE OWNED KORO FOR YEARS. HOW COULD THEY LEAVE HIM BEHIND?
MUNCH
MUNCH
KORO'S VERY OLD.
I CAN'T STAND TO SEE HIM WAITING OUT IN THE COLD LIKE THIS FOR HIS MASTERS TO RETURN.
MUNCH

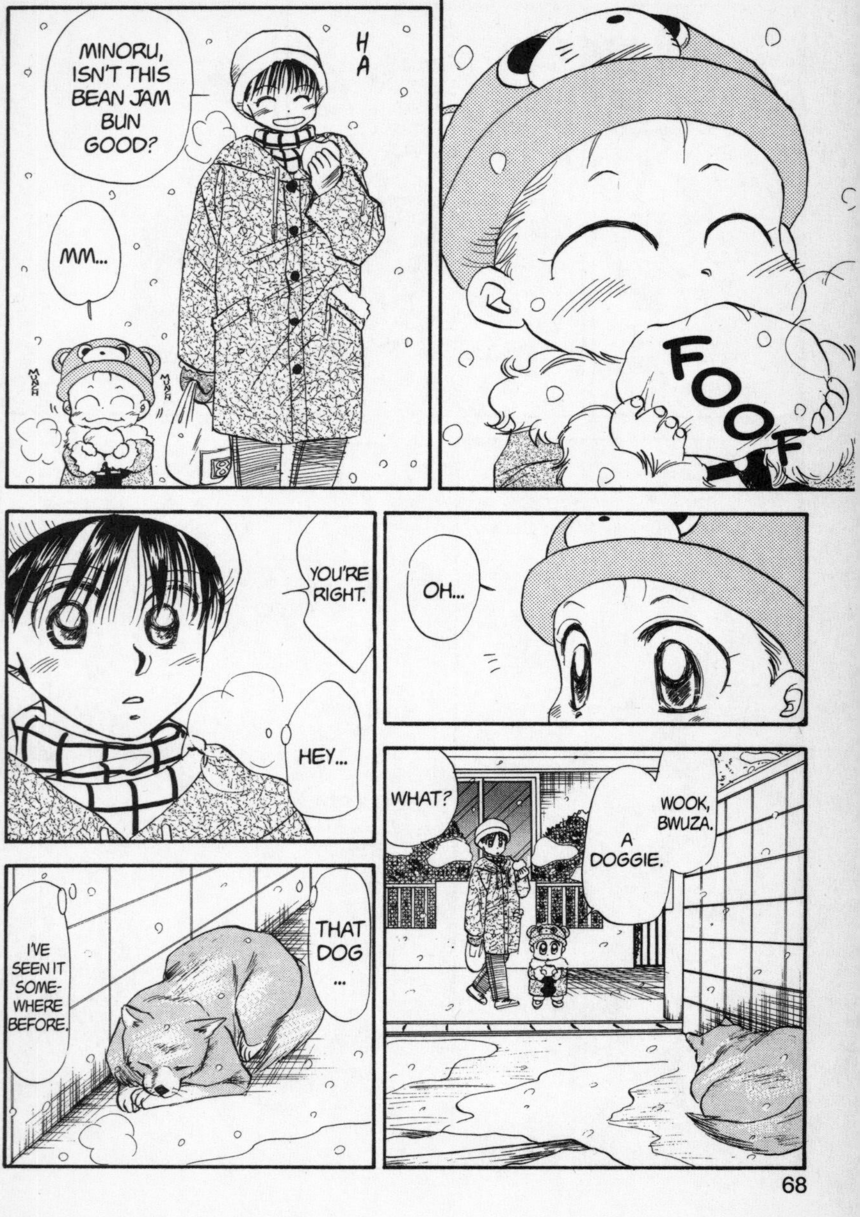
FOOF
HA HA
MINORU, ISN'T THIS BEAN JAM BUN GOOD?
MM...
MUNCH MUNCH
OH...
YOU'RE RIGHT.
HEY...
WOOK, BWUZA. A DOGGIE.
WHAT?
THAT DOG...
I'VE SEEN IT SOME-WHERE BEFORE.

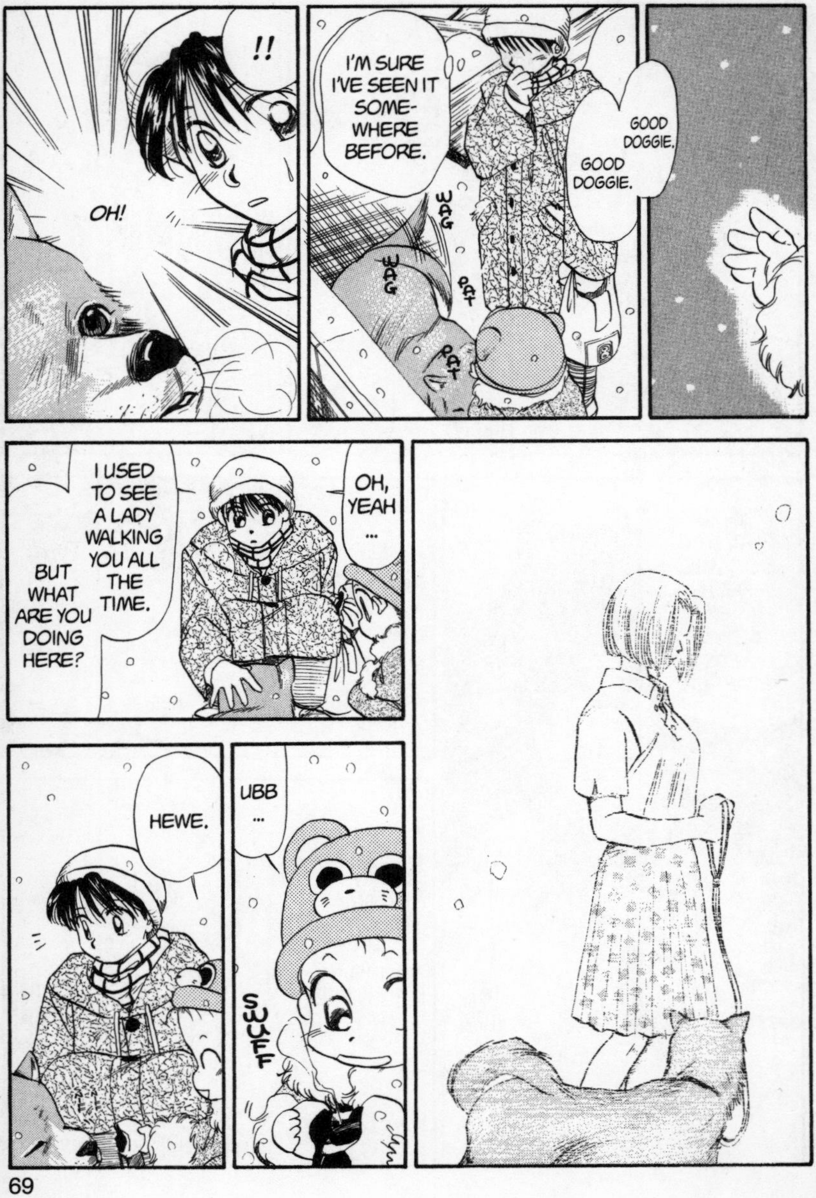
GOOD DOGGIE.
GOOD DOGGIE.
I'M SURE I'VE SEEN IT SOME-WHERE BEFORE.
WAG
WAG
PAT
PAT
!!
OH!
OH, YEAH ...
I USED TO SEE A LADY WALKING YOU ALL THE TIME.
BUT WHAT ARE YOU DOING HERE?
UBB ...
SWUFF
HEWE.

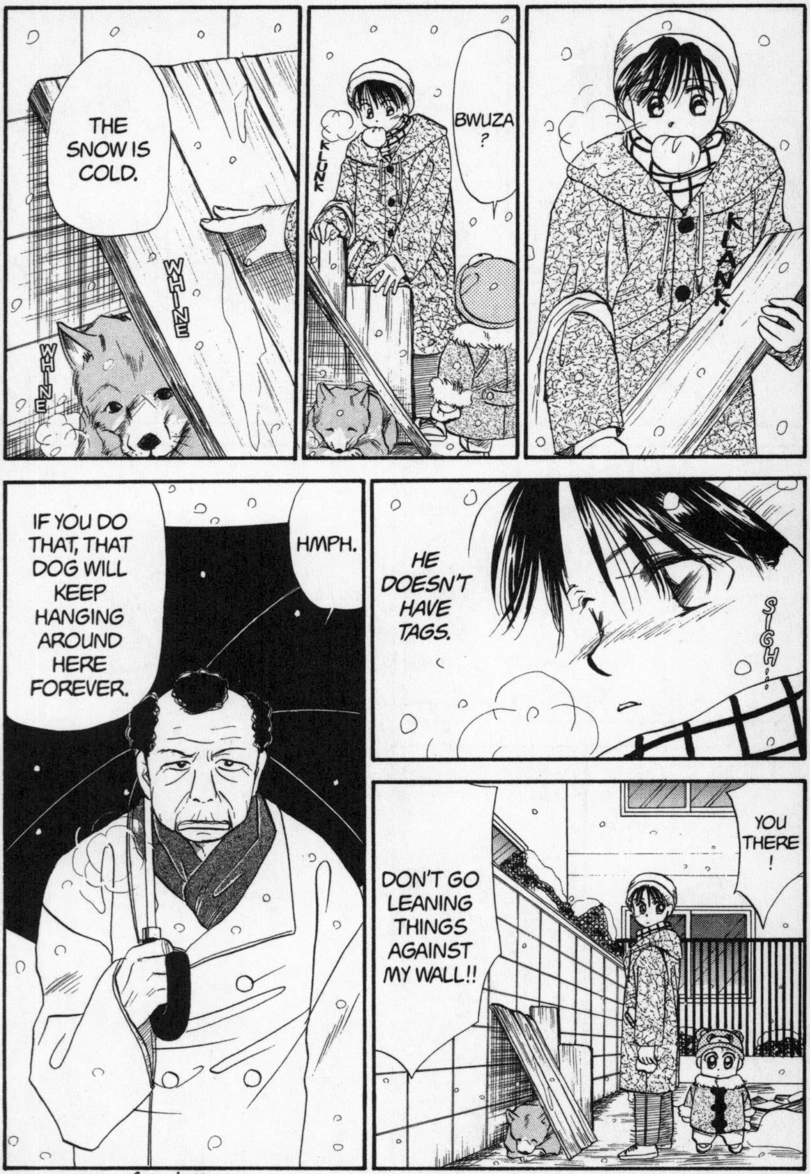
KLANK!
BWUZA?
KLUNK
THE SNOW IS COLD.
WHINE
WHINE
HE DOESN'T HAVE TAGS.
SIGH...
YOU THERE!
DON'T GO LEANING THINGS AGAINST MY WALL!!
HMPH.
IF YOU DO THAT, THAT DOG WILL KEEP HANGING AROUND HERE FOREVER.

Scary-looking ♪♪

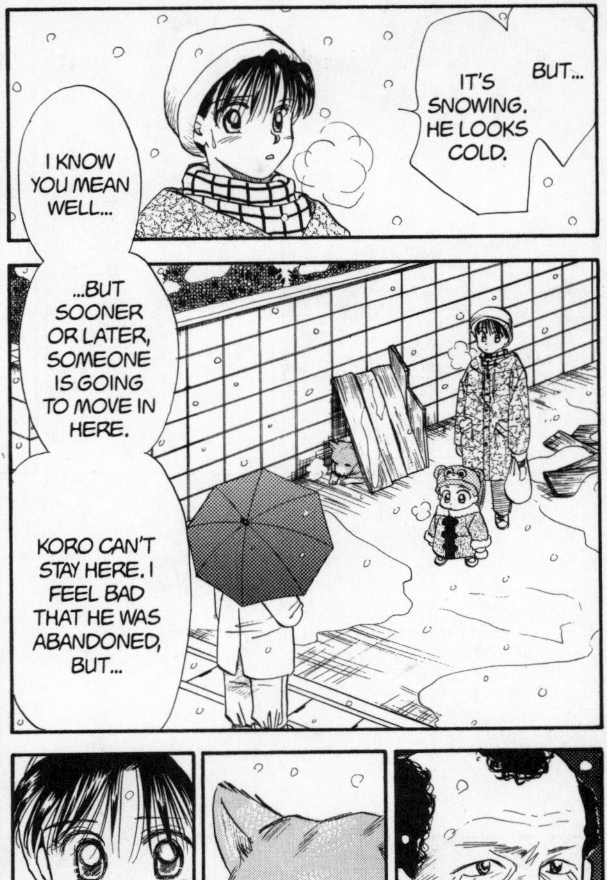
IT'S SNOWING. HE LOOKS COLD.
BUT...
I KNOW YOU MEAN WELL...
...BUT SOONER OR LATER, SOMEONE IS GOING TO MOVE IN HERE.
KORO CAN'T STAY HERE. I FEEL BAD THAT HE WAS ABANDONED, BUT...
THAT WAS IRRESPONSIBLE OF HIS OWNERS.
HUFF
HUFF

Author's Note 3

About this scene of the Fujii family in Chapter 40...

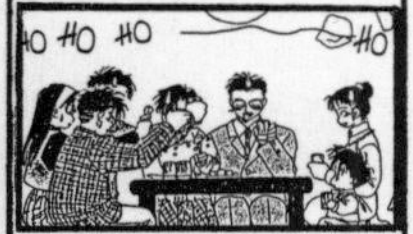
HO HO HO HO

Ichika's not there!! Some readers pointed that out to me.

But look carefully.

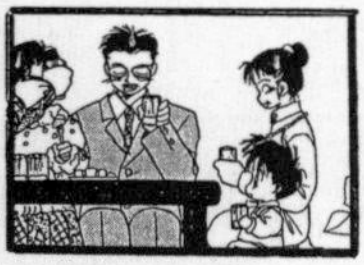

zoom

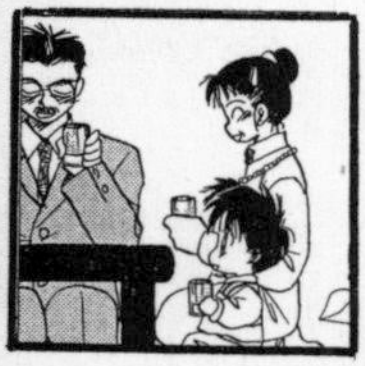

zoom

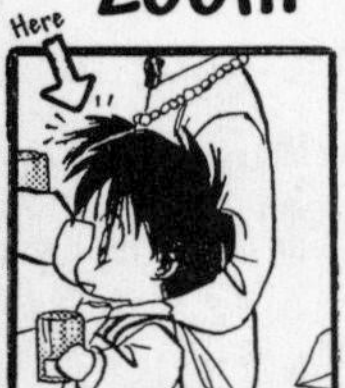
Here

She is there!! You can see some of her hair over her brother's head.

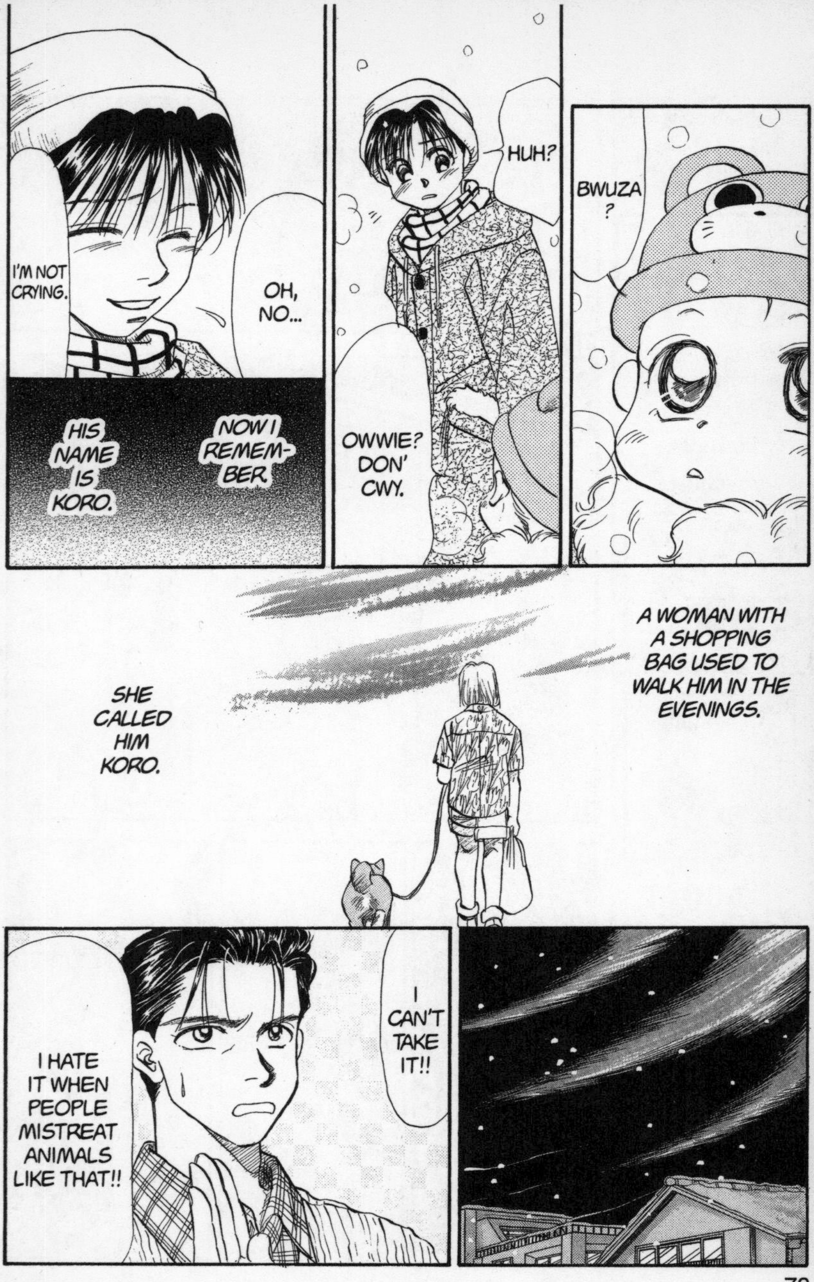
BWUZA?
HUH?
OWWIE? DON' CWY.
OH, NO...
I'M NOT CRYING.
NOW I REMEMBER.
HIS NAME IS KORO.
A WOMAN WITH A SHOPPING BAG USED TO WALK HIM IN THE EVENINGS.
SHE CALLED HIM KORO.
I CAN'T TAKE IT!!
I HATE IT WHEN PEOPLE MISTREAT ANIMALS LIKE THAT!!

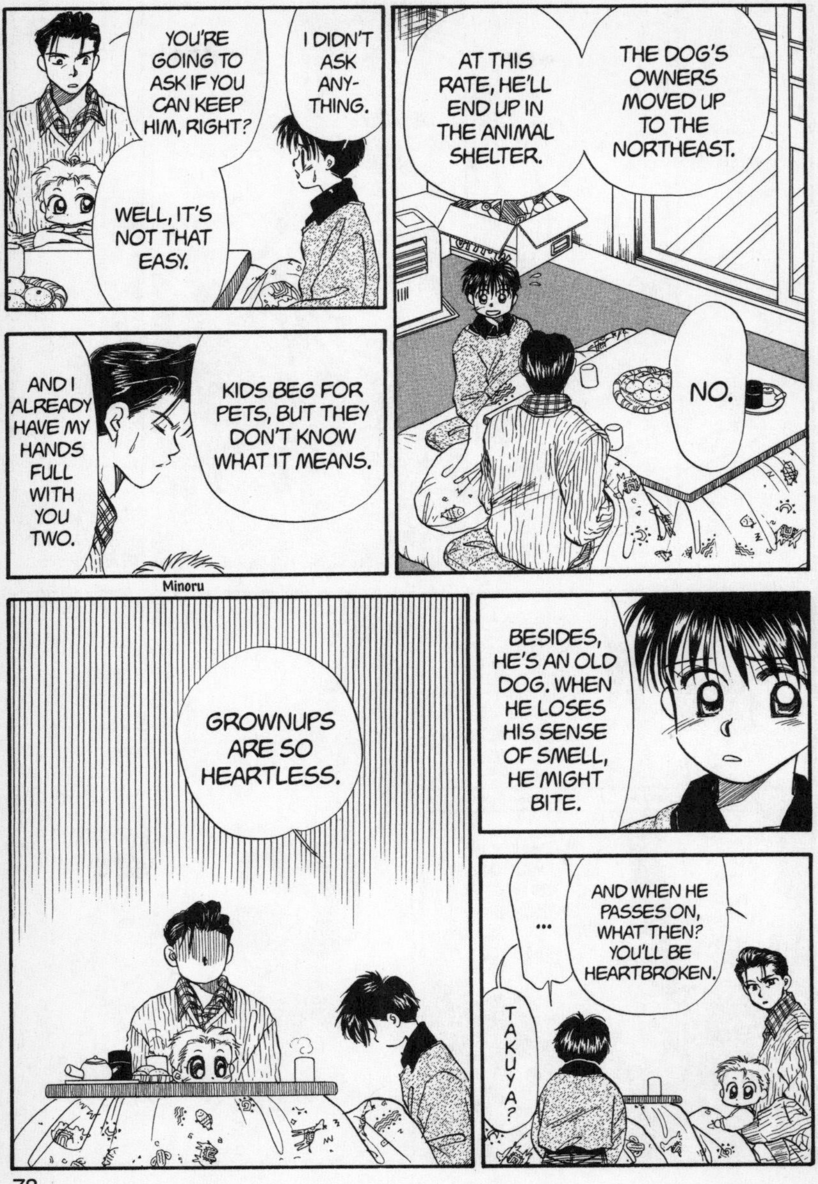
THE DOG'S OWNERS MOVED UP TO THE NORTHEAST.
AT THIS RATE, HE'LL END UP IN THE ANIMAL SHELTER.
NO.
I DIDN'T ASK ANY-THING.
YOU'RE GOING TO ASK IF YOU CAN KEEP HIM, RIGHT?
WELL, IT'S NOT THAT EASY.
KIDS BEG FOR PETS, BUT THEY DON'T KNOW WHAT IT MEANS.
AND I ALREADY HAVE MY HANDS FULL WITH YOU TWO.
Minoru
BESIDES, HE'S AN OLD DOG. WHEN HE LOSES HIS SENSE OF SMELL, HE MIGHT BITE.
AND WHEN HE PASSES ON, WHAT THEN? YOU'LL BE HEARTBROKEN.
...
TAKUYA?
GROWNUPS ARE SO HEARTLESS.

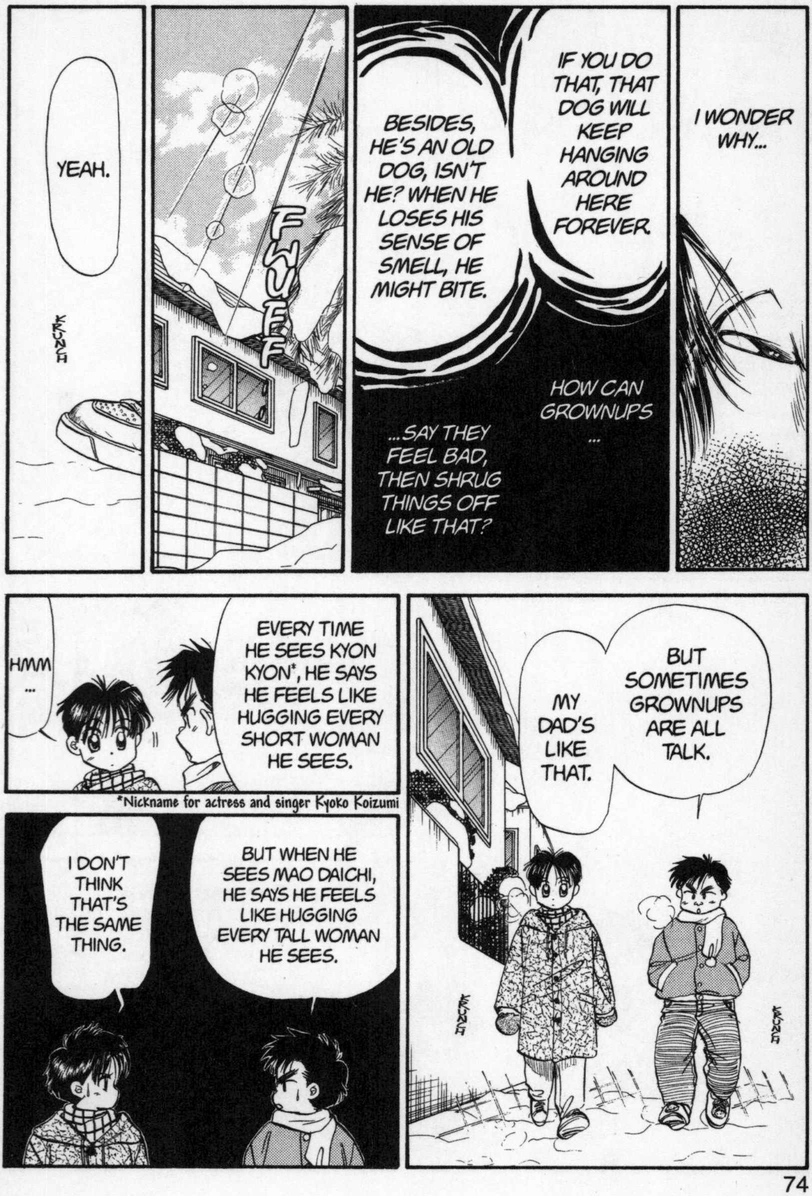
I WONDER WHY...
IF YOU DO THAT, THAT DOG WILL KEEP HANGING AROUND HERE FOREVER.
BESIDES, HE'S AN OLD DOG, ISN'T HE? WHEN HE LOSES HIS SENSE OF SMELL, HE MIGHT BITE.
HOW CAN GROWNUPS ...
...SAY THEY FEEL BAD, THEN SHRUG THINGS OFF LIKE THAT?
FWUFF
YEAH.
KRUNCH
BUT SOMETIMES GROWNUPS ARE ALL TALK.
MY DAD'S LIKE THAT.
KRUNCH
KRUNCH
EVERY TIME HE SEES KYON KYON*, HE SAYS HE FEELS LIKE HUGGING EVERY SHORT WOMAN HE SEES.
HMM ...
BUT WHEN HE SEES MAO DAICHI, HE SAYS HE FEELS LIKE HUGGING EVERY TALL WOMAN HE SEES.
I DON'T THINK THAT'S THE SAME THING.

*Nickname for actress and singer Kyoko Koizumi

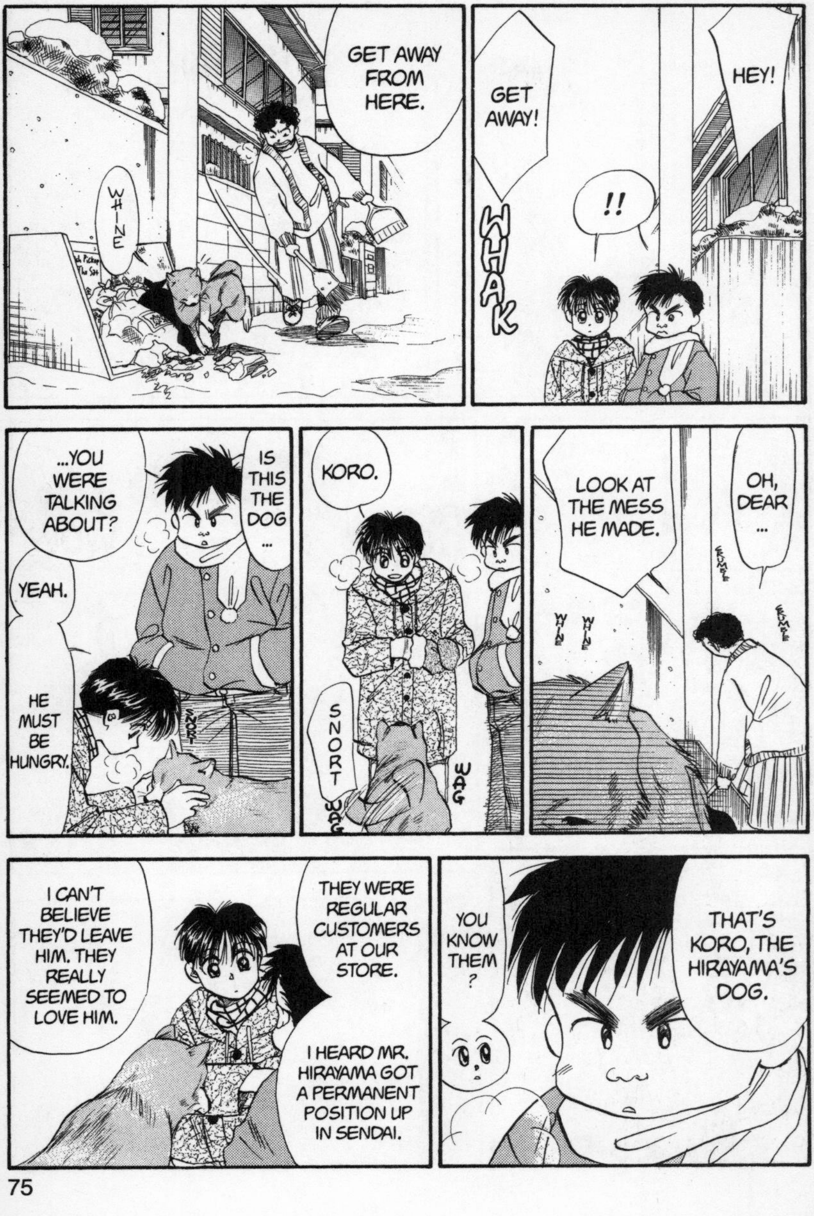
HEY!
GET AWAY!
WHAK
!!
GET AWAY FROM HERE.
WHINE
OH, DEAR ...
LOOK AT THE MESS HE MADE.
CRUMPLE
CRUMPLE
WHINE
WHINE
KORO.
SNORT
WAG
WAG
IS THIS THE DOG ...
...YOU WERE TALKING ABOUT?
YEAH.
SNORT
HE MUST BE HUNGRY.
THAT'S KORO, THE HIRAYAMA'S DOG.
YOU KNOW THEM ?
THEY WERE REGULAR CUSTOMERS AT OUR STORE.
I HEARD MR. HIRAYAMA GOT A PERMANENT POSITION UP IN SENDAI.
I CAN'T BELIEVE THEY'D LEAVE HIM. THEY REALLY SEEMED TO LOVE HIM.

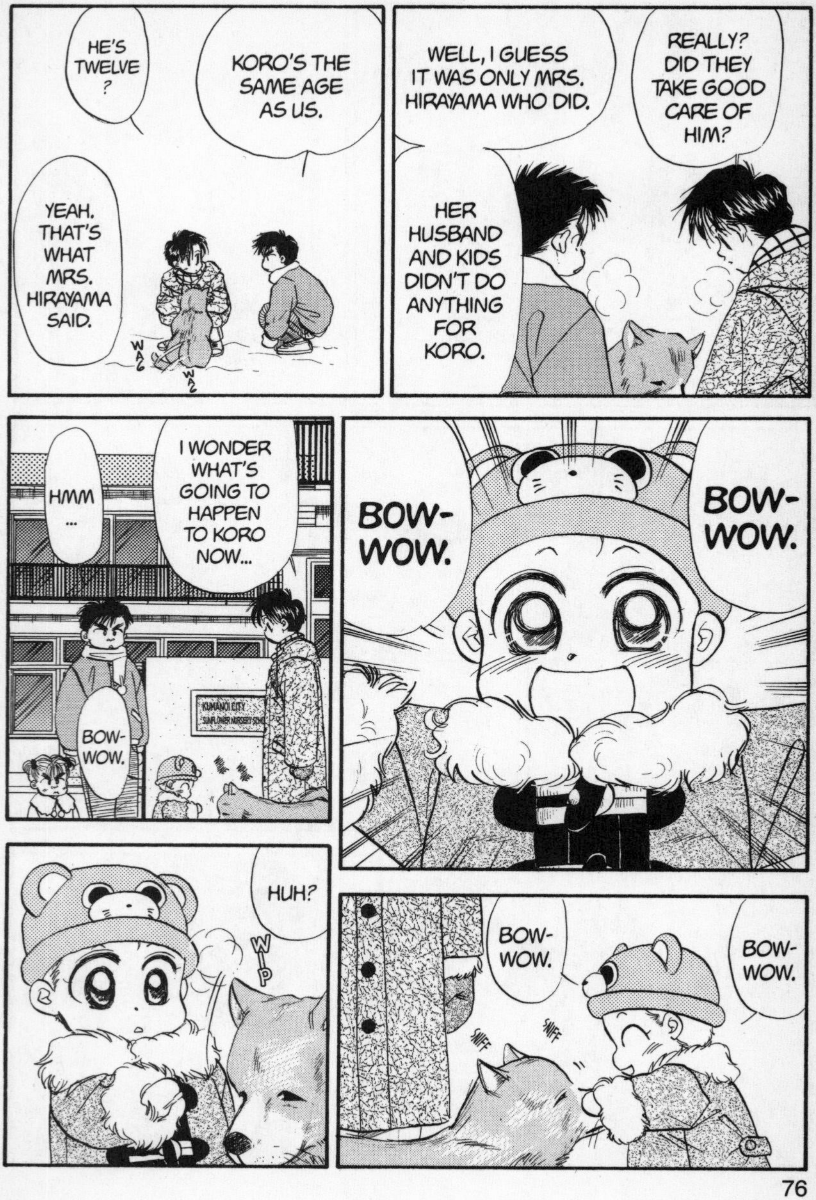
REALLY? DID THEY TAKE GOOD CARE OF HIM?
WELL, I GUESS IT WAS ONLY MRS. HIRAYAMA WHO DID.
HER HUSBAND AND KIDS DIDN'T DO ANYTHING FOR KORO.
KORO'S THE SAME AGE AS US.
HE'S TWELVE?
YEAH. THAT'S WHAT MRS. HIRAYAMA SAID.
WAG
WAG
BOW-WOW.
BOW-WOW.
I WONDER WHAT'S GOING TO HAPPEN TO KORO NOW...
HMM...
BOW-WOW.
BOW-WOW.
BOW-WOW.
SNIFF
SNIFF
HUH?
WIP

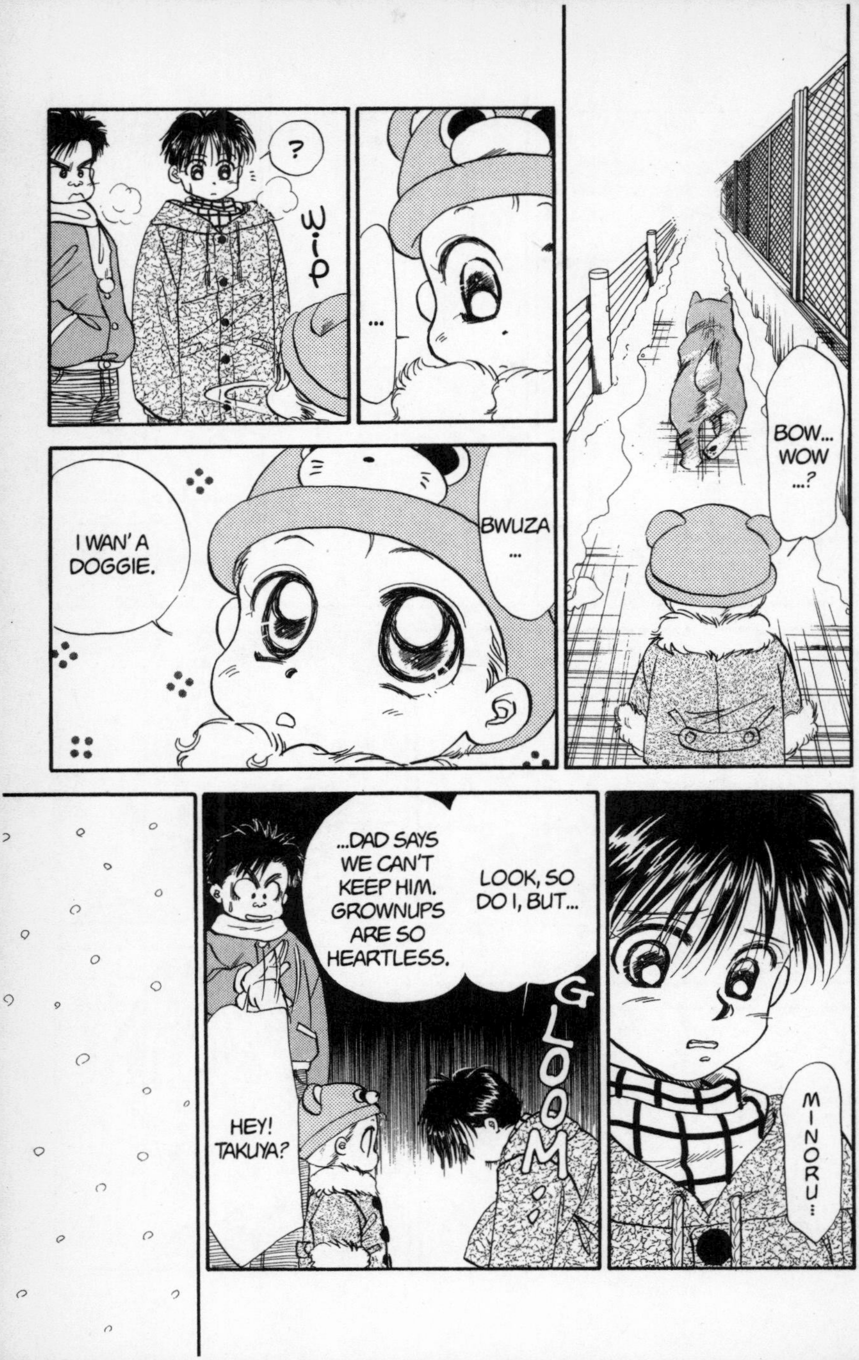
BOW... WOW ...?
...
?
WIP
BWUZA ...
I WAN' A DOGGIE.
MINORU...
...DAD SAYS WE CAN'T KEEP HIM. GROWNUPS ARE SO HEARTLESS.
LOOK, SO DO I, BUT...
GLOOM
HEY! TAKUYA?

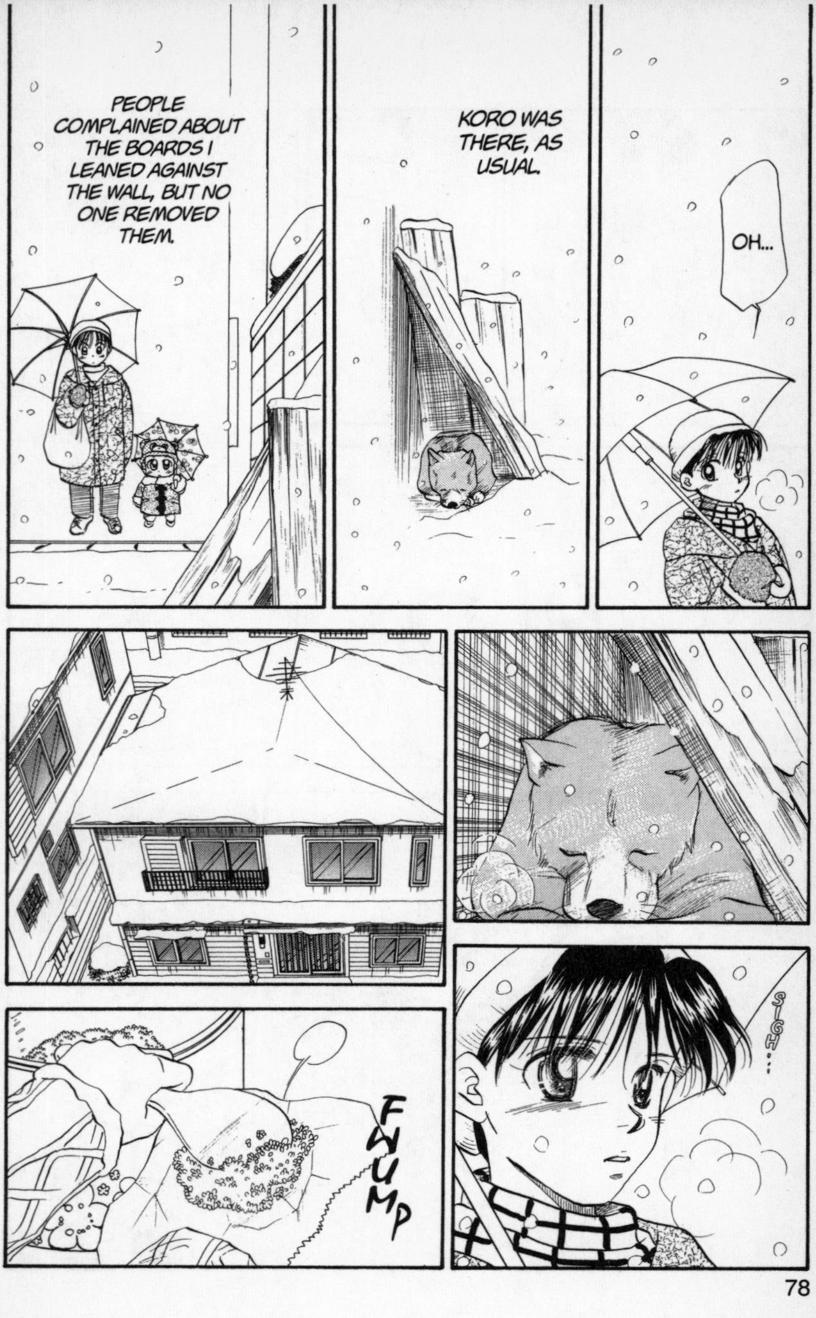
OH...
KORO WAS THERE, AS USUAL.
PEOPLE COMPLAINED ABOUT THE BOARDS I LEANED AGAINST THE WALL, BUT NO ONE REMOVED THEM.
SIGH...
FWUMP

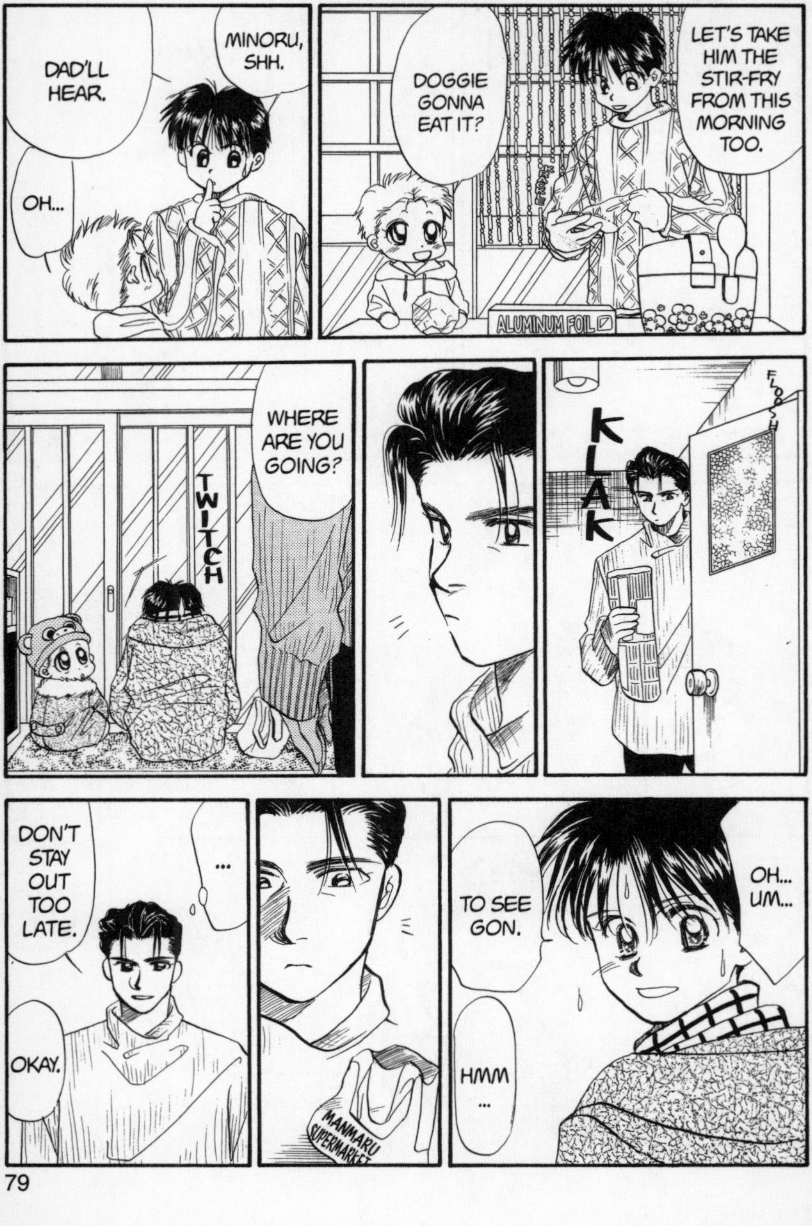
LET'S TAKE HIM THE STIR-FRY FROM THIS MORNING TOO.
DOGGIE GONNA EAT IT?
ALUMINUM FOIL
MINORU, SHH.
DAD'LL HEAR.
OH...
FLOOSH
KLAK
WHERE ARE YOU GOING?
TWITCH
OH... UM...
TO SEE GON.
HMM ...
MANMARU SUPERMARKET
...
DON'T STAY OUT TOO LATE.
OKAY.

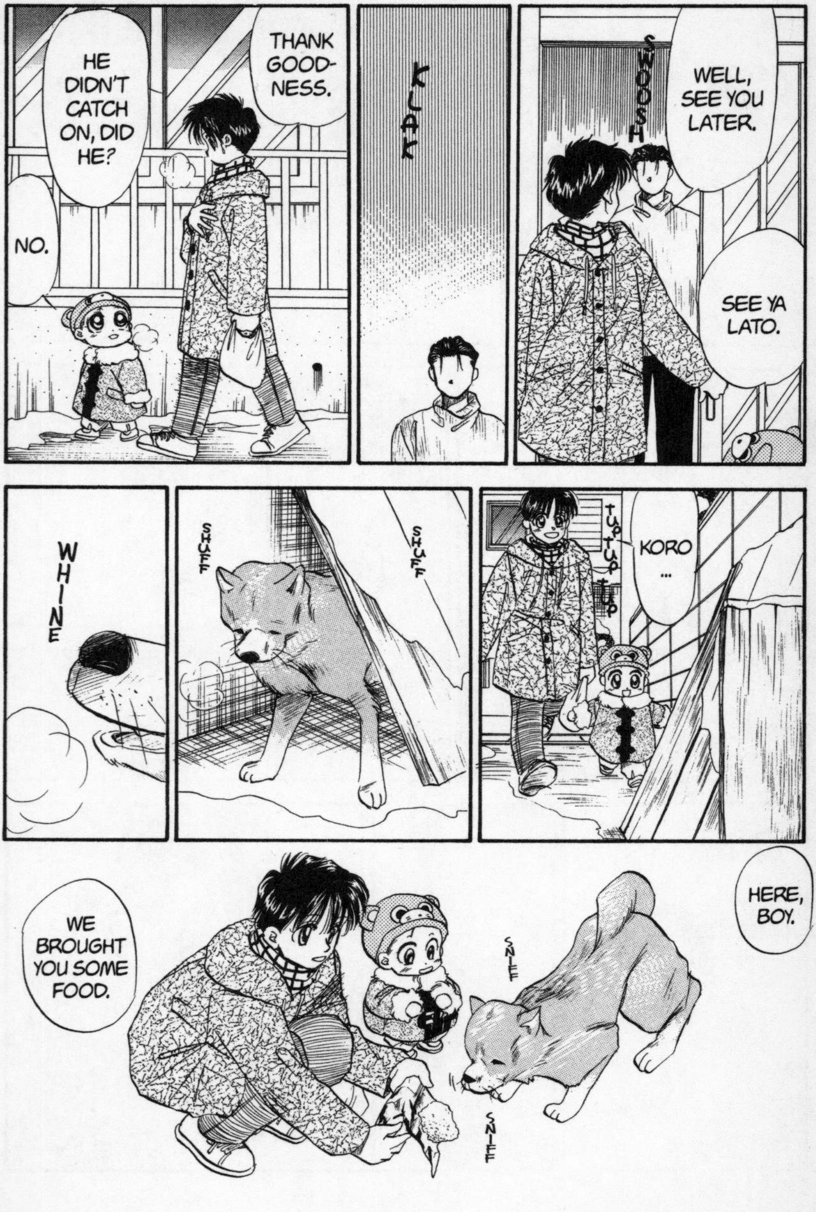
WELL, SEE YOU LATER.
SWOOSH
SEE YA LATO.
KLAK
THANK GOODNESS.
HE DIDN'T CATCH ON, DID HE?
NO.
KORO ...
TUP TUP TUP TUP
SHUFF
SHUFF
WHINE
HERE, BOY.
SNIFF
SNIFF
WE BROUGHT YOU SOME FOOD.

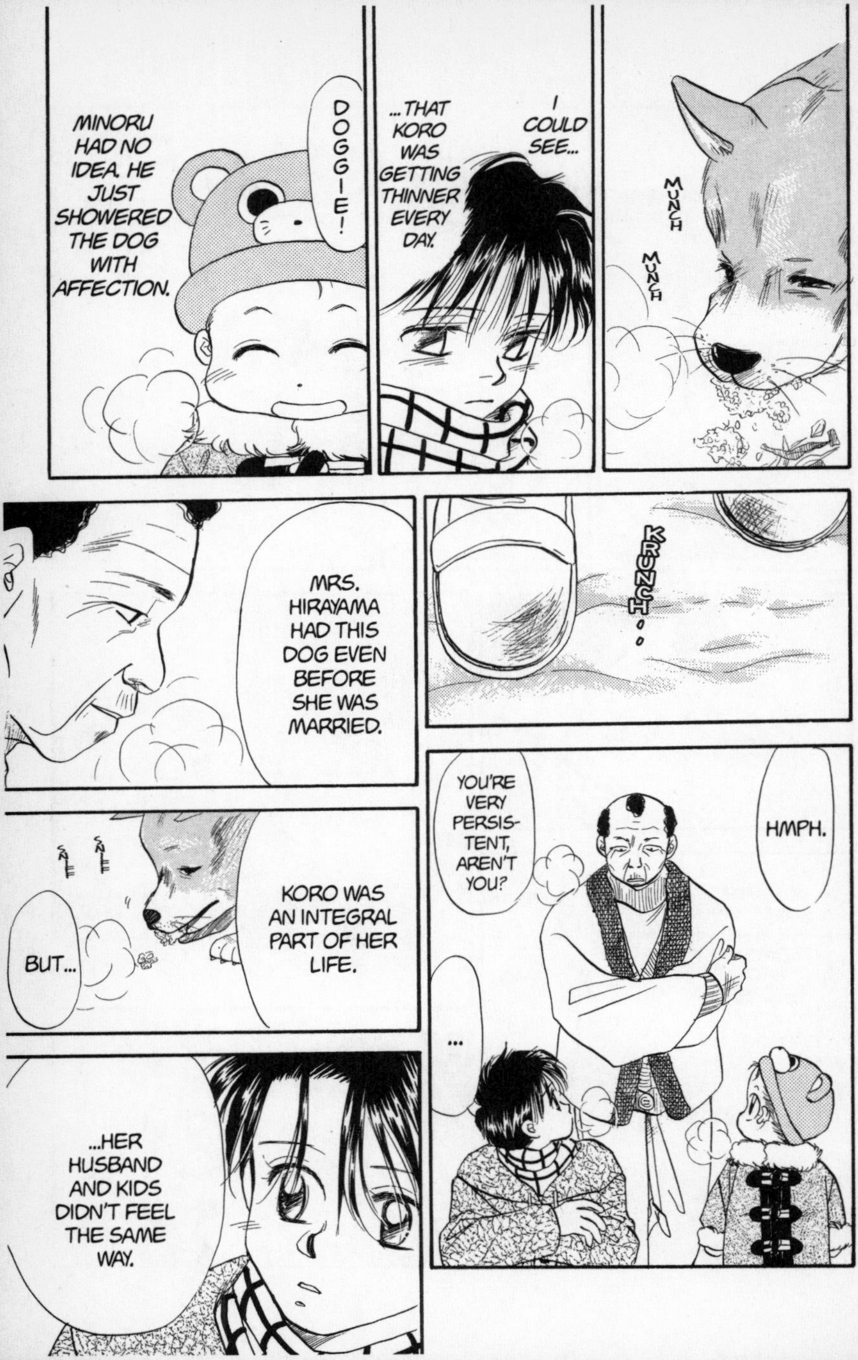
MUNCH
MUNCH
I COULD SEE...
...THAT KORO WAS GETTING THINNER EVERY DAY.
DOGGIE!
MINORU HAD NO IDEA. HE JUST SHOWERED THE DOG WITH AFFECTION.
KRUNCH..
MRS. HIRAYAMA HAD THIS DOG EVEN BEFORE SHE WAS MARRIED.
HMPH.
YOU'RE VERY PERSIS-TENT, AREN'T YOU?
...
KORO WAS AN INTEGRAL PART OF HER LIFE.
BUT...
...HER HUSBAND AND KIDS DIDN'T FEEL THE SAME WAY.

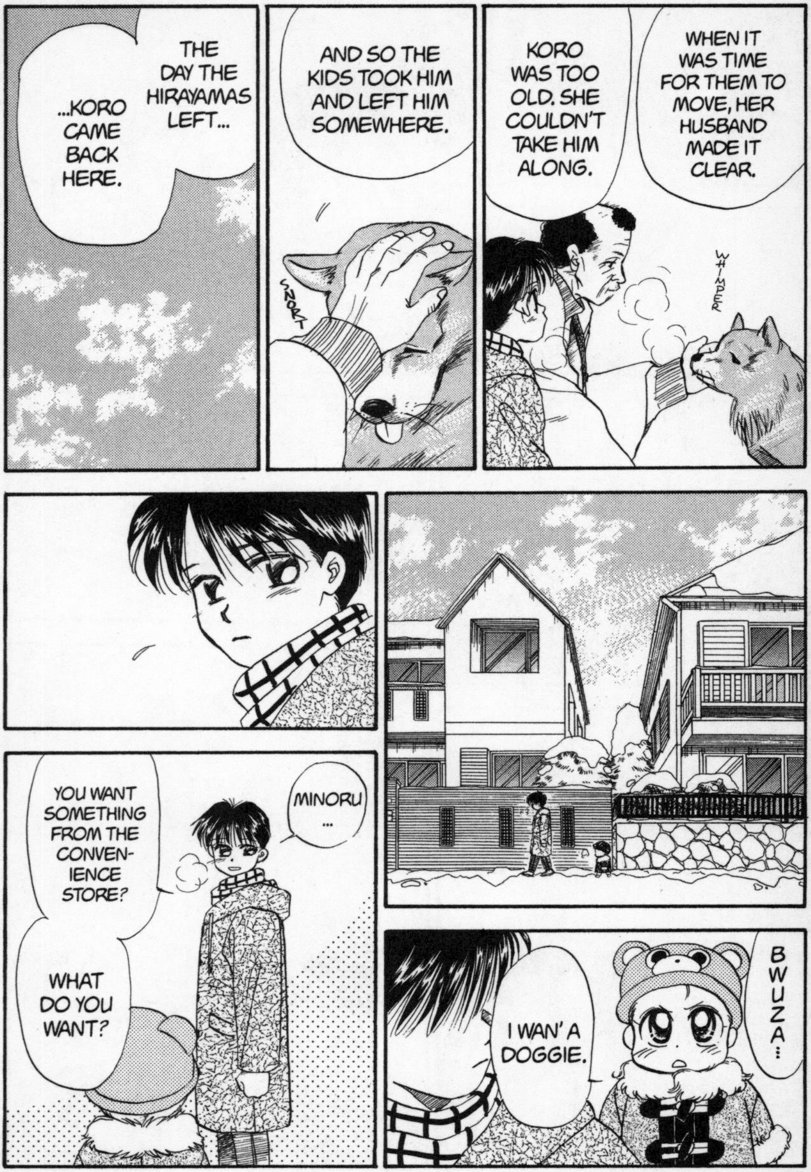
WHEN IT WAS TIME FOR THEM TO MOVE, HER HUSBAND MADE IT CLEAR.
KORO WAS TOO OLD. SHE COULDN'T TAKE HIM ALONG.
WHIMPER
AND SO THE KIDS TOOK HIM AND LEFT HIM SOMEWHERE.
SNORT
THE DAY THE HIRAYAMAS LEFT...
...KORO CAME BACK HERE.
MINORU...
YOU WANT SOMETHING FROM THE CONVEN-IENCE STORE?
WHAT DO YOU WANT?
BWUZA...
I WAN' A DOGGIE.

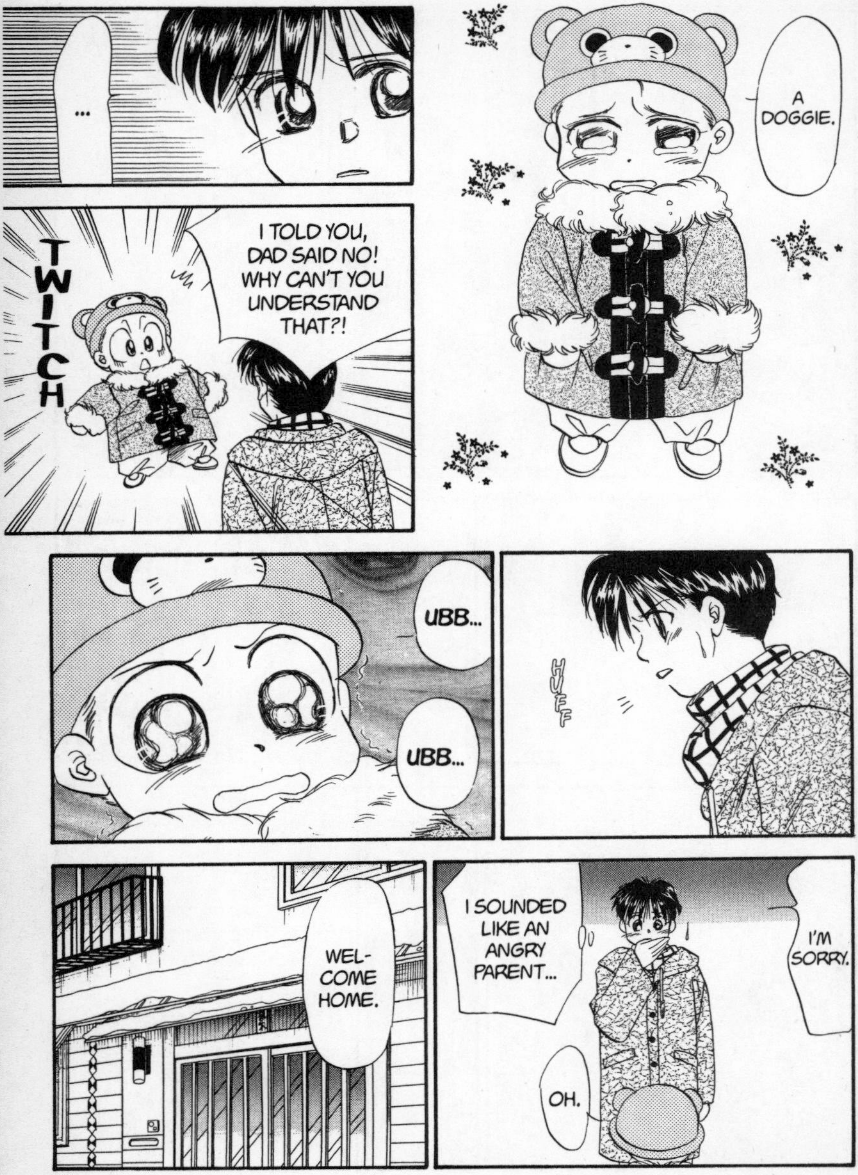
A DOGGIE.
...
TWITCH
I TOLD YOU, DAD SAID NO! WHY CAN'T YOU UNDERSTAND THAT?!
HUFF
UBB...
UBB...
I'M SORRY.
I SOUNDED LIKE AN ANGRY PARENT...
OH.
WEL-COME HOME.

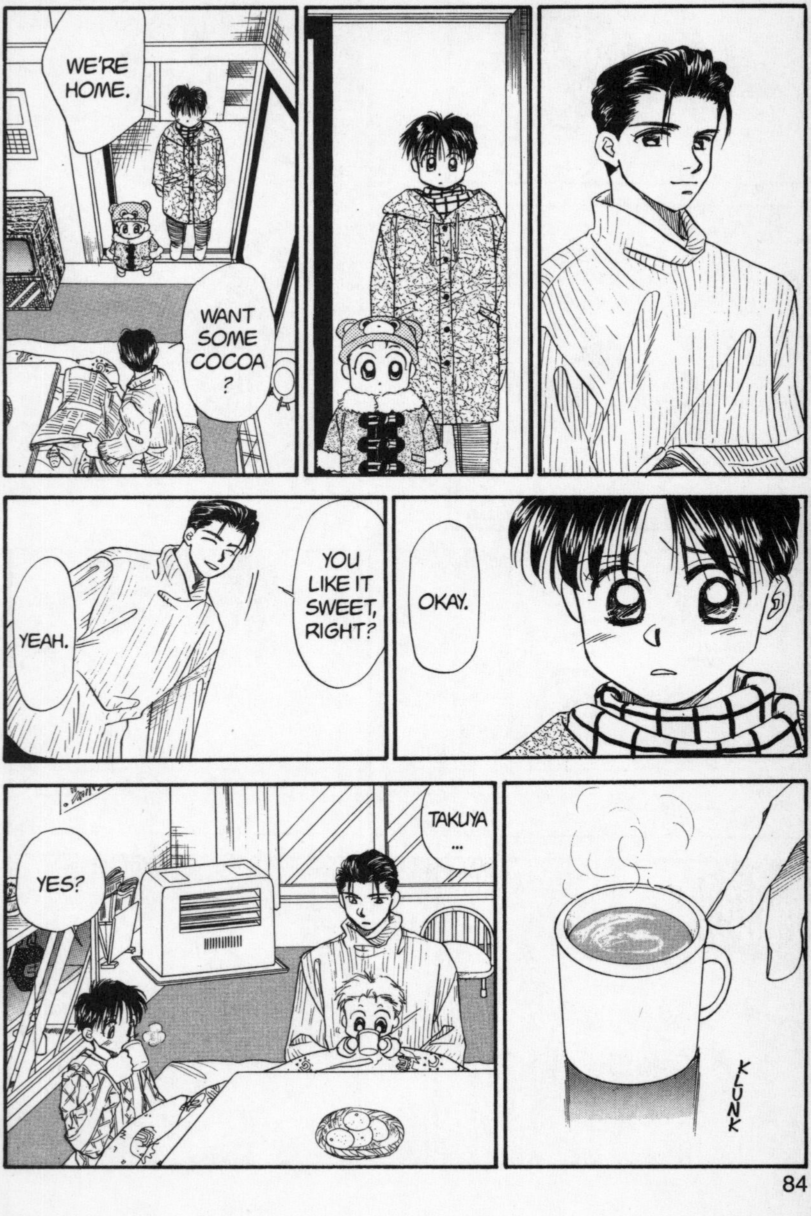
WE'RE HOME.
WANT SOME COCOA?
OKAY.
YOU LIKE IT SWEET, RIGHT?
YEAH.
KLUNK
TAKUYA...
YES?

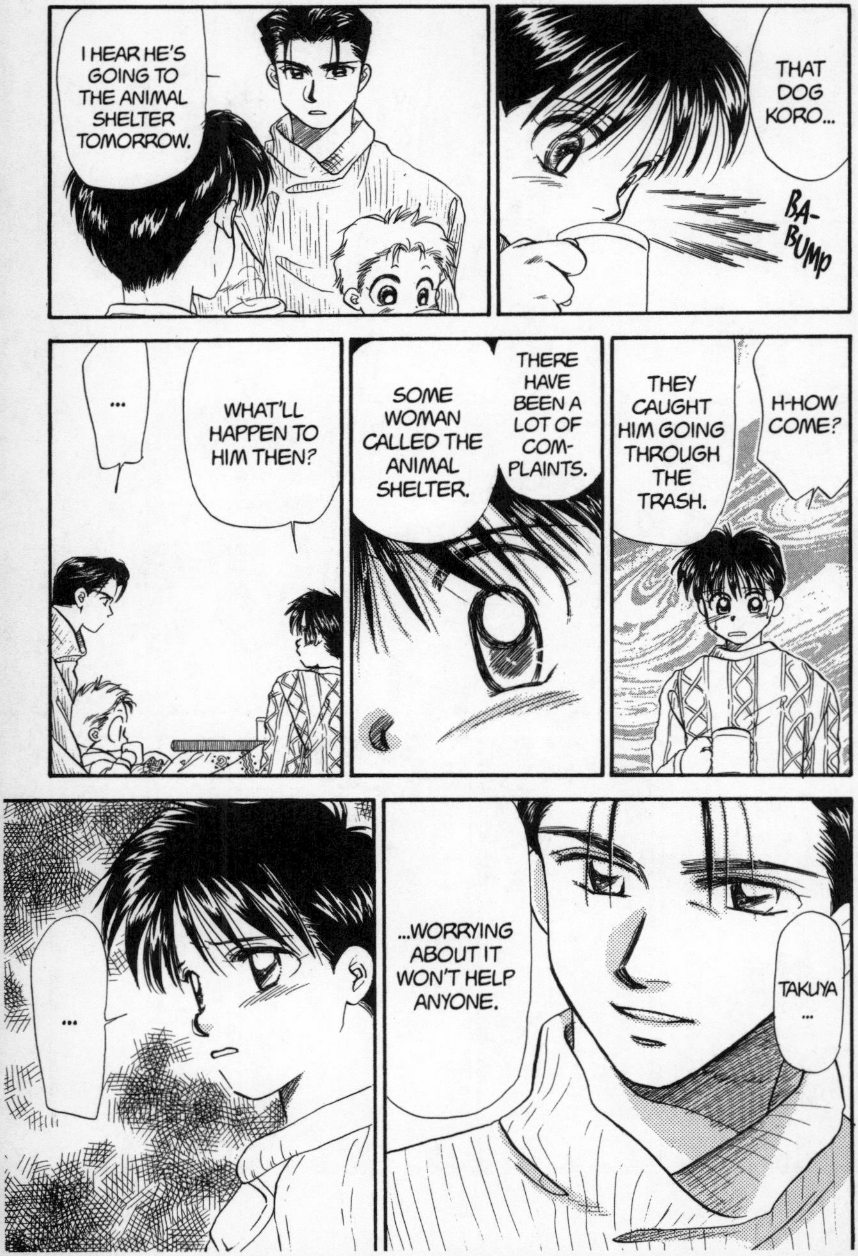
THAT DOG KORO...
BA-BUMP
I HEAR HE'S GOING TO THE ANIMAL SHELTER TOMORROW.
H-HOW COME?
THEY CAUGHT HIM GOING THROUGH THE TRASH.
THERE HAVE BEEN A LOT OF COM-PLAINTS.
SOME WOMAN CALLED THE ANIMAL SHELTER.
WHAT'LL HAPPEN TO HIM THEN?
...
TAKUYA ...
...WORRYING ABOUT IT WON'T HELP ANYONE.
...

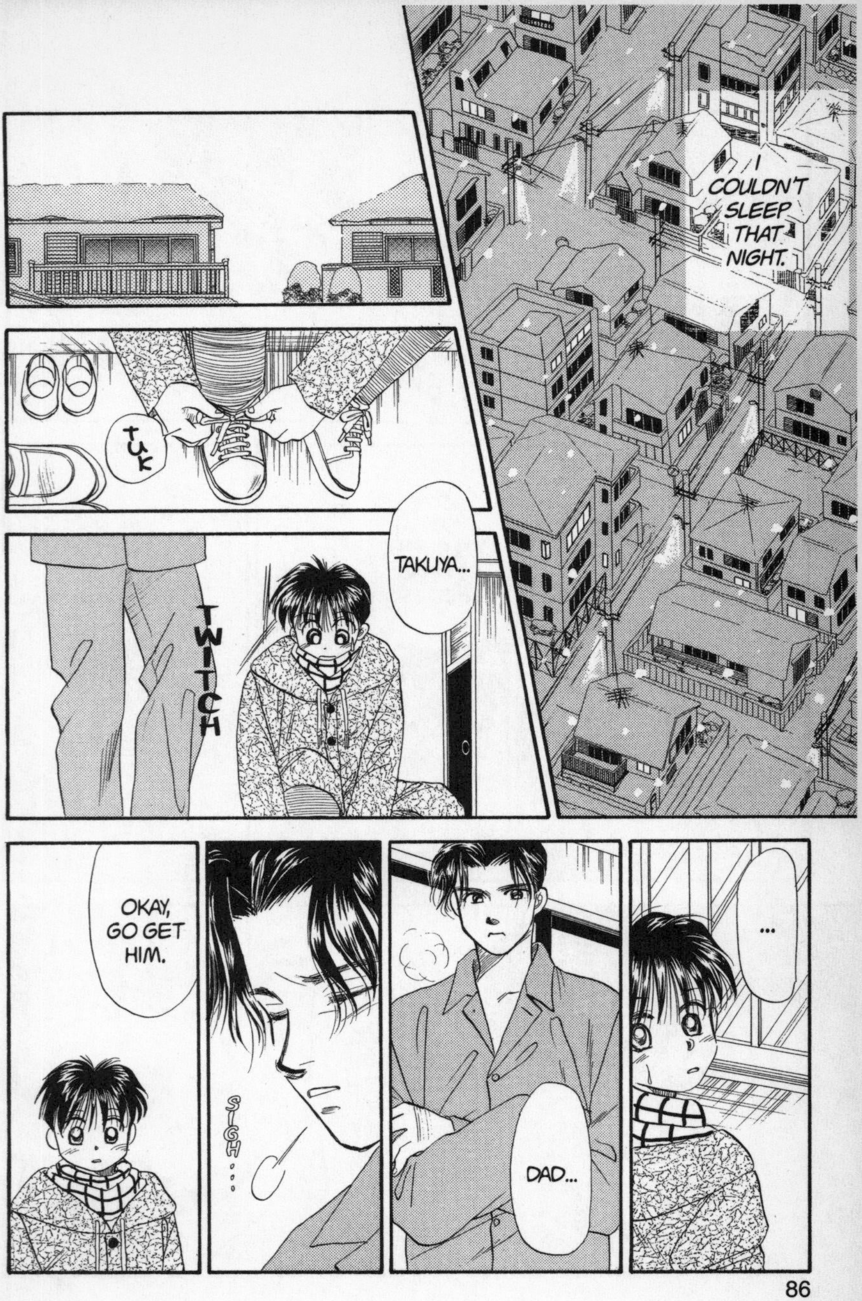
I COULDN'T SLEEP THAT NIGHT.
TUK
TAKUYA...
TWITCH
...
DAD...
SIGH...
OKAY, GO GET HIM.

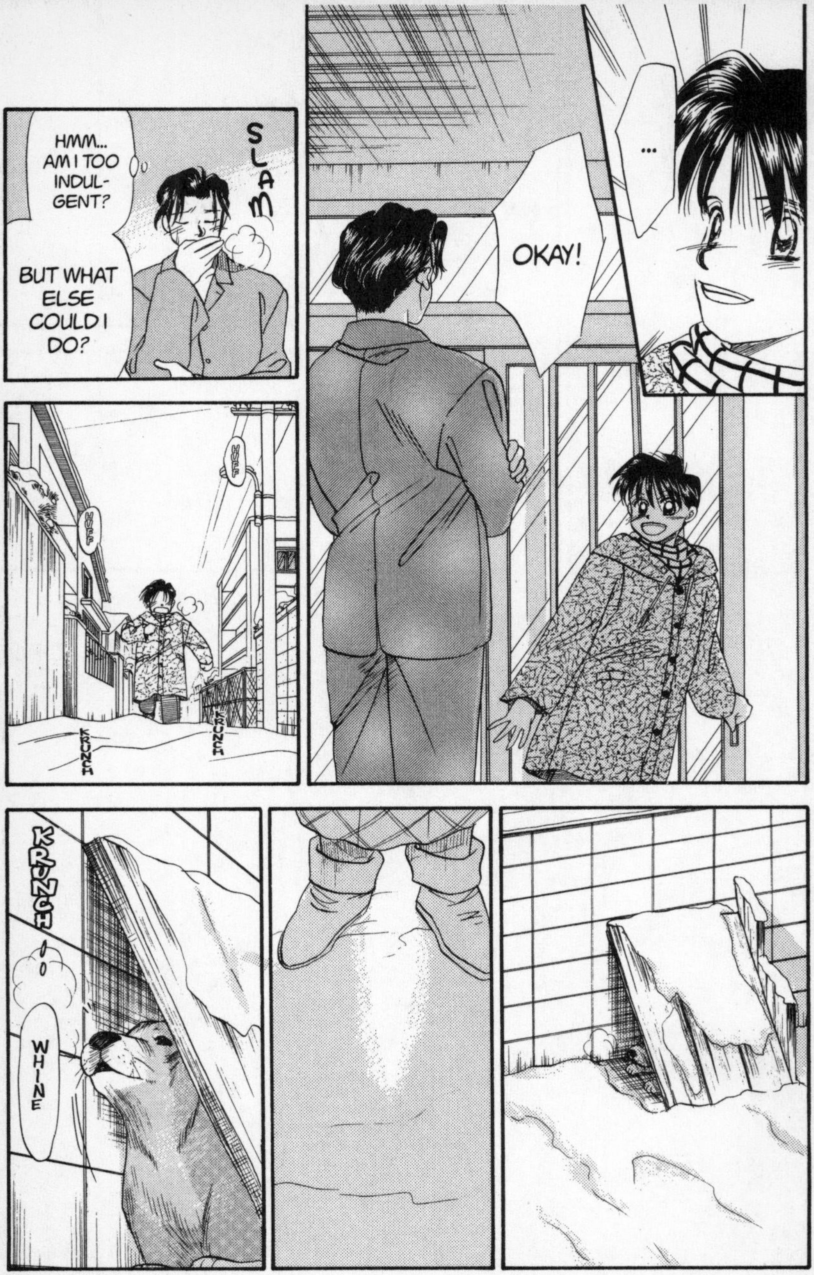
...
OKAY!
HMM... AM I TOO INDUL-GENT?
BUT WHAT ELSE COULD I DO?
SLAM
HUFF
HUFF
KRUNCH
KRUNCH
KRUNCH
WHINE

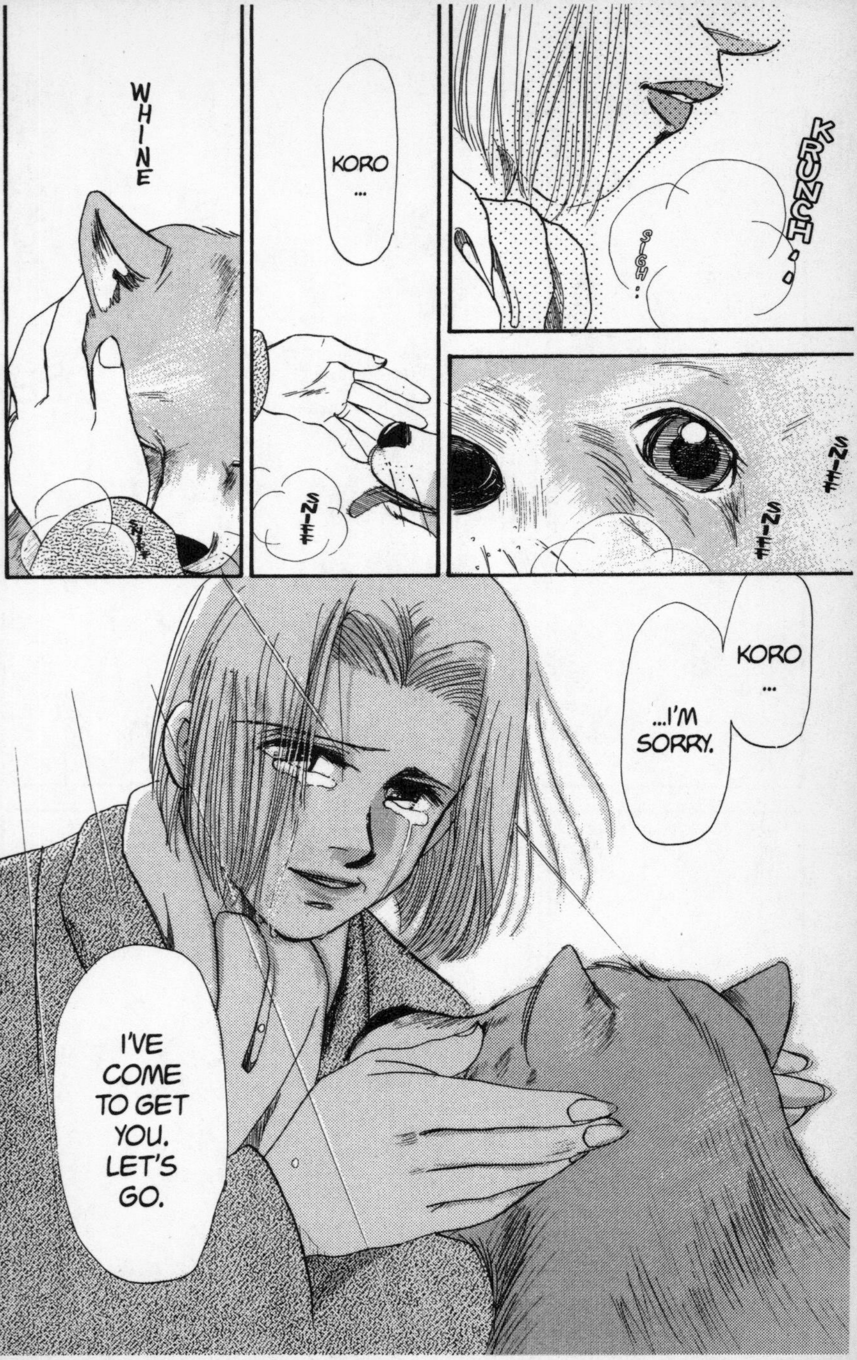
KRUNCH...
SIGH...
SNIFF
SNIFF
KORO...
SNIFF
WHINE
SNIFF
KORO...
...I'M SORRY.
I'VE COME TO GET YOU. LET'S GO.

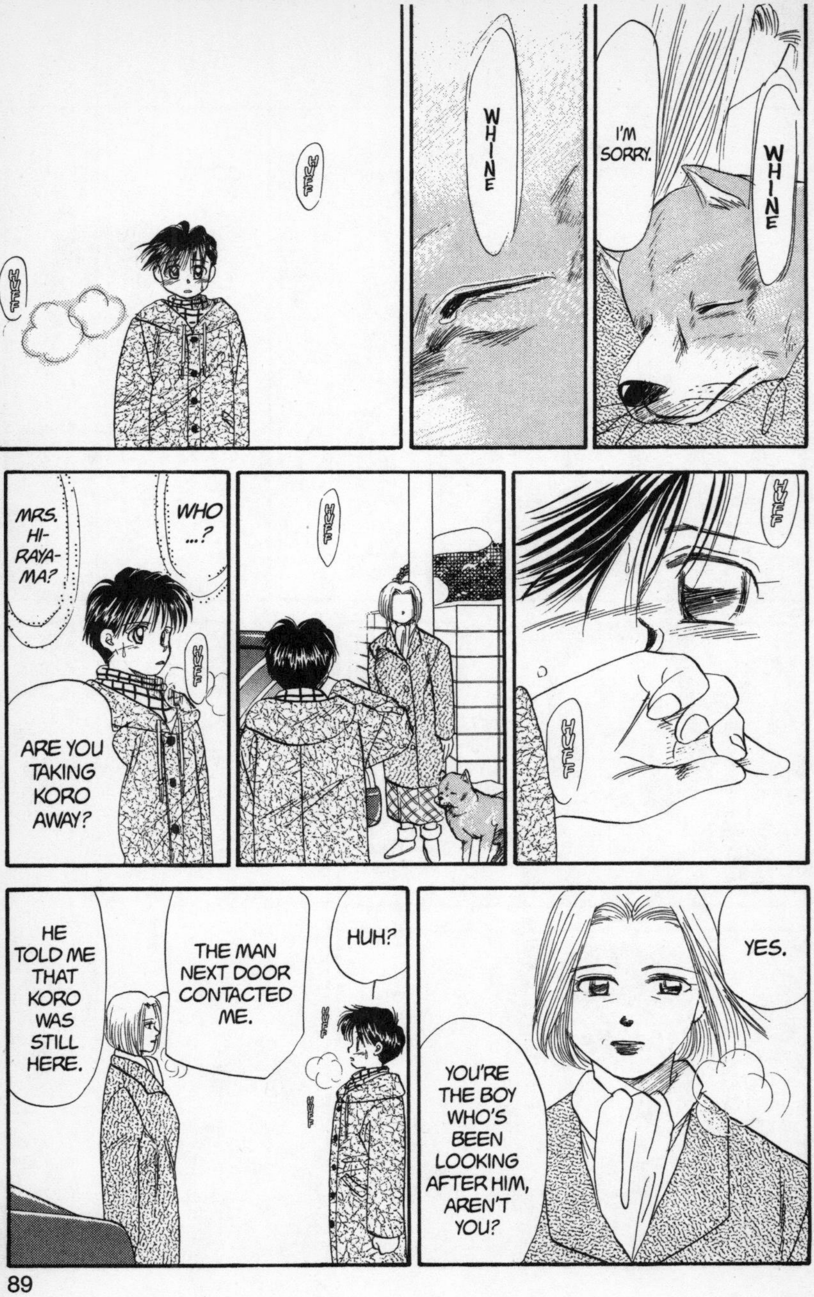
I'M SORRY.
WHINE
WHINE
HUFF
HUFF
HUFF
HUFF
HUFF
WHO ...?
MRS. HI-RAYA-MA?
HUFF
ARE YOU TAKING KORO AWAY?
YES.
YOU'RE THE BOY WHO'S BEEN LOOKING AFTER HIM, AREN'T YOU?
HUH?
HUFF
HUFF
THE MAN NEXT DOOR CONTACTED ME.
HE TOLD ME THAT KORO WAS STILL HERE.

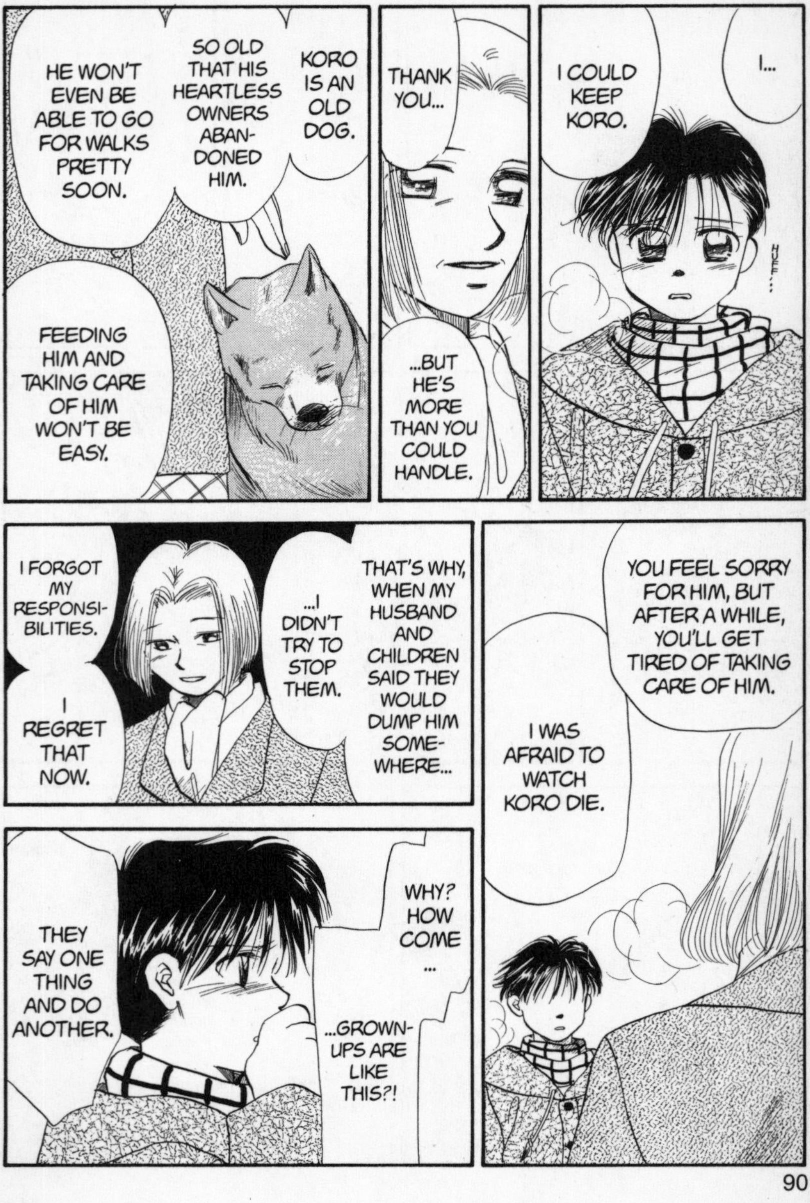
I...
I COULD KEEP KORO.
HUFF..
THANK YOU...
...BUT HE'S MORE THAN YOU COULD HANDLE.
KORO IS AN OLD DOG.
SO OLD THAT HIS HEARTLESS OWNERS ABAN- DONED HIM.
HE WON'T EVEN BE ABLE TO GO FOR WALKS PRETTY SOON.
FEEDING HIM AND TAKING CARE OF HIM WON'T BE EASY.
YOU FEEL SORRY FOR HIM, BUT AFTER A WHILE, YOU'LL GET TIRED OF TAKING CARE OF HIM.
I WAS AFRAID TO WATCH KORO DIE.
THAT'S WHY, WHEN MY HUSBAND AND CHILDREN SAID THEY WOULD DUMP HIM SOME- WHERE...
...I DIDN'T TRY TO STOP THEM.
I FORGOT MY RESPONSI- BILITIES.
I REGRET THAT NOW.
WHY? HOW COME ...
...GROWN- UPS ARE LIKE THIS?!
THEY SAY ONE THING AND DO ANOTHER.

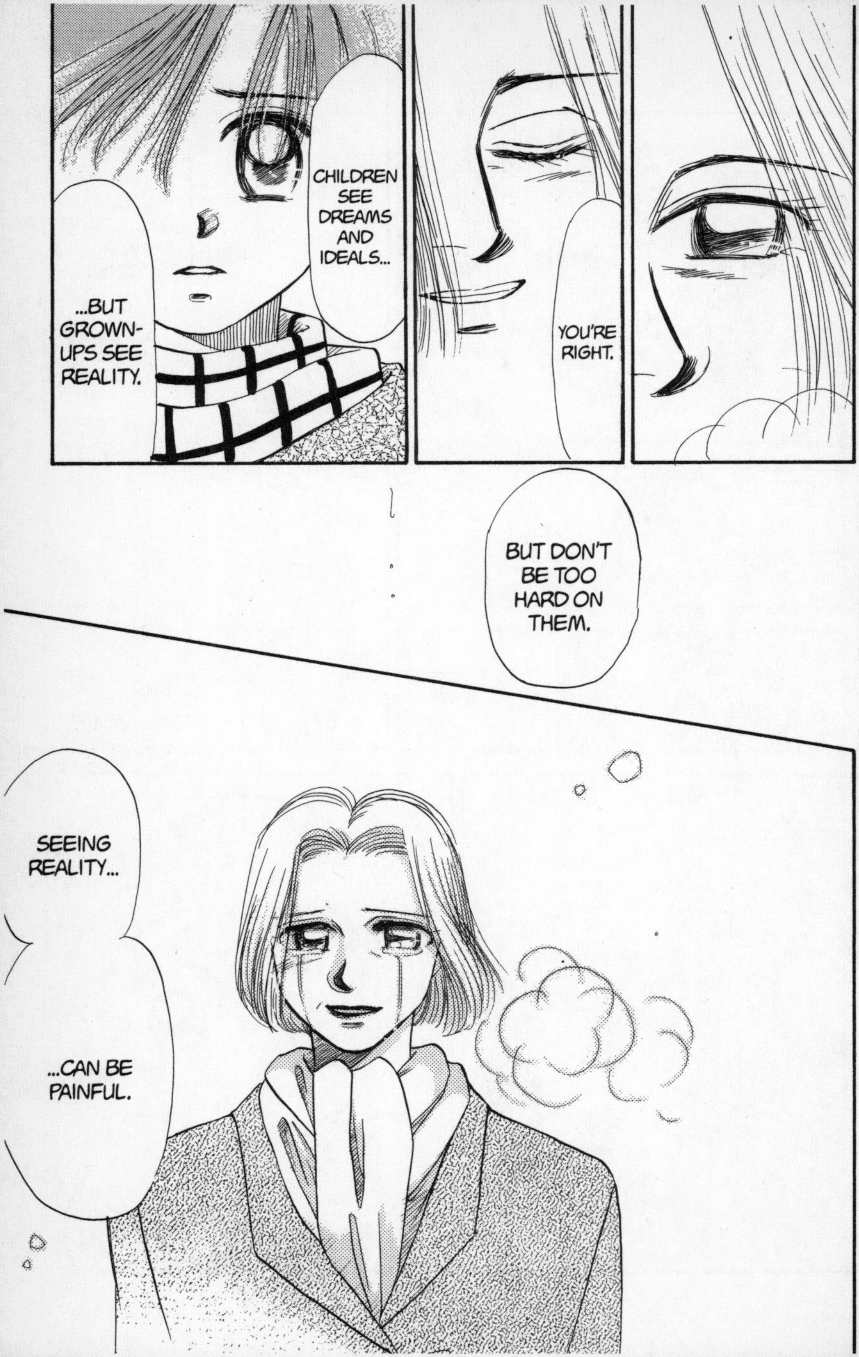
YOU'RE RIGHT.
CHILDREN SEE DREAMS AND IDEALS...
...BUT GROWN-UPS SEE REALITY.
BUT DON'T BE TOO HARD ON THEM.
SEEING REALITY...
...CAN BE PAINFUL.

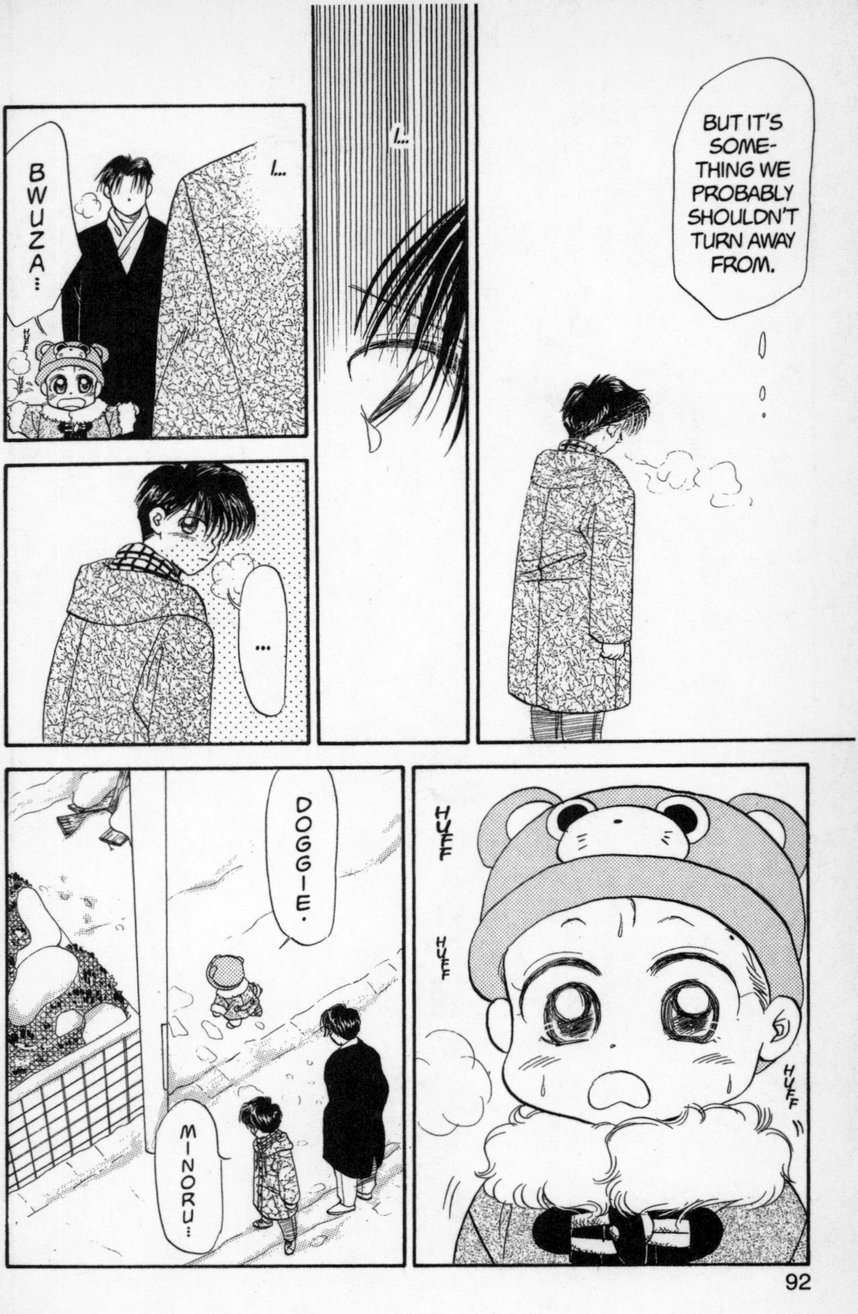

BUT IT'S SOME- THING WE PROBABLY SHOULDN'T TURN AWAY FROM.
I...
I...
BWUZA...
HUFF HUFF
...
HUFF
HUFF
HUFF
DOGGIE.
MINORU...

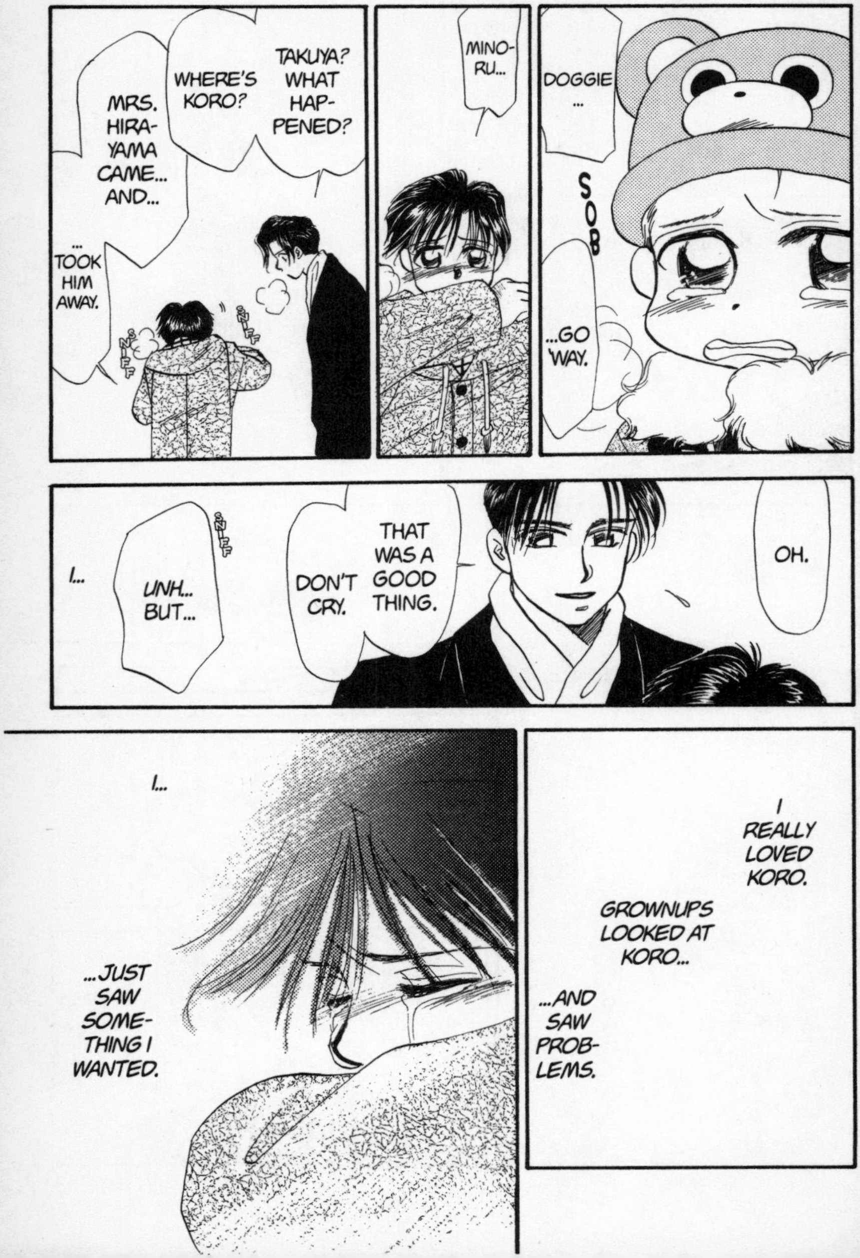
DOGGIE ...
SOB
...GO 'WAY.
MINO-RU...
TAKUYA? WHAT HAP-PENED?
WHERE'S KORO?
MRS. HIRA-YAMA CAME... AND...
... TOOK HIM AWAY.
SNIFF
SNIFF
OH.
THAT WAS A GOOD THING.
DON'T CRY.
SNIFF
UNH... BUT...
I...
I REALLY LOVED KORO.
GROWNUPS LOOKED AT KORO...
...AND SAW PROB-LEMS.
I...
...JUST SAW SOME-THING I WANTED.

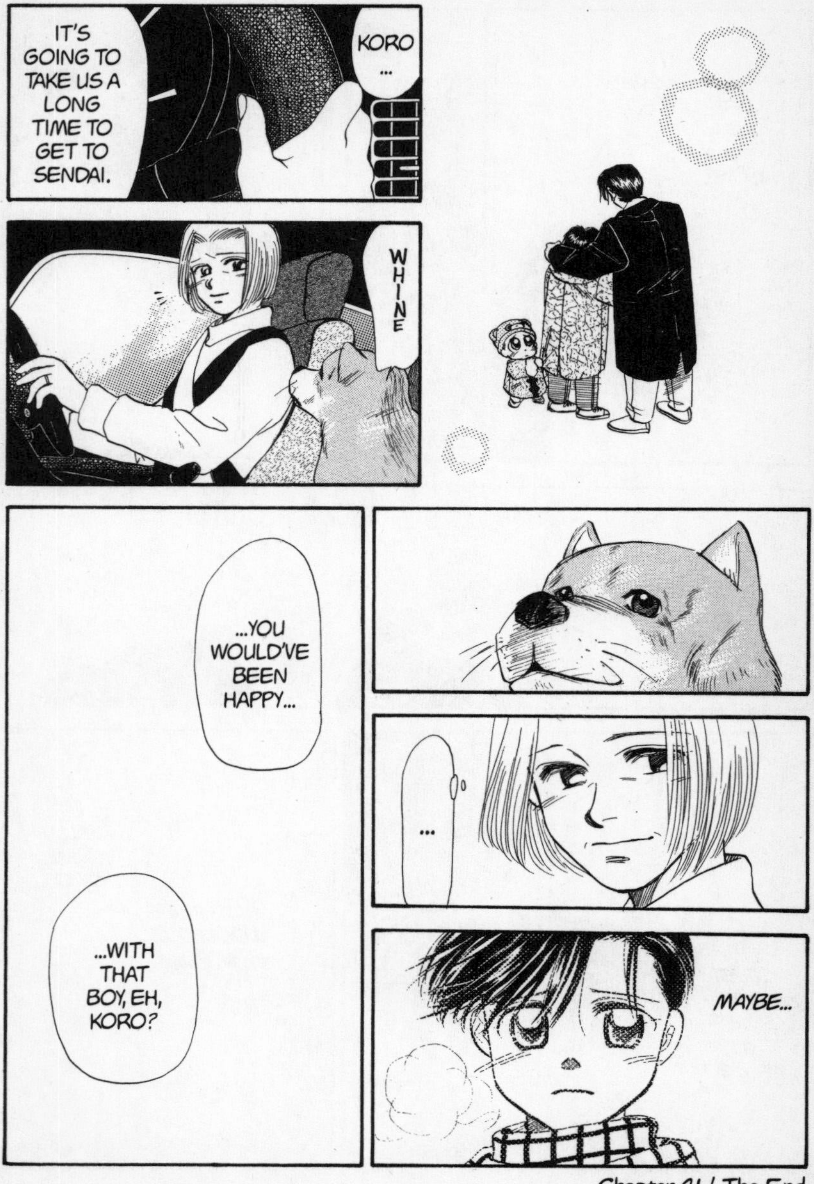
KORO ...
IT'S GOING TO TAKE US A LONG TIME TO GET TO SENDAI.
WHINE
...
MAYBE...
...YOU WOULD'VE BEEN HAPPY...
...WITH THAT BOY, EH, KORO?

Chapter 41 / The End

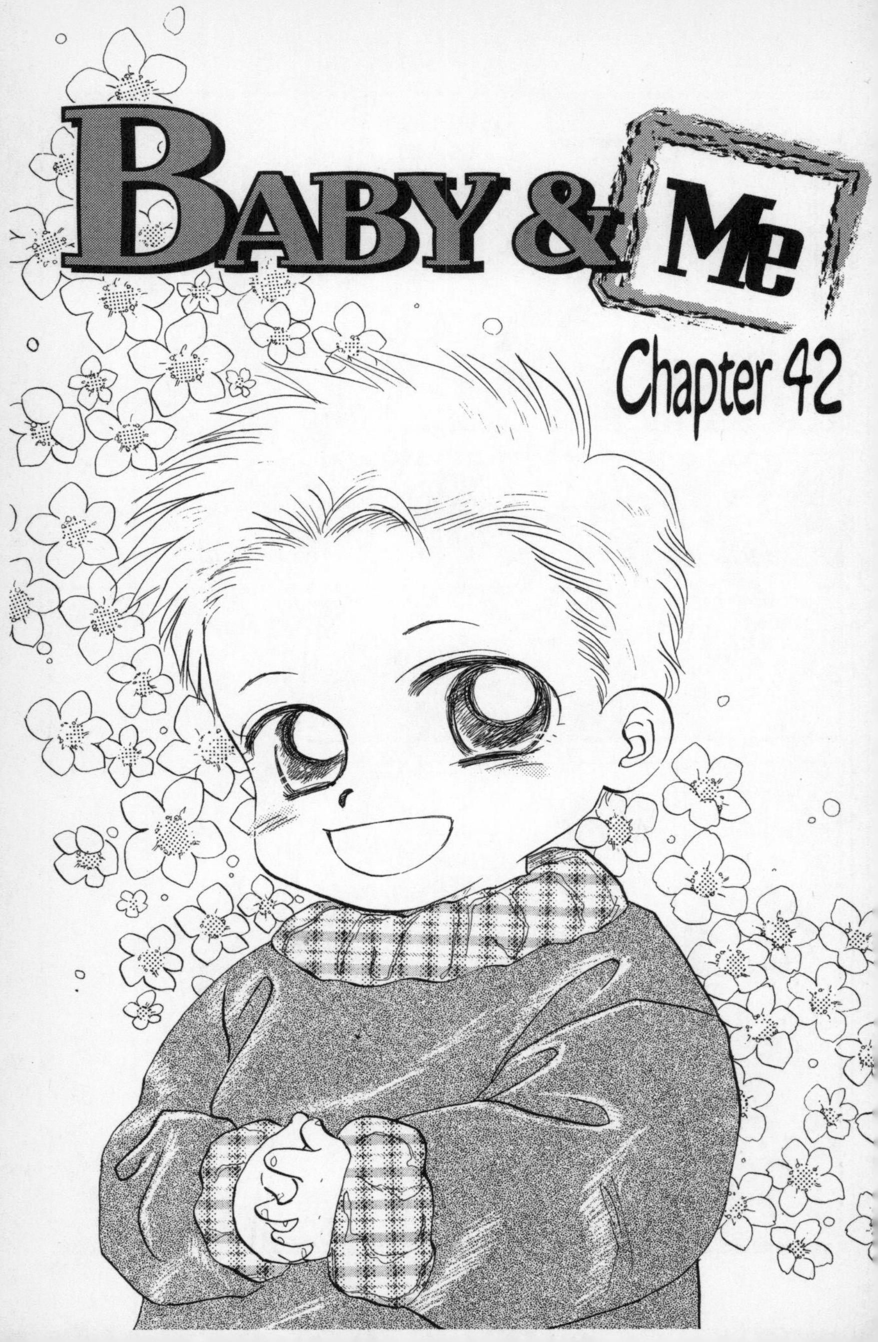
BABY & Me
Chapter 42

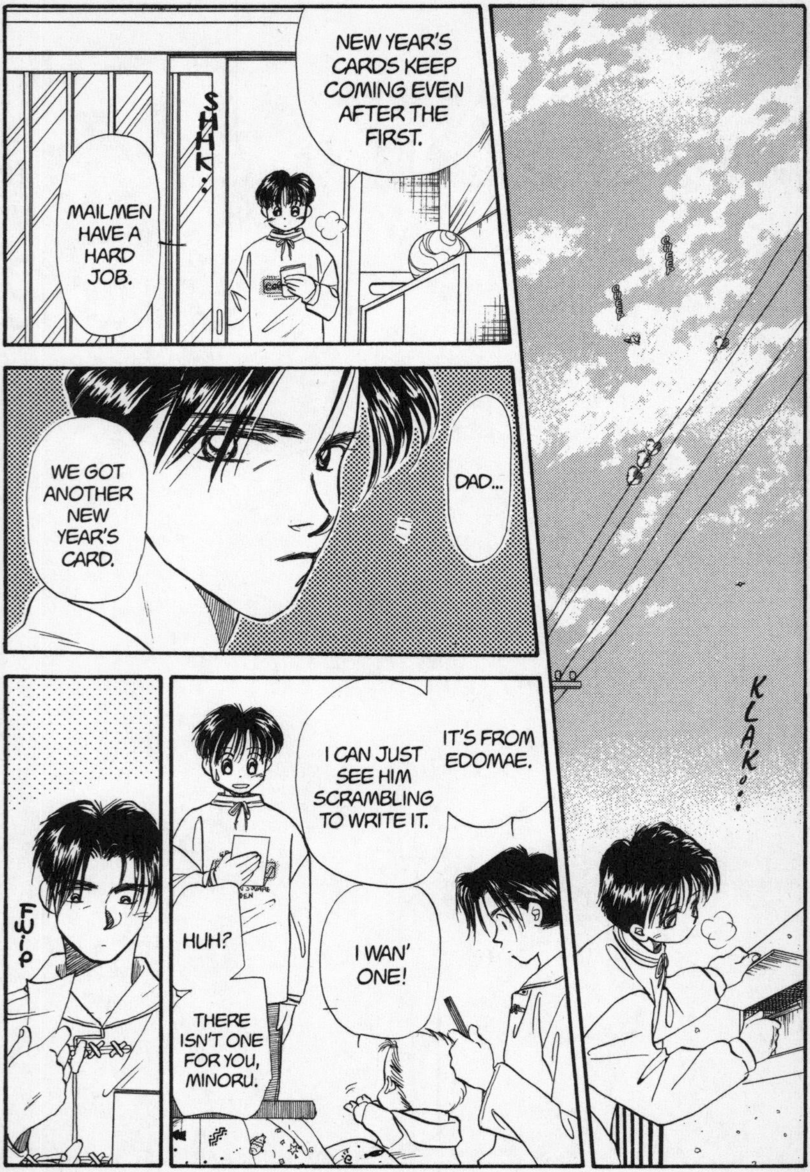
CHEEP
CHEEP
KLAK...
NEW YEAR'S CARDS KEEP COMING EVEN AFTER THE FIRST.
SHHK.
MAILMEN HAVE A HARD JOB.
DAD...
WE GOT ANOTHER NEW YEAR'S CARD.
IT'S FROM EDOMAE.
I CAN JUST SEE HIM SCRAMBLING TO WRITE IT.
I WAN' ONE!
HUH?
THERE ISN'T ONE FOR YOU, MINORU.
FWIP

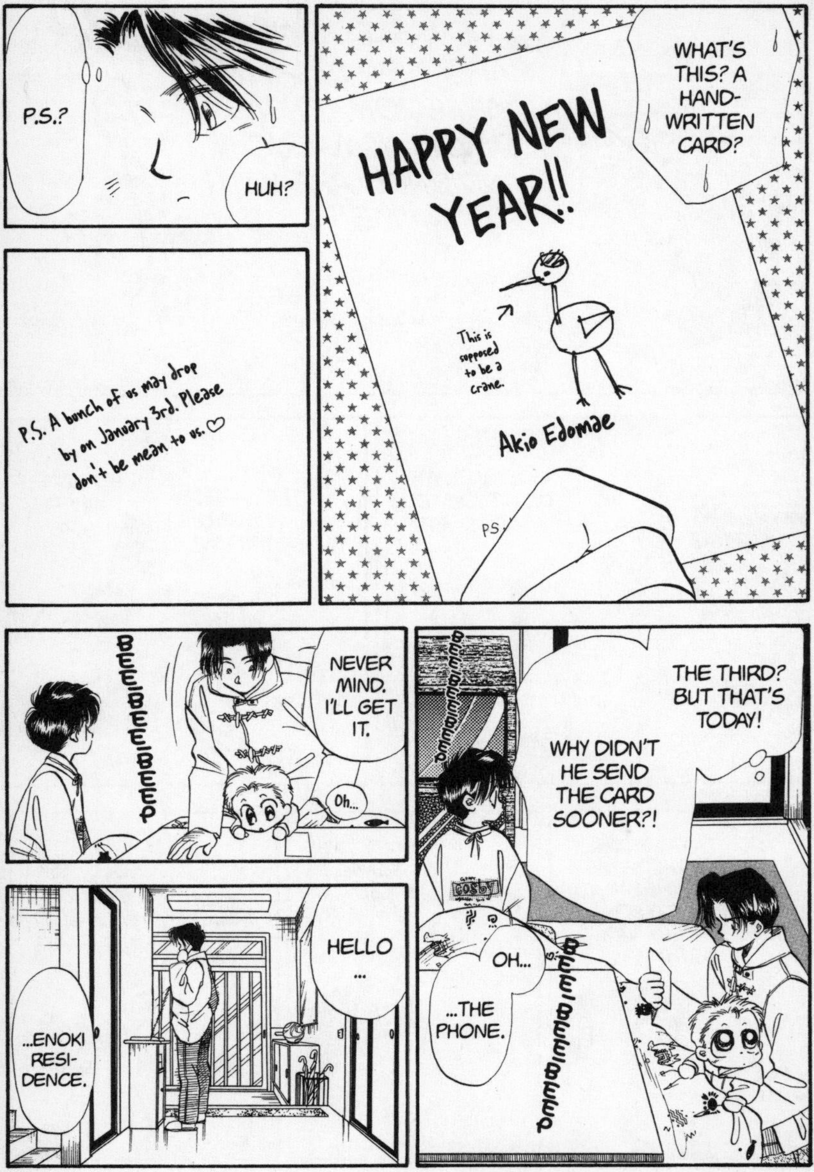
WHAT'S THIS? A HAND-WRITTEN CARD?
HAPPY NEW YEAR!!
This is supposed to be a crane.
Akio Edomae
PS.
P.S.?
HUH?
P.S. A bunch of us may drop by on January 3rd. Please don't be mean to us. ♡
THE THIRD? BUT THAT'S TODAY!
WHY DIDN'T HE SEND THE CARD SOONER?!
OH...
...THE PHONE.
BEEBEEBEEP
NEVER MIND. I'LL GET IT.
Oh...
HELLO ...
...ENOKI RESIDENCE.

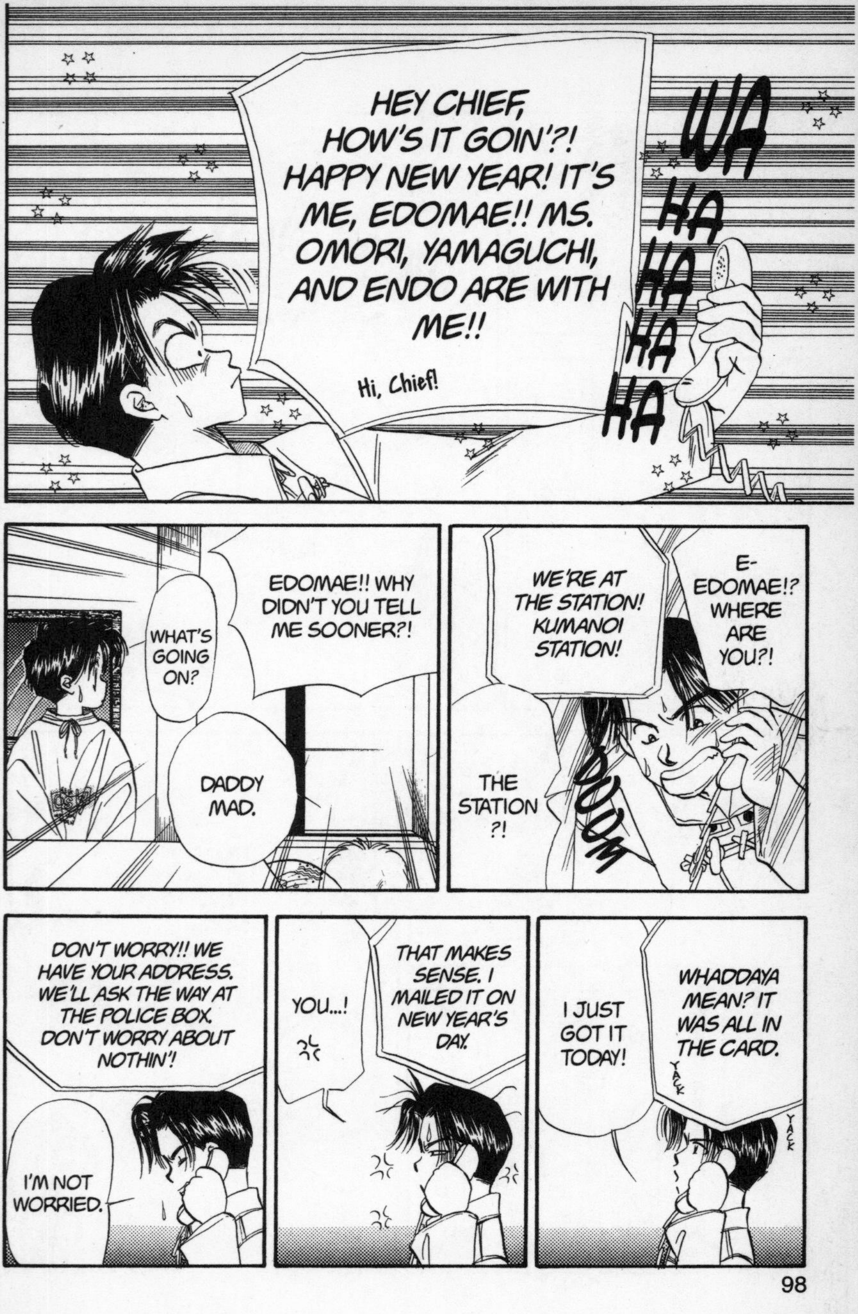
WA HA HA HA HA HA
HEY CHIEF, HOW'S IT GOIN'?! HAPPY NEW YEAR! IT'S ME, EDOMAE!! MS. OMORI, YAMAGUCHI, AND ENDO ARE WITH ME!!
Hi, Chief!
E- EDOMAE!? WHERE ARE YOU?!
WE'RE AT THE STATION! KUMANOI STATION!
DOOM
THE STATION ?!
EDOMAE!! WHY DIDN'T YOU TELL ME SOONER?!
WHAT'S GOING ON?
DADDY MAD.
WHADDAYA MEAN? IT WAS ALL IN THE CARD.
YACK
YACK
I JUST GOT IT TODAY!
THAT MAKES SENSE. I MAILED IT ON NEW YEAR'S DAY.
YOU...!
DON'T WORRY!! WE HAVE YOUR ADDRESS. WE'LL ASK THE WAY AT THE POLICE BOX. DON'T WORRY ABOUT NOTHIN'!
I'M NOT WORRIED.

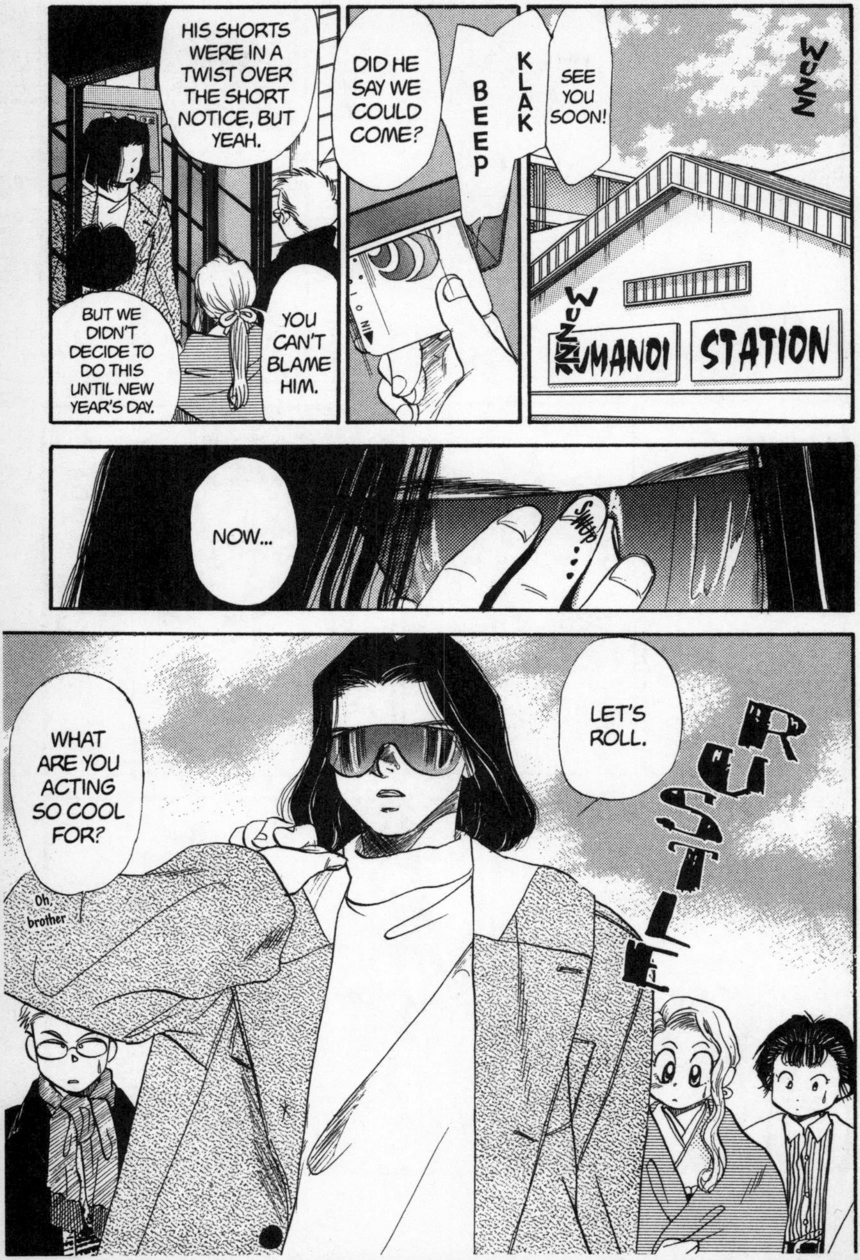
WUZN
SEE YOU SOON!
WUZN
UMANOI STATION
KLAK
BEEP
DID HE SAY WE COULD COME?
HIS SHORTS WERE IN A TWIST OVER THE SHORT NOTICE, BUT YEAH.
YOU CAN'T BLAME HIM.
BUT WE DIDN'T DECIDE TO DO THIS UNTIL NEW YEAR'S DAY.
NOW...
LET'S ROLL.
RUSTLE
WHAT ARE YOU ACTING SO COOL FOR?
Oh, brother...

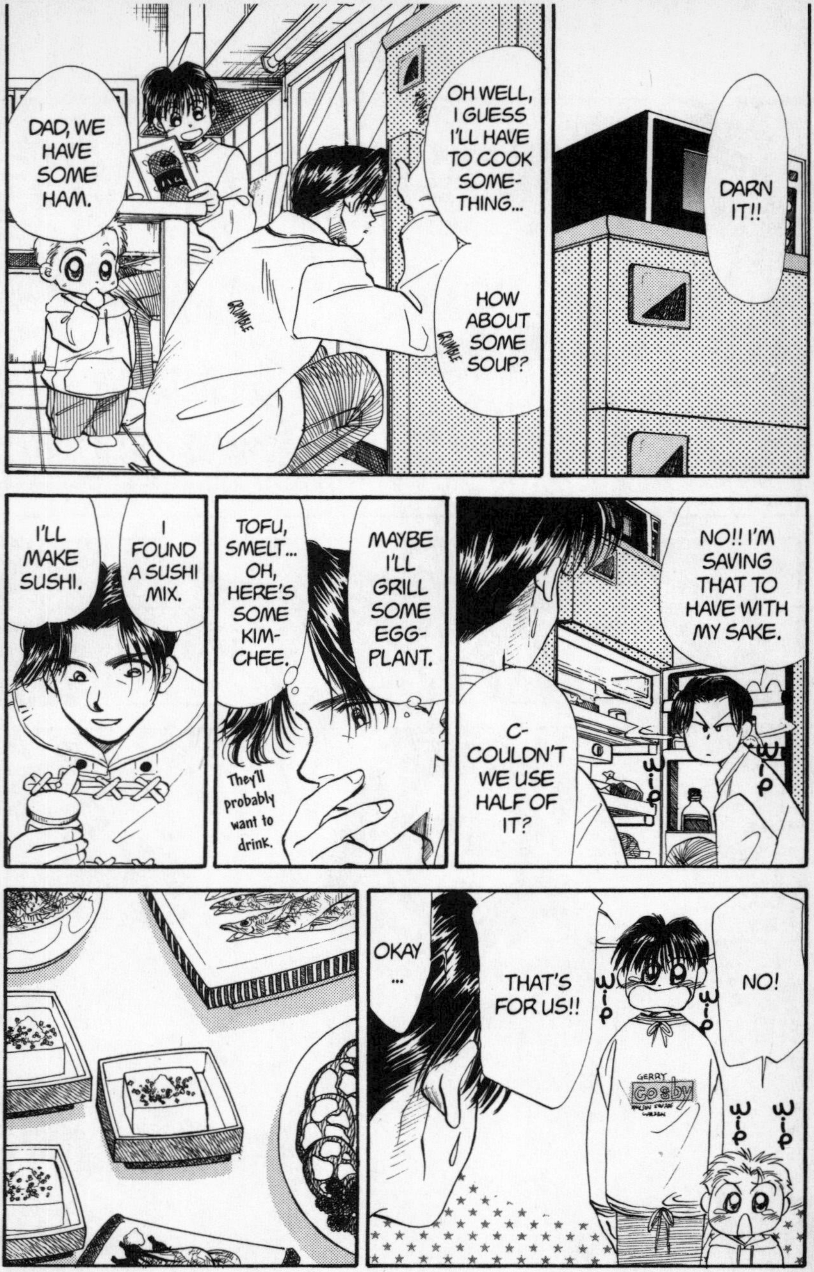
DARN IT!!
OH WELL, I GUESS I'LL HAVE TO COOK SOME-THING...
HOW ABOUT SOME SOUP?
RUMBLE
RUMBLE
DAD, WE HAVE SOME HAM.
NO!! I'M SAVING THAT TO HAVE WITH MY SAKE.
WIP
WIP
C-COULDN'T WE USE HALF OF IT?
MAYBE I'LL GRILL SOME EGG-PLANT.
TOFU, SMELT... OH, HERE'S SOME KIM-CHEE.
They'll probably want to drink.
I FOUND A SUSHI MIX.
I'LL MAKE SUSHI.
NO!
WIP
WIP
WIP
WIP
THAT'S FOR US!!
OKAY ...

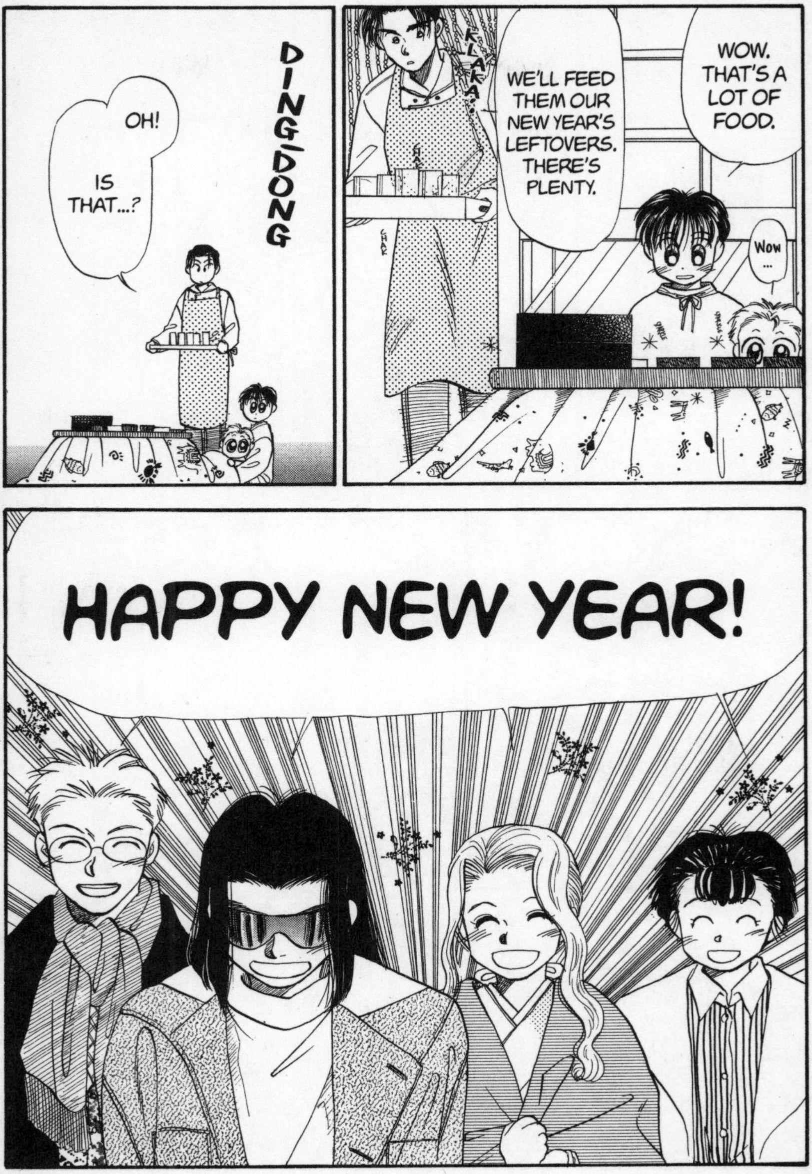
WOW. THAT'S A LOT OF FOOD.
WOW...
WE'LL FEED THEM OUR NEW YEAR'S LEFTOVERS. THERE'S PLENTY.
KLAKA
CHAK
DING-DONG
OH!
IS THAT...?
HAPPY NEW YEAR!

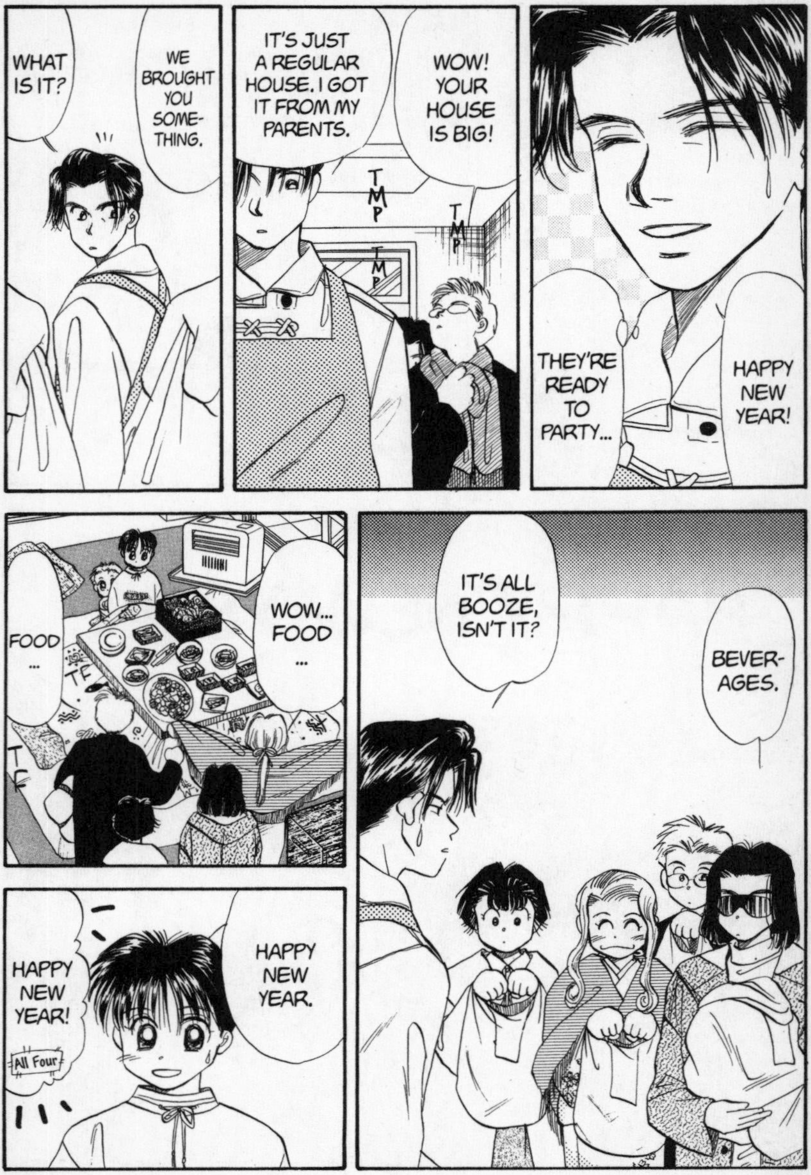

HAPPY NEW YEAR!
THEY'RE READY TO PARTY...
WOW! YOUR HOUSE IS BIG!
IT'S JUST A REGULAR HOUSE. I GOT IT FROM MY PARENTS.
TMP
TMP
TMP
WE BROUGHT YOU SOMETHING.
WHAT IS IT?
BEVER-AGES.
IT'S ALL BOOZE, ISN'T IT?
WOW... FOOD ...
FOOD ...
TF
TF
HAPPY NEW YEAR.
HAPPY NEW YEAR!
All Four

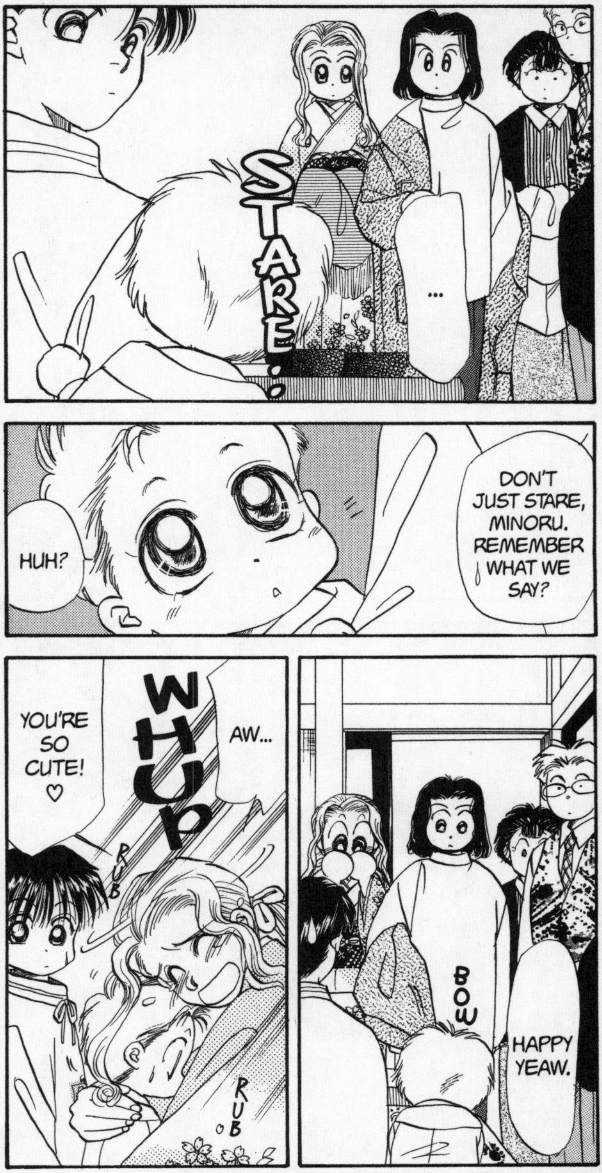
STARE...
...
DON'T JUST STARE, MINORU. REMEMBER WHAT WE SAY?
HUH?
BOW
HAPPY YEAW.
AW...
WHUP
YOU'RE SO CUTE! ♡
RUB
RUB

Author's Note 4

A silly story...
I moved to Tokyo almost five years ago, and people always asked me if I was afraid to live alone. (Now I live with my sister.) "Afraid of what?" I'd ask. "Of being alone? Of ghosts?" "Of being alone" was the answer. As for ghosts, I've never met one--of course, whenever I watch a ghost story on TV, I get scared--but I was never afraid just because I was alone. As a kid, I spent a lot of time by myself (even though I had a large family). I'm not comfortable being around people all the time. I prefer spending time alone, doing nothing. (My friends are exceptions, and they're precious to me.) But there was a time when I suddenly felt like I might forget how to talk. One morning I got up and spent the whole day indoors. Late that night, I suddenly realized that I hadn't said a word all day. I hadn't watched TV, or talked to myself, or sneezed, or even hiccuped. All I'd done was breathe in and out. That was scary. So to test myself I said "Ah!" in a loud voice. Then my worries evaporated. "I guess I still know how to speak," I thought. Now I can be alone without worrying.

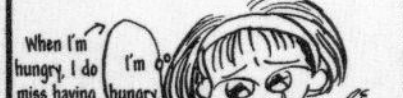
When I'm hungry, I do miss having someone around.
I'm hungry.

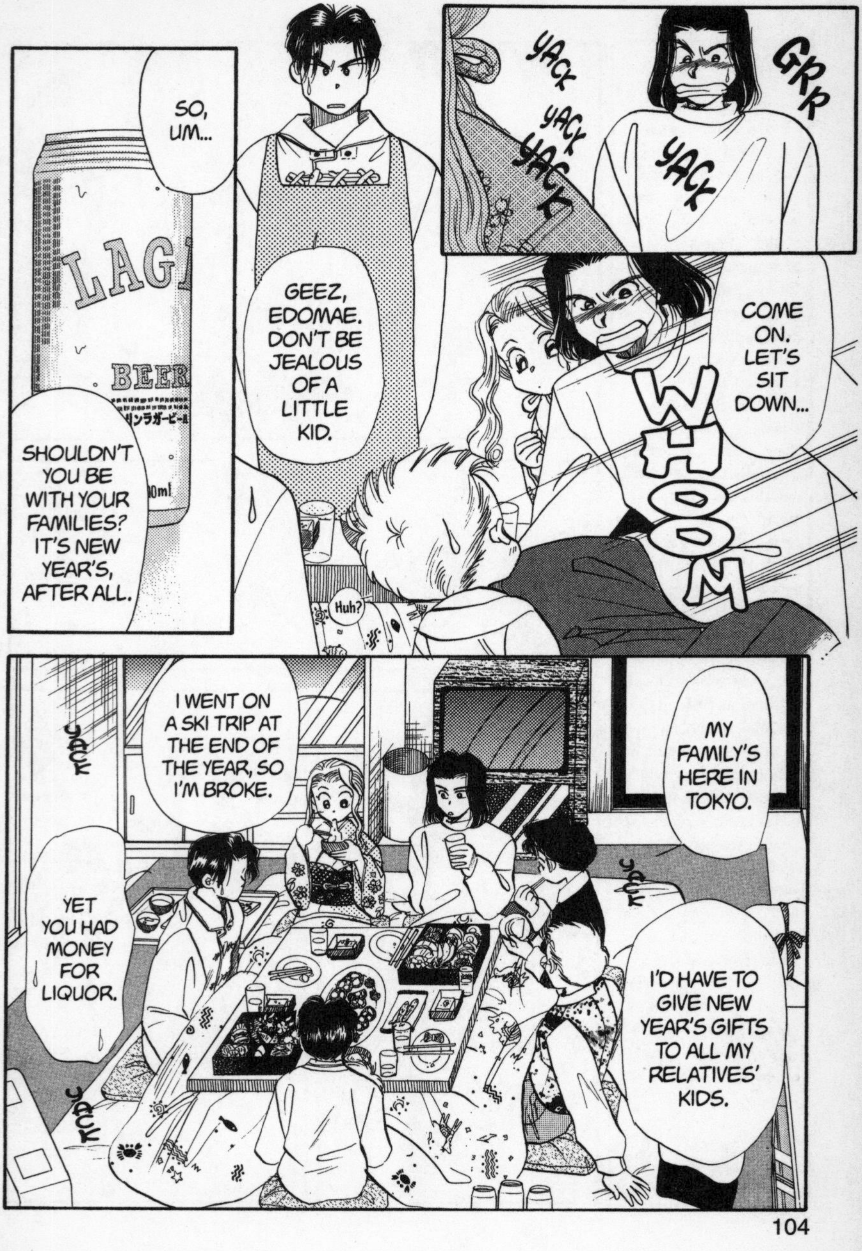
GRR
YACK
YACK
YACK YACK
YACK
COME ON. LET'S SIT DOWN...
WHOOM
GEEZ, EDOMAE. DON'T BE JEALOUS OF A LITTLE KID.
Huh?
SO, UM...
BEER
SHOULDN'T YOU BE WITH YOUR FAMILIES? IT'S NEW YEAR'S, AFTER ALL.
MY FAMILY'S HERE IN TOKYO.
I'D HAVE TO GIVE NEW YEAR'S GIFTS TO ALL MY RELATIVES' KIDS.
YACK
I WENT ON A SKI TRIP AT THE END OF THE YEAR, SO I'M BROKE.
YACK
YET YOU HAD MONEY FOR LIQUOR.
YACK

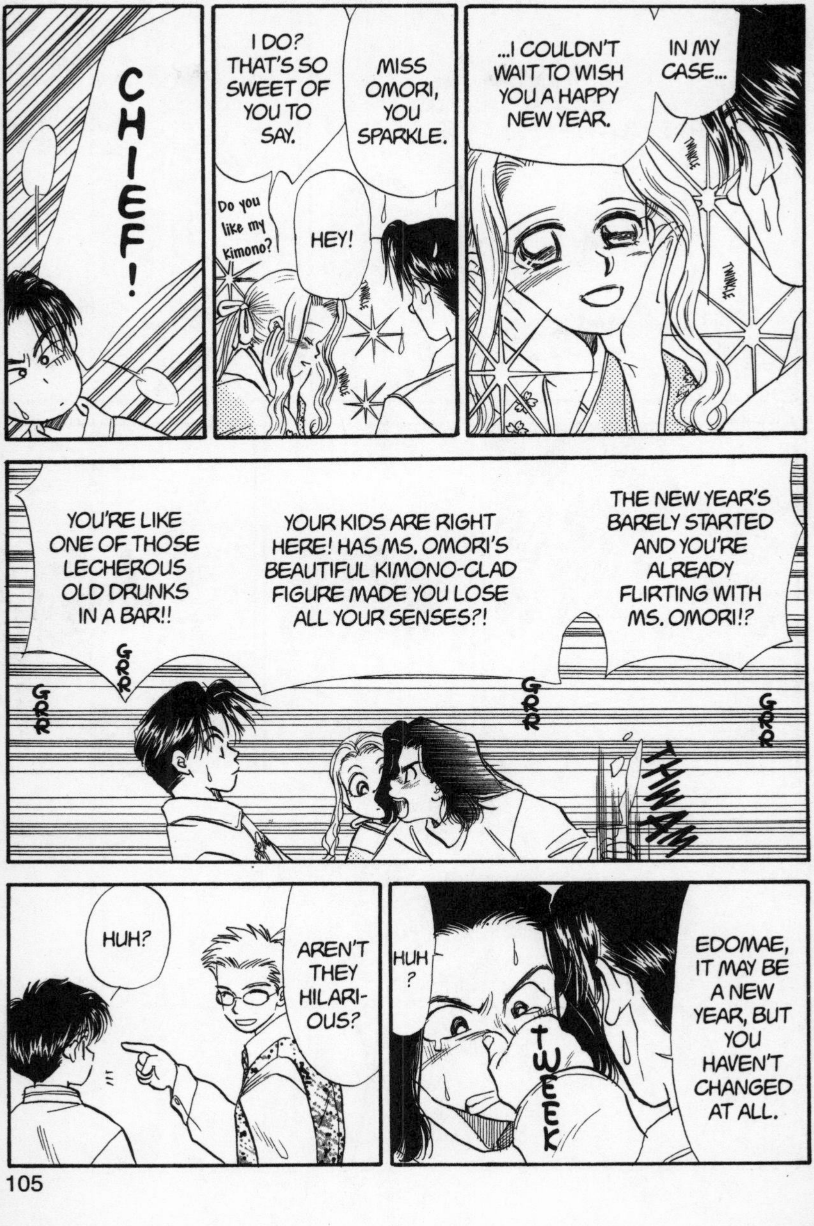
IN MY CASE...
...I COULDN'T WAIT TO WISH YOU A HAPPY NEW YEAR.
TWINKLE
TWINKLE
MISS OMORI, YOU SPARKLE.
I DO? THAT'S SO SWEET OF YOU TO SAY.
HEY!
Do you like my Kimono?
TWINKLE
TWINKLE
CHIEF!
THE NEW YEAR'S BARELY STARTED AND YOU'RE ALREADY FLIRTING WITH MS. OMORI!?
YOUR KIDS ARE RIGHT HERE! HAS MS. OMORI'S BEAUTIFUL KIMONO-CLAD FIGURE MADE YOU LOSE ALL YOUR SENSES?!
YOU'RE LIKE ONE OF THOSE LECHEROUS OLD DRUNKS IN A BAR!!
GRR
GRR
GRR
GRR
THWAM
EDOMAE, IT MAY BE A NEW YEAR, BUT YOU HAVEN'T CHANGED AT ALL.
TWEEK
HUH?
AREN'T THEY HILARI-OUS?
HUH?

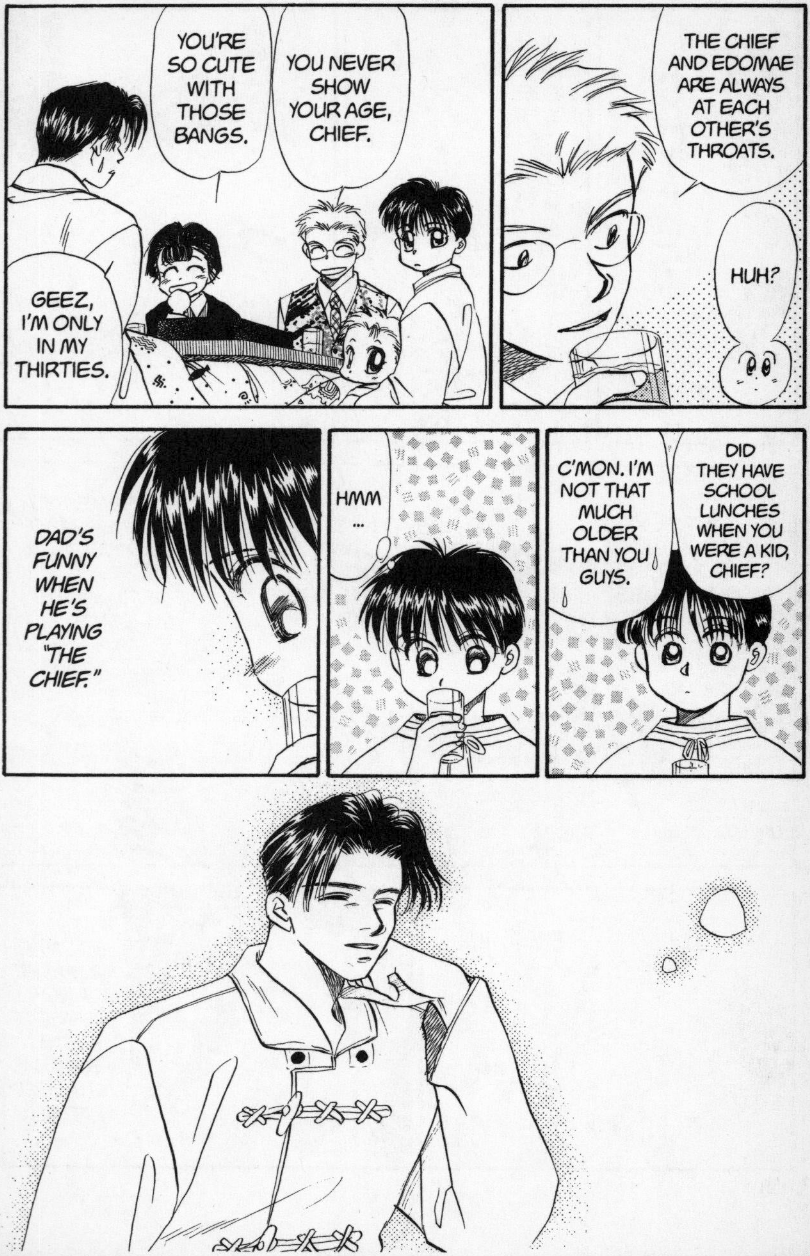
THE CHIEF AND EDOMAE ARE ALWAYS AT EACH OTHER'S THROATS.
HUH?
YOU NEVER SHOW YOUR AGE, CHIEF.
YOU'RE SO CUTE WITH THOSE BANGS.
GEEZ, I'M ONLY IN MY THIRTIES.
DID THEY HAVE SCHOOL LUNCHES WHEN YOU WERE A KID, CHIEF?
C'MON. I'M NOT THAT MUCH OLDER THAN YOU GUYS.
HMM ...
DAD'S FUNNY WHEN HE'S PLAYING "THE CHIEF."

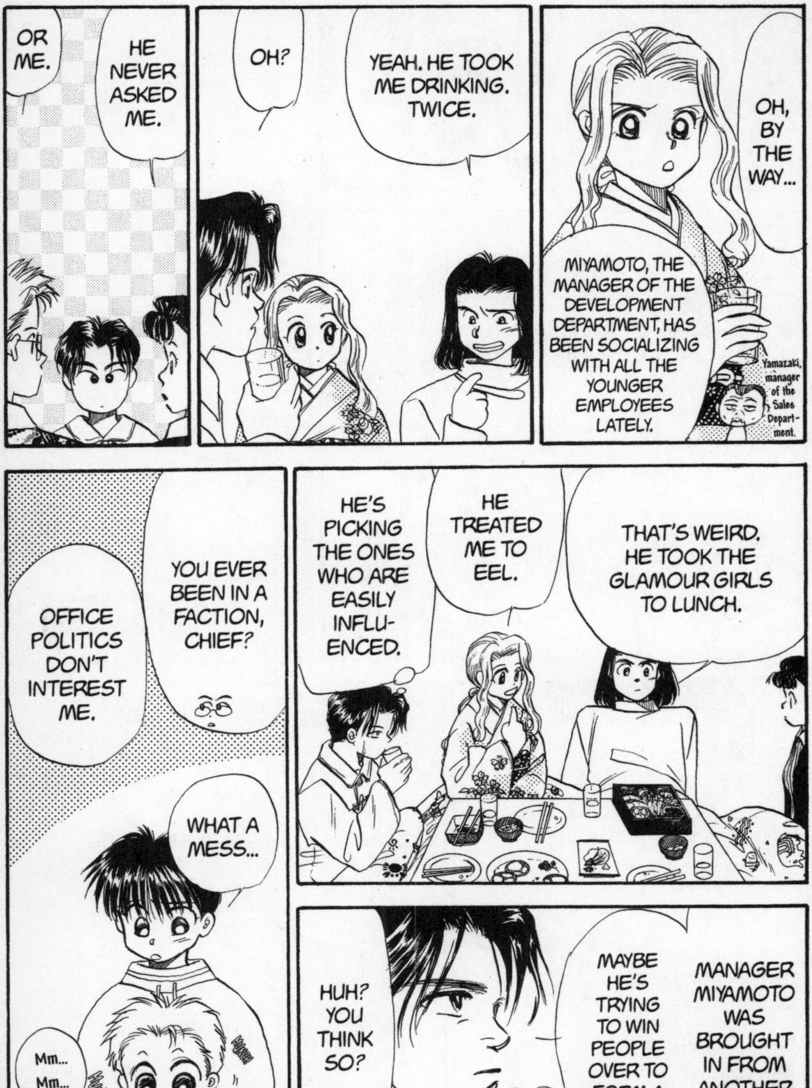
OH, BY THE WAY...
MIYAMOTO, THE MANAGER OF THE DEVELOPMENT DEPARTMENT, HAS BEEN SOCIALIZING WITH ALL THE YOUNGER EMPLOYEES LATELY.
Yamazaki, manager of the Sales Department.
YEAH. HE TOOK ME DRINKING. TWICE.
OH?
HE NEVER ASKED ME.
OR ME.
THAT'S WEIRD. HE TOOK THE GLAMOUR GIRLS TO LUNCH.
HE TREATED ME TO EEL.
HE'S PICKING THE ONES WHO ARE EASILY INFLU-ENCED.
MANAGER MIYAMOTO WAS BROUGHT IN FROM ANOTHER COMPANY.
MAYBE HE'S TRYING TO WIN PEOPLE OVER TO FORM A FACTION.
HUH? YOU THINK SO?
YOU EVER BEEN IN A FACTION, CHIEF?
OFFICE POLITICS DON'T INTEREST ME.
WHAT A MESS...
Mm... Mm...

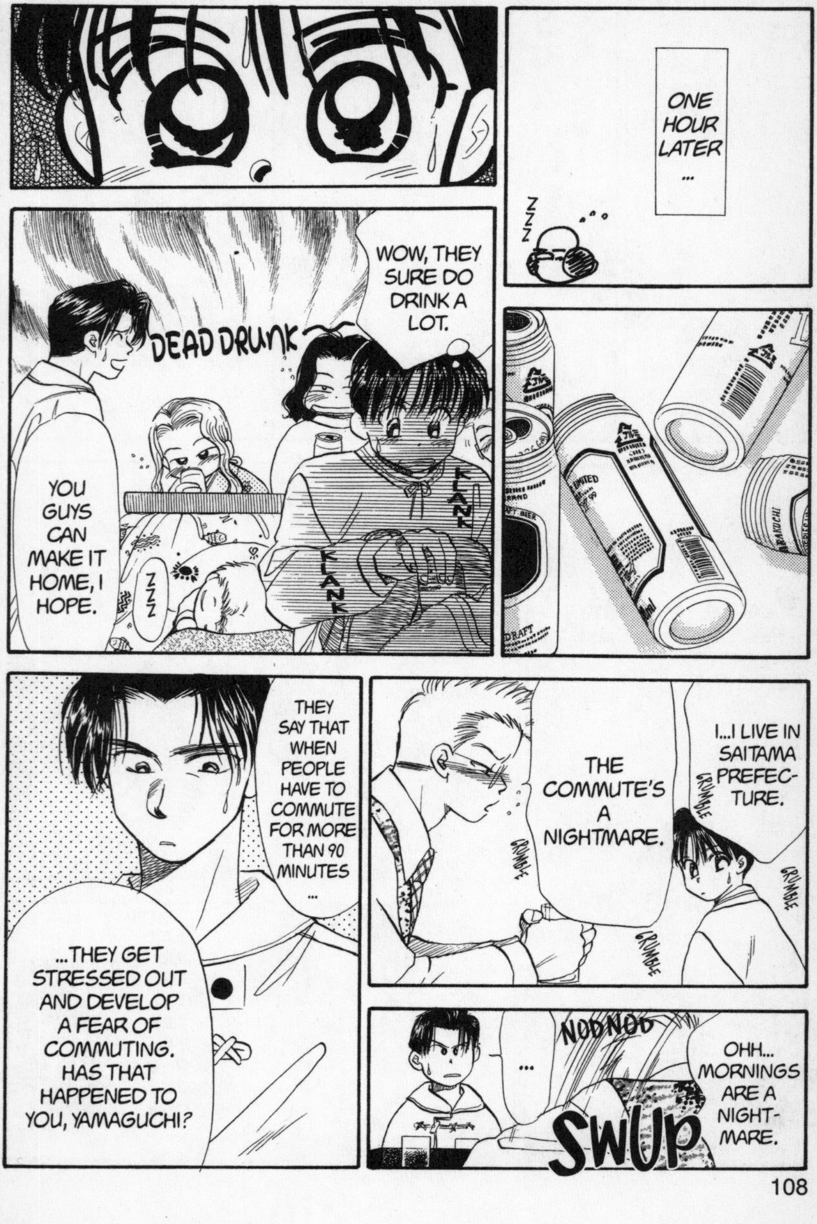
ONE HOUR LATER ...
ZZZ
WOW, THEY SURE DO DRINK A LOT.
DEAD DRUNK
KLANK
KLANK
ZZZ
YOU GUYS CAN MAKE IT HOME, I HOPE.
I...I LIVE IN SAITAMA PREFECTURE.
THE COMMUTE'S A NIGHTMARE.
CRUMBLE
CRUMBLE
CRUMBLE
CRUMBLE
OHH... MORNINGS ARE A NIGHTMARE.
NOD NOD
...
SWUP
THEY SAY THAT WHEN PEOPLE HAVE TO COMMUTE FOR MORE THAN 90 MINUTES ...
...THEY GET STRESSED OUT AND DEVELOP A FEAR OF COMMUTING. HAS THAT HAPPENED TO YOU, YAMAGUCHI?

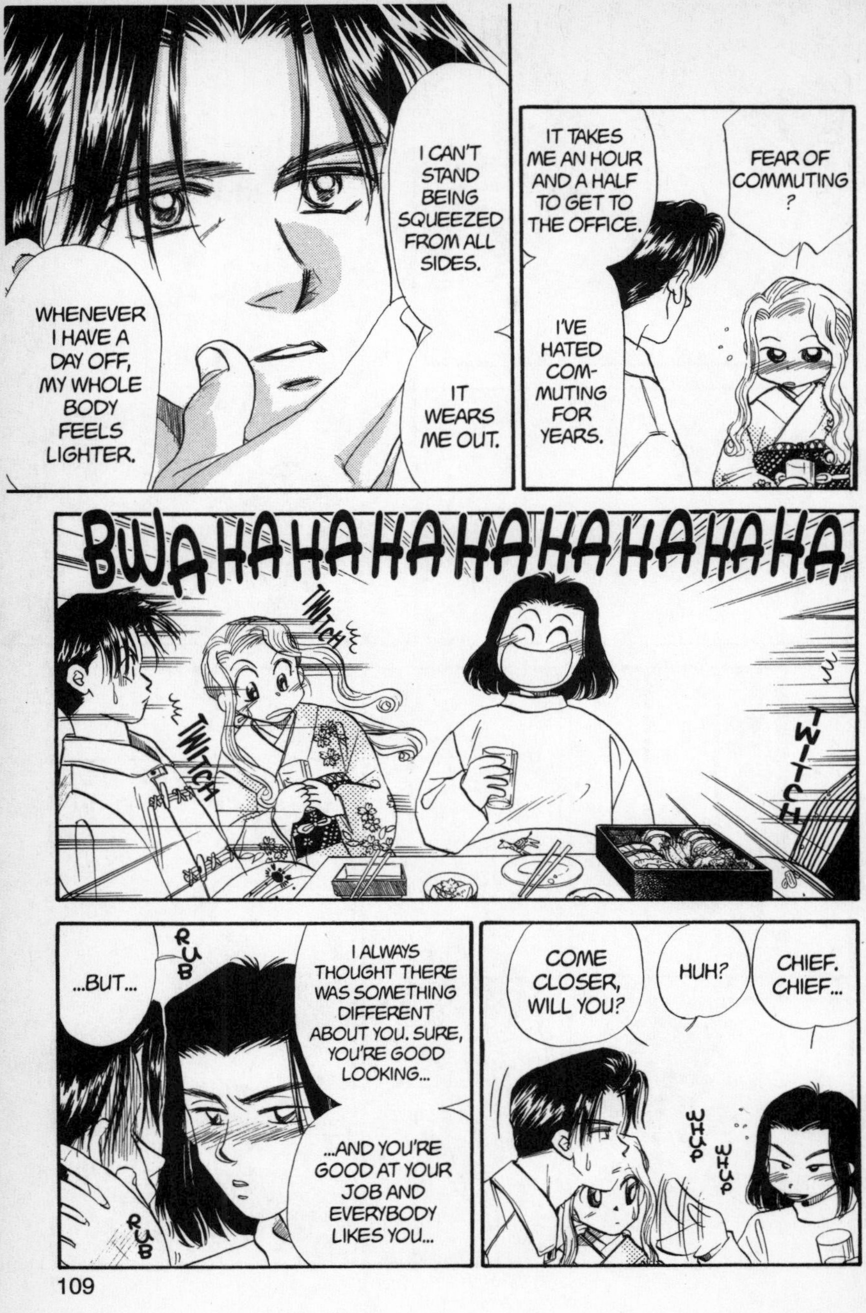
FEAR OF COMMUTING ?
IT TAKES ME AN HOUR AND A HALF TO GET TO THE OFFICE.
I'VE HATED COMMUTING FOR YEARS.
I CAN'T STAND BEING SQUEEZED FROM ALL SIDES.
IT WEARS ME OUT.
WHENEVER I HAVE A DAY OFF, MY WHOLE BODY FEELS LIGHTER.
BWAHAHAHAHAHAHAHAHAHAHA
TWITCH
TWITCH
TWITCH
CHIEF. CHIEF...
HUH?
COME CLOSER, WILL YOU?
WHUP
WHUP
I ALWAYS THOUGHT THERE WAS SOMETHING DIFFERENT ABOUT YOU. SURE, YOU'RE GOOD LOOKING...
...AND YOU'RE GOOD AT YOUR JOB AND EVERYBODY LIKES YOU...
...BUT...
RUB
RUB

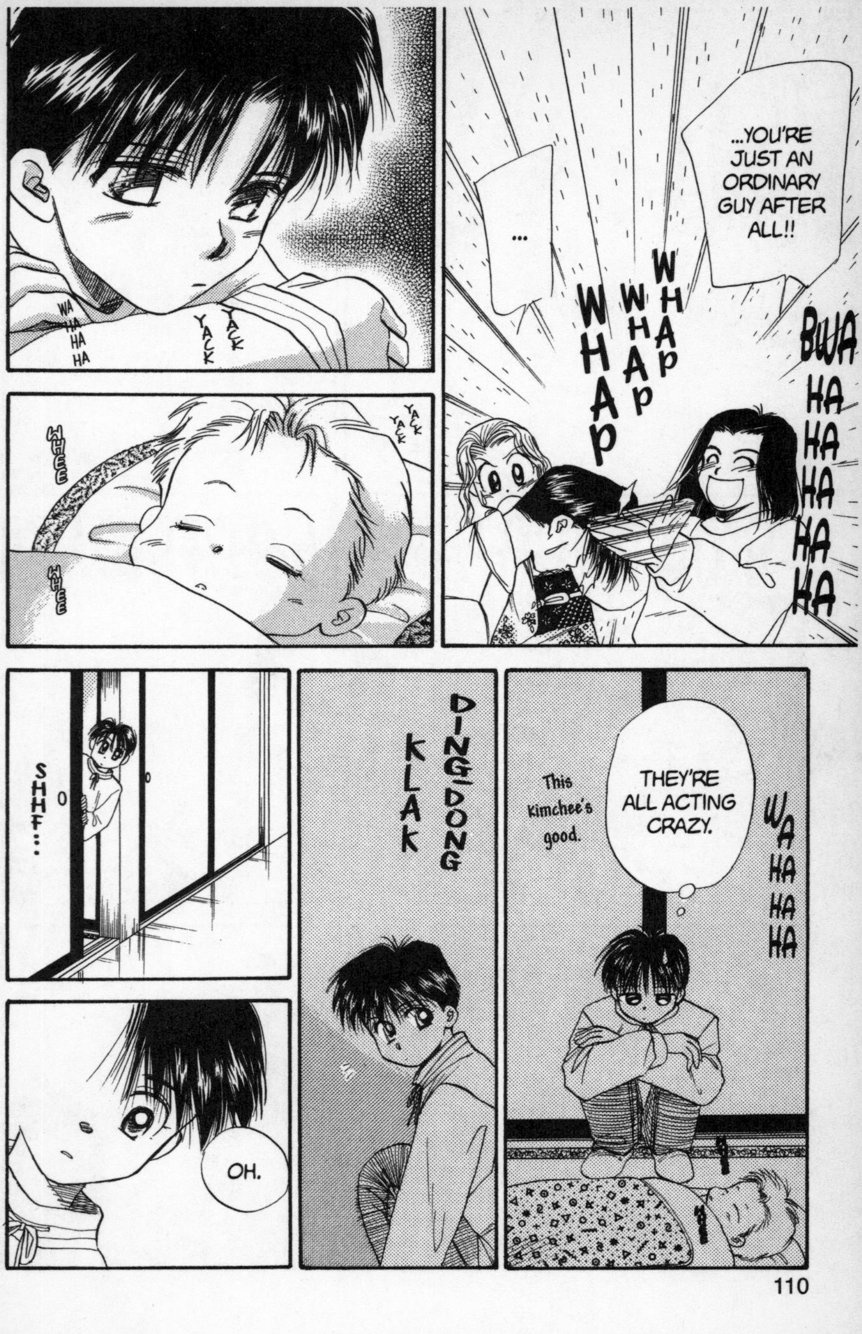
...YOU'RE JUST AN ORDINARY GUY AFTER ALL!!
...
WHAP
WHAP
WHAP
BWA HA HA HA HA HA HA
WA HA HA HA
YACK YACK
YACK YACK
WHEE
WHEE
This Kimchee's good.
THEY'RE ALL ACTING CRAZY.
WA HA HA HA HA
DING-DONG
KLAK
SHHF...
OH.

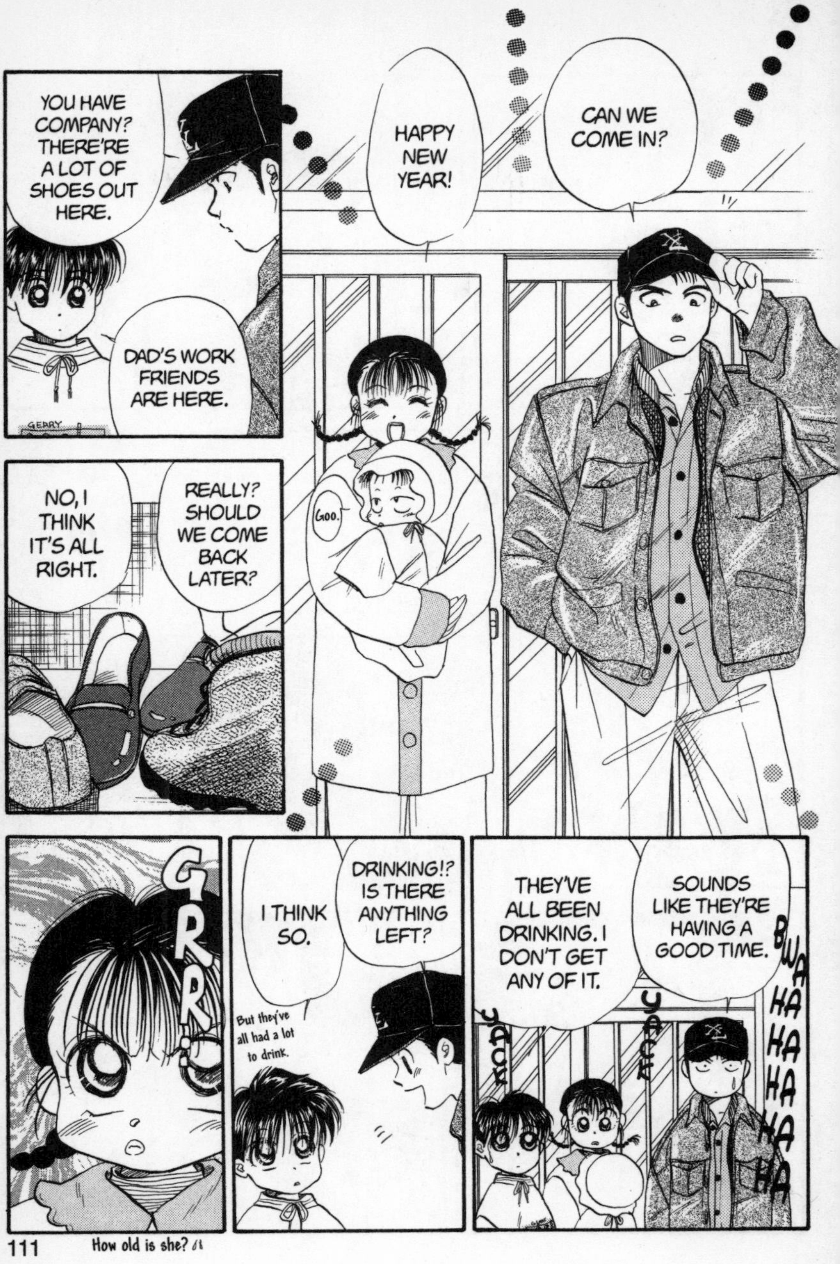
CAN WE COME IN?
HAPPY NEW YEAR!
GOO.
YOU HAVE COMPANY? THERE'RE A LOT OF SHOES OUT HERE.
DAD'S WORK FRIENDS ARE HERE.
REALLY? SHOULD WE COME BACK LATER?
NO, I THINK IT'S ALL RIGHT.
SOUNDS LIKE THEY'RE HAVING A GOOD TIME.
BWAHAHAHAHAHAHAHA
THEY'VE ALL BEEN DRINKING. I DON'T GET ANY OF IT.
DRINKING!? IS THERE ANYTHING LEFT?
I THINK SO.
But they've all had a lot to drink.
GRR

How old is she?

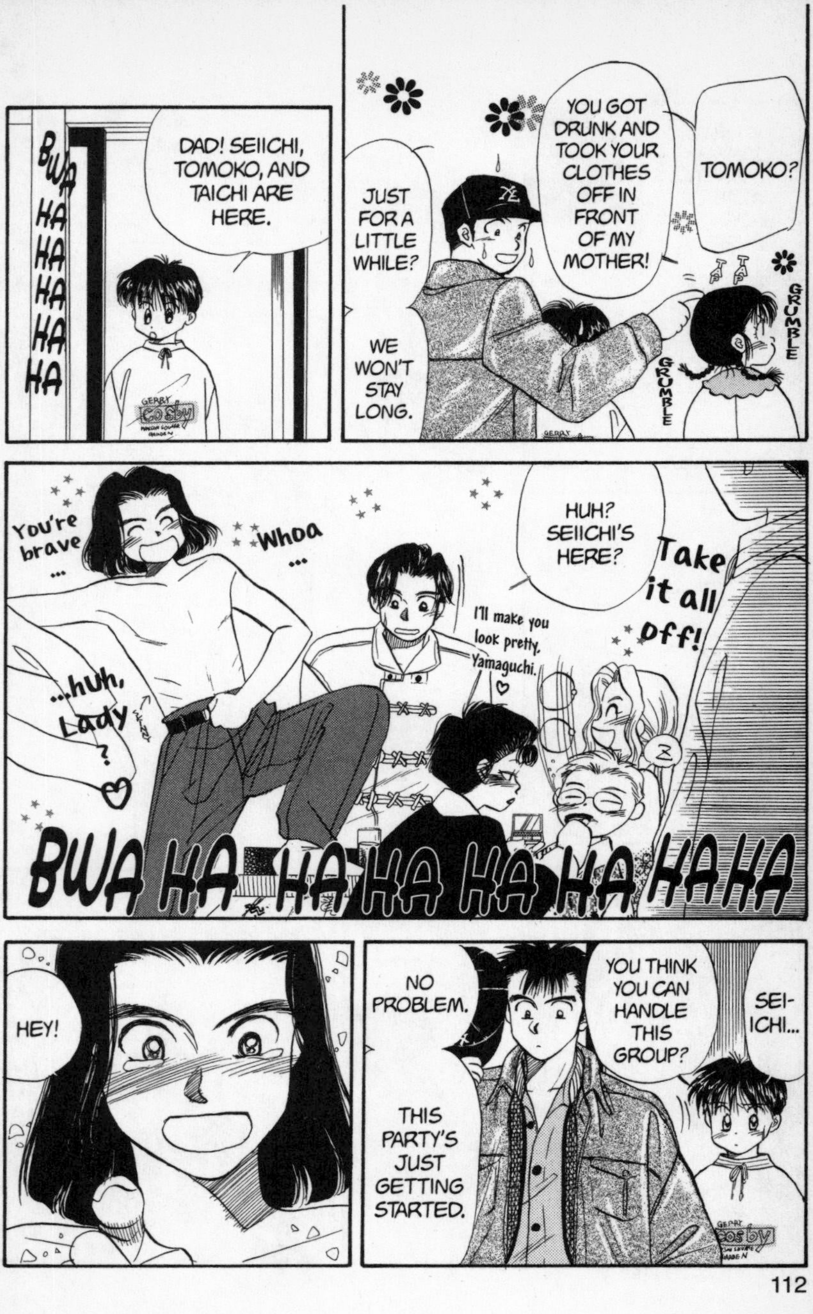
TOMOKO?
YOU GOT DRUNK AND TOOK YOUR CLOTHES OFF IN FRONT OF MY MOTHER!
TAP TAP
GRUMBLE
GRUMBLE
JUST FOR A LITTLE WHILE?
WE WON'T STAY LONG.
DAD! SEIICHI, TOMOKO, AND TAICHI ARE HERE.
BWA HA HA HA HA HA HA HA
Take it all off!
HUH? SEIICHI'S HERE?
I'll make you look pretty, Yamaguchi.
Whoa ...
You're brave ...
...huh, Lady ?
BWA HA HA HA HA HA HA HAHA
SEI-ICHI...
YOU THINK YOU CAN HANDLE THIS GROUP?
NO PROBLEM.
THIS PARTY'S JUST GETTING STARTED.
HEY!

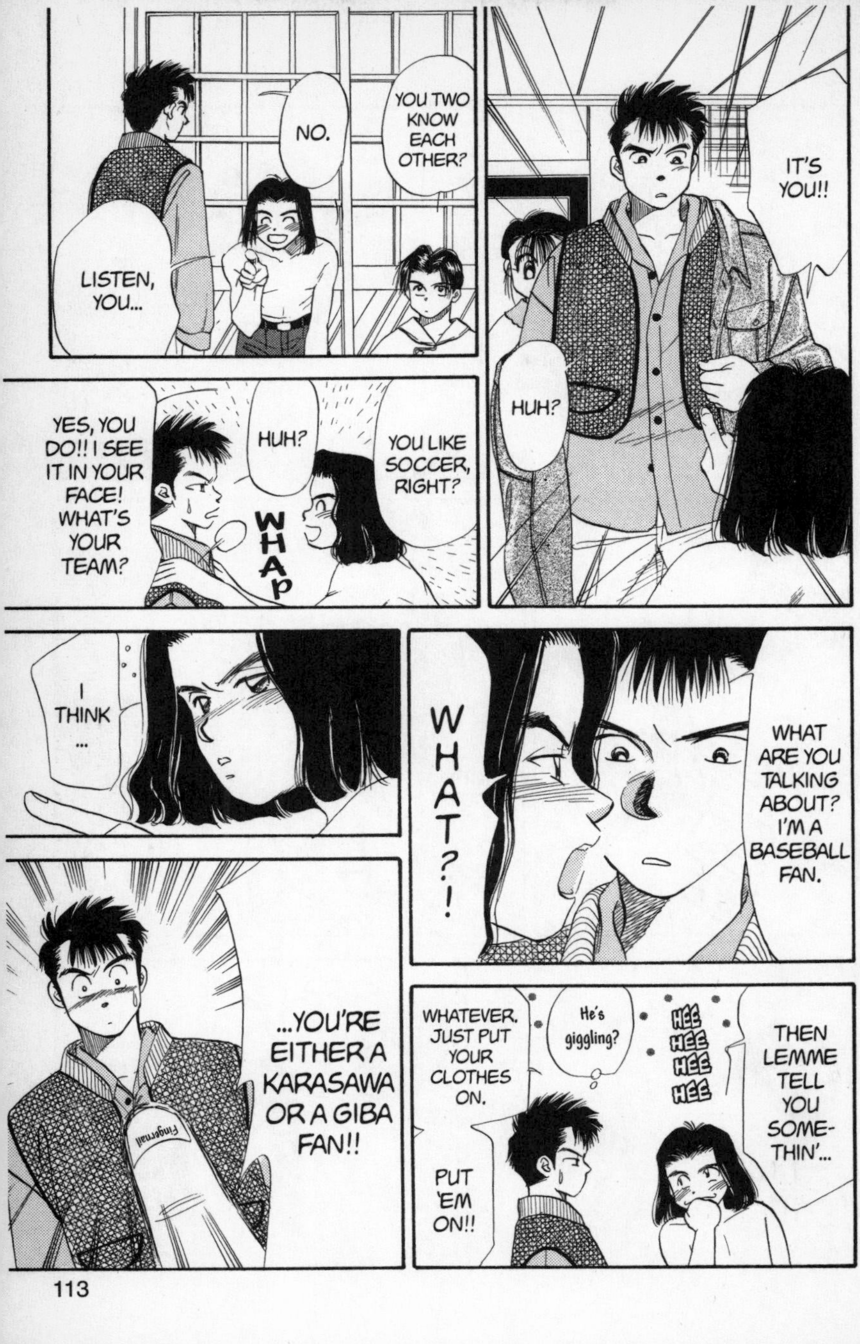
IT'S YOU!!
HUH?
YOU TWO KNOW EACH OTHER?
NO.
LISTEN, YOU...
YOU LIKE SOCCER, RIGHT?
HUH?
WHAP
YES, YOU DO!! I SEE IT IN YOUR FACE! WHAT'S YOUR TEAM?
WHAT ARE YOU TALKING ABOUT? I'M A BASEBALL FAN.
WHAT?!
I THINK ...
THEN LEMME TELL YOU SOME-THIN'...
HEE HEE HEE HEE
He's giggling?
WHATEVER. JUST PUT YOUR CLOTHES ON.
PUT 'EM ON!!
...YOU'RE EITHER A KARASAWA OR A GIBA FAN!!
Fingernail

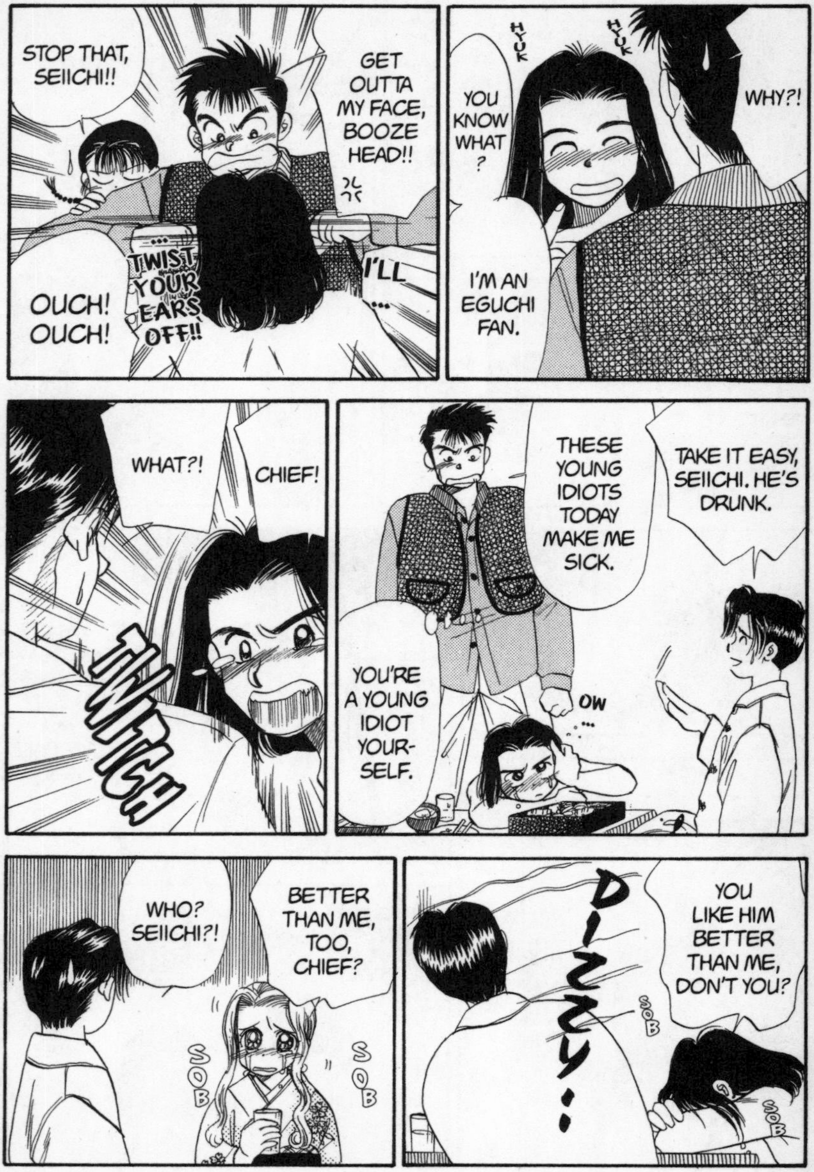
HYUK HYUK
WHY?!
YOU KNOW WHAT?
I'M AN EGUCHI FAN.
GET OUTTA MY FACE, BOOZE HEAD!!
STOP THAT, SEIICHI!!
I'LL...
...TWIST YOUR EARS OFF!!
OUCH! OUCH!
TAKE IT EASY, SEIICHI. HE'S DRUNK.
THESE YOUNG IDIOTS TODAY MAKE ME SICK.
YOU'RE A YOUNG IDIOT YOURSELF.
OW...
CHIEF!
WHAT?!
TWITCH
YOU LIKE HIM BETTER THAN ME, DON'T YOU?
SOB SOB
DIZZY..
BETTER THAN ME, TOO, CHIEF?
WHO? SEIICHI?!
SOB SOB

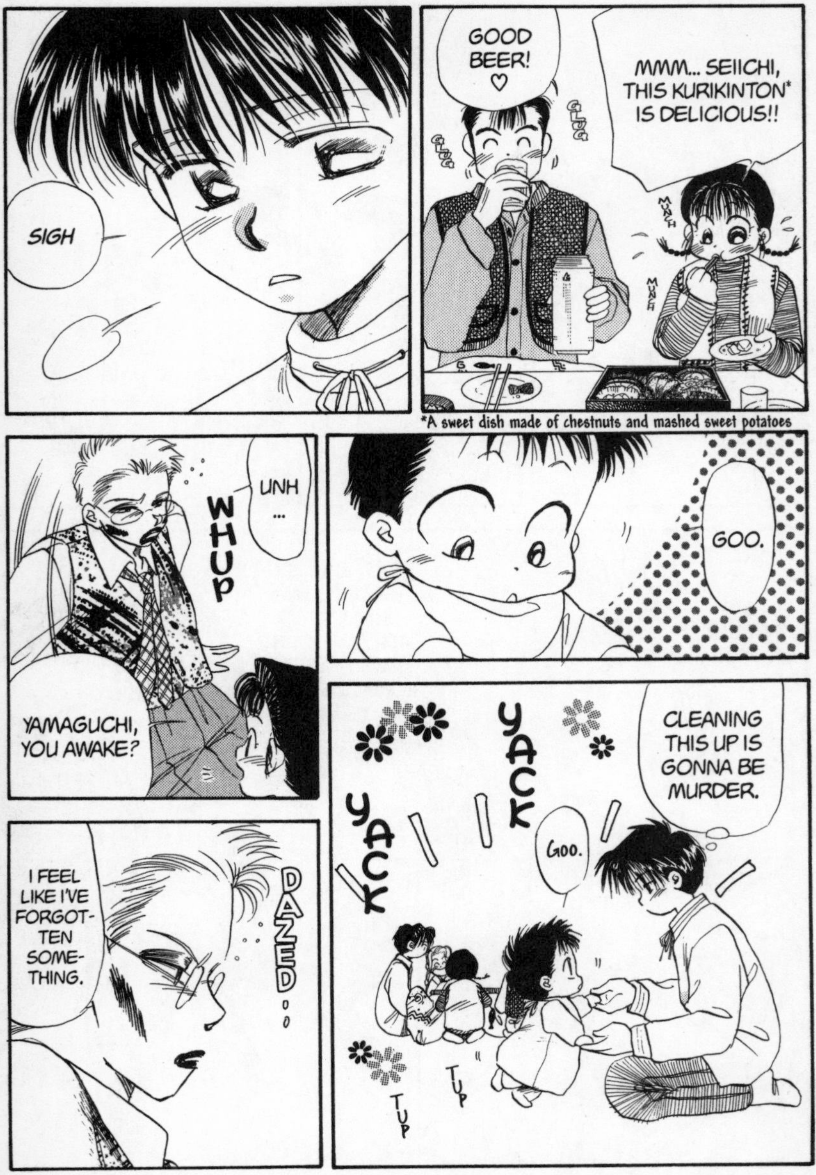
MMM... SEIICHI, THIS KURIKINTON* IS DELICIOUS!!
GOOD BEER! ♡
GLUG GLUG GLUG
MUNCH MUNCH
SIGH
GOO.
CLEANING THIS UP IS GONNA BE MURDER.
YACK
Goo.
YACK
TUP TUP
UNH ...
WHUP
YAMAGUCHI, YOU AWAKE?
DAZED
I FEEL LIKE I'VE FORGOTTEN SOMETHING.

*A sweet dish made of chestnuts and mashed sweet potatoes

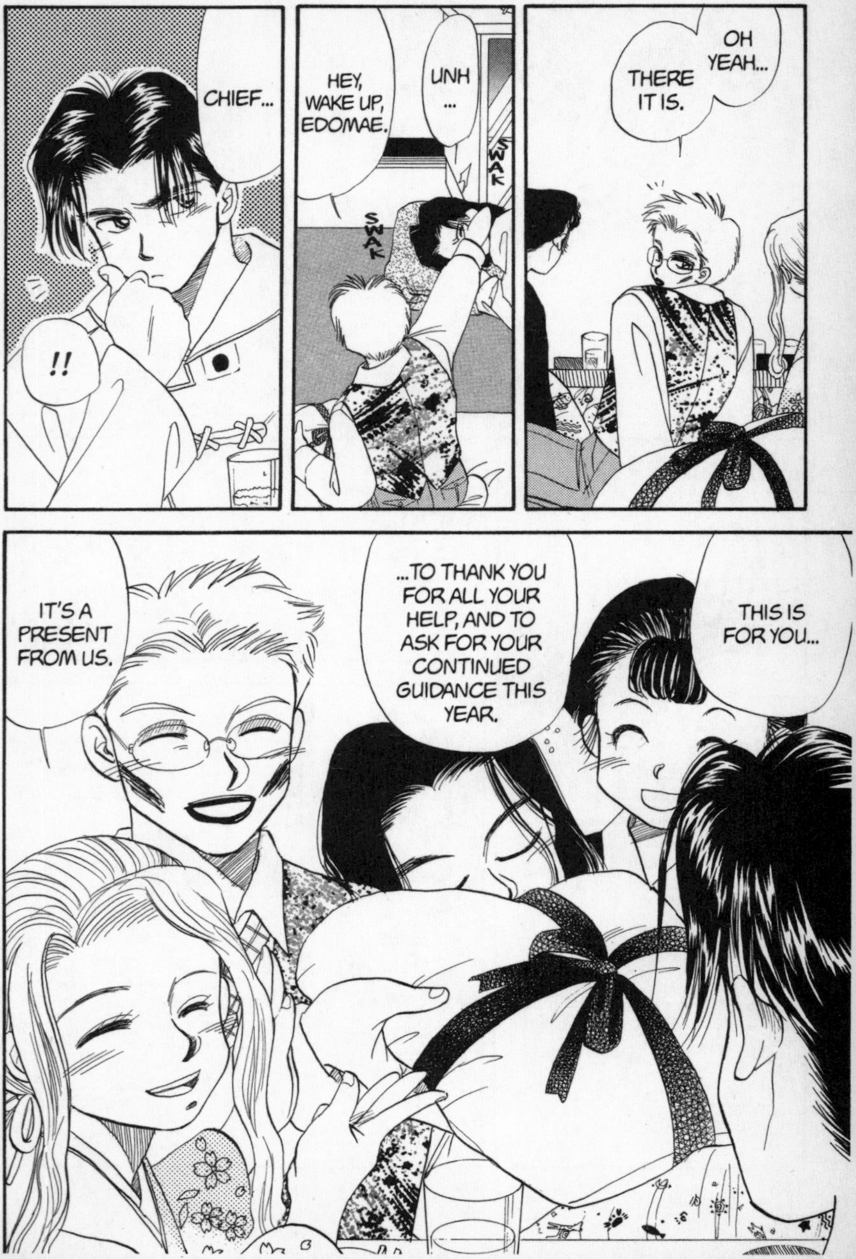
OH YEAH...
THERE IT IS.
UNH ...
HEY, WAKE UP, EDOMAE.
SWAK
SWAK
CHIEF...
!!
THIS IS FOR YOU...
...TO THANK YOU FOR ALL YOUR HELP, AND TO ASK FOR YOUR CONTINUED GUIDANCE THIS YEAR.
IT'S A PRESENT FROM US.

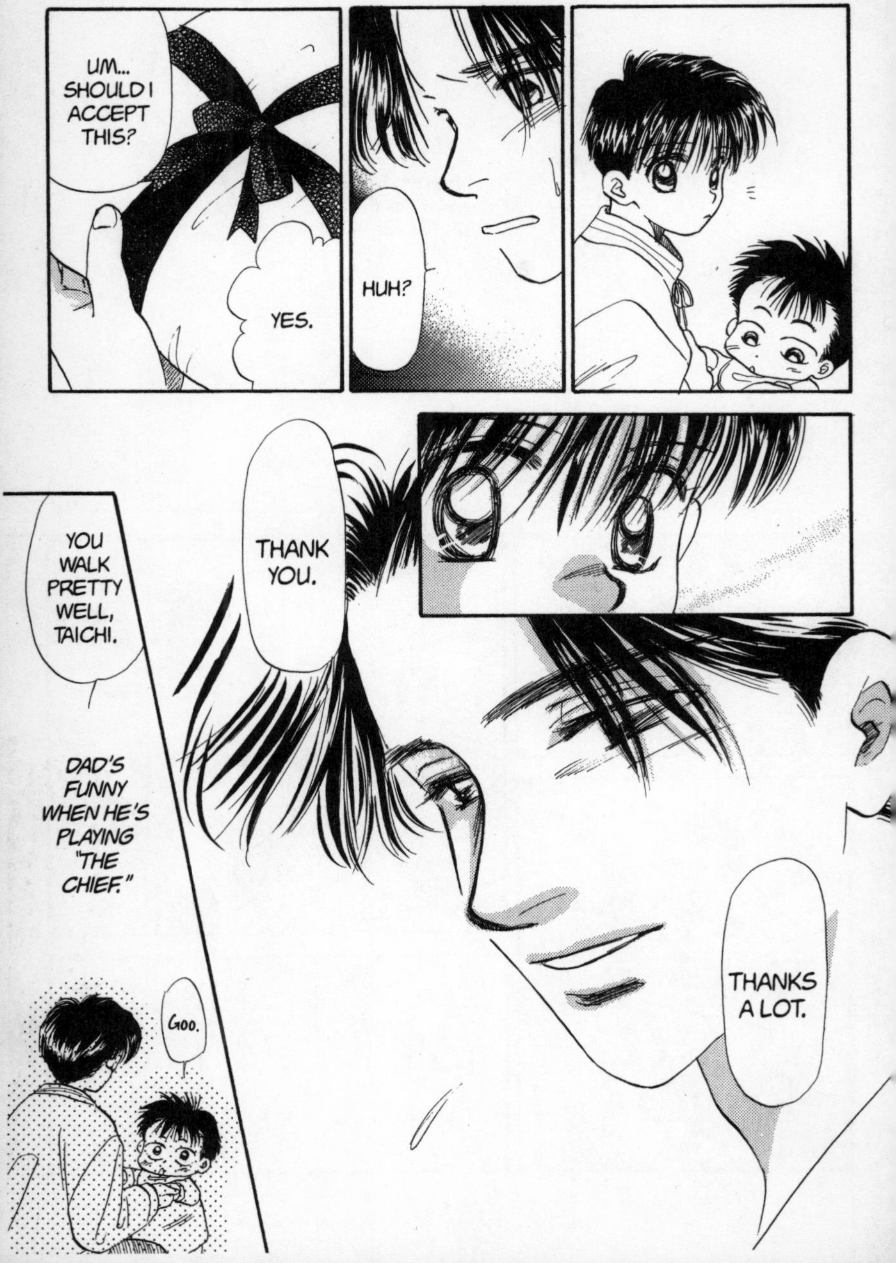
HUH?
UM... SHOULD I ACCEPT THIS?
YES.
THANK YOU.
THANKS A LOT.
YOU WALK PRETTY WELL, TAICHI.
DAD'S FUNNY WHEN HE'S PLAYING "THE CHIEF."
Goo.

I GOT A GLIMPSE OF WHAT MY DAD WAS LIKE AT WORK.

RUSTLE...

WELL... OKAY.

WOW. PEOPLE DON'T USUALLY BUY THEIR BOSSES NEW YEAR'S GIFTS.

C'MON, HURRY UP AND OPEN IT, HARUMI.

HUH?

WHAT IS THIS?

FWUP

I AM?

RUSTLE

RUSTLE

YOU'RE GONNA BE SO SUR- PRISED!

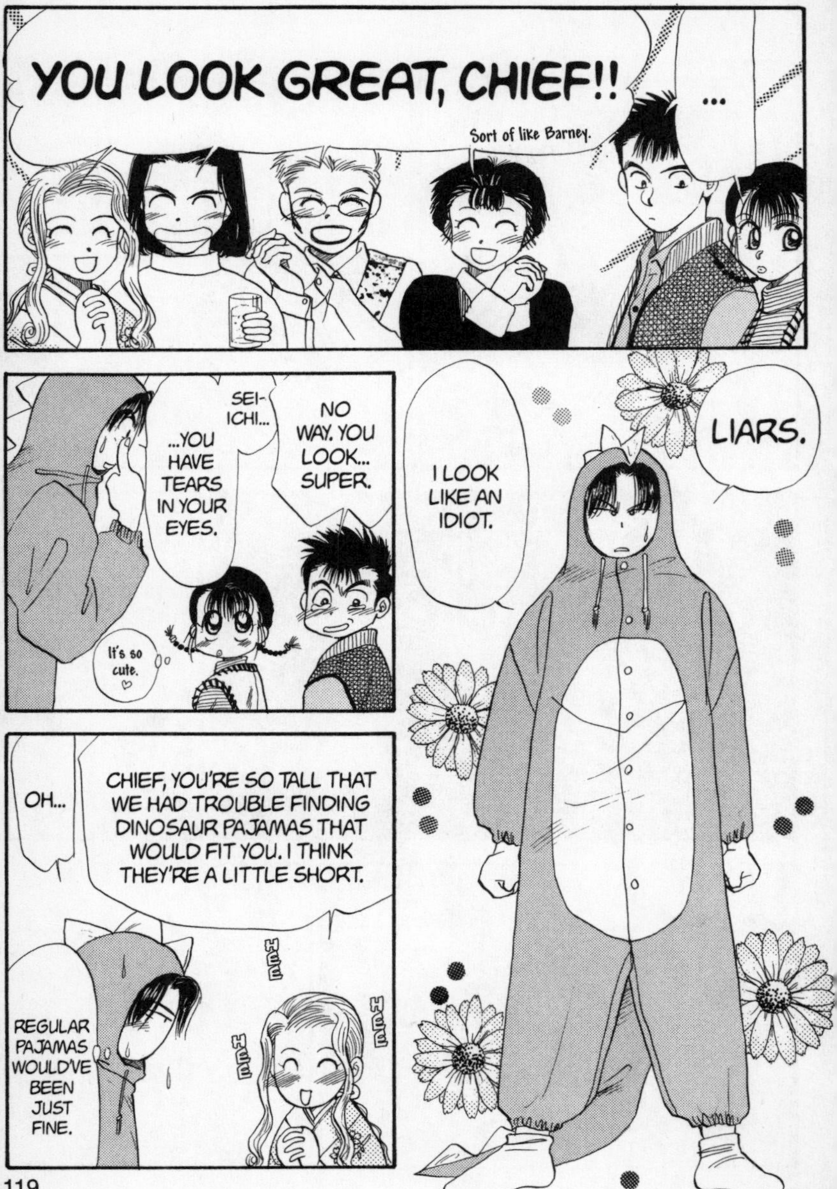
...
YOU LOOK GREAT, CHIEF!!
Sort of like Barney.
LIARS.
I LOOK LIKE AN IDIOT.
NO WAY. YOU LOOK... SUPER.
SEI-ICHI...
...YOU HAVE TEARS IN YOUR EYES.
It's so cute. ♡
CHIEF, YOU'RE SO TALL THAT WE HAD TROUBLE FINDING DINOSAUR PAJAMAS THAT WOULD FIT YOU. I THINK THEY'RE A LITTLE SHORT.
OH...
HMM
HMM
HMM
REGULAR PAJAMAS WOULD'VE BEEN JUST FINE.

HUH?

YAMAGUCHI, ISN'T IT ABOUT TIME YOU TOOK THAT MAKEUP OFF?

You look creepy.

AAH! WHAT THE HECK?!

HUH?

GIMME YOUR MAKEUP.

HUH?

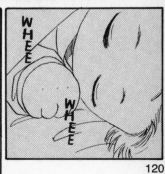

WHEE

WHEE

120

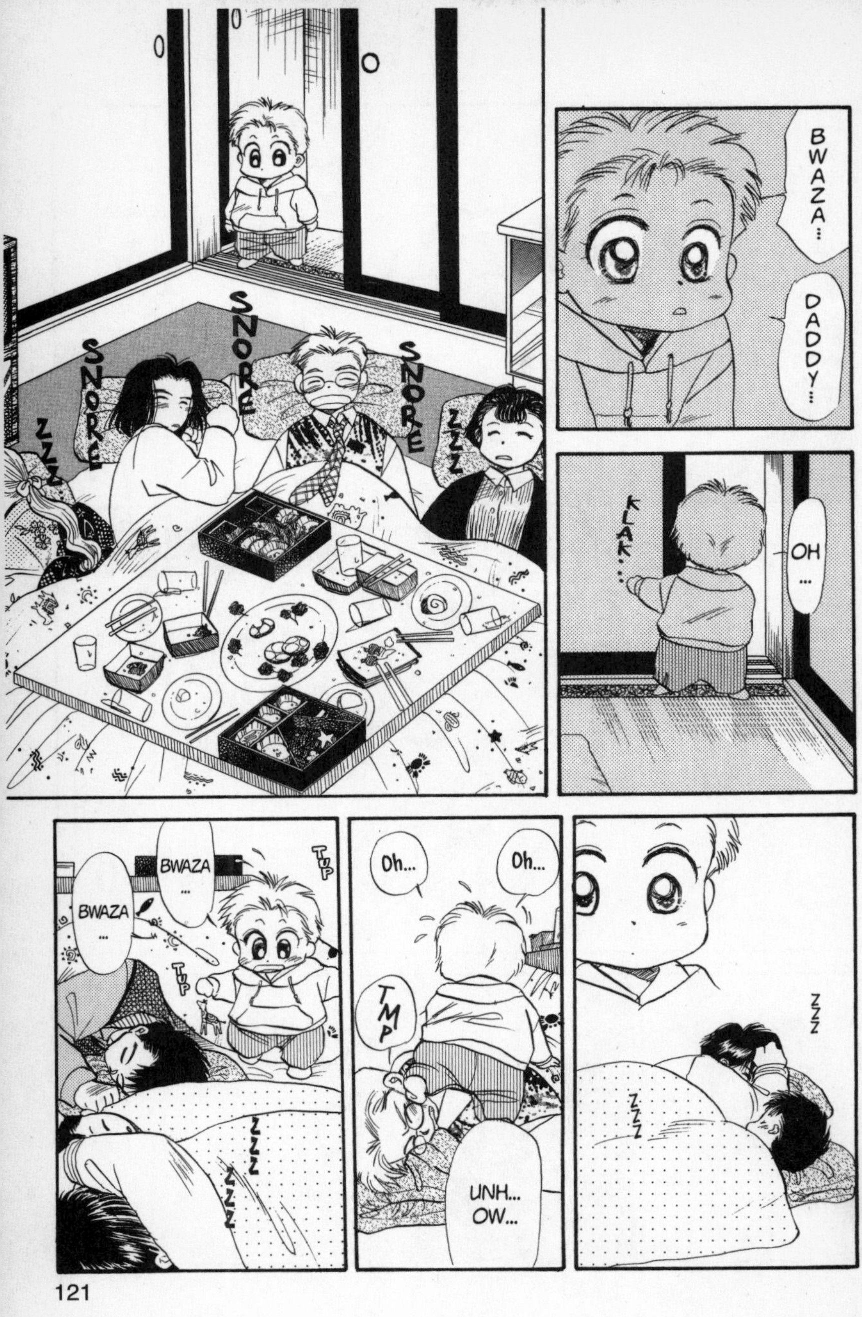
BWAZA...
DADDY...
KLAK...
OH...
SNORE
SNORE
SNORE
ZZZ
ZZZ
ZZZ
ZZZ
Oh...
Oh...
TMP
UNH... OW...
TUP
BWAZA...
BWAZA...
TUP
ZZZ
ZZZ

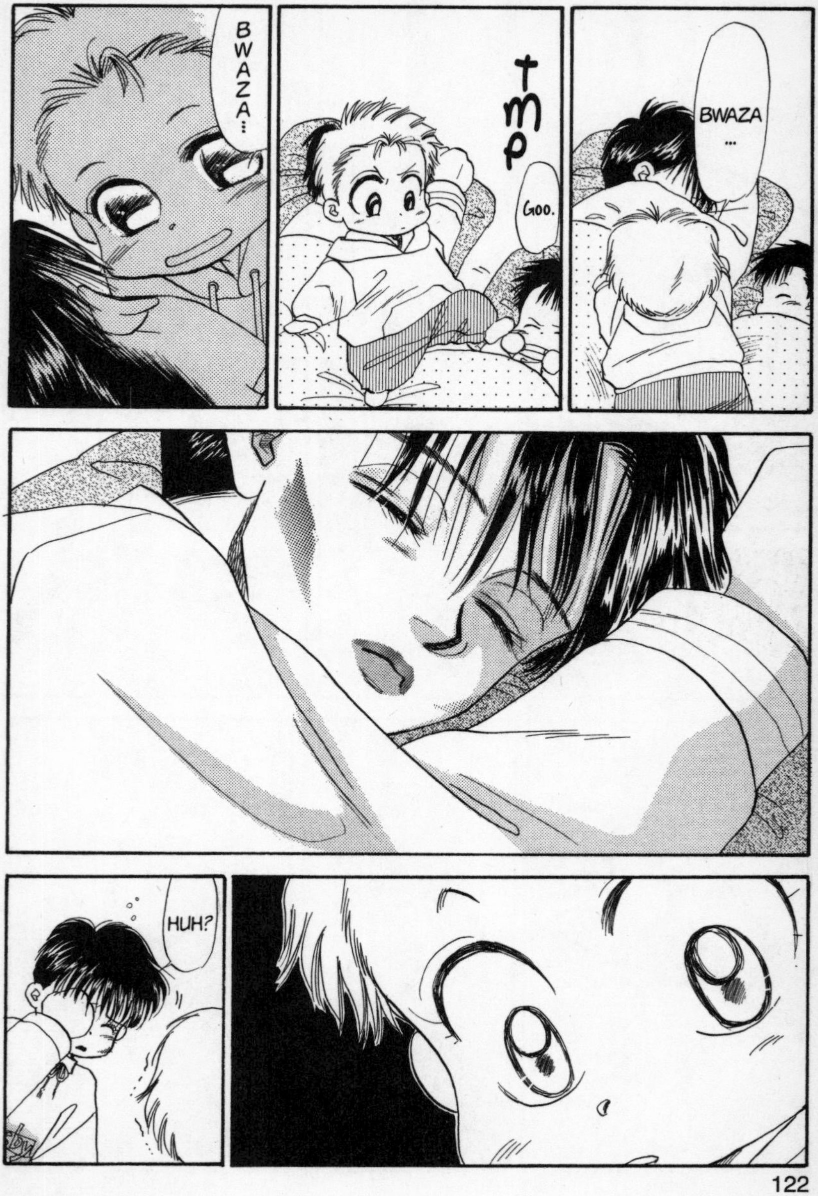
BWAZA ...
TMP
GOO.
BWAZA...
HUH?

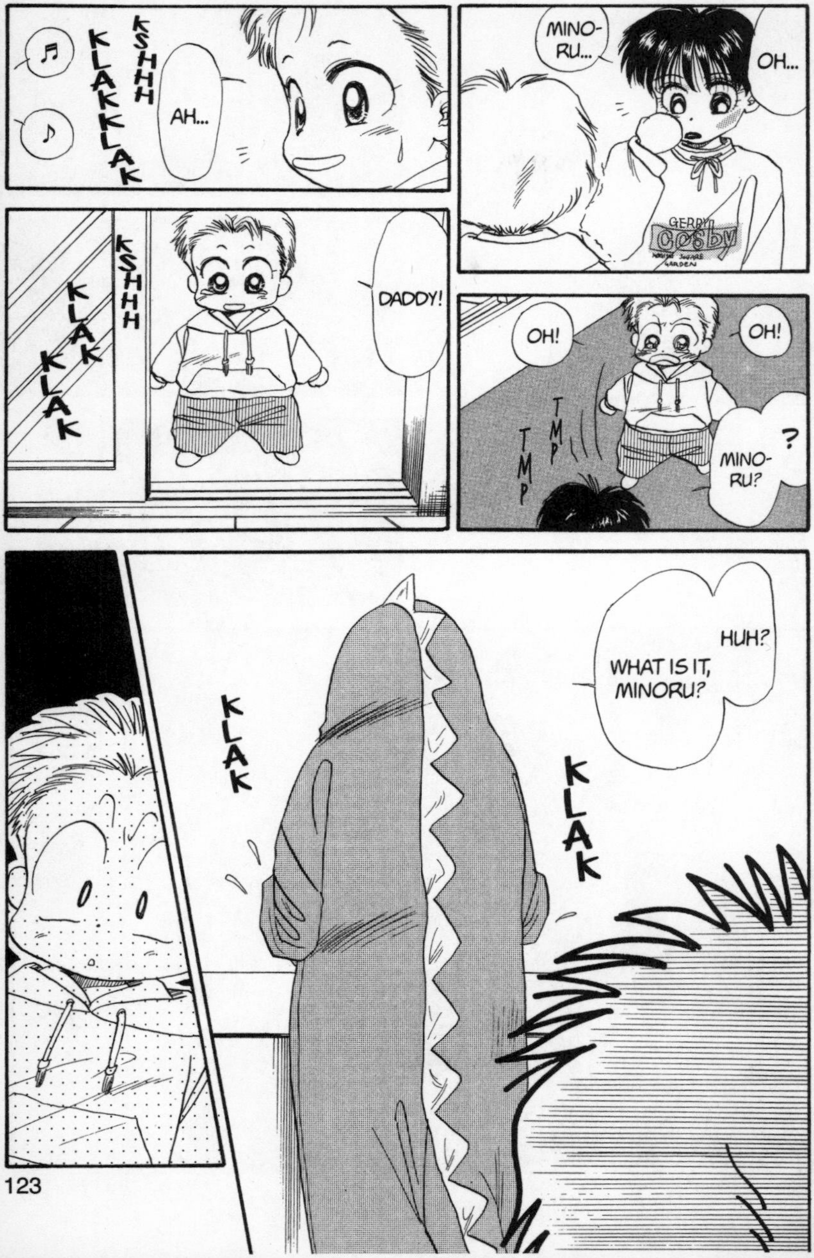
OH...
MINORU...
AH...
KSHHH
KLAKKLAK
♬
♪
DADDY!
KSHHH
KLAK
KLAK
OH!
OH!
MINORU?
?
TMP
TMP
HUH?
WHAT IS IT, MINORU?
KLAK
KLAK

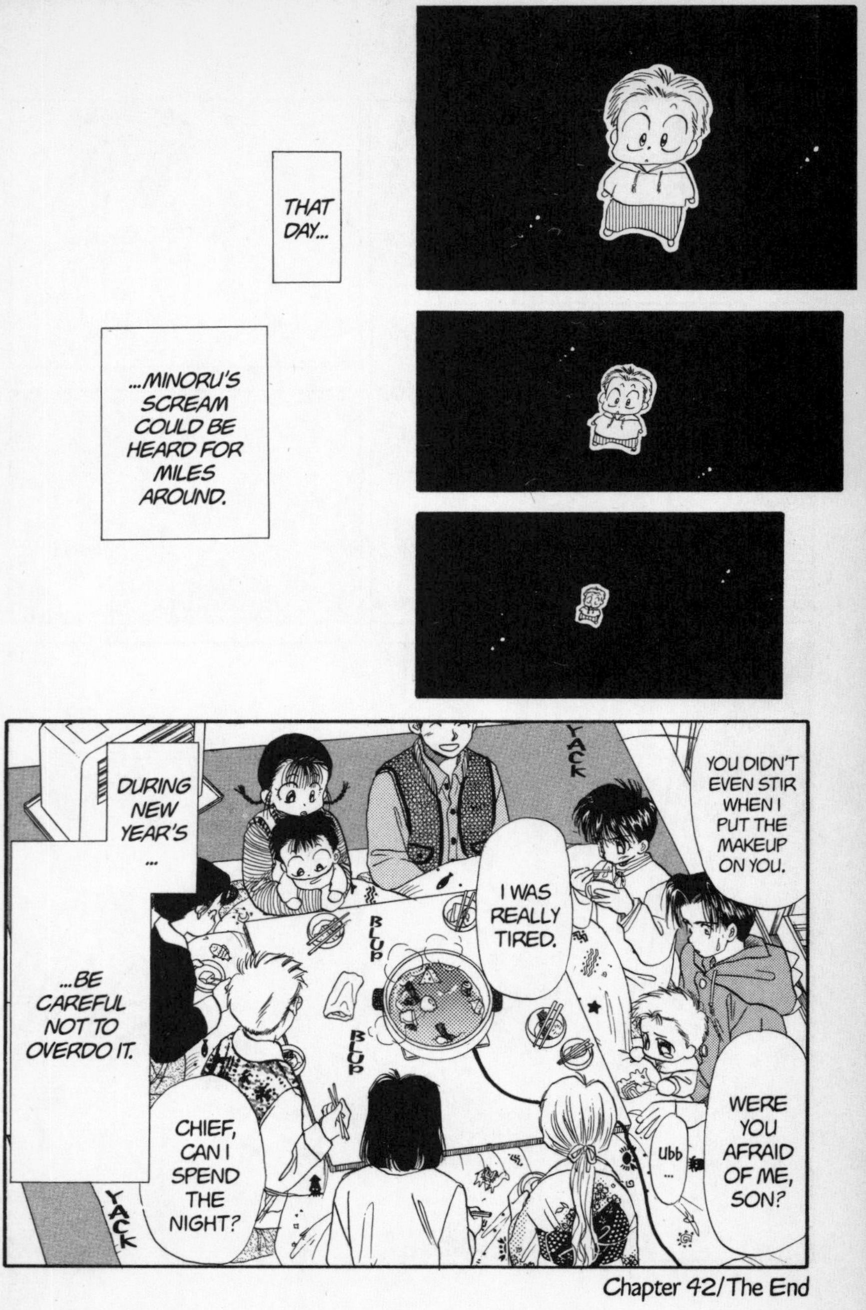
THAT DAY...
...MINORU'S SCREAM COULD BE HEARD FOR MILES AROUND.
YACK
YOU DIDN'T EVEN STIR WHEN I PUT THE MAKEUP ON YOU.
I WAS REALLY TIRED.
DURING NEW YEAR'S ...
BLUP
BLUP
...BE CAREFUL NOT TO OVERDO IT.
WERE YOU AFRAID OF ME, SON?
Ubb ...
CHIEF, CAN I SPEND THE NIGHT?
YACK

Chapter 42/The End

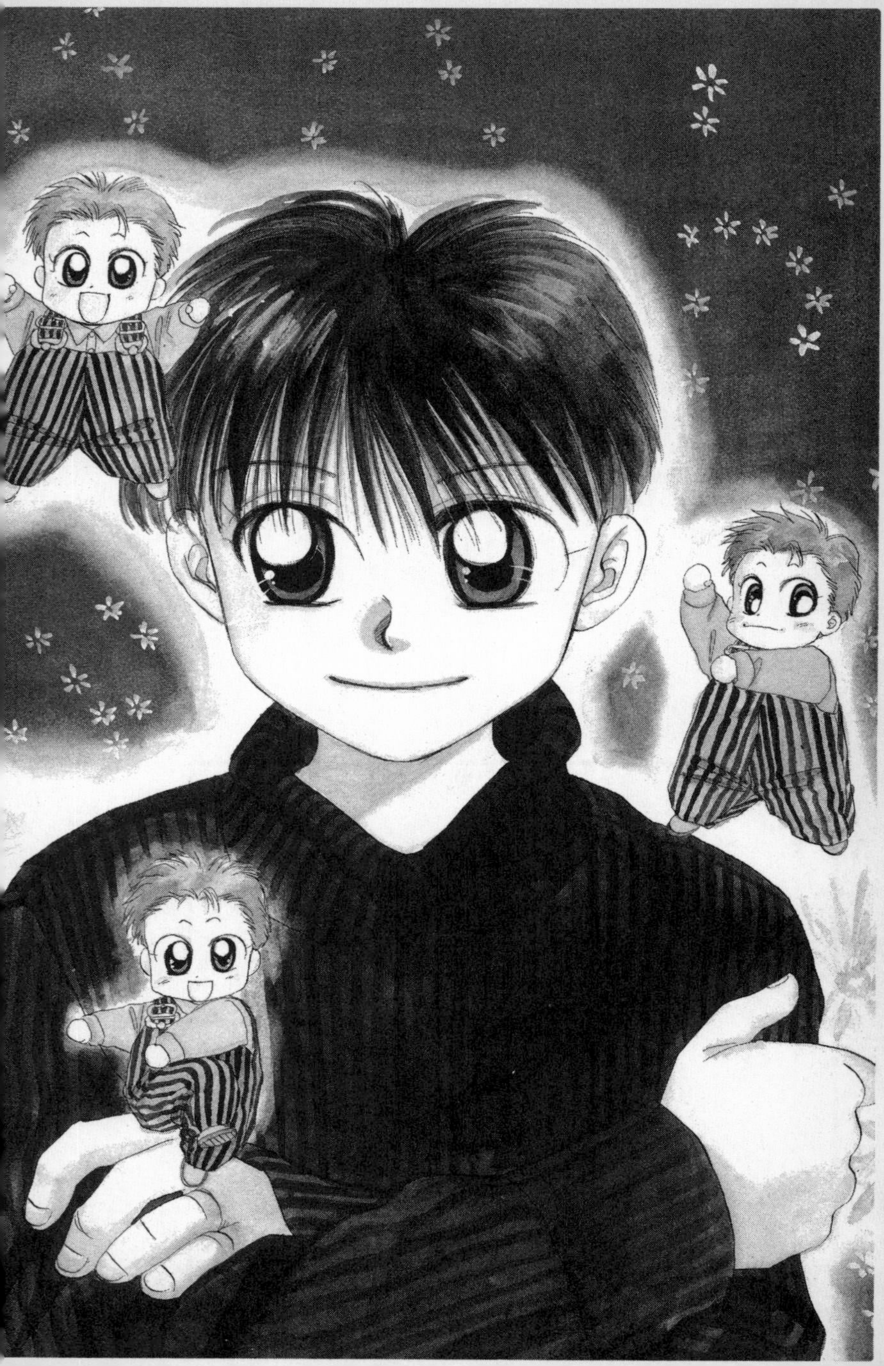

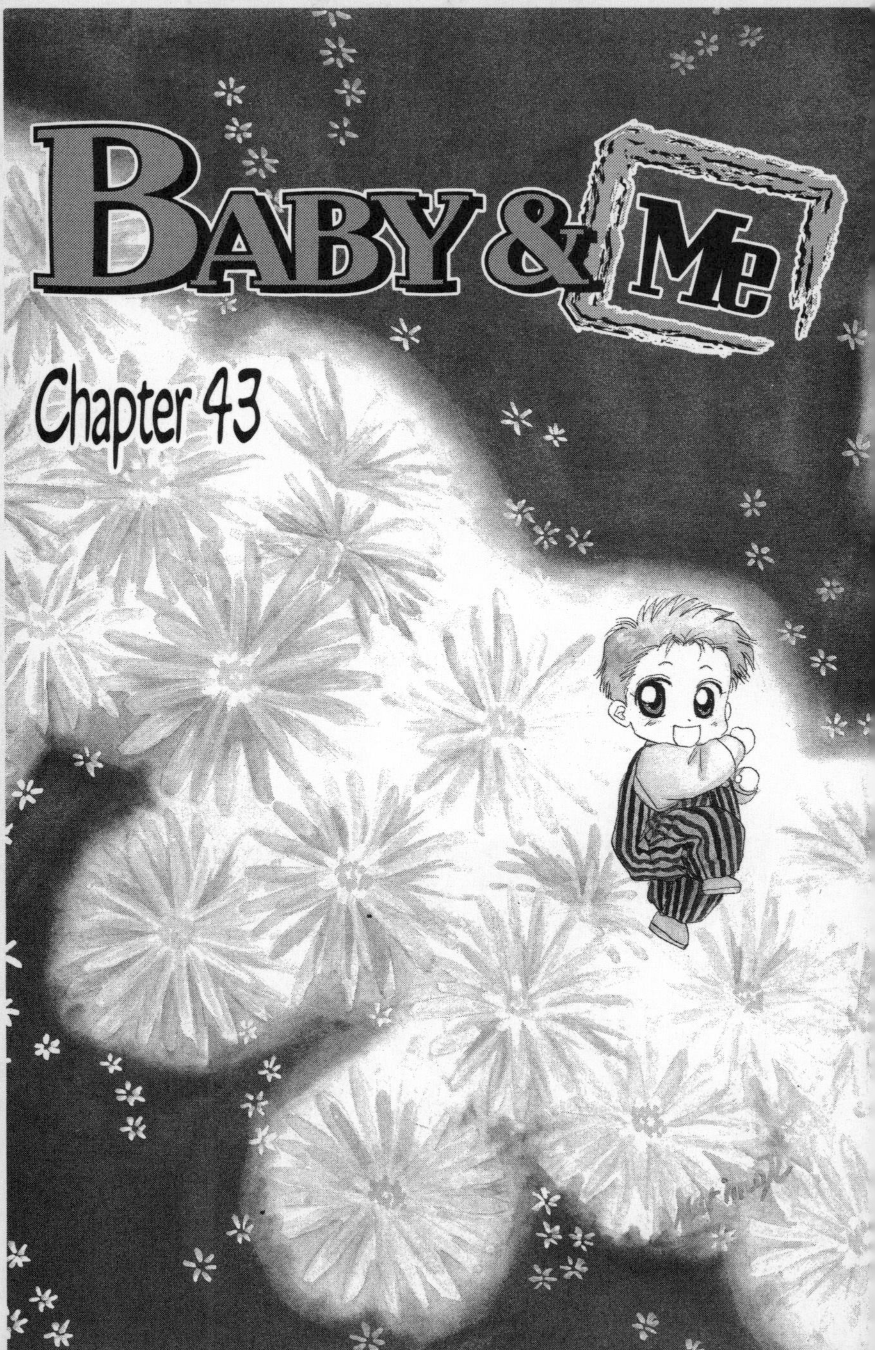
BABY & ME
Chapter 43

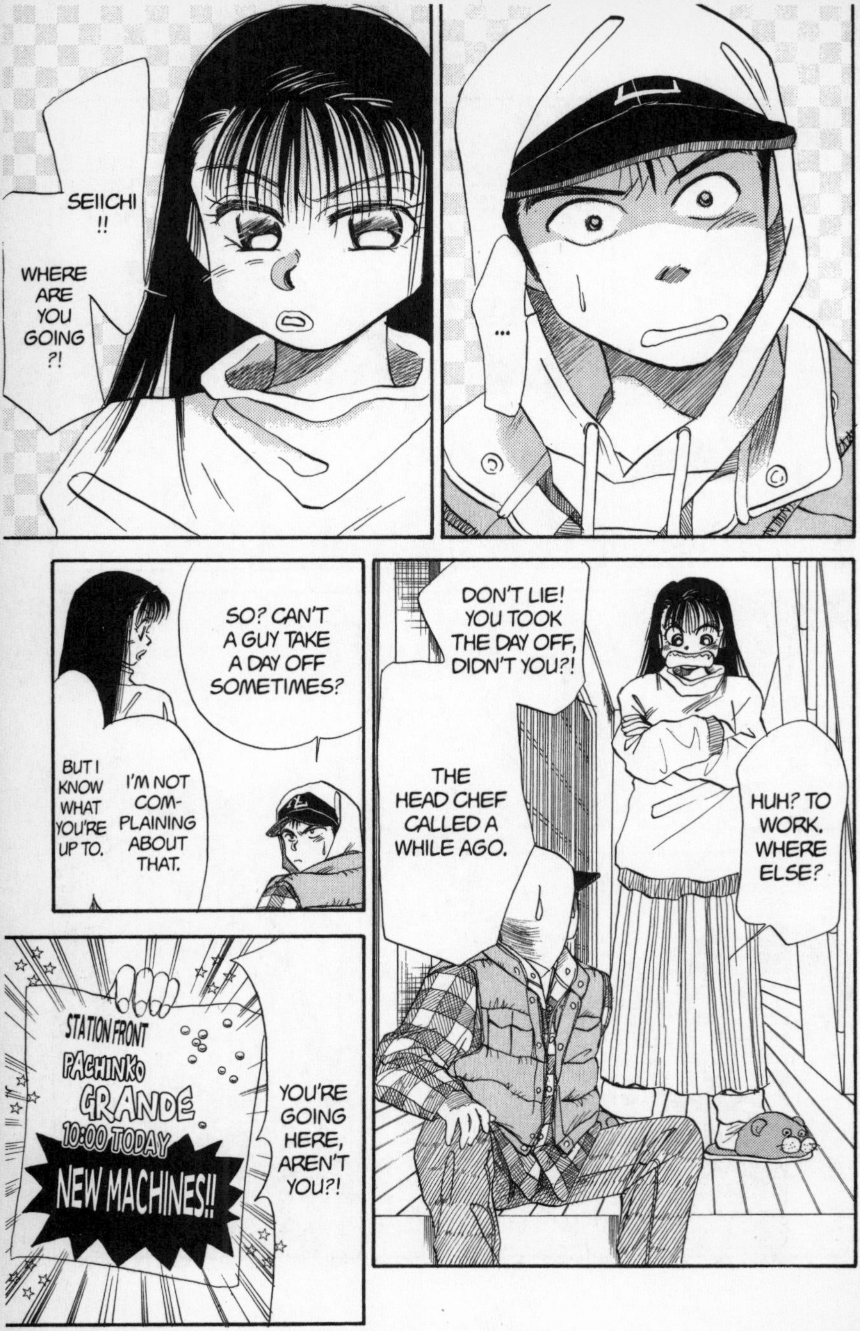
...
SEIICHI!!
WHERE ARE YOU GOING?!
HUH? TO WORK. WHERE ELSE?
DON'T LIE! YOU TOOK THE DAY OFF, DIDN'T YOU?!
THE HEAD CHEF CALLED A WHILE AGO.
SO? CAN'T A GUY TAKE A DAY OFF SOMETIMES?
I'M NOT COMPLAINING ABOUT THAT.
BUT I KNOW WHAT YOU'RE UP TO.
YOU'RE GOING HERE, AREN'T YOU?!
STATION FRONT PACHINKO GRANDE
10:00 TODAY
NEW MACHINES!!

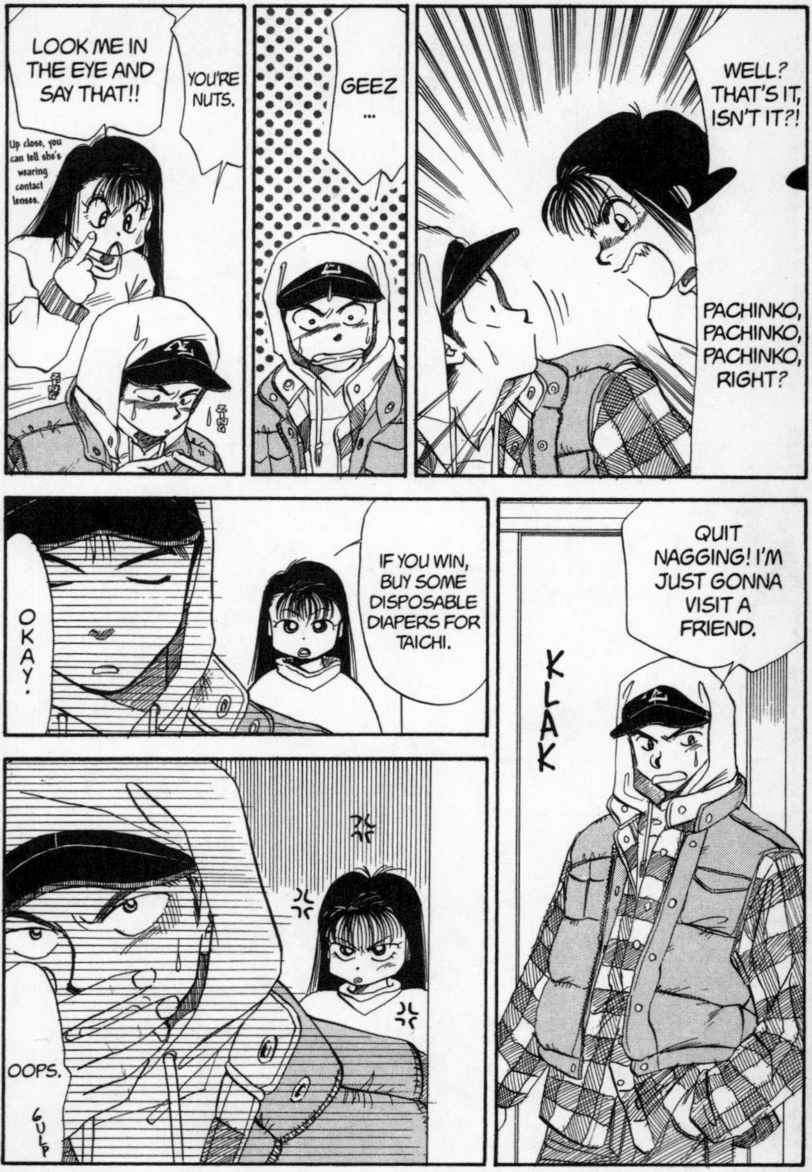
WELL? THAT'S IT, ISN'T IT?!
PACHINKO, PACHINKO, PACHINKO, RIGHT?
GEEZ ...
YOU'RE NUTS.
LOOK ME IN THE EYE AND SAY THAT!!
Up close, you can tell she's wearing contact lenses.
ZING
ZING
QUIT NAGGING! I'M JUST GONNA VISIT A FRIEND.
KLAK
IF YOU WIN, BUY SOME DISPOSABLE DIAPERS FOR TAICHI.
OKAY.
OOPS.
GULP

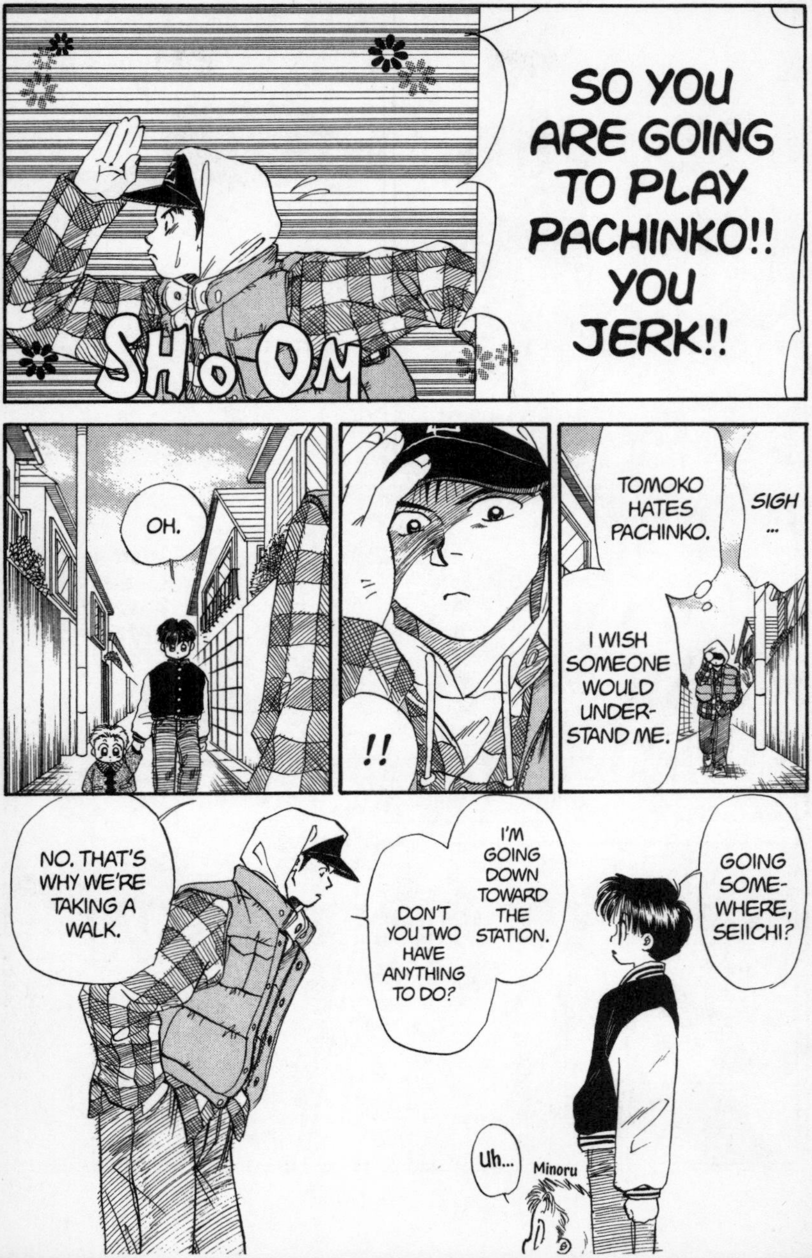
SO YOU ARE GOING TO PLAY PACHINKO!! YOU JERK!!
SHOOM
SIGH ...
TOMOKO HATES PACHINKO.
I WISH SOMEONE WOULD UNDER-STAND ME.
!!
OH.
GOING SOME-WHERE, SEIICHI?
I'M GOING DOWN TOWARD THE STATION.
DON'T YOU TWO HAVE ANYTHING TO DO?
NO. THAT'S WHY WE'RE TAKING A WALK.
Uh...
Minoru

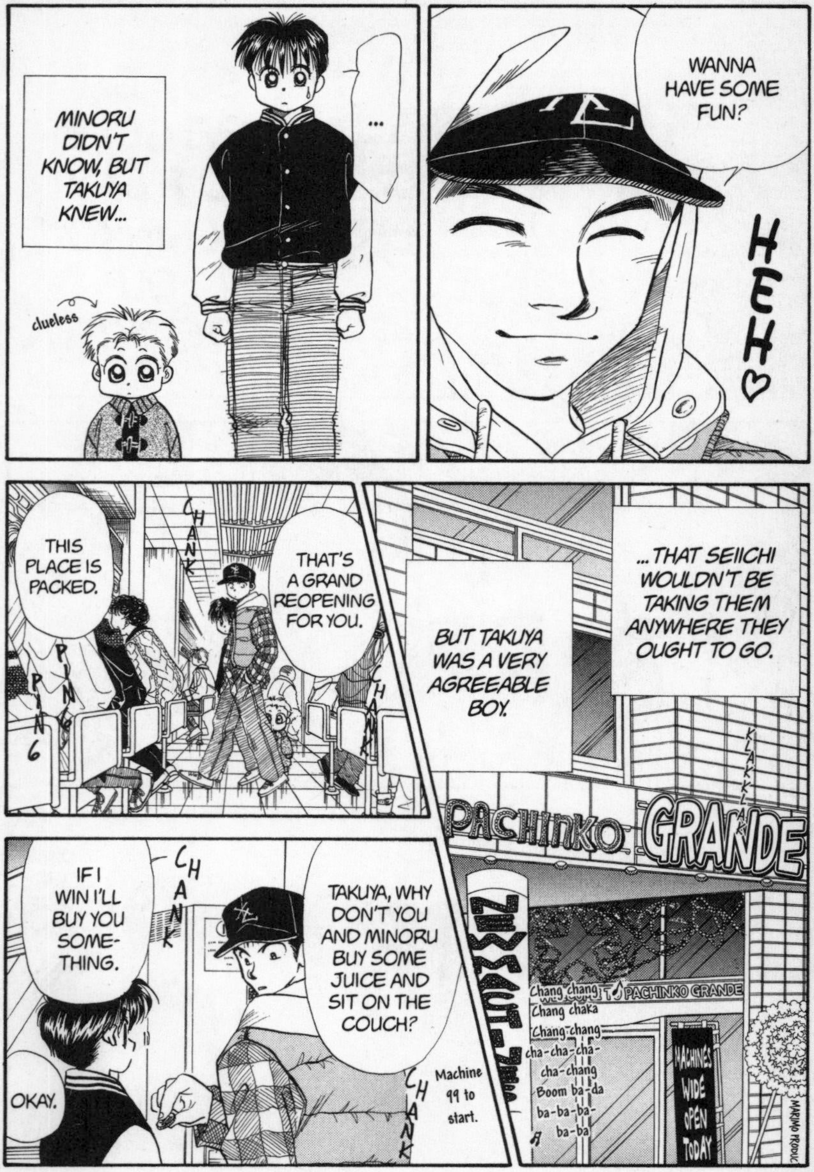
WANNA HAVE SOME FUN?
HEH ♥
MINORU DIDN'T KNOW, BUT TAKUYA KNEW...
...
clueless
...THAT SEIICHI WOULDN'T BE TAKING THEM ANYWHERE THEY OUGHT TO GO.
BUT TAKUYA WAS A VERY AGREEABLE BOY.
KLAKKLAK
PACHINKO GRANDE
PACHINKO GRANDE
Chang chang
Chang chaka
Chang chang
cha-cha-cha-
cha-chang
Boom ba-da
ba-ba-ba-
ba-ba
MACHINES WIDE OPEN TODAY
Machine 99 to start.
THAT'S A GRAND REOPENING FOR YOU.
THIS PLACE IS PACKED.
CHANK
CHANK
PING PING
TAKUYA, WHY DON'T YOU AND MINORU BUY SOME JUICE AND SIT ON THE COUCH?
IF I WIN I'LL BUY YOU SOME-THING.
CHANK
CHANK
OKAY.

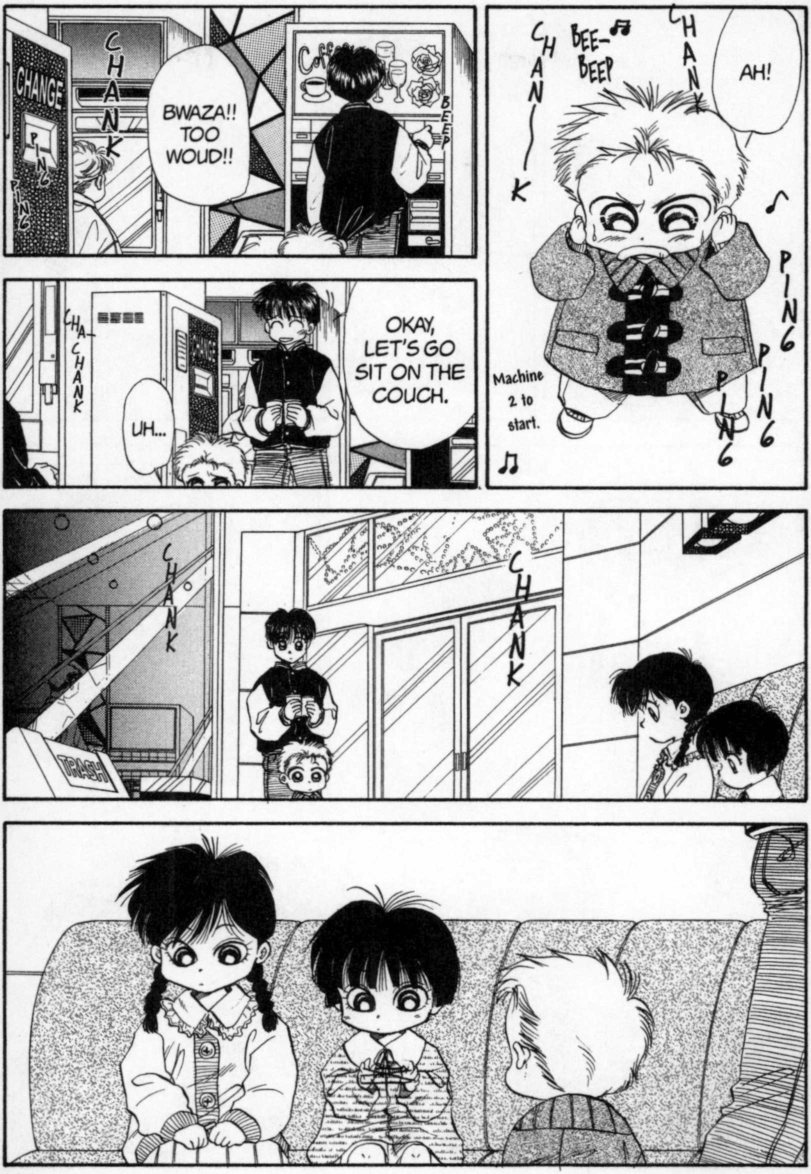
CHANK
AH!
BEE-BEEP
CHA-A-A-K
PING
PING
PING
Machine 2 to start.
BEEP
BWAZA!! TOO WOUD!!
CHANK
PING
PING
OKAY, LET'S GO SIT ON THE COUCH.
UH...
CHA-CHANK
CHANK
CHANK

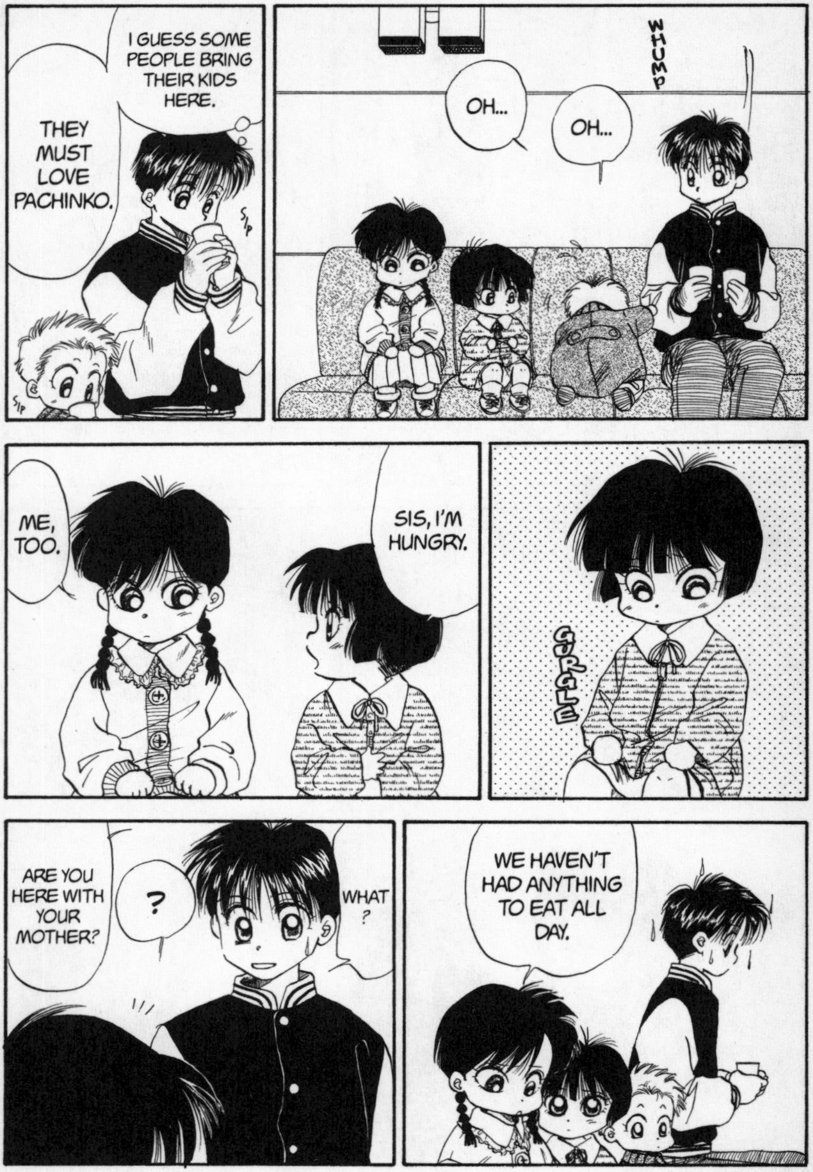
WHUMP
OH...
OH...
I GUESS SOME PEOPLE BRING THEIR KIDS HERE.
THEY MUST LOVE PACHINKO.
SIP
SIP
GURGLE
SIS, I'M HUNGRY.
ME, TOO.
WE HAVEN'T HAD ANYTHING TO EAT ALL DAY.
WHAT?
?
ARE YOU HERE WITH YOUR MOTHER?

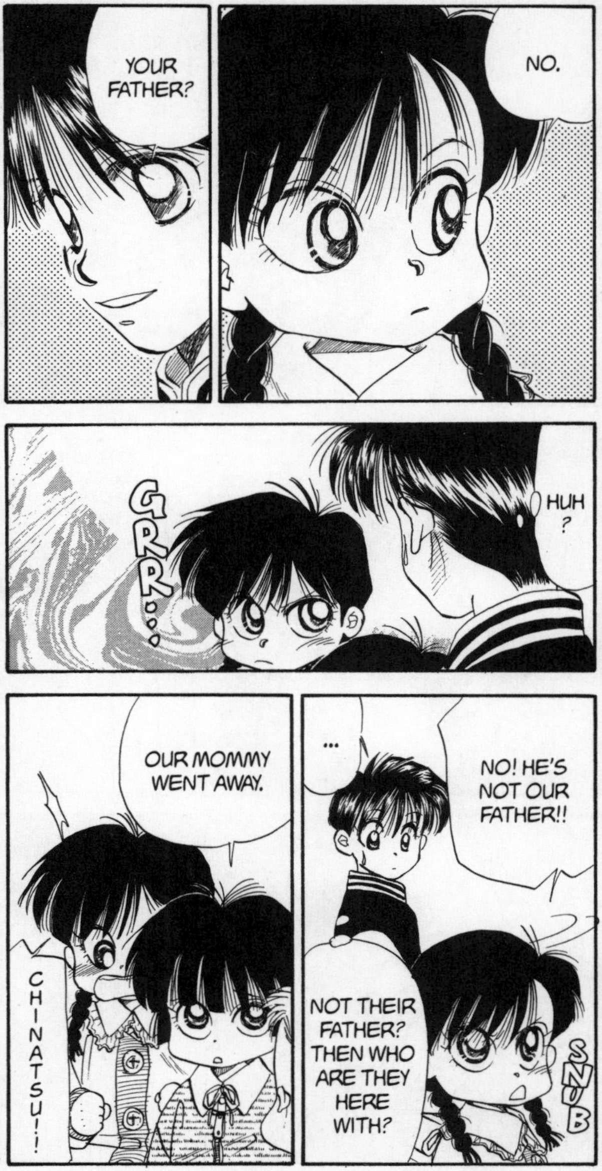
YOUR FATHER?
NO.
GRRR...
HUH?
OUR MOMMY WENT AWAY.
CHINATSU!!
...
NO! HE'S NOT OUR FATHER!!
NOT THEIR FATHER? THEN WHO ARE THEY HERE WITH?
SNUB

Author's Note 5

A Recent Mystery

Are you supposed to eat the little clams in miso soup?

Well, it's really up to you, but as someone who loves miso soup with clams, I think you should eat them. Some people say they don't eat them because they're too much trouble to get out of the shell or that the clams are only used to flavor the stock, but I don't agree.

A Recent Mystery Solved

When I was a student, my teacher once wondered out loud why there were three polite prefixes in the word "omiotsuke." Words are often prefixed with "o" to make them more polite. The kanji character for this "o" 「御」 is sometimes read "go" or "mi." So the teacher believed that the "o" "mi" and "o" in "omiotsuke" were all the same character. The other day I remembered that. But when I looked the word up in a dictionary, I got a surprise. The word was written with different characters! Instead of "o-mi-o-tsuke" 「御御御汁」, it was "omi" 「御味」 (meaning miso) and "otsuke" 「御汁」 (meaning miso soup). So there weren't three polite prefixes added to the word "tsuke" at all! What a surprise!

Did everyone follow that? Little kids are probably wondering what I'm going on about. Teachers, please check your facts before you tell us stuff!! ♪

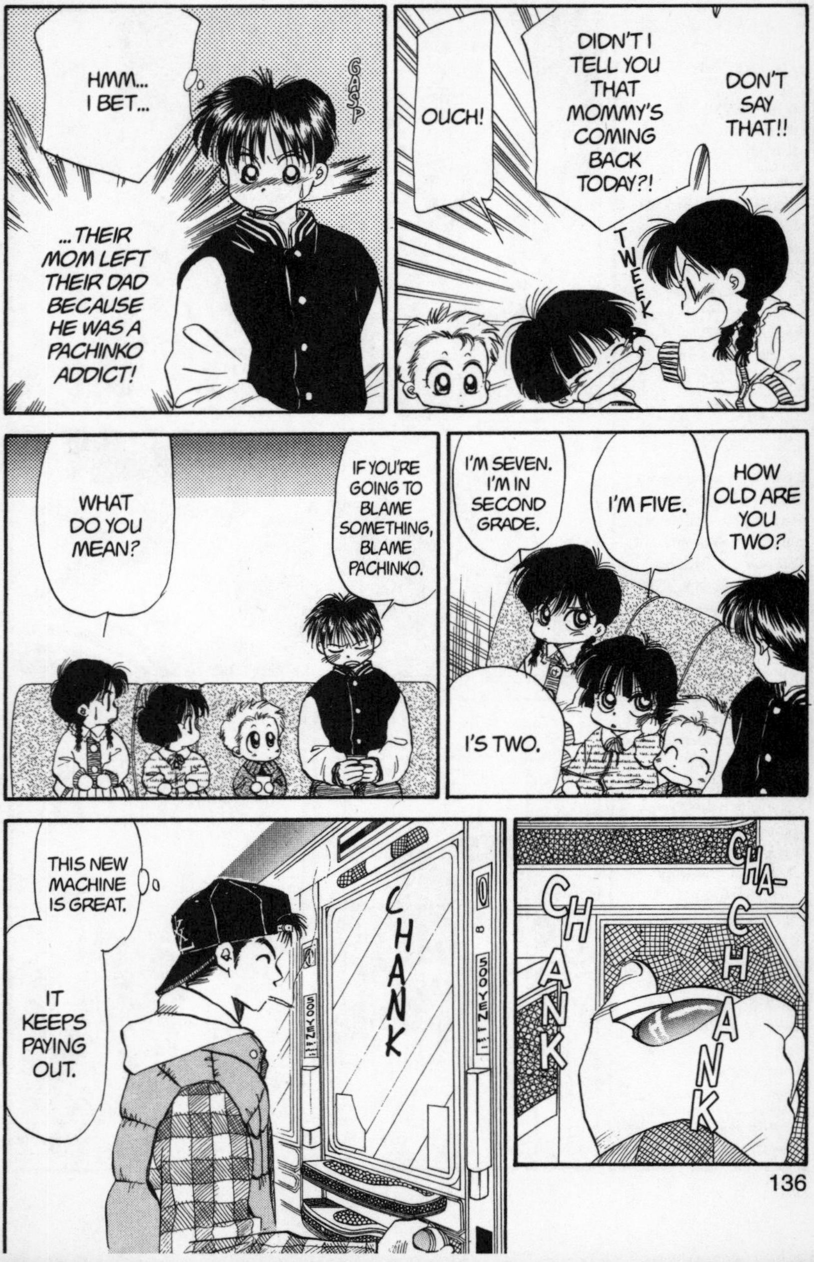
DON'T SAY THAT!!
DIDN'T I TELL YOU THAT MOMMY'S COMING BACK TODAY?!
OUCH!
TWEEK
HMM... I BET...
GASP
...THEIR MOM LEFT THEIR DAD BECAUSE HE WAS A PACHINKO ADDICT!
HOW OLD ARE YOU TWO?
I'M FIVE.
I'M SEVEN. I'M IN SECOND GRADE.
I'S TWO.
IF YOU'RE GOING TO BLAME SOMETHING, BLAME PACHINKO.
WHAT DO YOU MEAN?
CHA-CHANK
CHANK
CHANK
500 YEN
500 YEN
THIS NEW MACHINE IS GREAT.
IT KEEPS PAYING OUT.

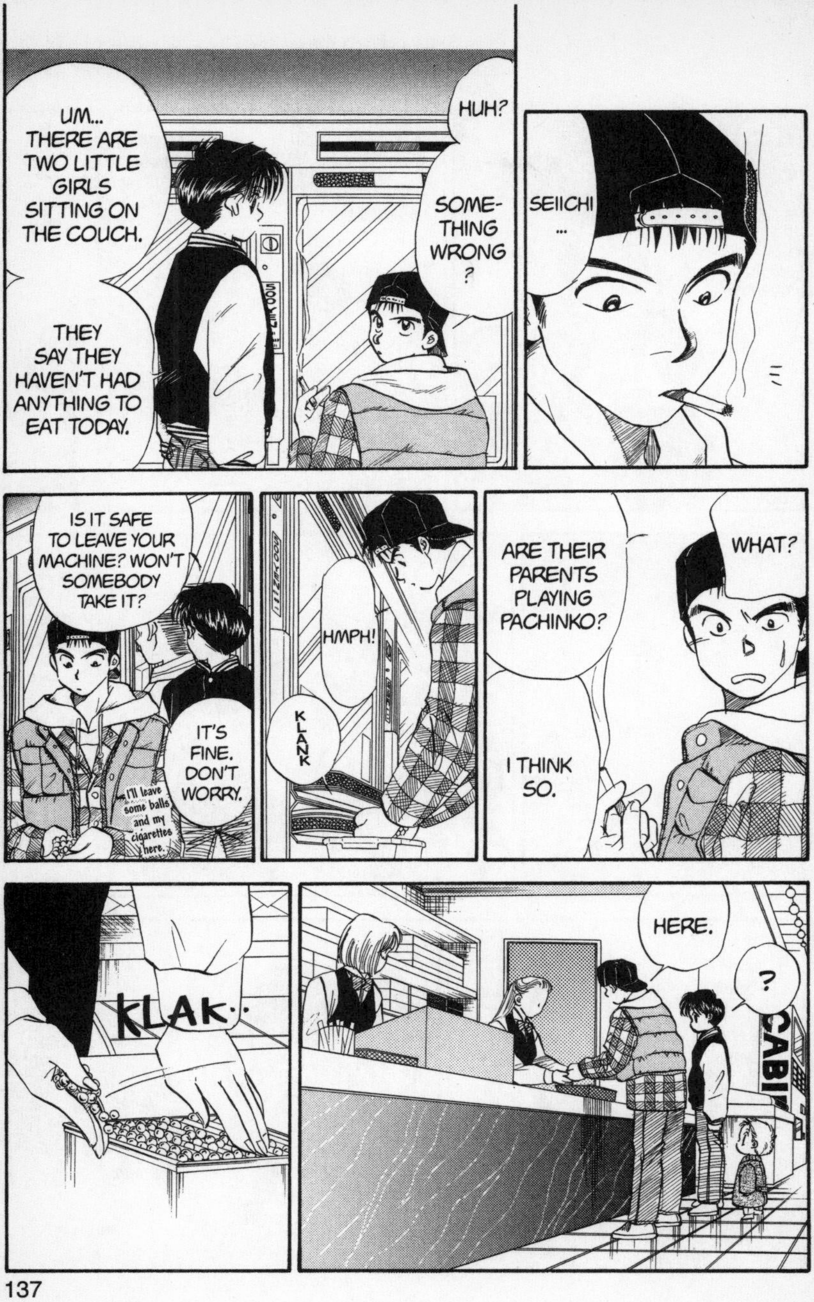
SEIICHI ...
HUH?
SOME-THING WRONG?
UM... THERE ARE TWO LITTLE GIRLS SITTING ON THE COUCH.
THEY SAY THEY HAVEN'T HAD ANYTHING TO EAT TODAY.
WHAT?
ARE THEIR PARENTS PLAYING PACHINKO?
I THINK SO.
HMPH!
KLANK
IS IT SAFE TO LEAVE YOUR MACHINE? WON'T SOMEBODY TAKE IT?
IT'S FINE. DON'T WORRY.
I'll leave some balls and my cigarettes here.
HERE.
?
KLAK..

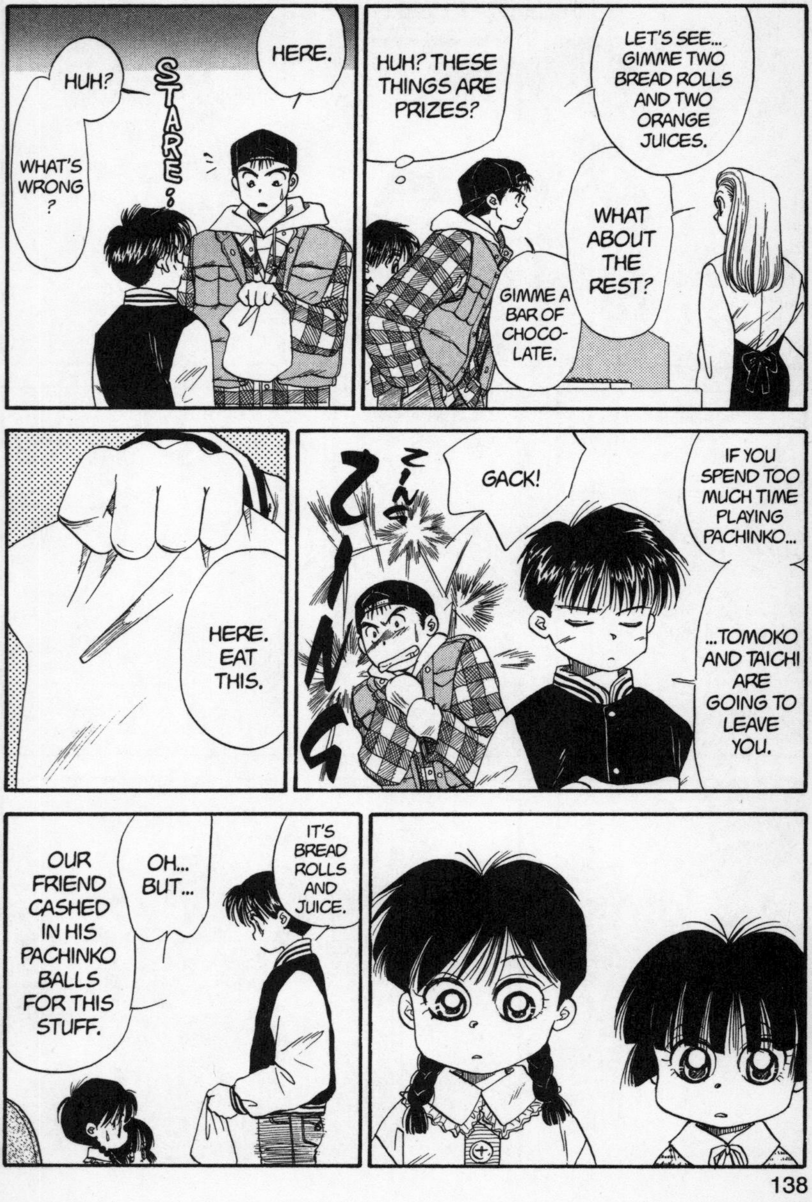
LET'S SEE... GIMME TWO BREAD ROLLS AND TWO ORANGE JUICES.
HUH? THESE THINGS ARE PRIZES?
WHAT ABOUT THE REST?
GIMME A BAR OF CHOCO-LATE.
HERE.
STARE...
HUH?
WHAT'S WRONG?
IF YOU SPEND TOO MUCH TIME PLAYING PACHINKO...
...TOMOKO AND TAICHI ARE GOING TO LEAVE YOU.
GACK!
ZINS
ZINS
HERE. EAT THIS.
IT'S BREAD ROLLS AND JUICE.
OH... BUT...
OUR FRIEND CASHED IN HIS PACHINKO BALLS FOR THIS STUFF.

Author's Note 6

This is the order in which I work on my manga!! (I'll take excerpts from Chapter 43.)

1. I mull over the story.
2. I create a plot. I decide how the story will proceed and work out a page plan. Otherwise, it won't come out to the right number of pages.

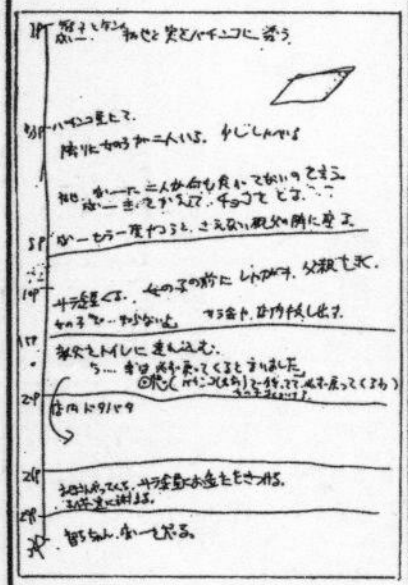

3. I design the characters. (These are from my notebook.)

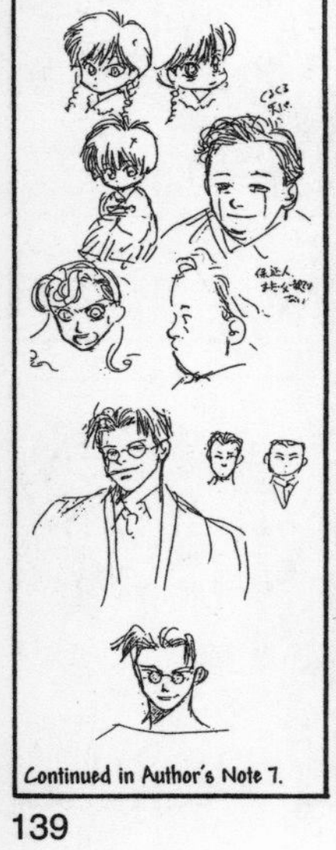

Continued in Author's Note 7.

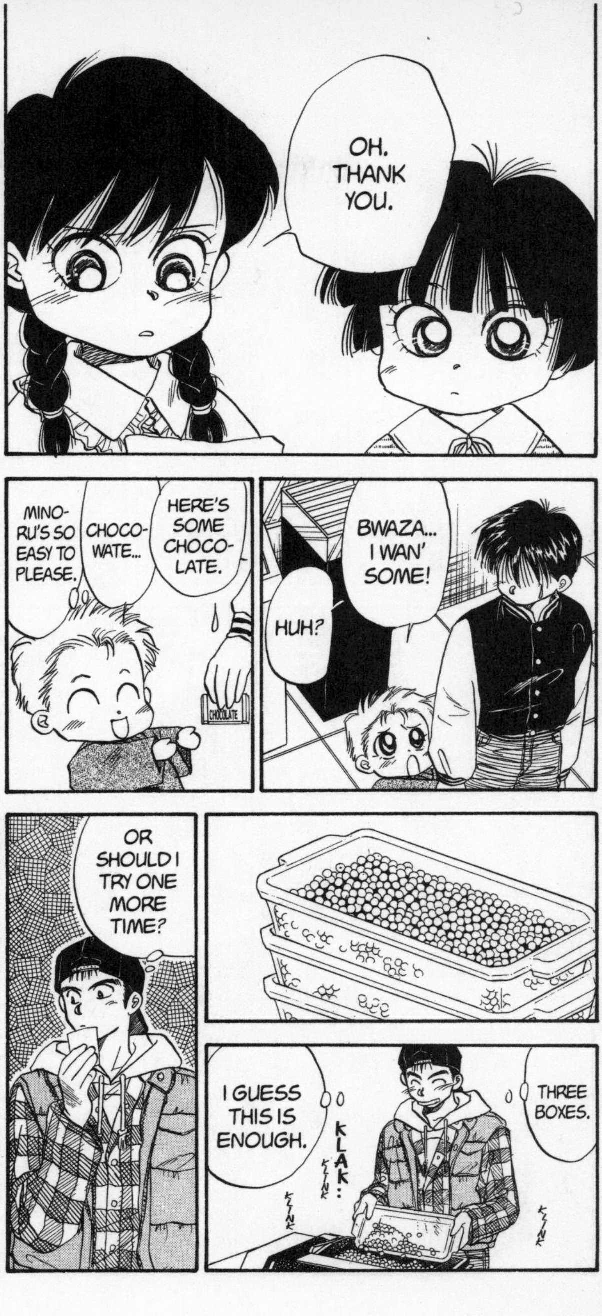

OH. THANK YOU.
BWAZA... I WAN' SOME!
HUH?
HERE'S SOME CHOCOLATE.
CHOCOLATE
CHOCO-WATE...
MINO-RU'S SO EASY TO PLEASE.
THREE BOXES.
KLAK...
I GUESS THIS IS ENOUGH.
OR SHOULD I TRY ONE MORE TIME?

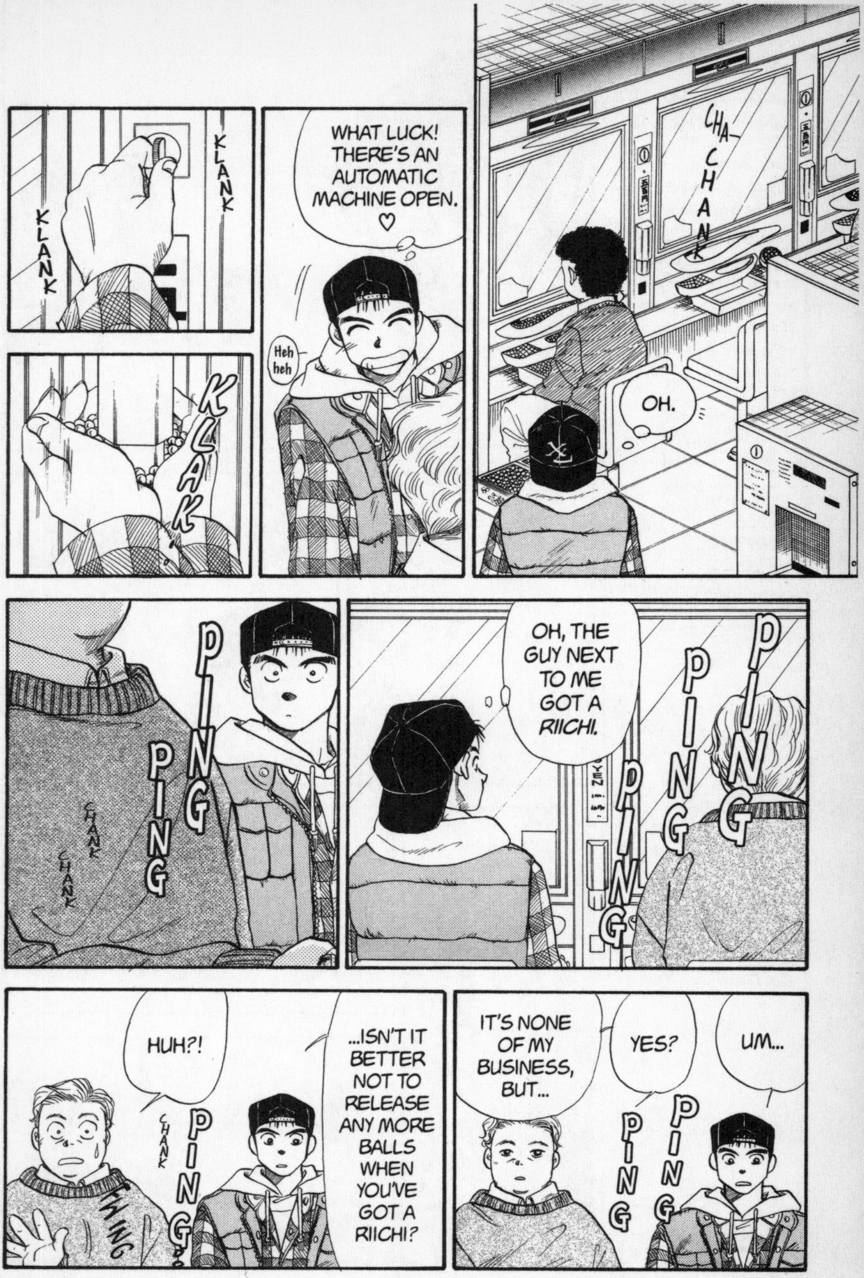
CHA-CHANK
OH.
WHAT LUCK! THERE'S AN AUTOMATIC MACHINE OPEN. ♡
Heh heh
KLANK
KLANK
KLAK
OH, THE GUY NEXT TO ME GOT A *RIICHI.*
PING
PING
PING
PING
PING
CHANK
CHANK
UM...
YES?
PING
PING
IT'S NONE OF MY BUSINESS, BUT...
...ISN'T IT BETTER NOT TO RELEASE ANY MORE BALLS WHEN YOU'VE GOT A RIICHI?
HUH?!
PING
CHANK
THING

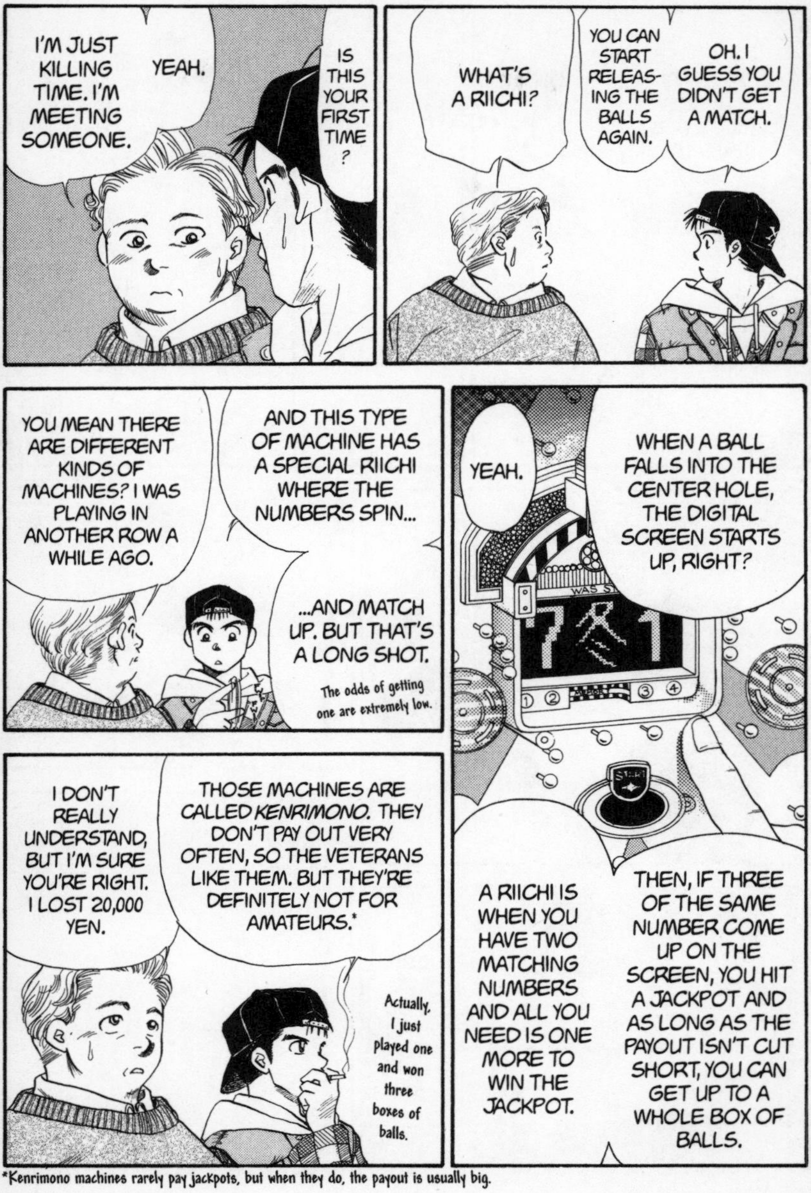
OH. I GUESS YOU DIDN'T GET A MATCH.
YOU CAN START RELEAS-ING THE BALLS AGAIN.
WHAT'S A RIICHI?
IS THIS YOUR FIRST TIME?
YEAH.
I'M JUST KILLING TIME. I'M MEETING SOMEONE.
WHEN A BALL FALLS INTO THE CENTER HOLE, THE DIGITAL SCREEN STARTS UP, RIGHT?
YEAH.
THEN, IF THREE OF THE SAME NUMBER COME UP ON THE SCREEN, YOU HIT A JACKPOT AND AS LONG AS THE PAYOUT ISN'T CUT SHORT, YOU CAN GET UP TO A WHOLE BOX OF BALLS.
A RIICHI IS WHEN YOU HAVE TWO MATCHING NUMBERS AND ALL YOU NEED IS ONE MORE TO WIN THE JACKPOT.
AND THIS TYPE OF MACHINE HAS A SPECIAL RIICHI WHERE THE NUMBERS SPIN...
...AND MATCH UP. BUT THAT'S A LONG SHOT.
The odds of getting one are extremely low.
YOU MEAN THERE ARE DIFFERENT KINDS OF MACHINES? I WAS PLAYING IN ANOTHER ROW A WHILE AGO.
THOSE MACHINES ARE CALLED *KENRIMONO*. THEY DON'T PAY OUT VERY OFTEN, SO THE VETERANS LIKE THEM. BUT THEY'RE DEFINITELY NOT FOR AMATEURS.*
I DON'T REALLY UNDERSTAND, BUT I'M SURE YOU'RE RIGHT. I LOST 20,000 YEN.
Actually, I just played one and won three boxes of balls.

*Kenrimono machines rarely pay jackpots, but when they do, the payout is usually big.

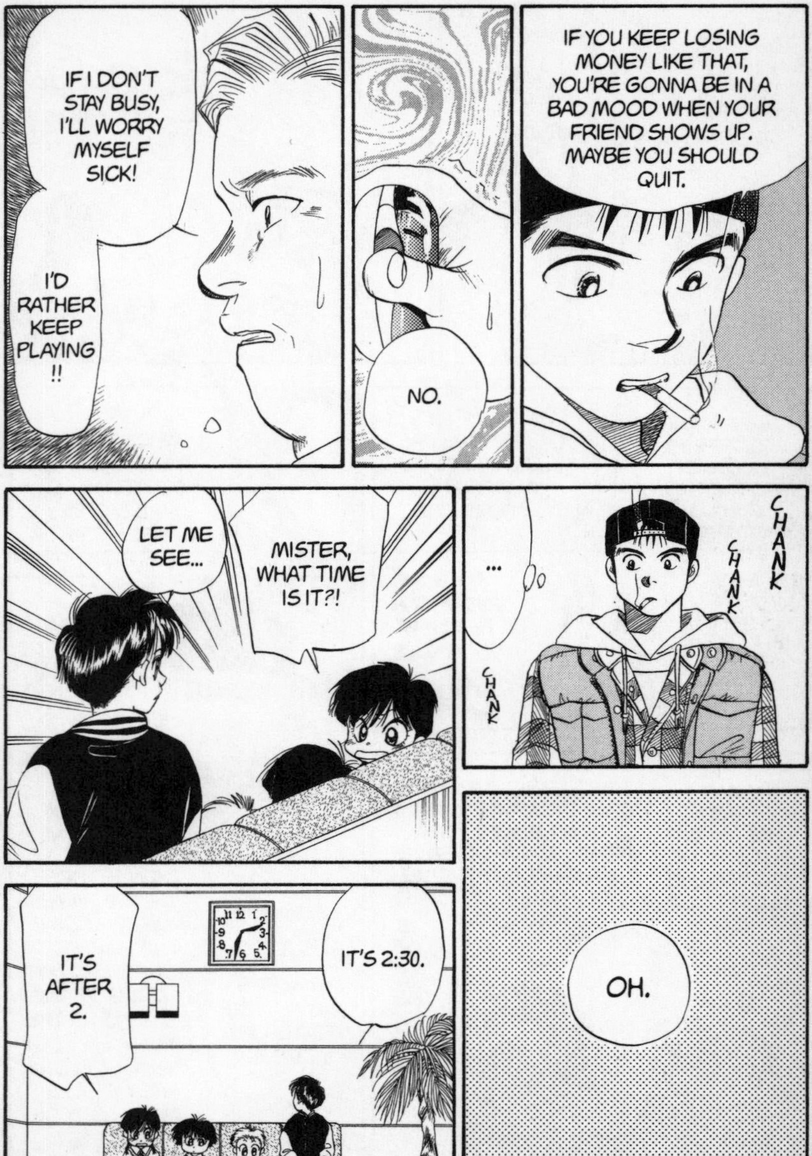
IF YOU KEEP LOSING MONEY LIKE THAT, YOU'RE GONNA BE IN A BAD MOOD WHEN YOUR FRIEND SHOWS UP. MAYBE YOU SHOULD QUIT.
NO.
IF I DON'T STAY BUSY, I'LL WORRY MYSELF SICK!
I'D RATHER KEEP PLAYING!!
CHANK
CHANK
...
CHANK
MISTER, WHAT TIME IS IT?!
LET ME SEE...
OH.
IT'S 2:30.
IT'S AFTER 2.

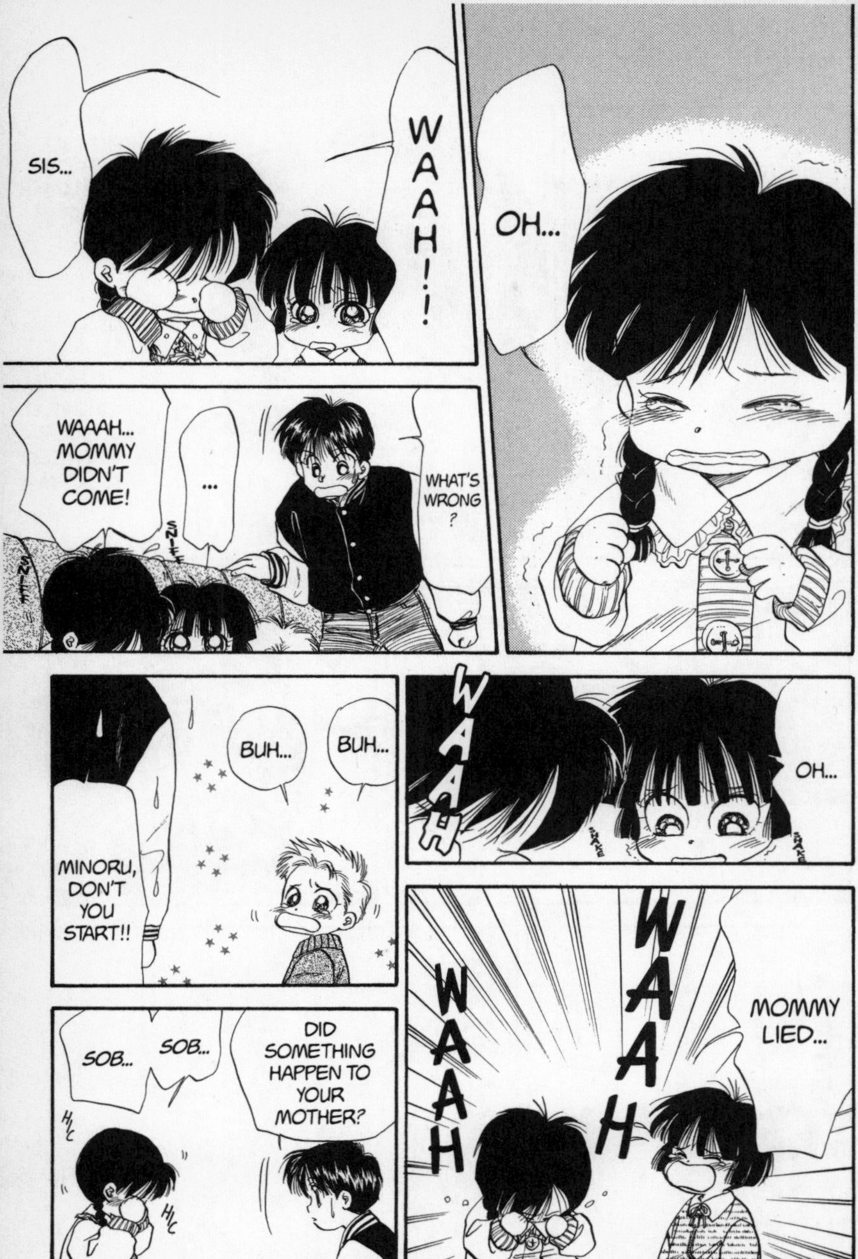
OH...
WAAAH!!
SIS...
WHAT'S WRONG?
...
SNIFF
WAAAH... MOMMY DIDN'T COME!
SNIFF
OH...
SHAKE
WAAAH
SHAKE
BUH...
BUH...
MINORU, DON'T YOU START!!
MOMMY LIED...
WAAAH
WAAAH
DID SOMETHING HAPPEN TO YOUR MOTHER?
SOB...
SOB...
HIC
HIC

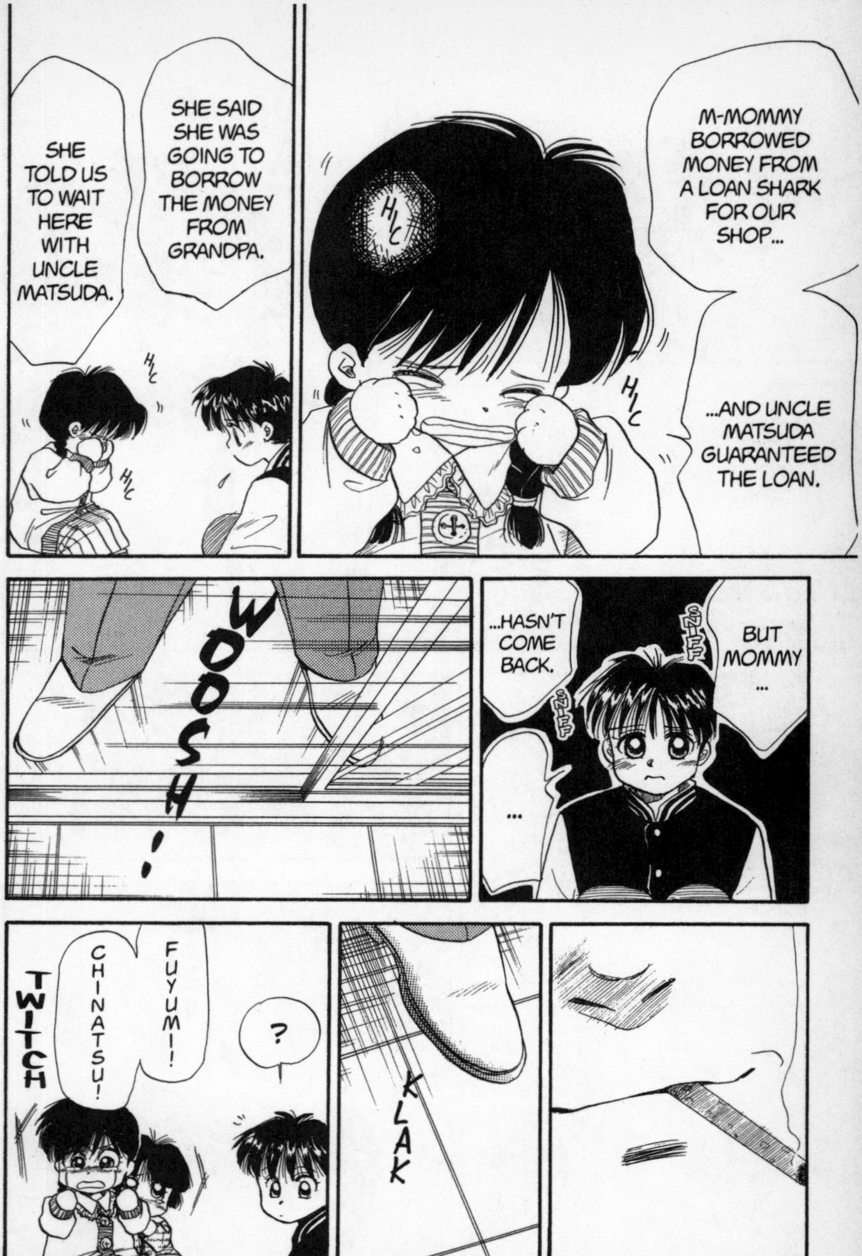

M-MOMMY BORROWED MONEY FROM A LOAN SHARK FOR OUR SHOP...
HIC
...AND UNCLE MATSUDA GUARANTEED THE LOAN.
HIC
SHE SAID SHE WAS GOING TO BORROW THE MONEY FROM GRANDPA.
SHE TOLD US TO WAIT HERE WITH UNCLE MATSUDA.
HIC
HIC
BUT MOMMY ...
SNIFF
SNIFF
...HASN'T COME BACK.
...
WOOSH!
KLAK
FUYUMI!
CHINATSU!
?
TWITCH

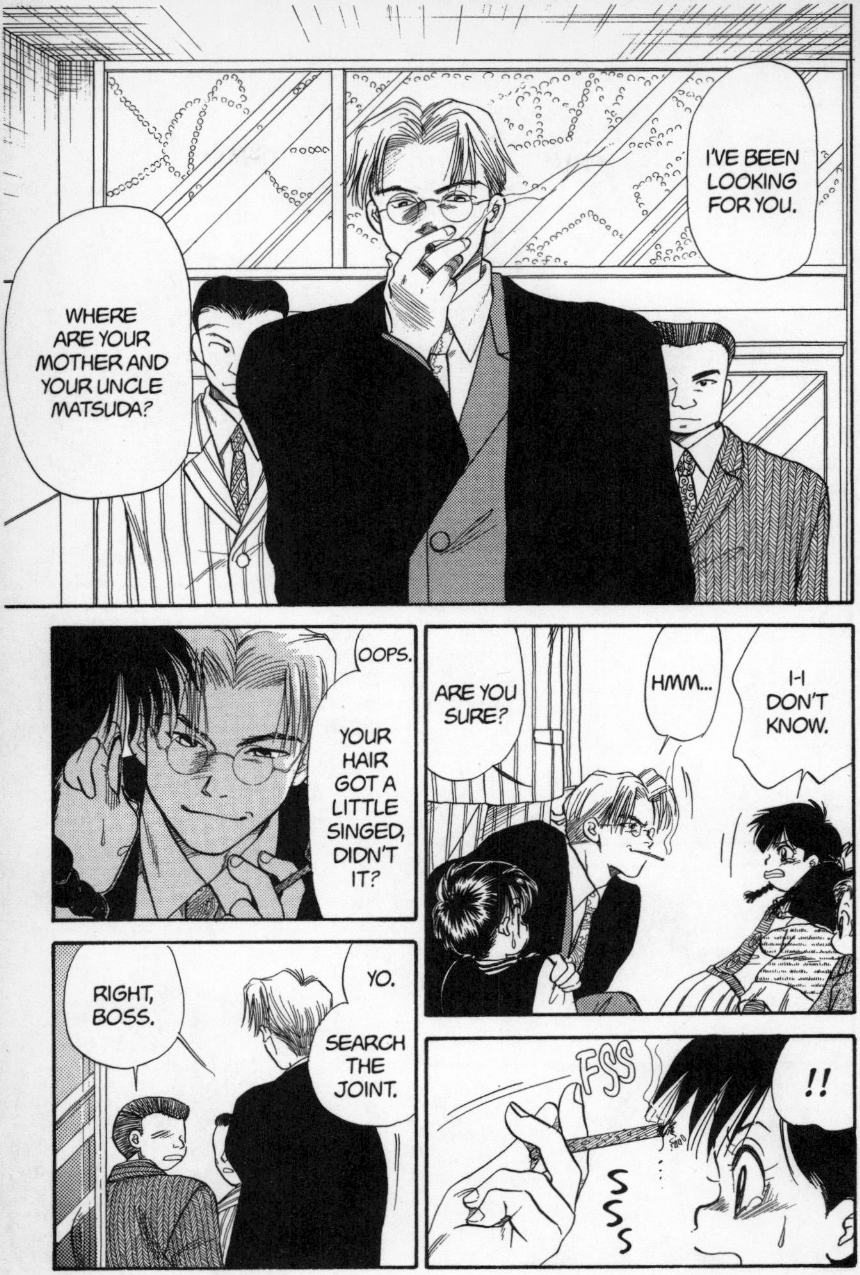
I'VE BEEN LOOKING FOR YOU.
WHERE ARE YOUR MOTHER AND YOUR UNCLE MATSUDA?
I-I DON'T KNOW.
HMM...
ARE YOU SURE?
FSS
!!
SSS
OOPS.
YOUR HAIR GOT A LITTLE SINGED, DIDN'T IT?
YO.
SEARCH THE JOINT.
RIGHT, BOSS.

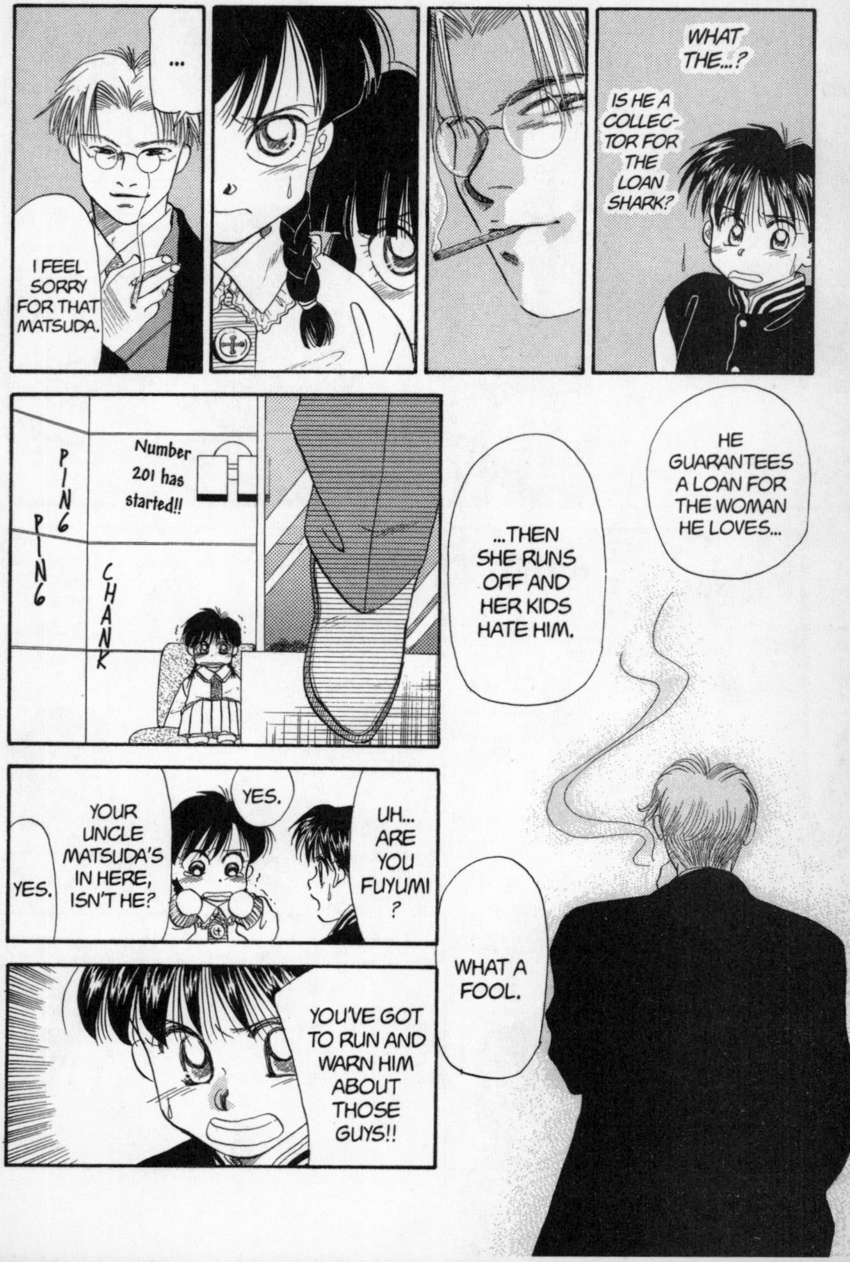
WHAT THE...?
IS HE A COLLECTOR FOR THE LOAN SHARK?
...
I FEEL SORRY FOR THAT MATSUDA.
HE GUARANTEES A LOAN FOR THE WOMAN HE LOVES...
...THEN SHE RUNS OFF AND HER KIDS HATE HIM.
WHAT A FOOL.
Number 201 has started!!
PING
PING
CHANK
UH... ARE YOU FUYUMI?
YES.
YOUR UNCLE MATSUDA'S IN HERE, ISN'T HE?
YES.
YOU'VE GOT TO RUN AND WARN HIM ABOUT THOSE GUYS!!

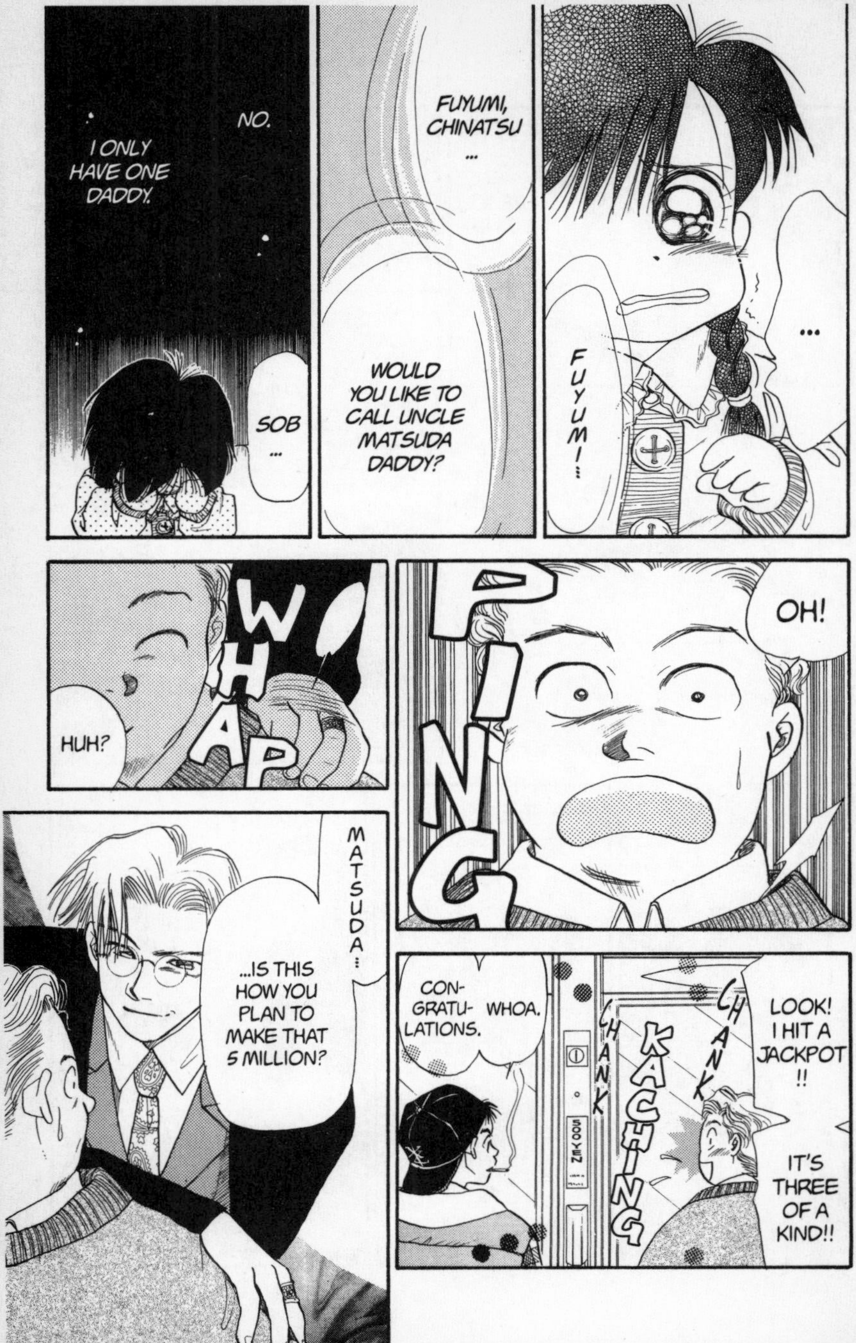

...
FUYUMI!...
FUYUMI, CHINATSU ...
WOULD YOU LIKE TO CALL UNCLE MATSUDA DADDY?
NO.
I ONLY HAVE ONE DADDY.
SOB ...
OH!
PING
WHAP
HUH?
LOOK! I HIT A JACKPOT !!
IT'S THREE OF A KIND!!
CHANK
KACHING
CHANK
500YEN
WHOA.
CON-GRATU-LATIONS.
MATSUDA...
...IS THIS HOW YOU PLAN TO MAKE THAT 5 MILLION?

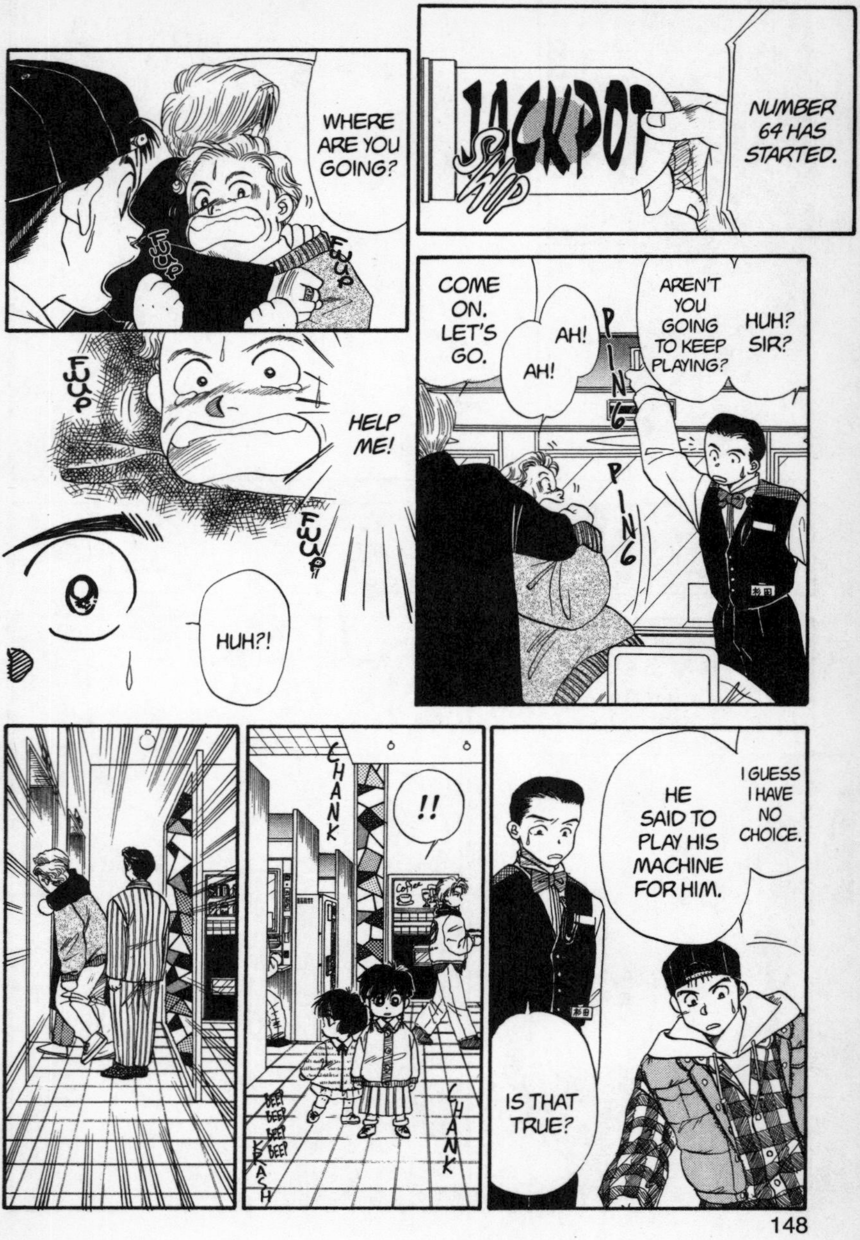
NUMBER 64 HAS STARTED.
JACKPOT
SHWIP
WHERE ARE YOU GOING?
FWUP
FWUP
HUH? SIR?
AREN'T YOU GOING TO KEEP PLAYING?
PING
PING
AH!
AH!
COME ON. LET'S GO.
FWUP
HELP ME!
FWUP
HUH?!
I GUESS I HAVE NO CHOICE.
HE SAID TO PLAY HIS MACHINE FOR HIM.
IS THAT TRUE?
CHANK
!!
CHANK
BEEP BEEP BEEP BEEP
KRASH

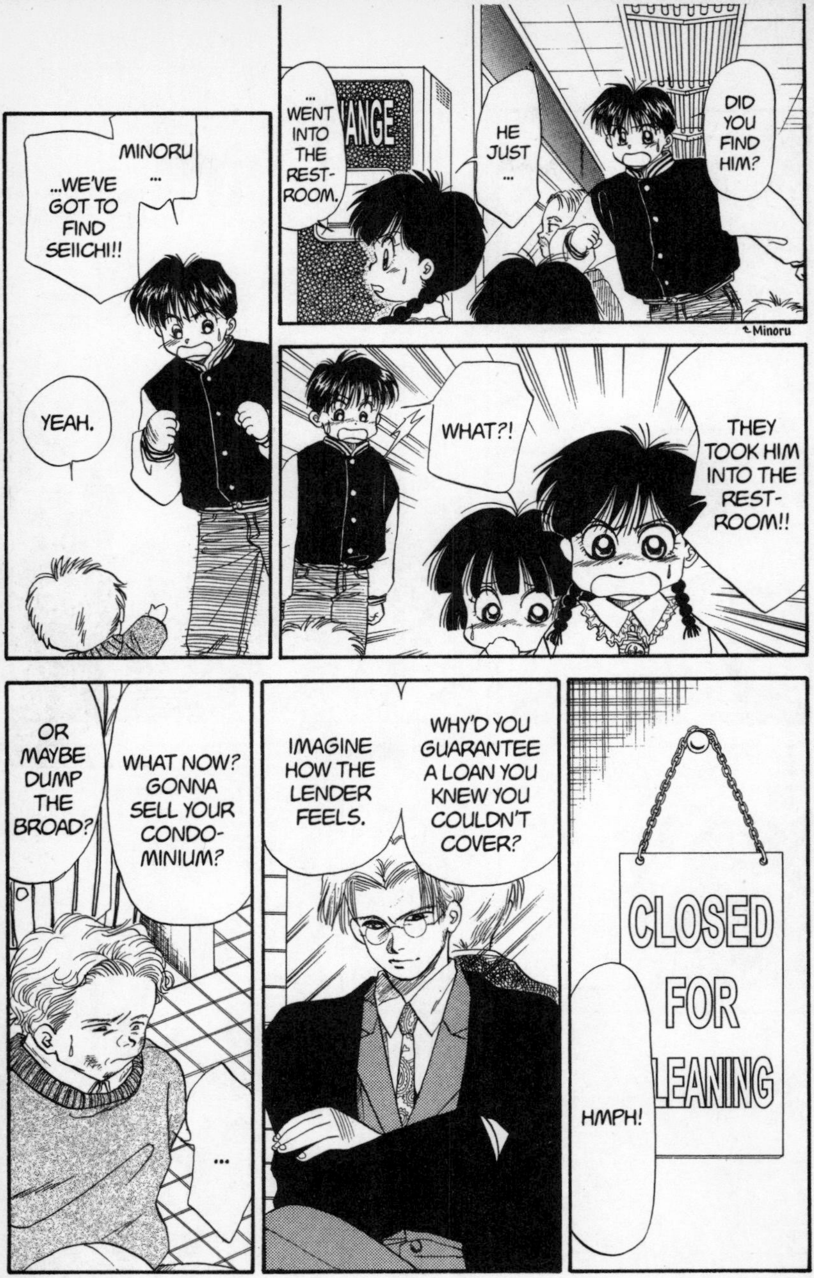

DID YOU FIND HIM?
Minoru
HE JUST ...
... WENT INTO THE REST-ROOM.
ANGE
THEY TOOK HIM INTO THE REST-ROOM!!
WHAT?!
MINORU ...
...WE'VE GOT TO FIND SEIICHI!!
YEAH.
CLOSED FOR LEANING
HMPH!
WHY'D YOU GUARANTEE A LOAN YOU KNEW YOU COULDN'T COVER?
IMAGINE HOW THE LENDER FEELS.
WHAT NOW? GONNA SELL YOUR CONDO-MINIUM?
OR MAYBE DUMP THE BROAD?
...

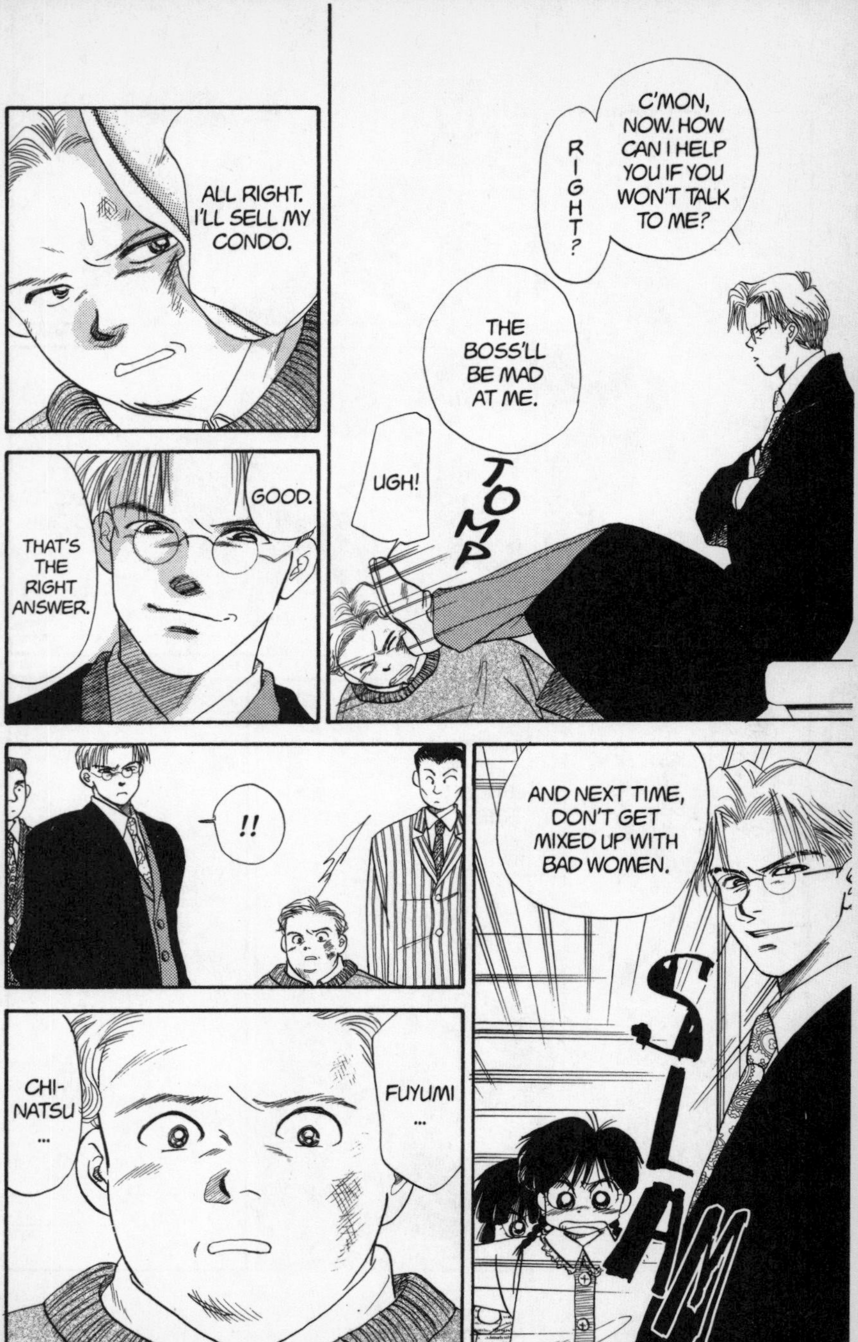
C'MON, NOW. HOW CAN I HELP YOU IF YOU WON'T TALK TO ME?
RIGHT?
THE BOSS'LL BE MAD AT ME.
UGH!
TOMP
ALL RIGHT. I'LL SELL MY CONDO.
GOOD.
THAT'S THE RIGHT ANSWER.
AND NEXT TIME, DON'T GET MIXED UP WITH BAD WOMEN.
SLAM
!!
FUYUMI ...
CHI-NATSU ...

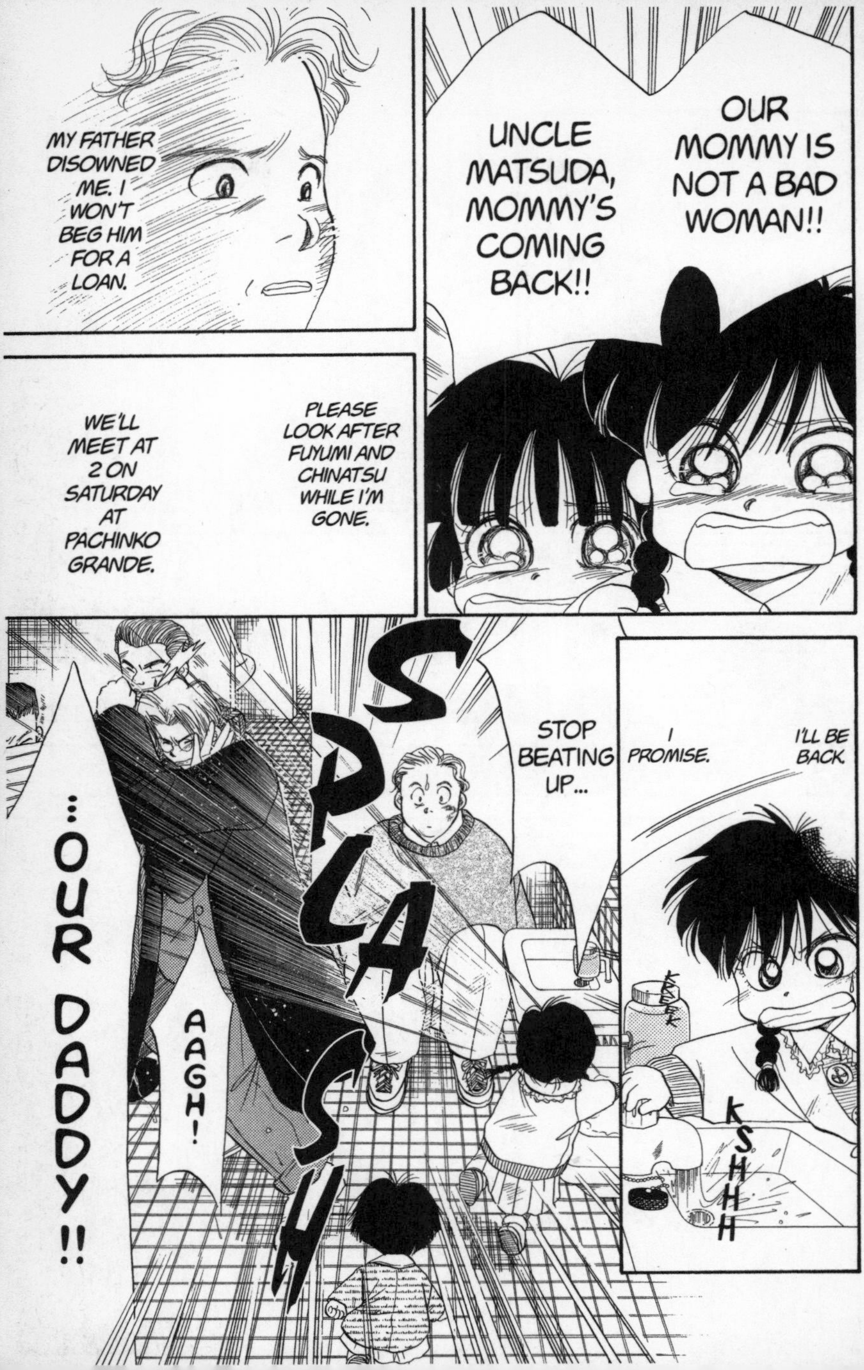
OUR MOMMY IS NOT A BAD WOMAN!!
UNCLE MATSUDA, MOMMY'S COMING BACK!!
MY FATHER DISOWNED ME. I WON'T BEG HIM FOR A LOAN.
PLEASE LOOK AFTER FUYUMI AND CHINATSU WHILE I'M GONE.
WE'LL MEET AT 2 ON SATURDAY AT PACHINKO GRANDE.
I'LL BE BACK.
I PROMISE.
KREEK
KSHHH
STOP BEATING UP...
SPLASH
AAGH!
...OUR DADDY!!

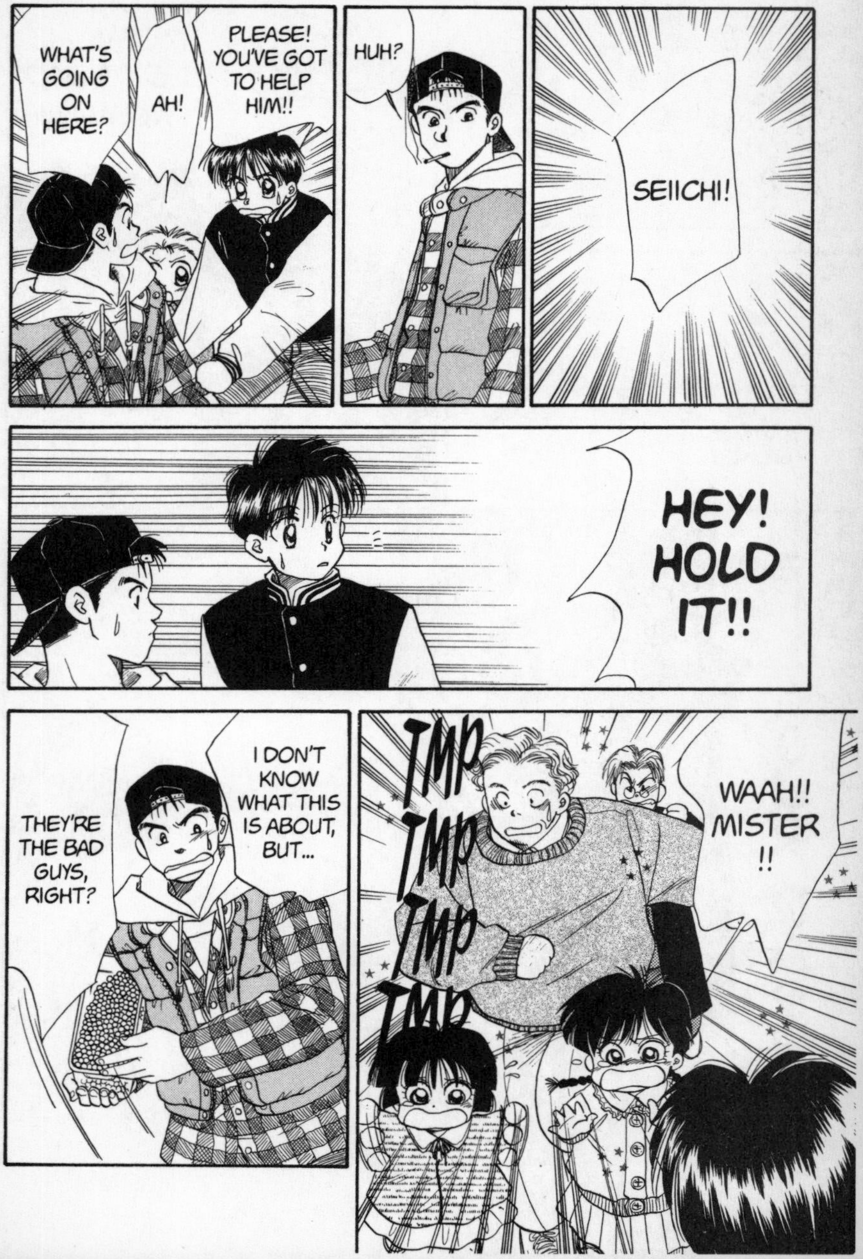
SEIICHI!
HUH?
PLEASE! YOU'VE GOT TO HELP HIM!!
AH!
WHAT'S GOING ON HERE?
HEY! HOLD IT!!
WAAH!! MISTER !!
TMP TMP TMP TMP
I DON'T KNOW WHAT THIS IS ABOUT, BUT...
THEY'RE THE BAD GUYS, RIGHT?

YIKES!

AND THE MAN BOWLS!!

CHECK OUT HIS MAGNIFICENT 180+ FORM!!

SWIP!

S T R I K E!!

KLATTER!

WHY, YOU...

...STUPID IDIOTS!

HUFF
HUFF
HUFF

YOU'RE THE IDIOT.

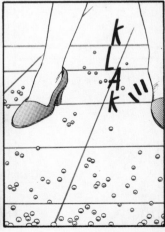

KLAK!

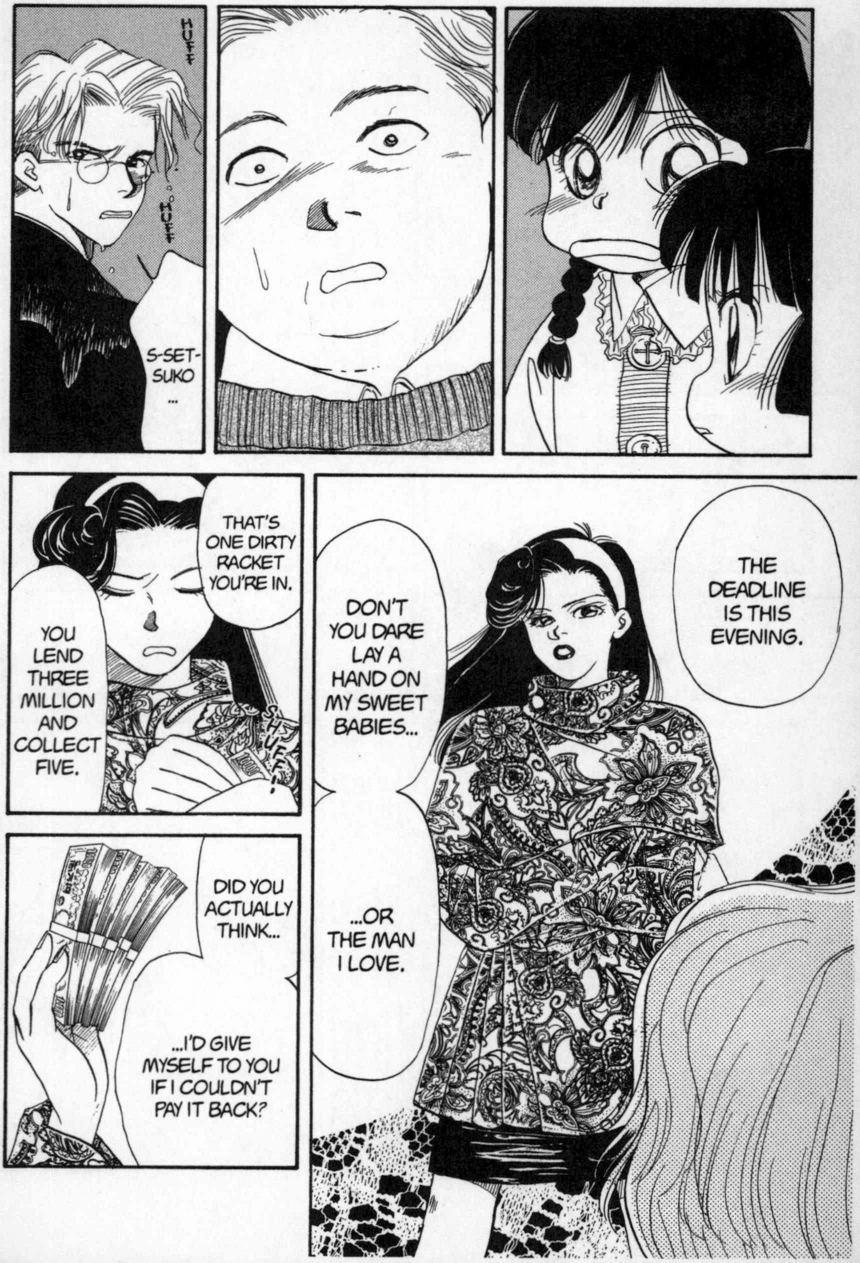
HUFF
HUFF
S-SET-SUKO...
THE DEADLINE IS THIS EVENING.
DON'T YOU DARE LAY A HAND ON MY SWEET BABIES...
...OR THE MAN I LOVE.
THAT'S ONE DIRTY RACKET YOU'RE IN.
YOU LEND THREE MILLION AND COLLECT FIVE.
SHUFF!
DID YOU ACTUALLY THINK...
...I'D GIVE MYSELF TO YOU IF I COULDN'T PAY IT BACK?

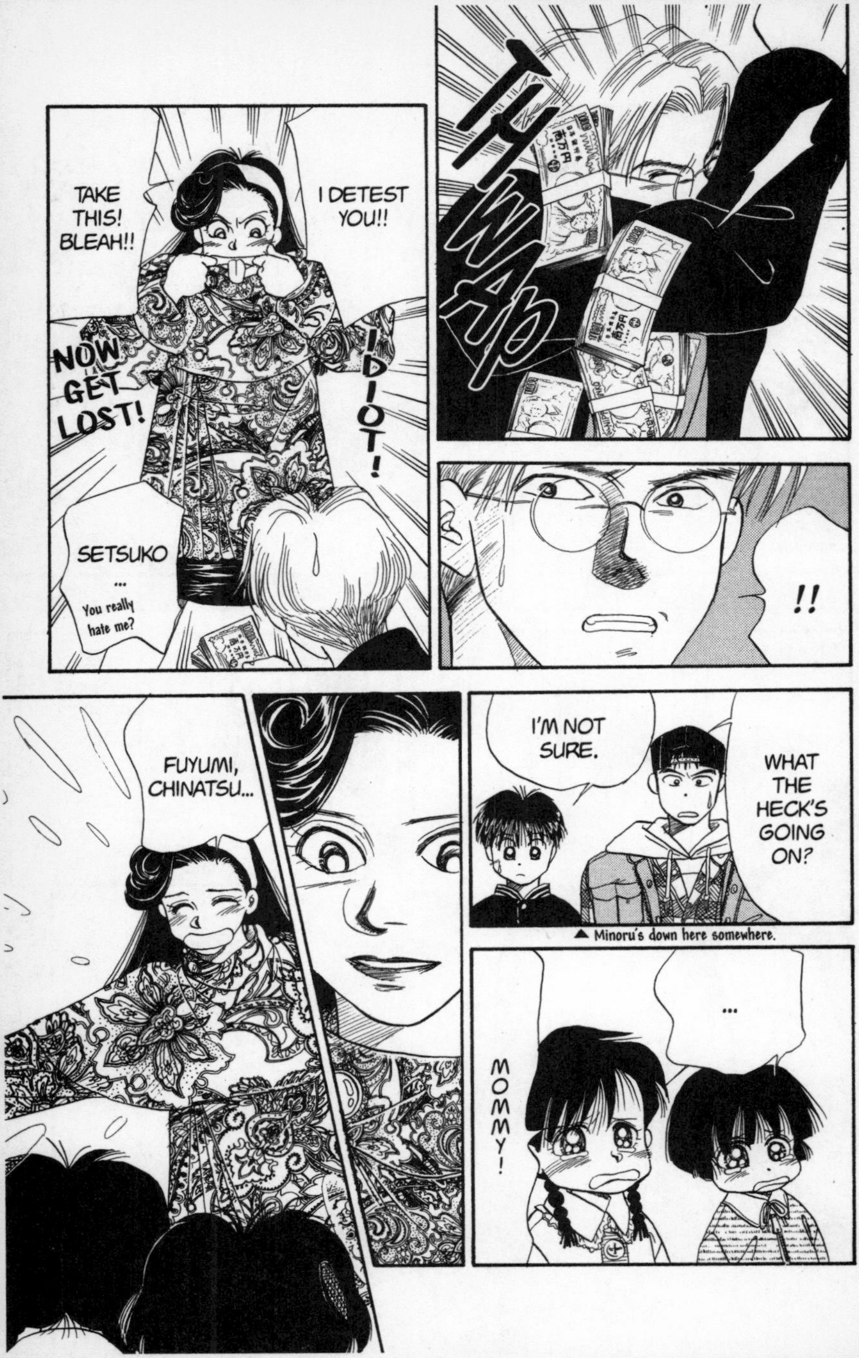
THWAP
!!
I DETEST YOU!!
TAKE THIS! BLEAH!!
IDIOT!
NOW GET LOST!
SETSUKO ... You really hate me?
WHAT THE HECK'S GOING ON?
I'M NOT SURE.
▲ Minoru's down here somewhere.
...
MOMMY!
FUYUMI, CHINATSU...

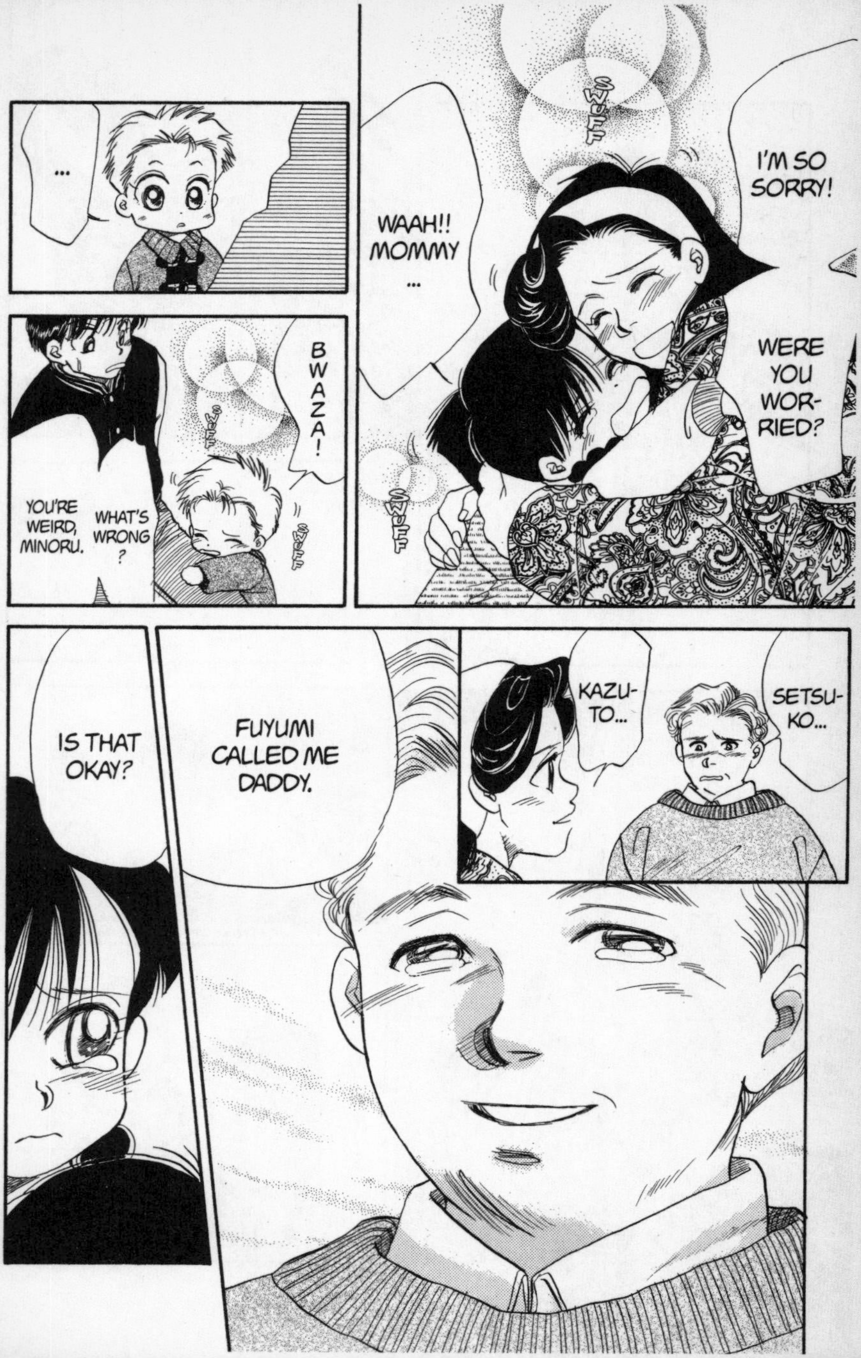
SWUFF
I'M SO SORRY!
WAAH!! MOMMY ...
WERE YOU WOR-RIED?
SWUFF
...
BWAZA!
SWUFF
SWUFF
WHAT'S WRONG?
YOU'RE WEIRD, MINORU.
SETSU-KO...
KAZU-TO...
FUYUMI CALLED ME DADDY.
IS THAT OKAY?

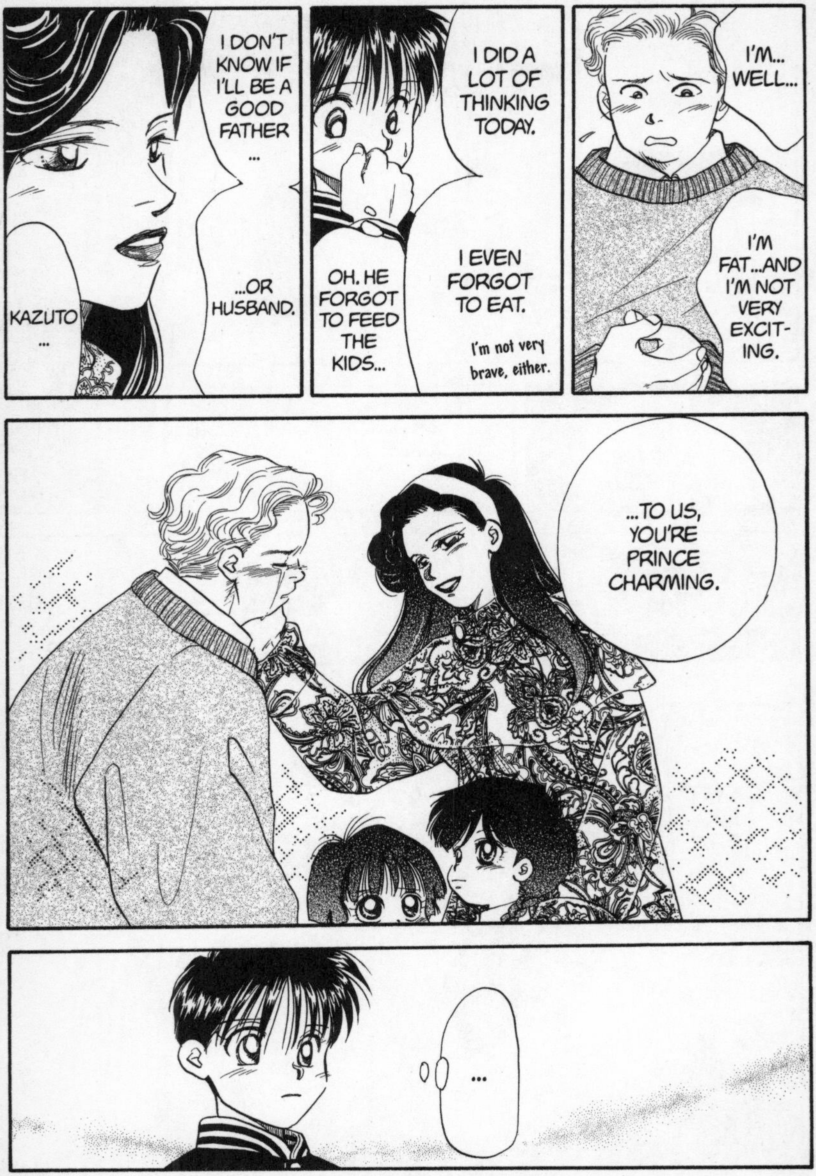
I'M... WELL...
I'M FAT...AND I'M NOT VERY EXCIT-ING.
I DID A LOT OF THINKING TODAY.
I EVEN FORGOT TO EAT.
I'm not very brave, either.
OH. HE FORGOT TO FEED THE KIDS...
I DON'T KNOW IF I'LL BE A GOOD FATHER ...
...OR HUSBAND.
KAZUTO ...
...TO US, YOU'RE PRINCE CHARMING.
...

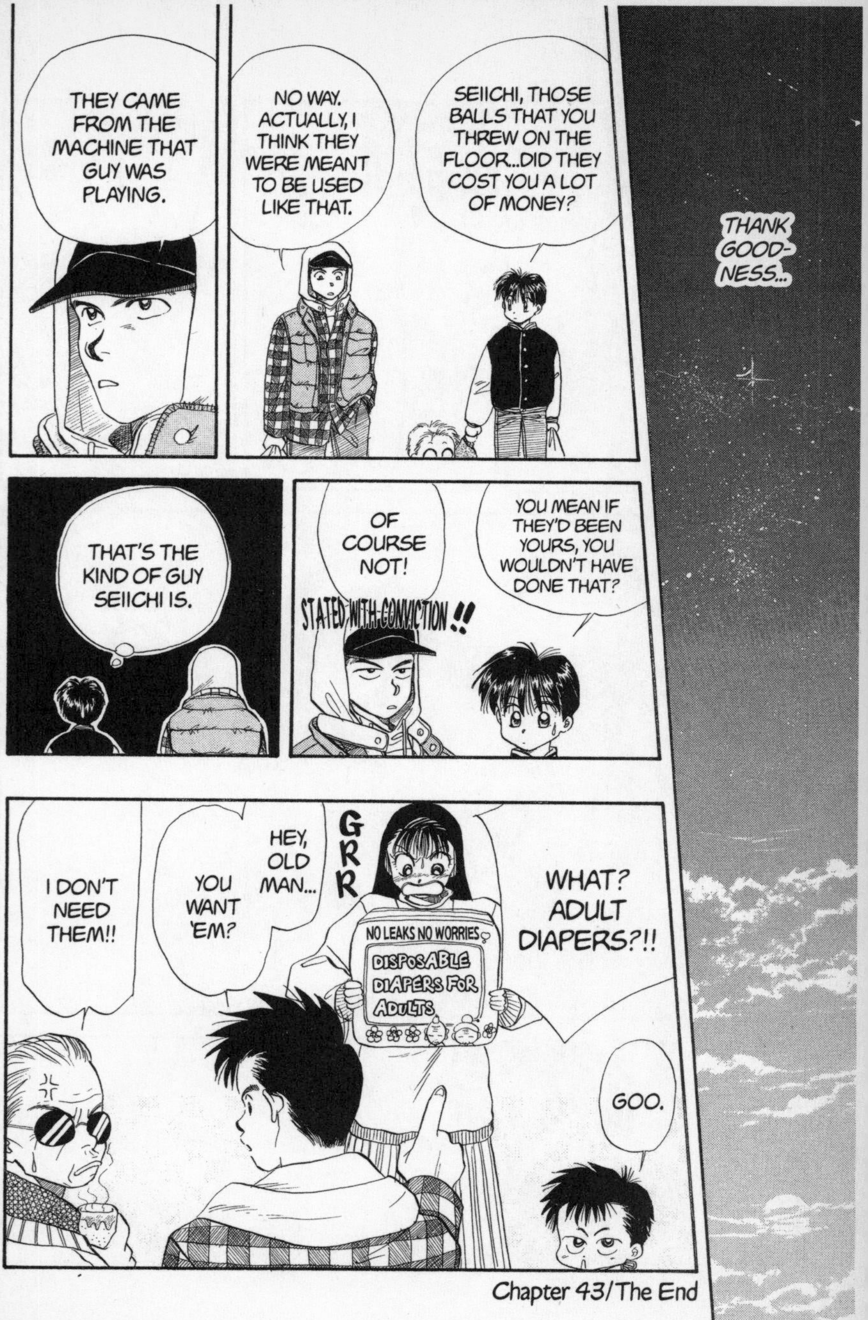
THANK GOODNESS...
SEIICHI, THOSE BALLS THAT YOU THREW ON THE FLOOR...DID THEY COST YOU A LOT OF MONEY?
NO WAY. ACTUALLY, I THINK THEY WERE MEANT TO BE USED LIKE THAT.
THEY CAME FROM THE MACHINE THAT GUY WAS PLAYING.
YOU MEAN IF THEY'D BEEN YOURS, YOU WOULDN'T HAVE DONE THAT?
OF COURSE NOT!
STATED WITH CONVICTION !!
THAT'S THE KIND OF GUY SEIICHI IS.
WHAT? ADULT DIAPERS?!!
GRR
HEY, OLD MAN...
YOU WANT 'EM?
I DON'T NEED THEM!!
NO LEAKS NO WORRIES
DISPOSABLE DIAPERS FOR ADULTS
GOO.

Chapter 43/The End

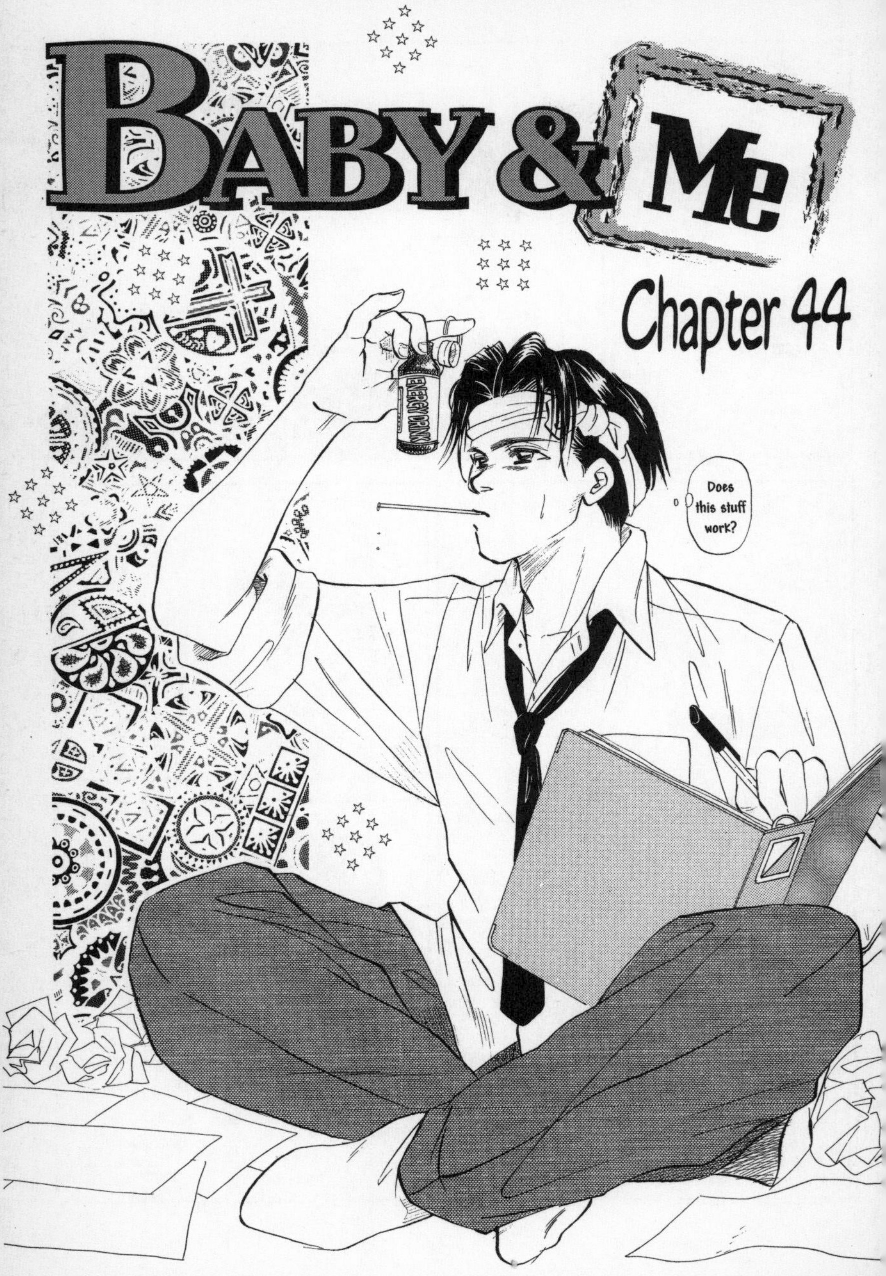
BABY & ME
Chapter 44
ENERGY DRINK
Does this stuff work?

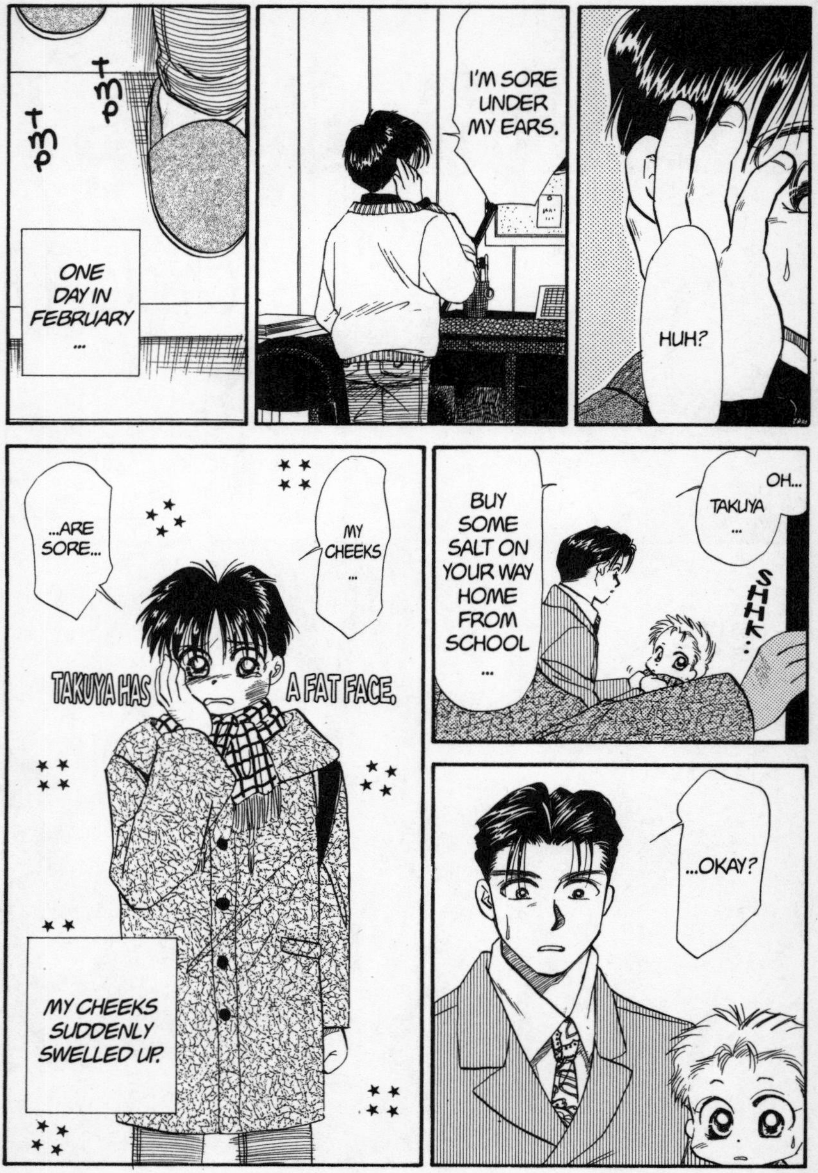

HUH?
I'M SORE UNDER MY EARS.
tmp
tmp
ONE DAY IN FEBRUARY ...
OH... TAKUYA ...
SHHK!
BUY SOME SALT ON YOUR WAY HOME FROM SCHOOL ...
...OKAY?
MY CHEEKS ...
...ARE SORE...
TAKUYA HAS A FAT FACE.
MY CHEEKS SUDDENLY SWELLED UP.

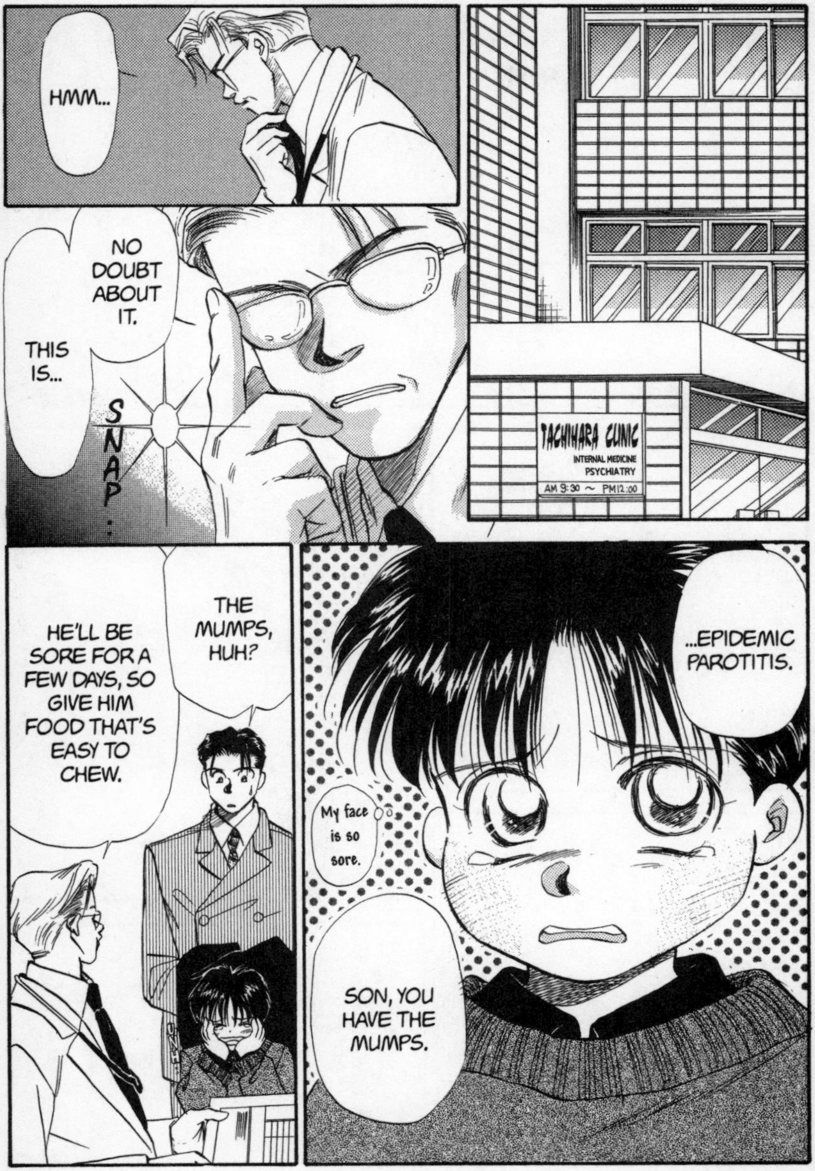

TACHIHARA CLINIC
INTERNAL MEDICINE
PSYCHIATRY
AM 9:30 ~ PM12:00
HMM...
NO DOUBT ABOUT IT.
THIS IS...
SNAP...
...EPIDEMIC PAROTITIS.
My face is so sore.
SON, YOU HAVE THE MUMPS.
THE MUMPS, HUH?
HE'LL BE SORE FOR A FEW DAYS, SO GIVE HIM FOOD THAT'S EASY TO CHEW.

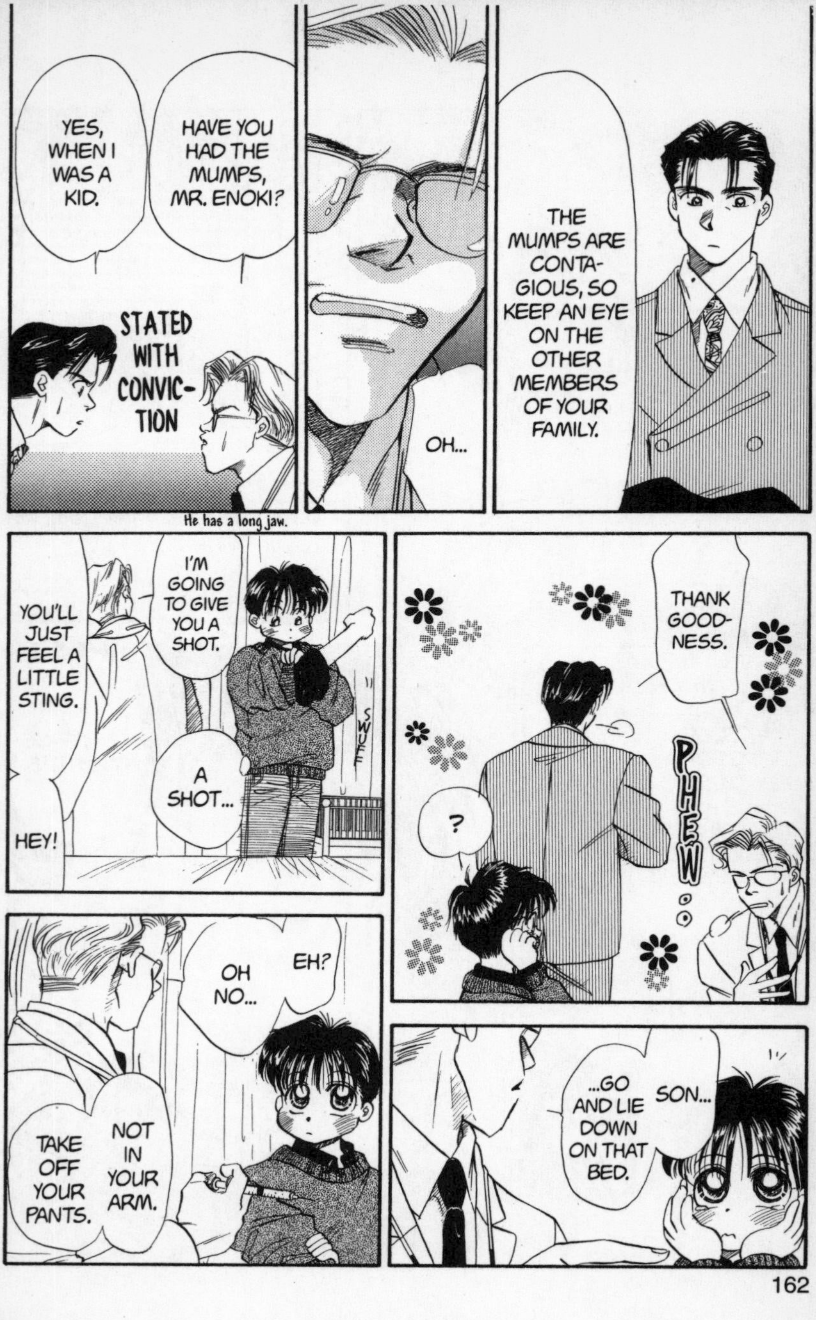
THE MUMPS ARE CONTAGIOUS, SO KEEP AN EYE ON THE OTHER MEMBERS OF YOUR FAMILY.
OH...
HAVE YOU HAD THE MUMPS, MR. ENOKI?
YES, WHEN I WAS A KID.
STATED WITH CONVICTION
He has a long jaw.
THANK GOODNESS.
PHEW..
?
I'M GOING TO GIVE YOU A SHOT.
YOU'LL JUST FEEL A LITTLE STING.
SWUFF
A SHOT...
HEY!
SON...
...GO AND LIE DOWN ON THAT BED.
EH?
OH NO...
NOT IN YOUR ARM.
TAKE OFF YOUR PANTS.

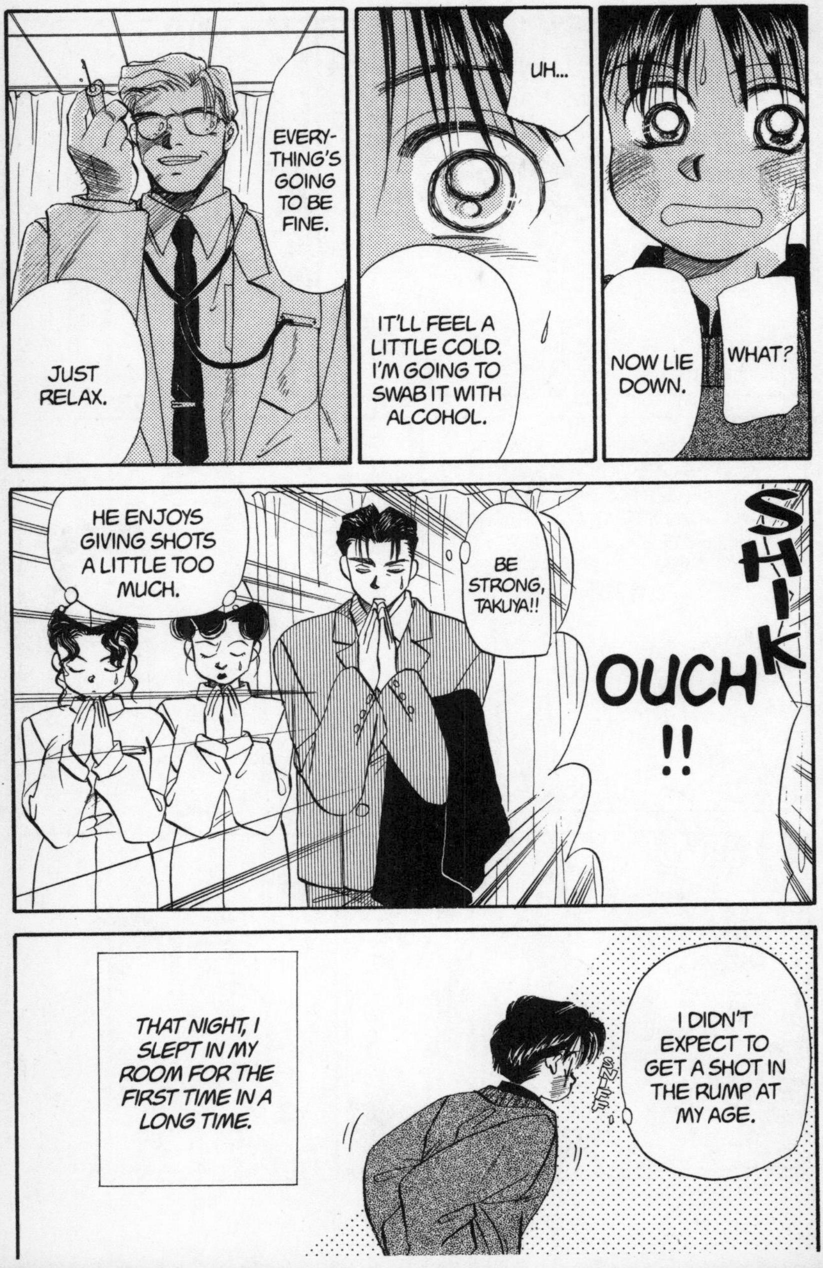
WHAT?
NOW LIE DOWN.
UH...
IT'LL FEEL A LITTLE COLD. I'M GOING TO SWAB IT WITH ALCOHOL.
EVERY-THING'S GOING TO BE FINE.
JUST RELAX.
SHIK
OUCH!!
BE STRONG, TAKUYA!!
HE ENJOYS GIVING SHOTS A LITTLE TOO MUCH.
I DIDN'T EXPECT TO GET A SHOT IN THE RUMP AT MY AGE.
THAT NIGHT, I SLEPT IN MY ROOM FOR THE FIRST TIME IN A LONG TIME.

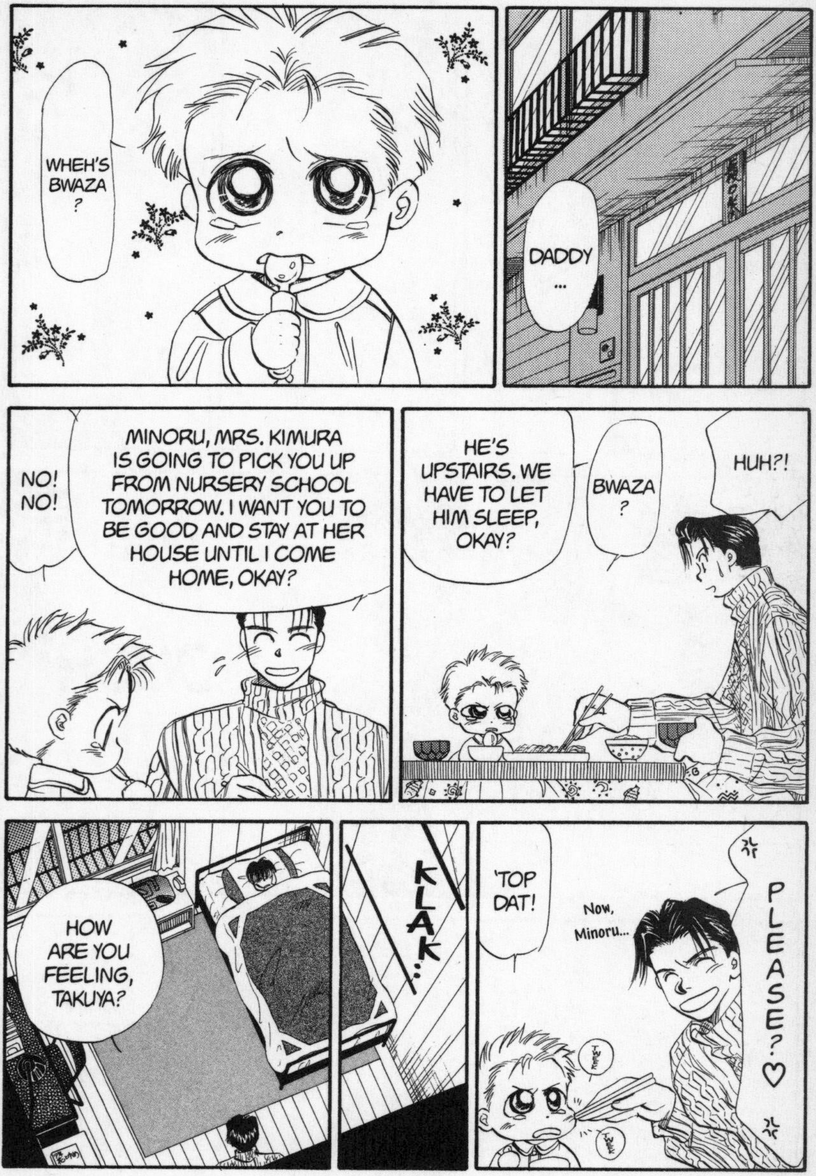
DADDY ...
WHEH'S BWAZA ?
HUH?!
BWAZA ?
HE'S UPSTAIRS. WE HAVE TO LET HIM SLEEP, OKAY?
MINORU, MRS. KIMURA IS GOING TO PICK YOU UP FROM NURSERY SCHOOL TOMORROW. I WANT YOU TO BE GOOD AND STAY AT HER HOUSE UNTIL I COME HOME, OKAY?
NO! NO!
PLEASE?♡
Now, Minoru...
'TOP DAT!
TWEE
TWEE
KLAK...
HOW ARE YOU FEELING, TAKUYA?

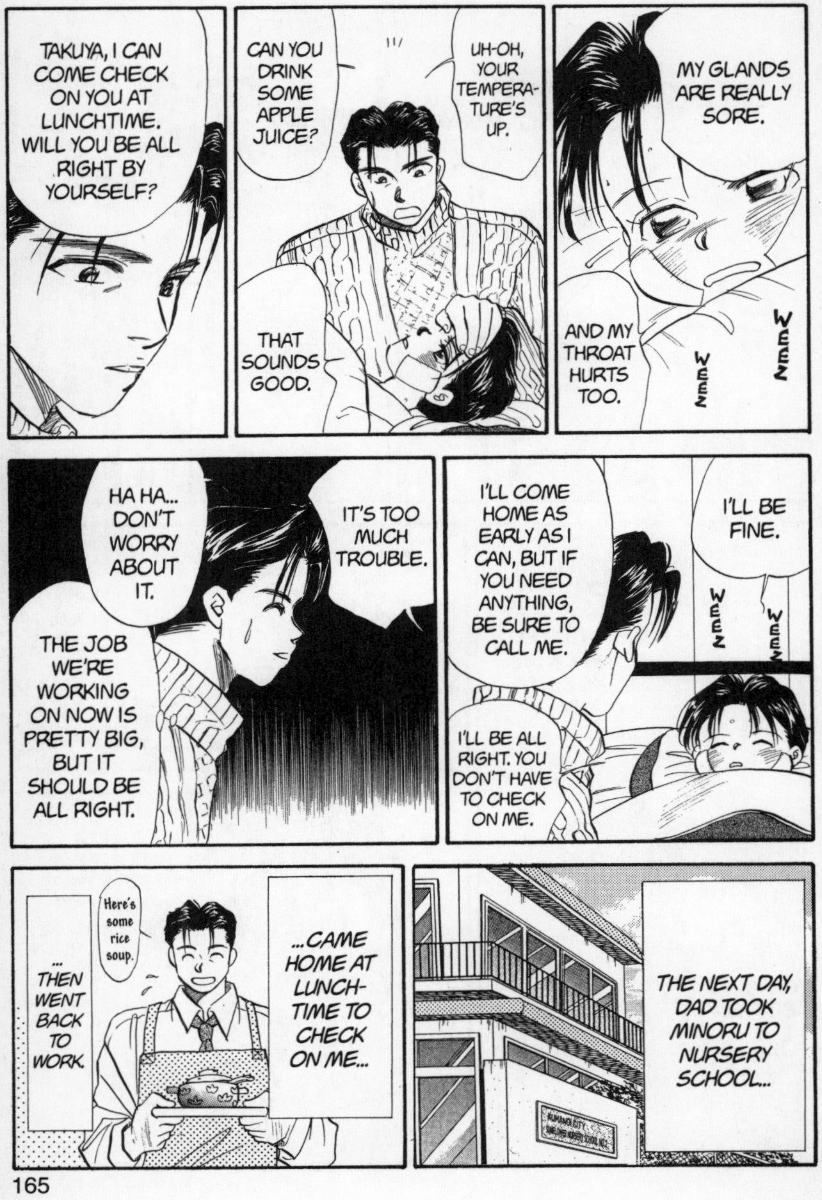
MY GLANDS ARE REALLY SORE.
AND MY THROAT HURTS TOO.
WEEZ
WEEZ
UH-OH, YOUR TEMPERATURE'S UP.
CAN YOU DRINK SOME APPLE JUICE?
THAT SOUNDS GOOD.
TAKUYA, I CAN COME CHECK ON YOU AT LUNCHTIME. WILL YOU BE ALL RIGHT BY YOURSELF?
I'LL BE FINE.
WEEZ
WEEZ
I'LL COME HOME AS EARLY AS I CAN, BUT IF YOU NEED ANYTHING, BE SURE TO CALL ME.
I'LL BE ALL RIGHT. YOU DON'T HAVE TO CHECK ON ME.
IT'S TOO MUCH TROUBLE.
HA HA... DON'T WORRY ABOUT IT.
THE JOB WE'RE WORKING ON NOW IS PRETTY BIG, BUT IT SHOULD BE ALL RIGHT.
THE NEXT DAY, DAD TOOK MINORU TO NURSERY SCHOOL...
...CAME HOME AT LUNCHTIME TO CHECK ON ME...
Here's some rice soup.
...THEN WENT BACK TO WORK.

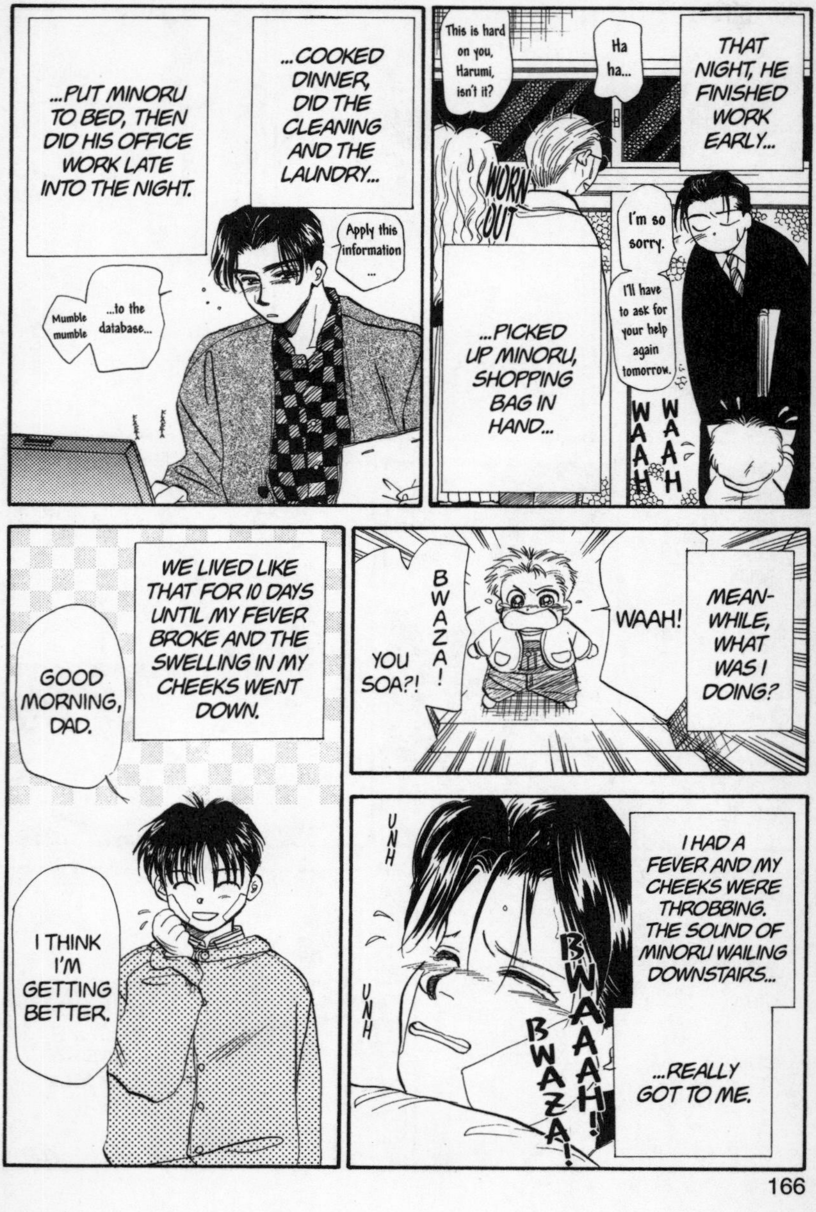

THAT NIGHT, HE FINISHED WORK EARLY...
Ha ha...
This is hard on you, Harumi, isn't it?
WORN OUT
I'm so sorry.
I'll have to ask for your help again tomorrow.
...PICKED UP MINORU, SHOPPING BAG IN HAND...
WAAH WAAH
...COOKED DINNER, DID THE CLEANING AND THE LAUNDRY...
...PUT MINORU TO BED, THEN DID HIS OFFICE WORK LATE INTO THE NIGHT.
Apply this information ...
...to the database...
Mumble mumble
MEAN-WHILE, WHAT WAS I DOING?
WAAH!
BWAZA!
YOU SOA?!
I HAD A FEVER AND MY CHEEKS WERE THROBBING. THE SOUND OF MINORU WAILING DOWNSTAIRS...
BWAAAH!!
BWAZA!
UNH
UNH
...REALLY GOT TO ME.
WE LIVED LIKE THAT FOR 10 DAYS UNTIL MY FEVER BROKE AND THE SWELLING IN MY CHEEKS WENT DOWN.
GOOD MORNING, DAD.
I THINK I'M GETTING BETTER.

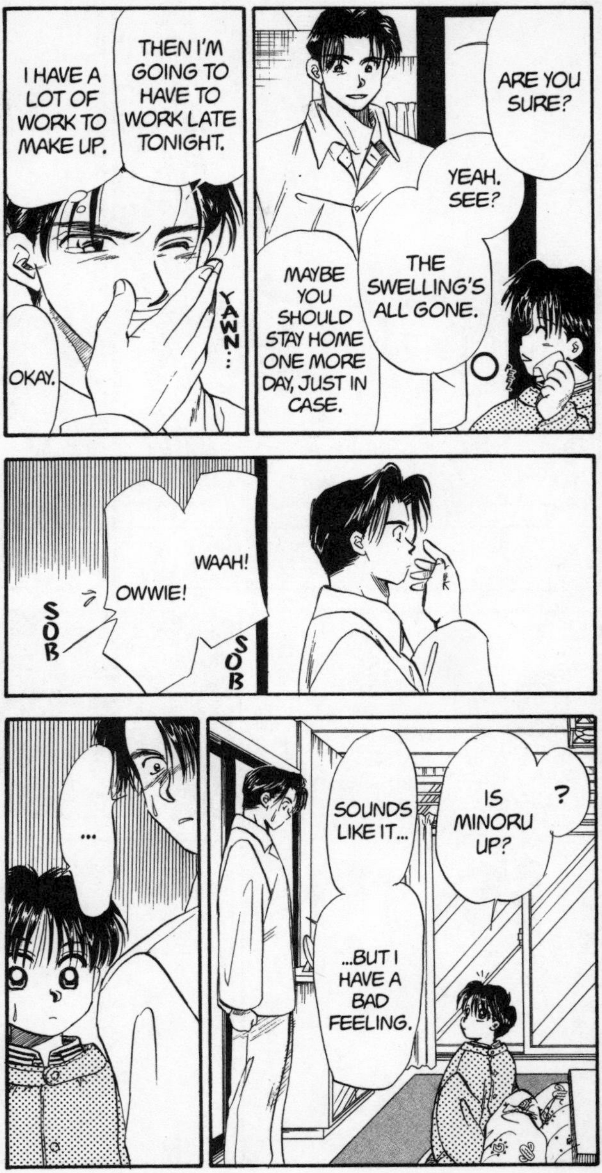
ARE YOU SURE?
YEAH. SEE?
THE SWELLING'S ALL GONE.
MAYBE YOU SHOULD STAY HOME ONE MORE DAY, JUST IN CASE.
THEN I'M GOING TO HAVE TO WORK LATE TONIGHT.
I HAVE A LOT OF WORK TO MAKE UP.
YAWN...
OKAY.
WAAH!
OWWIE!
SOB
SOB
IS MINORU UP?
?
SOUNDS LIKE IT...
...BUT I HAVE A BAD FEELING.
...

Author's Note 7

4. Do a rough draft. The one below was drawn on B5 straw paper.

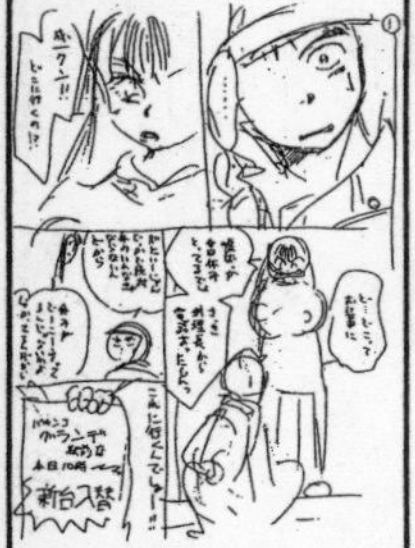

5. Draw everything on manuscript paper. I hate this part of my job.

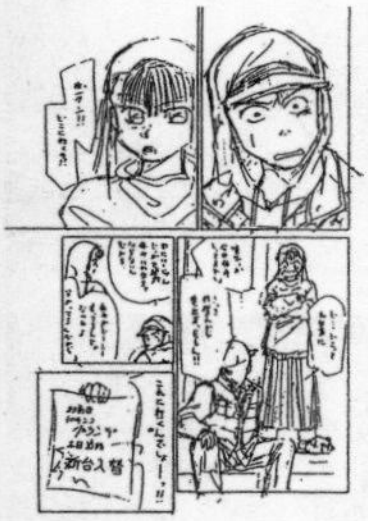

6. Ink it with pens. Add light and shadow.
7. Paste in the background tone and check it one last time. Now it's done. ♡

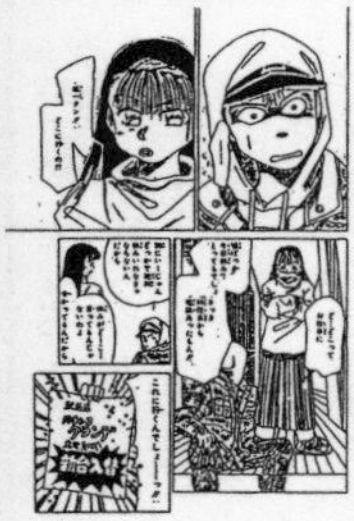

The end. See you in volume 9!

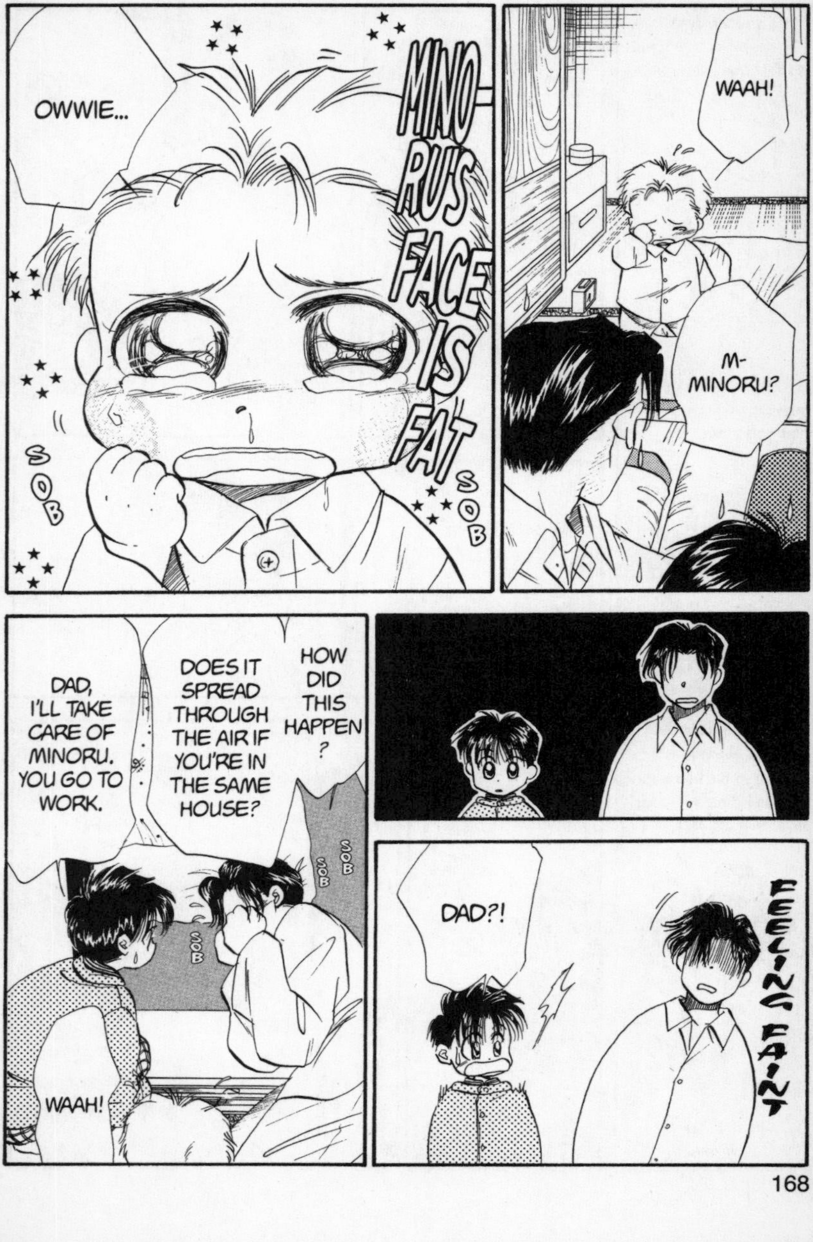
WAAH!
M-MINORU?
MINORU'S FACE IS FAT
SOB
OWWIE...
SOB
FEELING FAINT
DAD?!
HOW DID THIS HAPPEN?
DOES IT SPREAD THROUGH THE AIR IF YOU'RE IN THE SAME HOUSE?
DAD, I'LL TAKE CARE OF MINORU. YOU GO TO WORK.
SOB
SOB
SOB
WAAH!

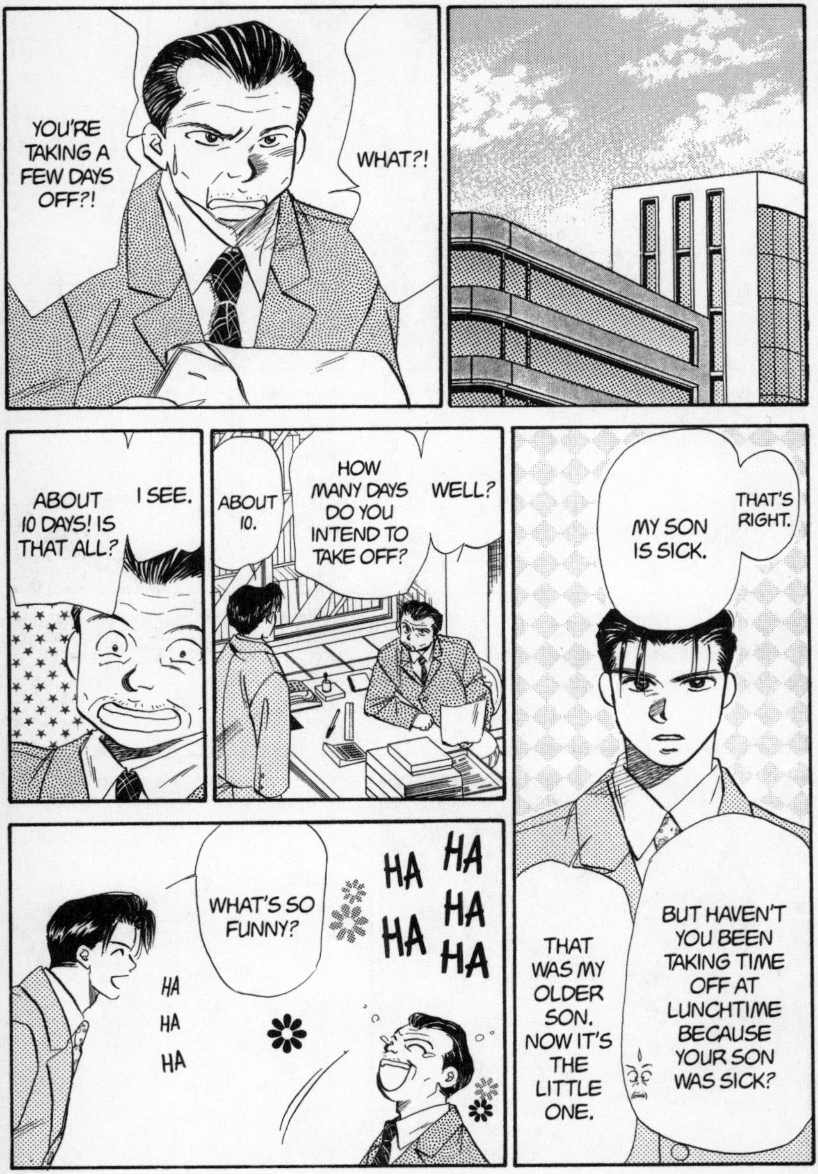
WHAT?!
YOU'RE TAKING A FEW DAYS OFF?!
THAT'S RIGHT.
MY SON IS SICK.
BUT HAVEN'T YOU BEEN TAKING TIME OFF AT LUNCHTIME BECAUSE YOUR SON WAS SICK?
THAT WAS MY OLDER SON. NOW IT'S THE LITTLE ONE.
WELL?
HOW MANY DAYS DO YOU INTEND TO TAKE OFF?
ABOUT 10.
I SEE.
ABOUT 10 DAYS! IS THAT ALL?
HA HA HA
HA HA
WHAT'S SO FUNNY?
HA HA HA

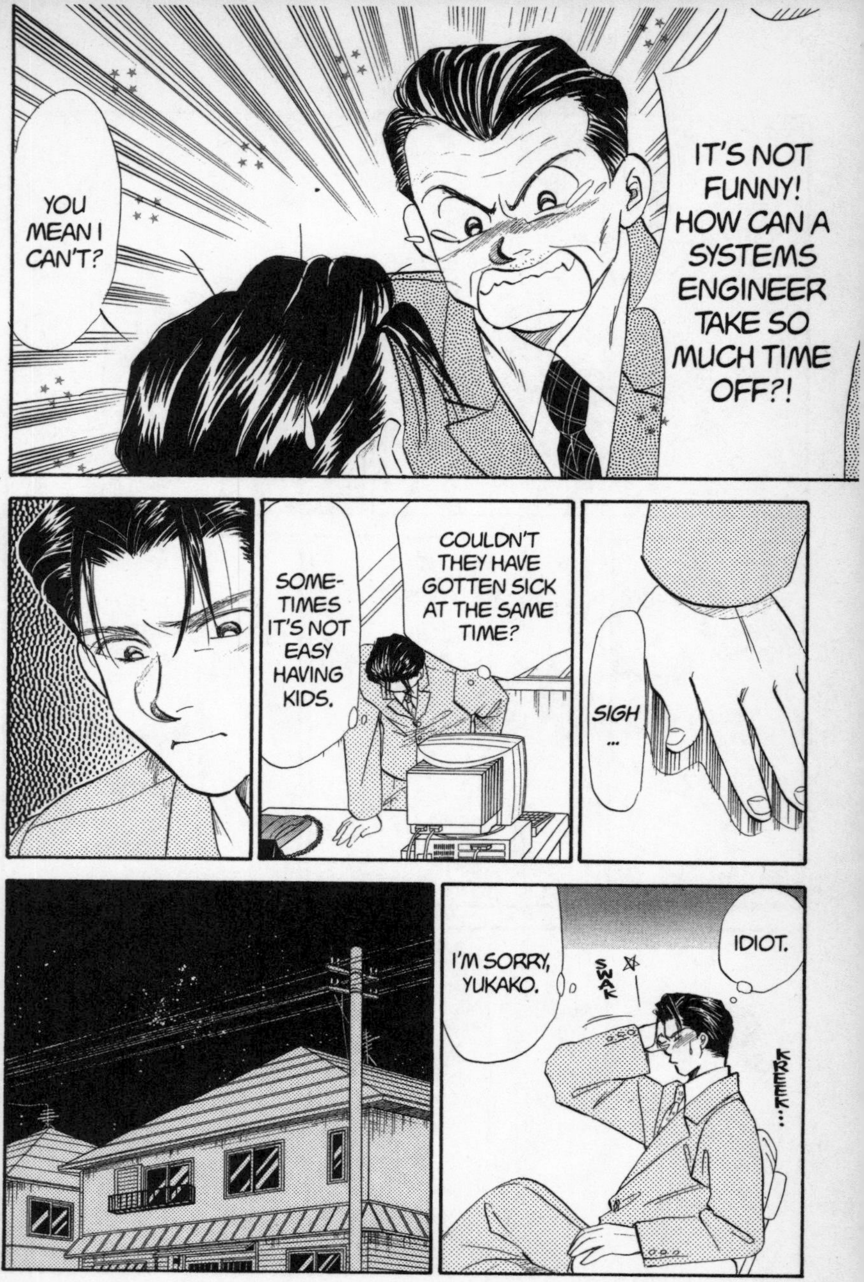
IT'S NOT FUNNY! HOW CAN A SYSTEMS ENGINEER TAKE SO MUCH TIME OFF?!
YOU MEAN I CAN'T?
SIGH ...
COULDN'T THEY HAVE GOTTEN SICK AT THE SAME TIME?
SOME-TIMES IT'S NOT EASY HAVING KIDS.
IDIOT.
I'M SORRY, YUKAKO.
SWAK
KREEK...

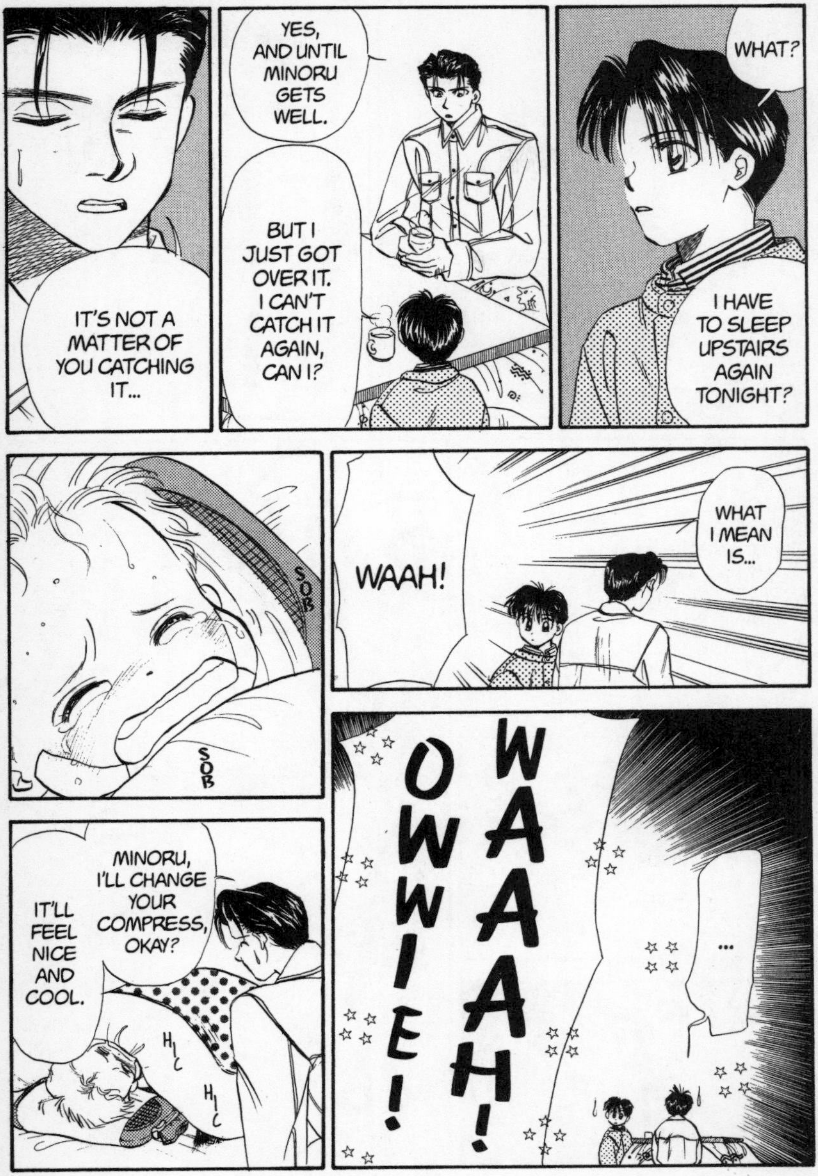
WHAT?
I HAVE TO SLEEP UPSTAIRS AGAIN TONIGHT?
YES, AND UNTIL MINORU GETS WELL.
BUT I JUST GOT OVER IT. I CAN'T CATCH IT AGAIN, CAN I?
IT'S NOT A MATTER OF YOU CATCHING IT...
WHAT I MEAN IS...
WAAH!
SOB
SOB
WAAAAH!
OWWIE!
...
MINORU, I'LL CHANGE YOUR COMPRESS, OKAY?
IT'LL FEEL NICE AND COOL.
HIC
HIC

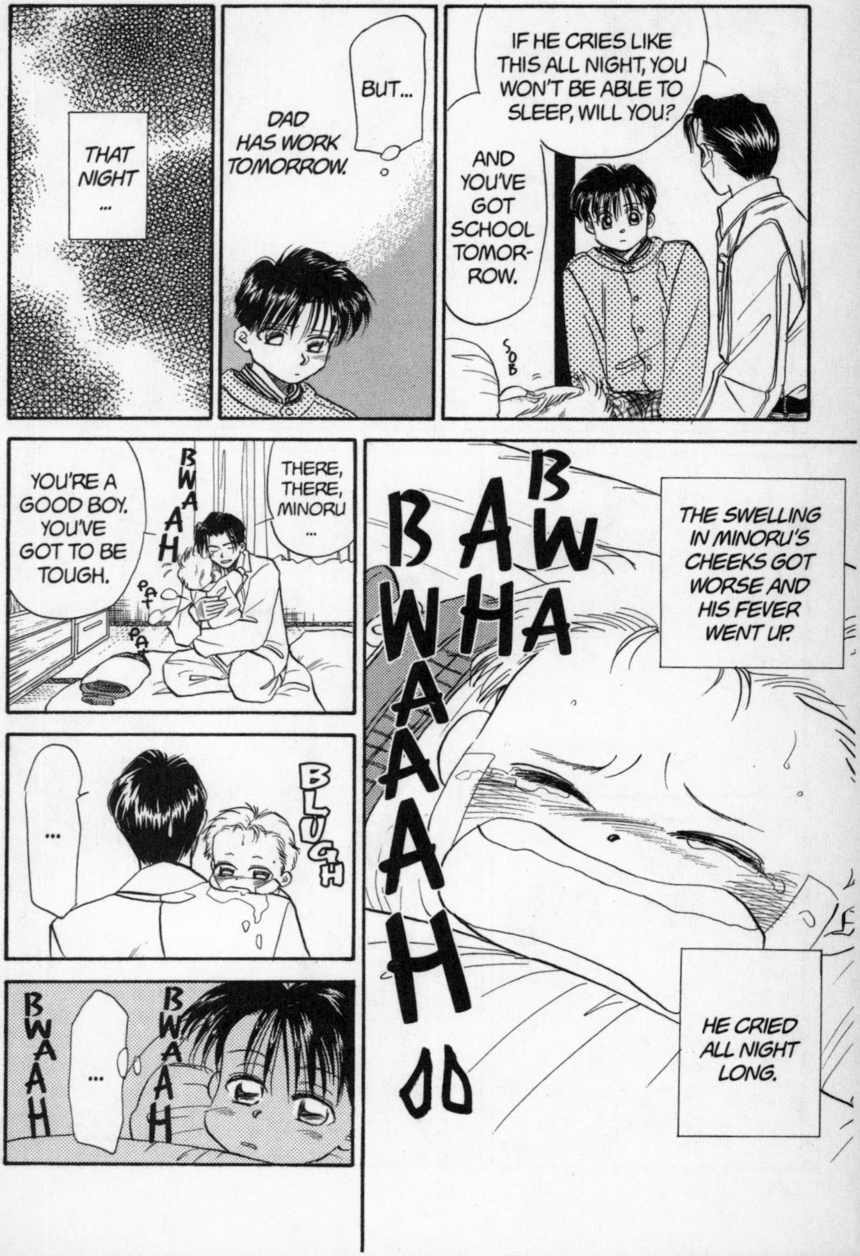
IF HE CRIES LIKE THIS ALL NIGHT, YOU WON'T BE ABLE TO SLEEP, WILL YOU?
AND YOU'VE GOT SCHOOL TOMORROW.
SOB
BUT...
DAD HAS WORK TOMORROW.
THAT NIGHT ...
BAWHA
BWAAAAH
THE SWELLING IN MINORU'S CHEEKS GOT WORSE AND HIS FEVER WENT UP.
HE CRIED ALL NIGHT LONG.
THERE, THERE, MINORU ...
BWAAH
YOU'RE A GOOD BOY. YOU'VE GOT TO BE TOUGH.
PAT PAT
BLUGH
...
BWAAH
...
BWAAH

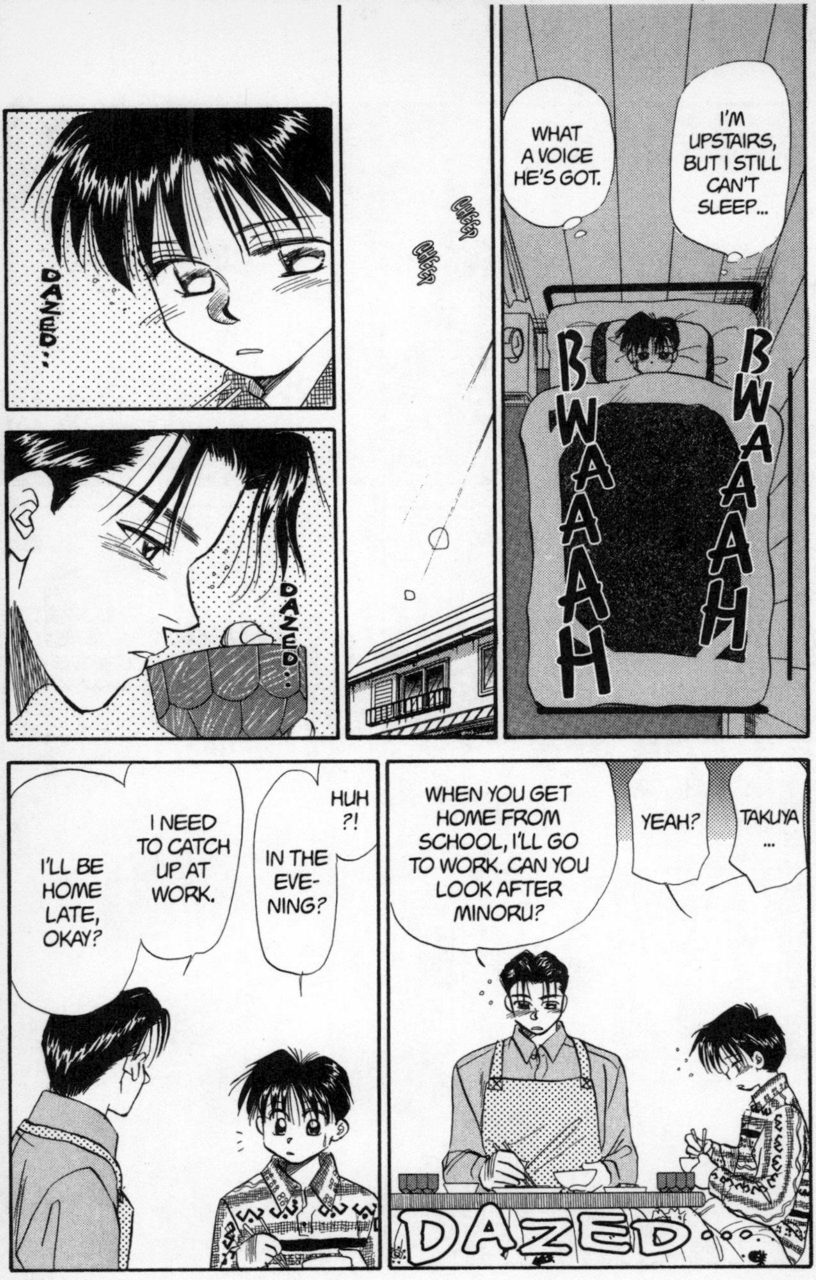
I'M UPSTAIRS, BUT I STILL CAN'T SLEEP...
WHAT A VOICE HE'S GOT.
BWAAAAH
BWAAAAH
CHEEP
CHEEP
DAZED...
DAZED...
TAKUYA...
YEAH?
WHEN YOU GET HOME FROM SCHOOL, I'LL GO TO WORK. CAN YOU LOOK AFTER MINORU?
DAZED...
HUH?!
IN THE EVENING?
I NEED TO CATCH UP AT WORK.
I'LL BE HOME LATE, OKAY?

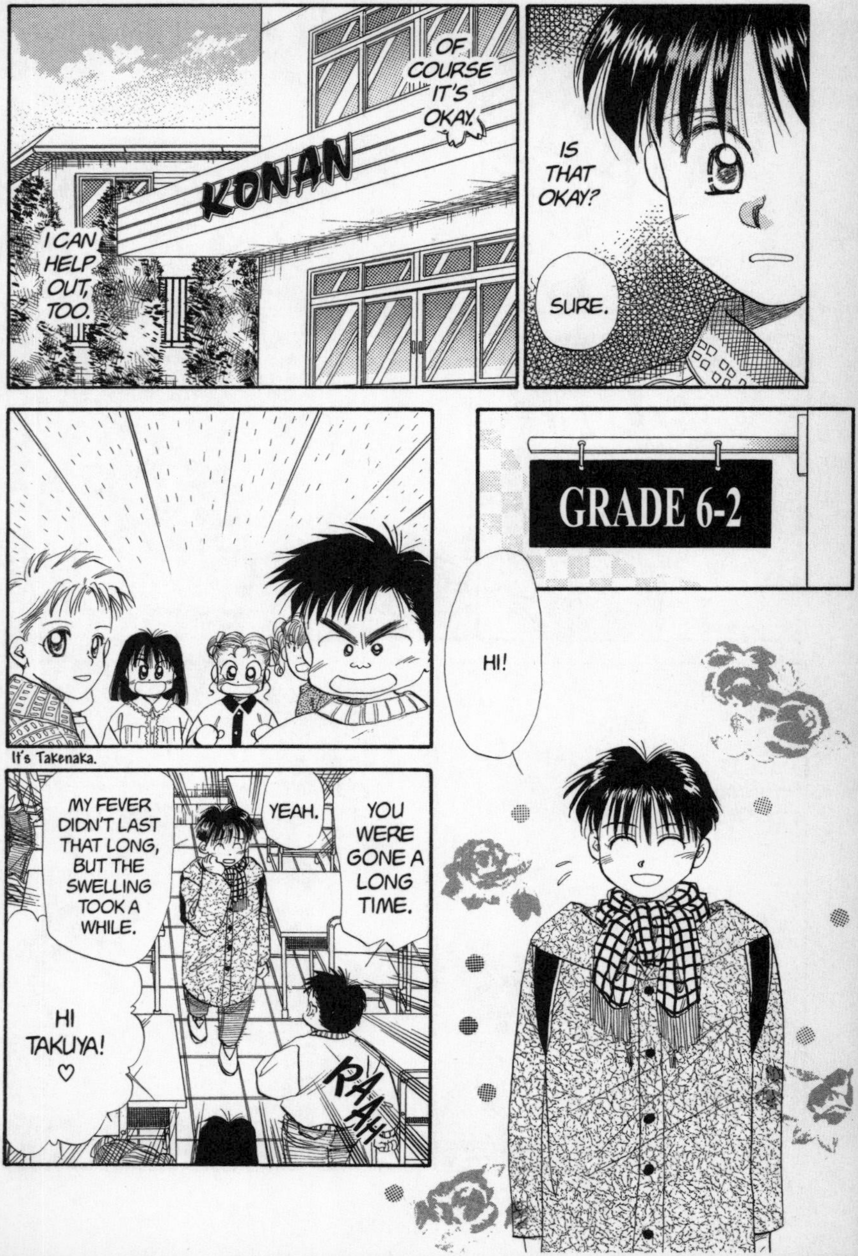
IS THAT OKAY?
SURE.
OF COURSE IT'S OKAY.
KONAN
I CAN HELP OUT, TOO.
GRADE 6-2
HI!
It's Takenaka.
YOU WERE GONE A LONG TIME.
YEAH.
MY FEVER DIDN'T LAST THAT LONG, BUT THE SWELLING TOOK A WHILE.
HI TAKUYA! ♡
RAAH

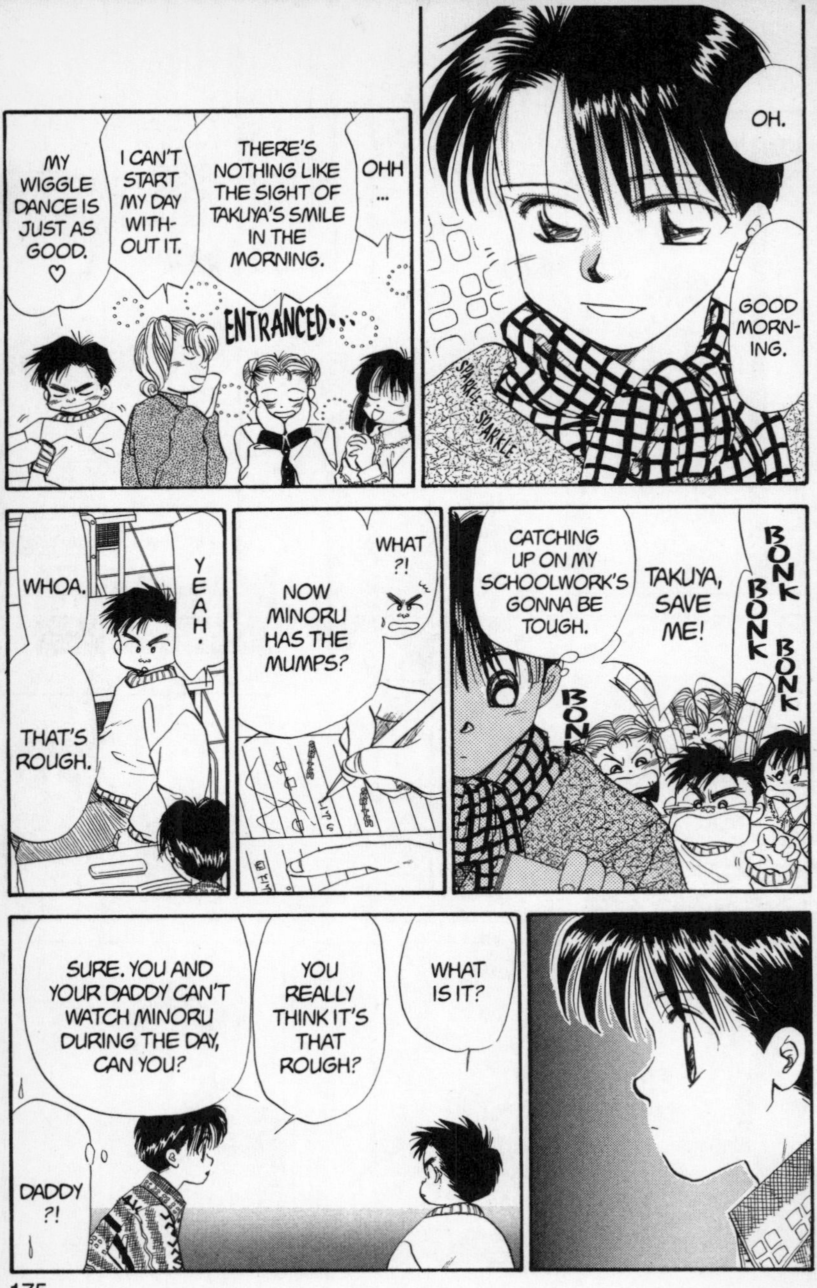
OH.
GOOD MORNING.
SPARKLE SPARKLE SPARKLE
OHH ...
THERE'S NOTHING LIKE THE SIGHT OF TAKUYA'S SMILE IN THE MORNING.
I CAN'T START MY DAY WITHOUT IT.
MY WIGGLE DANCE IS JUST AS GOOD. ♡
ENTRANCED...
BONK BONK BONK
TAKUYA, SAVE ME!
CATCHING UP ON MY SCHOOLWORK'S GONNA BE TOUGH.
BONK
WHAT ?!
NOW MINORU HAS THE MUMPS?
YEAH.
WHOA.
THAT'S ROUGH.
WHAT IS IT?
YOU REALLY THINK IT'S THAT ROUGH?
SURE. YOU AND YOUR DADDY CAN'T WATCH MINORU DURING THE DAY, CAN YOU?
DADDY ?!

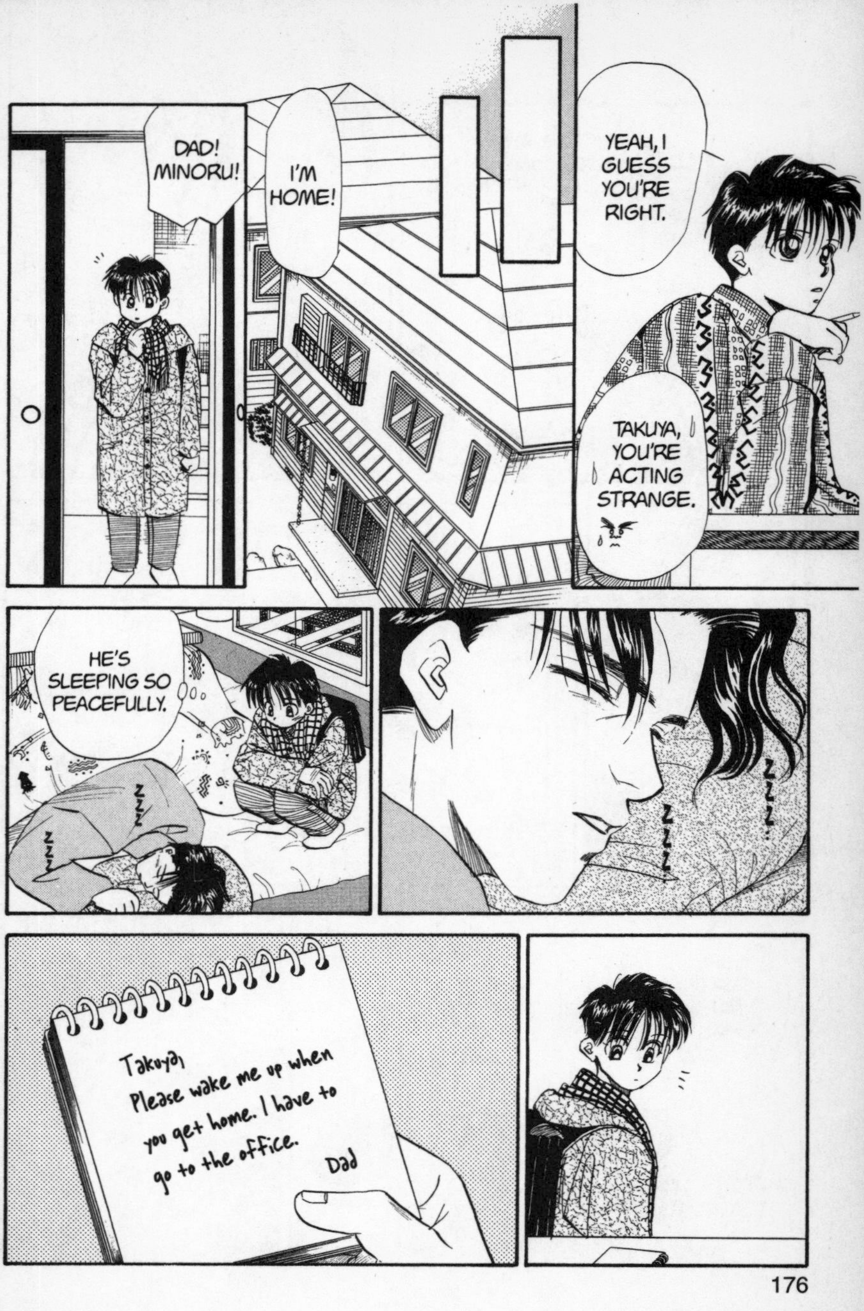
YEAH, I GUESS YOU'RE RIGHT.
TAKUYA, YOU'RE ACTING STRANGE.
I'M HOME!
DAD! MINORU!
HE'S SLEEPING SO PEACEFULLY.
Takuya,
Please wake me up when you get home. I have to go to the office.
Dad

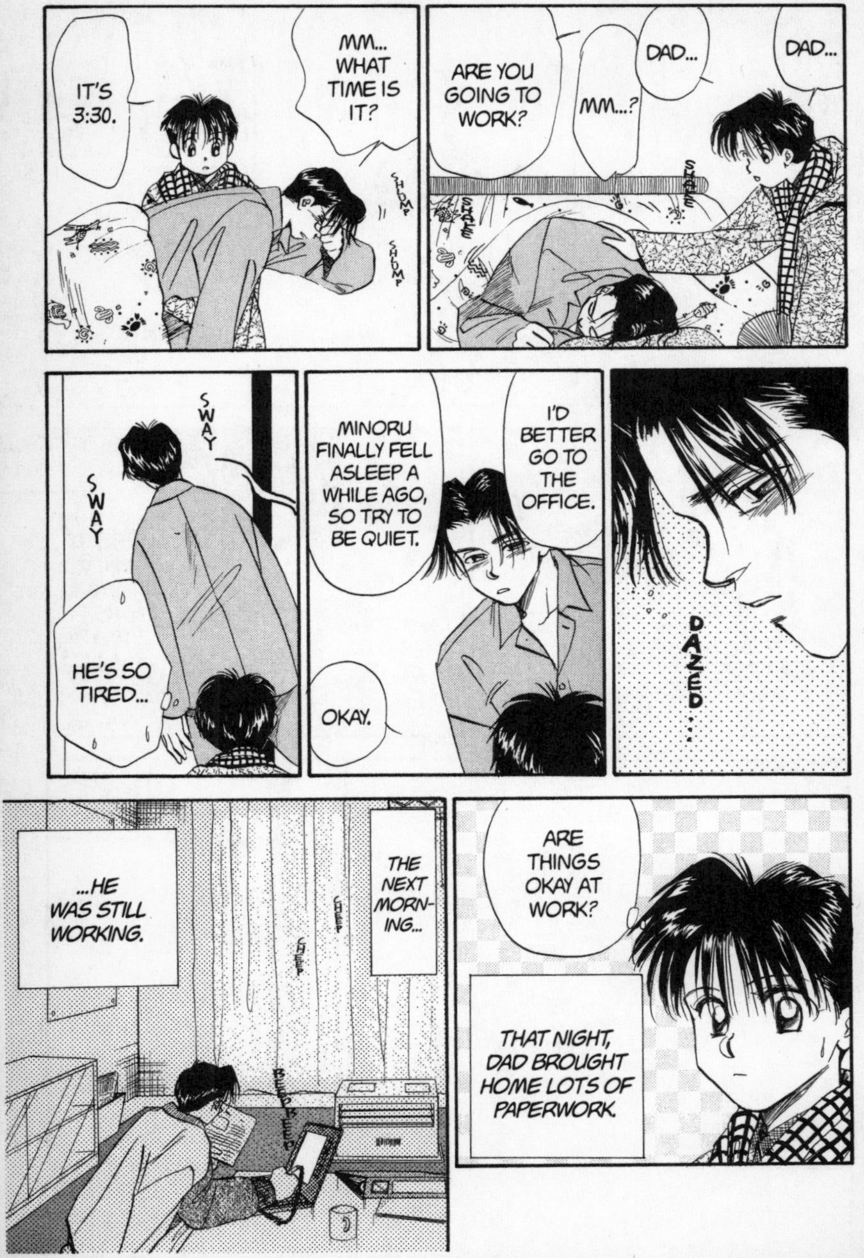
DAD...
DAD...
MM...?
ARE YOU GOING TO WORK?
SHAKE
SHAKE
MM... WHAT TIME IS IT?
IT'S 3:30.
SHUMP
SHUMP
DAZED...
I'D BETTER GO TO THE OFFICE.
MINORU FINALLY FELL ASLEEP A WHILE AGO, SO TRY TO BE QUIET.
OKAY.
SWAY
SWAY
HE'S SO TIRED...
ARE THINGS OKAY AT WORK?
THAT NIGHT, DAD BROUGHT HOME LOTS OF PAPERWORK.
THE NEXT MORN-ING...
CHEP
CHEP
...HE WAS STILL WORKING.

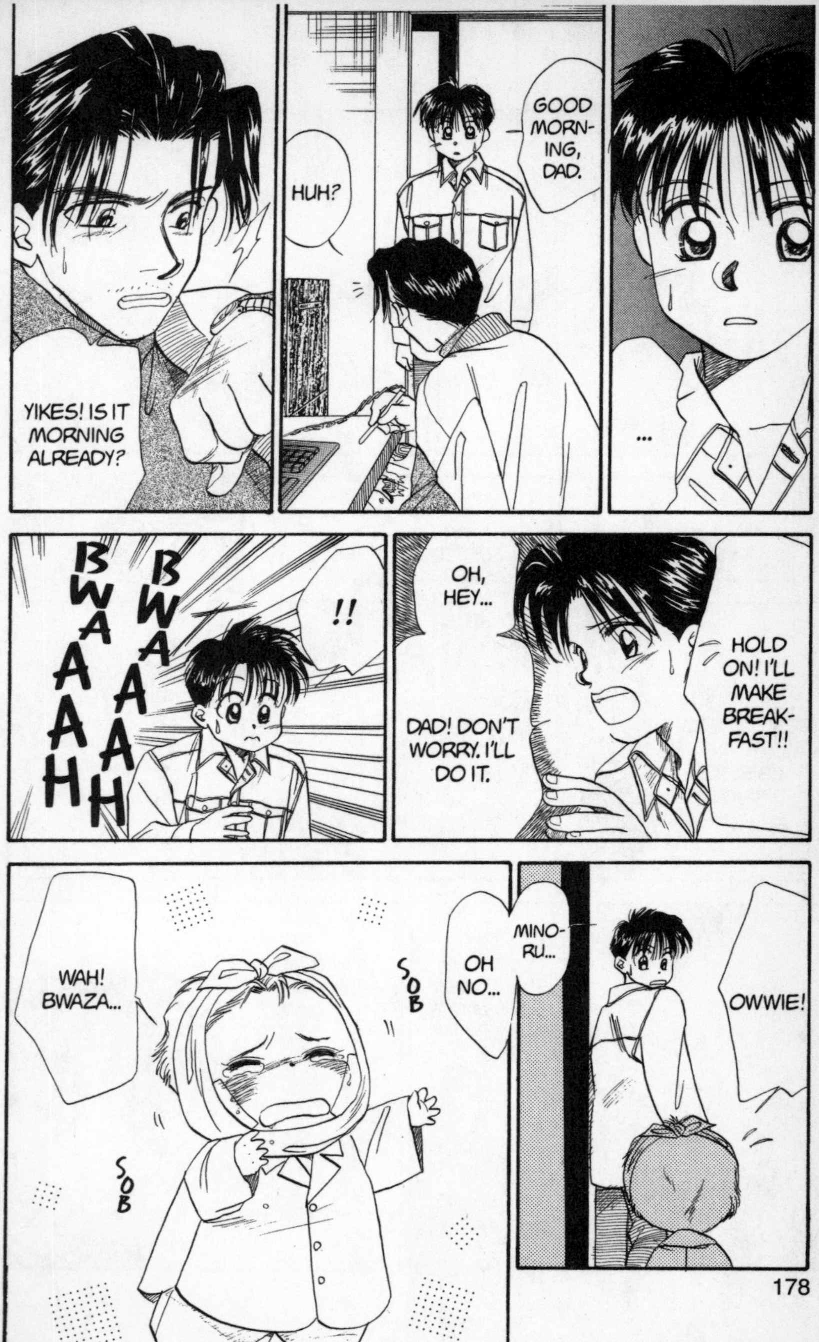
...
GOOD MORNING, DAD.
HUH?
YIKES! IS IT MORNING ALREADY?
HOLD ON! I'LL MAKE BREAKFAST!!
OH, HEY...
DAD! DON'T WORRY. I'LL DO IT.
!!
BWAAAH
BWAAAH
OWWIE!
MINORU...
OH NO...
SOB
WAH! BWAZA...
SOB

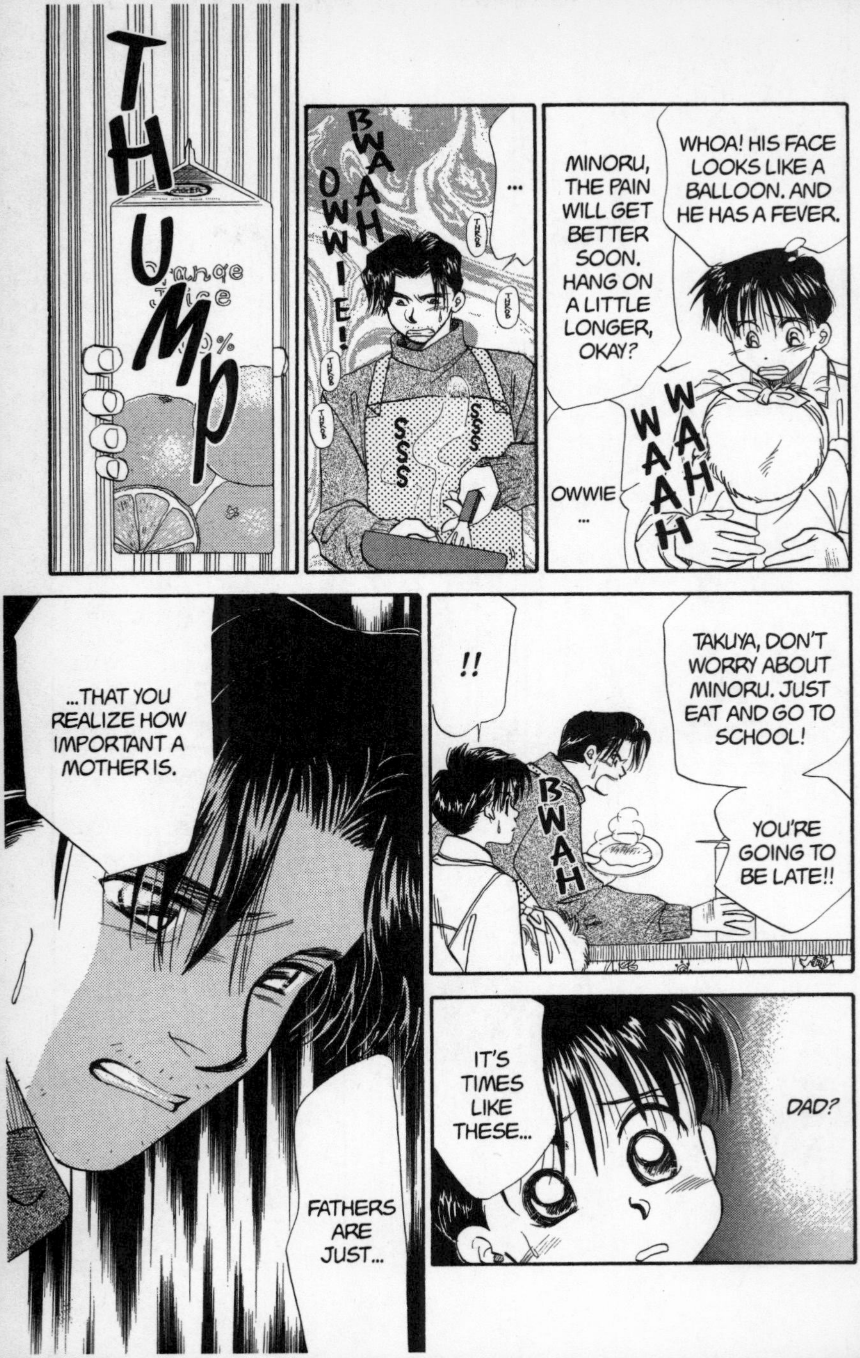
WHOA! HIS FACE LOOKS LIKE A BALLOON. AND HE HAS A FEVER.
MINORU, THE PAIN WILL GET BETTER SOON. HANG ON A LITTLE LONGER, OKAY?
WAAH
WAAH
OWWIE ...
...
BWAAH
OWWIE!
THROB
THROB
THROB
THROB
SSS
SSS
SSS
THUMP
TAKUYA, DON'T WORRY ABOUT MINORU. JUST EAT AND GO TO SCHOOL!
YOU'RE GOING TO BE LATE!!
!!
BWAH
DAD?
IT'S TIMES LIKE THESE...
FATHERS ARE JUST...
...THAT YOU REALIZE HOW IMPORTANT A MOTHER IS.

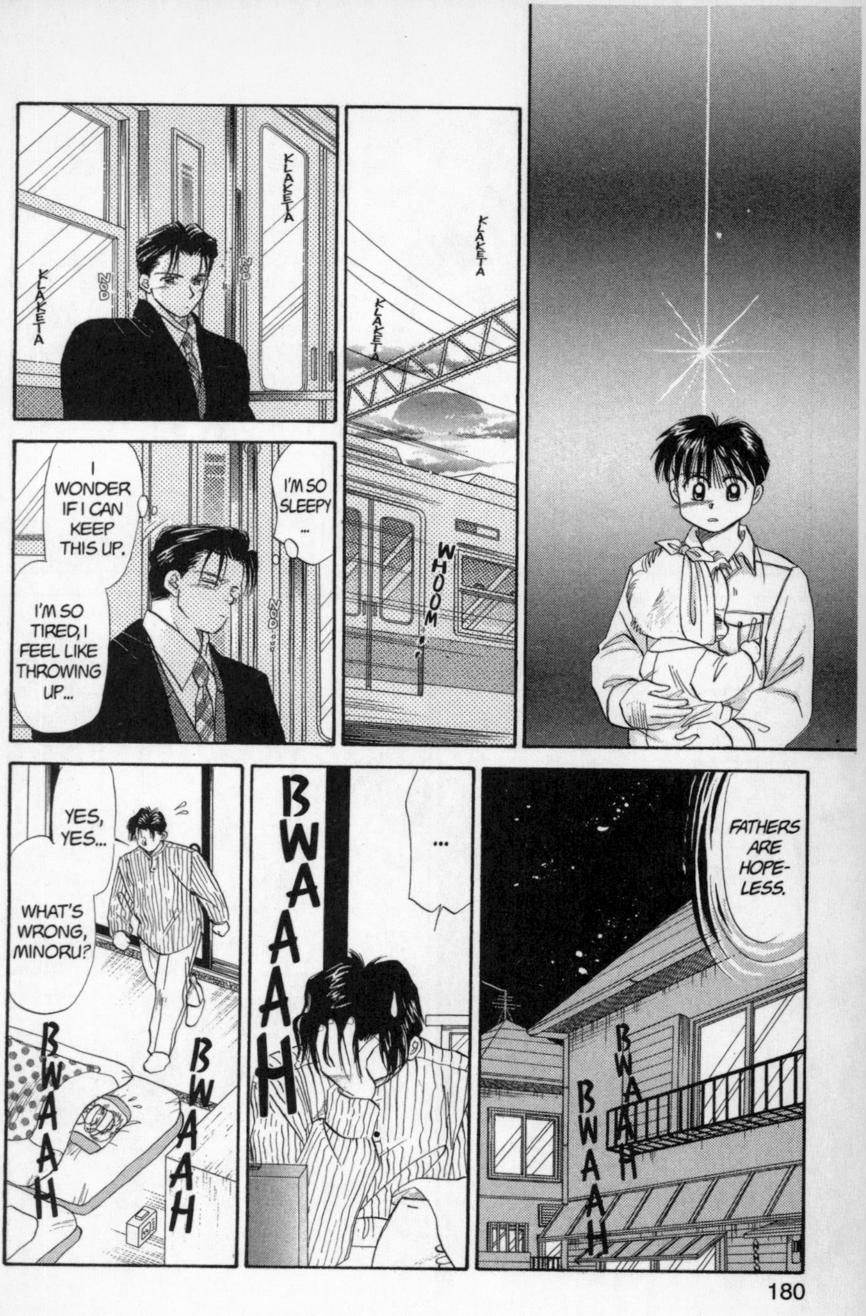
KLAKETA
KLAKETA
WHOOOM...
KLAKETA
NOD
NOD
KLAKETA
I'M SO SLEEPY...
I WONDER IF I CAN KEEP THIS UP.
I'M SO TIRED, I FEEL LIKE THROWING UP...
NOD
FATHERS ARE HOPE-LESS.
BWAAH
BWAAAH
BWAAAAH
...
YES, YES...
WHAT'S WRONG, MINORU?
BWAAAH
BWAAAH

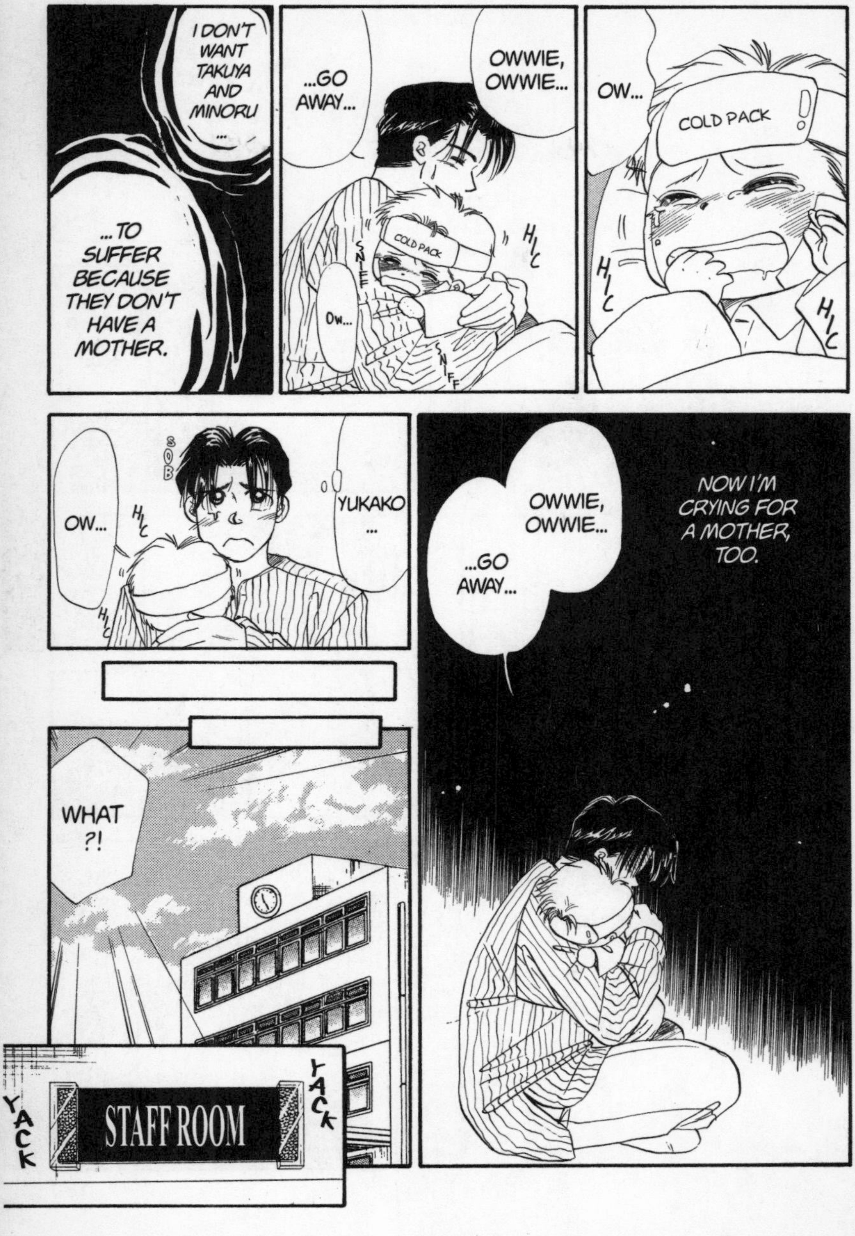
OW...
COLD PACK
HIC
HIC
OWWIE, OWWIE...
...GO AWAY...
COLD PACK
HIC
SNIFF
OW...
SNIFF
I DON'T WANT TAKUYA AND MINORU ...
...TO SUFFER BECAUSE THEY DON'T HAVE A MOTHER.
NOW I'M CRYING FOR A MOTHER, TOO.
OWWIE, OWWIE...
...GO AWAY...
YUKAKO ...
SOB
HIC
OW...
HIC
WHAT ?!
YACK
STAFF ROOM
YACK

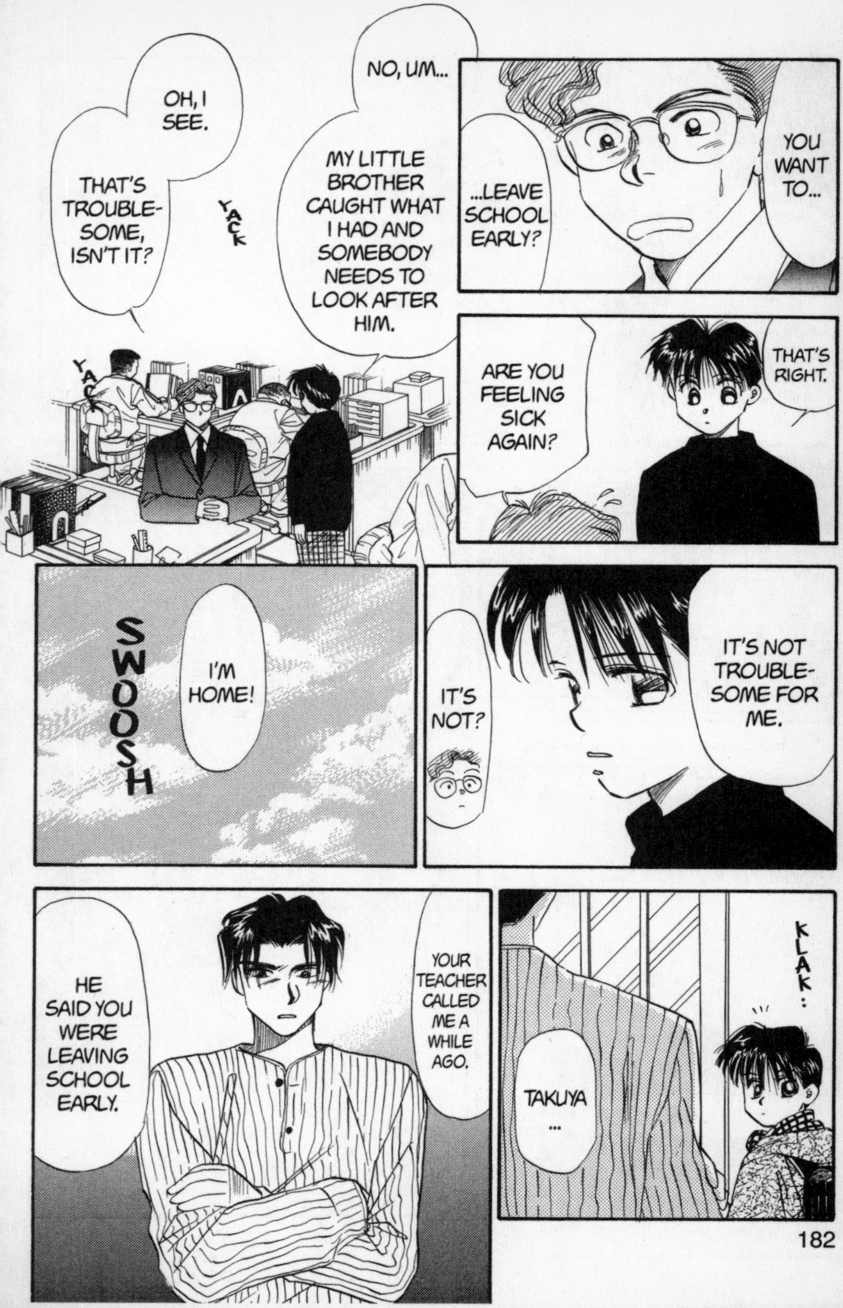
YOU WANT TO...
...LEAVE SCHOOL EARLY?
THAT'S RIGHT.
ARE YOU FEELING SICK AGAIN?
NO, UM...
MY LITTLE BROTHER CAUGHT WHAT I HAD AND SOMEBODY NEEDS TO LOOK AFTER HIM.
OH, I SEE.
THAT'S TROUBLE-SOME, ISN'T IT?
YACK
YACK
IT'S NOT TROUBLE-SOME FOR ME.
IT'S NOT?
SWOOSH
I'M HOME!
KLAK
TAKUYA ...
YOUR TEACHER CALLED ME A WHILE AGO.
HE SAID YOU WERE LEAVING SCHOOL EARLY.

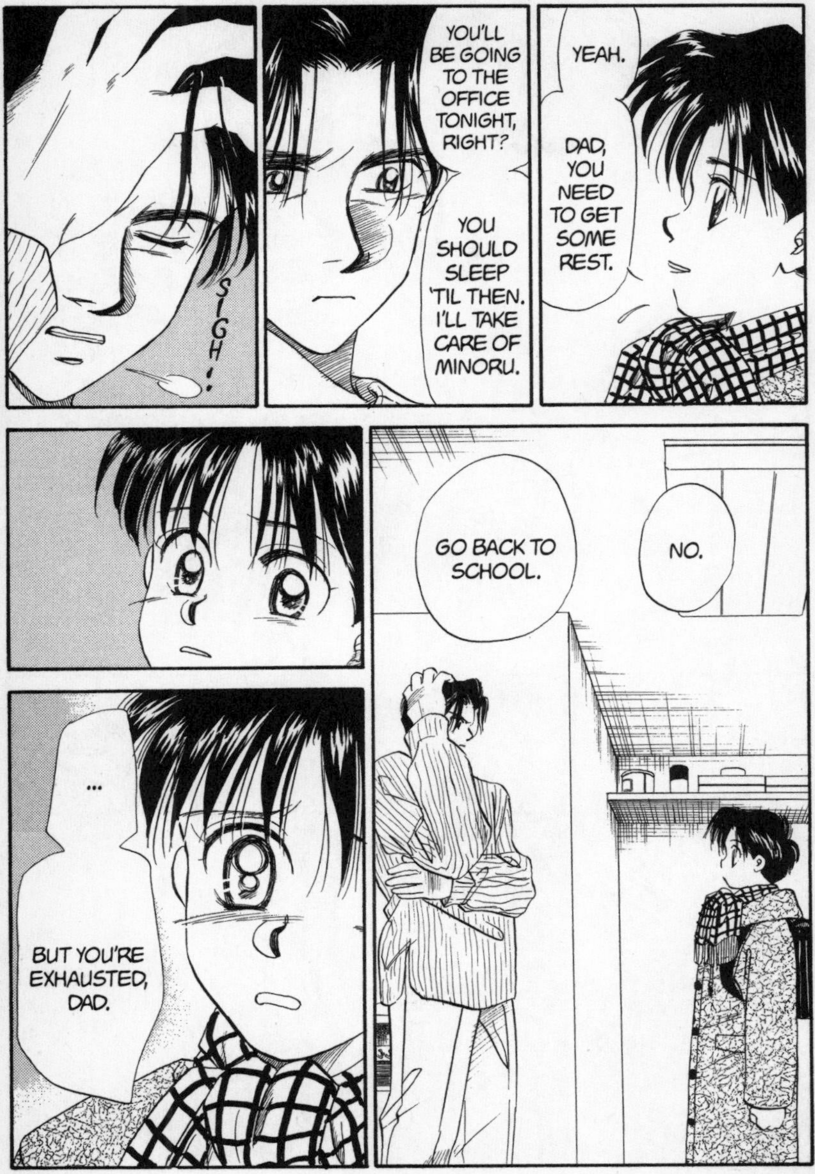
YEAH.
DAD, YOU NEED TO GET SOME REST.
YOU'LL BE GOING TO THE OFFICE TONIGHT, RIGHT?
YOU SHOULD SLEEP 'TIL THEN. I'LL TAKE CARE OF MINORU.
SIGH!
NO.
GO BACK TO SCHOOL.
...
BUT YOU'RE EXHAUSTED, DAD.

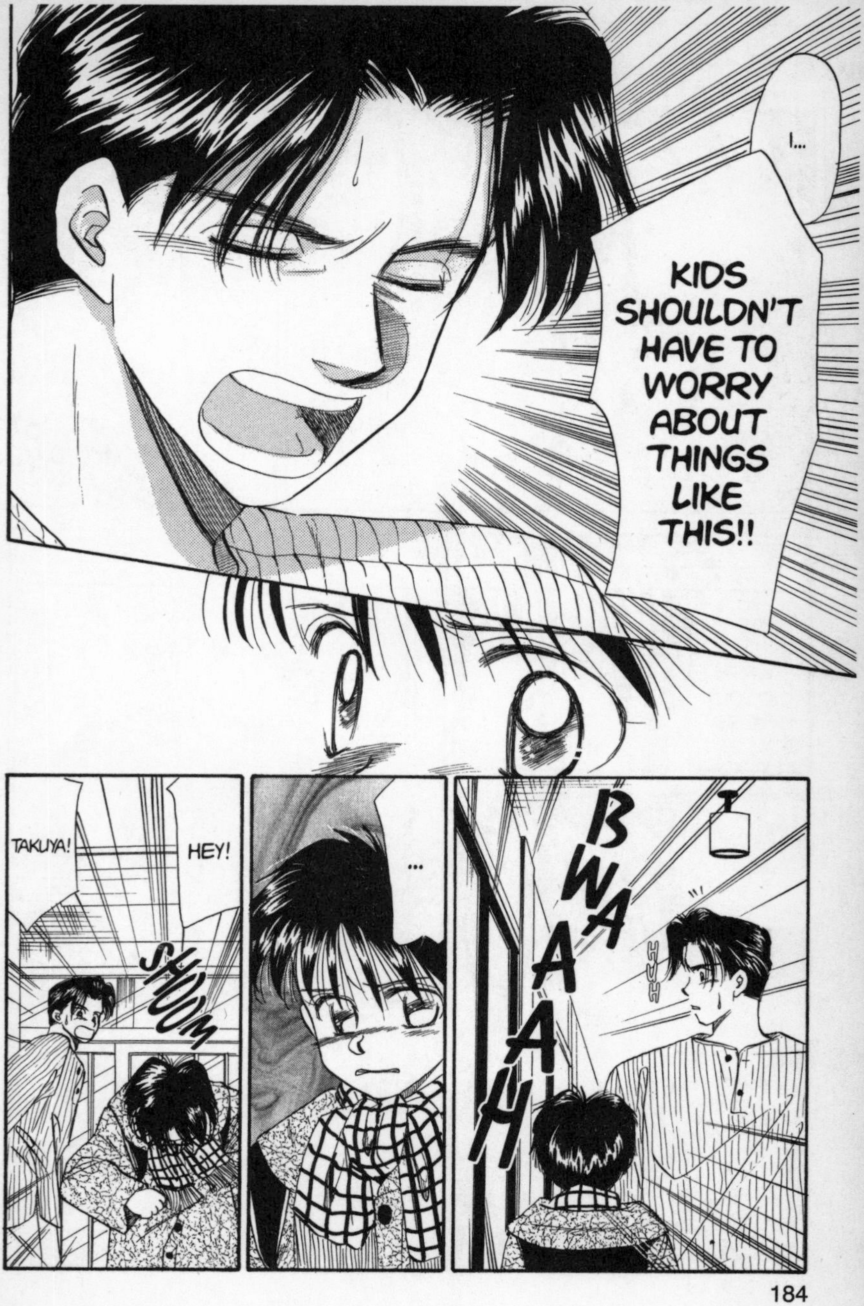
I...
KIDS SHOULDN'T HAVE TO WORRY ABOUT THINGS LIKE THIS!!
BWAAAH
HUH
...
HEY!
TAKUYA!
SHUUM

TAKUYA.

...

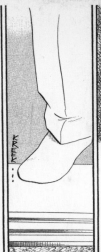

KREEK...

HIC

HIC

GRAB

...

WHY DO YOU HAVE TO DO IT ALL YOURSELF, DAD?

...?

WHY?

...I'M...

AFTER ALL...

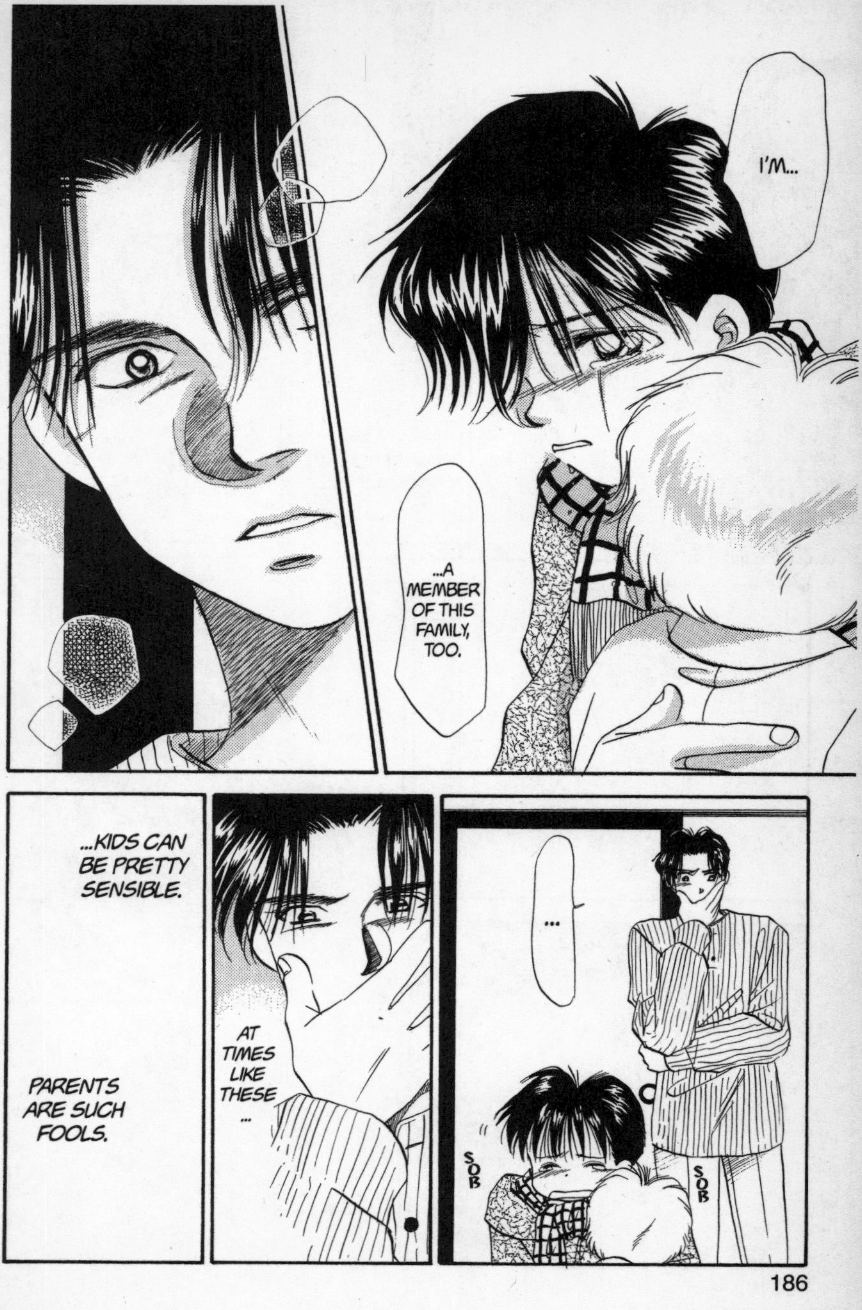
I'M...
...A MEMBER OF THIS FAMILY, TOO.
...
SOB
SOB
AT TIMES LIKE THESE ...
...KIDS CAN BE PRETTY SENSIBLE.
PARENTS ARE SUCH FOOLS.

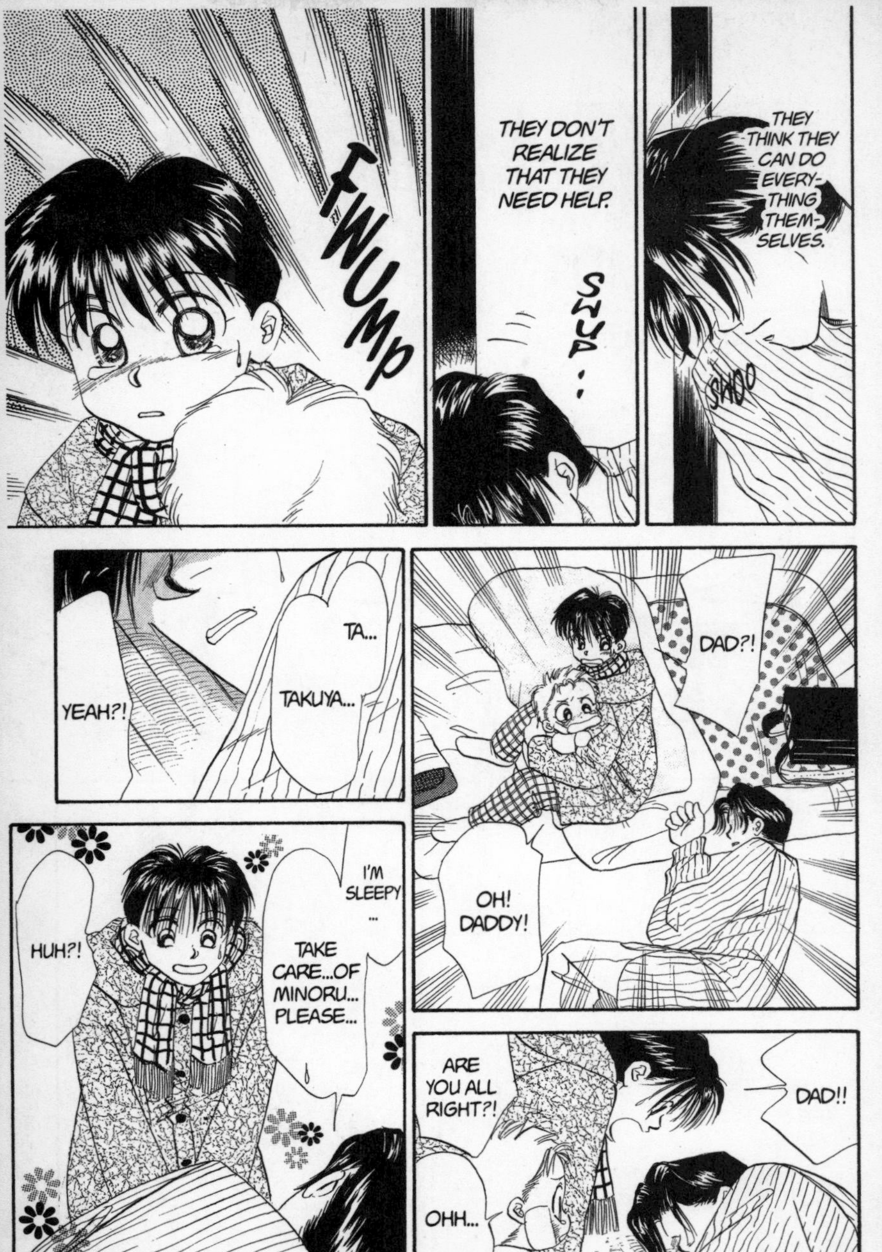
THEY THINK THEY CAN DO EVERYTHING THEMSELVES.
SHOO
THEY DON'T REALIZE THAT THEY NEED HELP.
SWUP..
FWUMP
DAD?!
OH! DADDY!
TA...
TAKUYA...
YEAH?!
DAD!!
ARE YOU ALL RIGHT?!
OHH...
I'M SLEEPY...
TAKE CARE...OF MINORU... PLEASE...
HUH?!

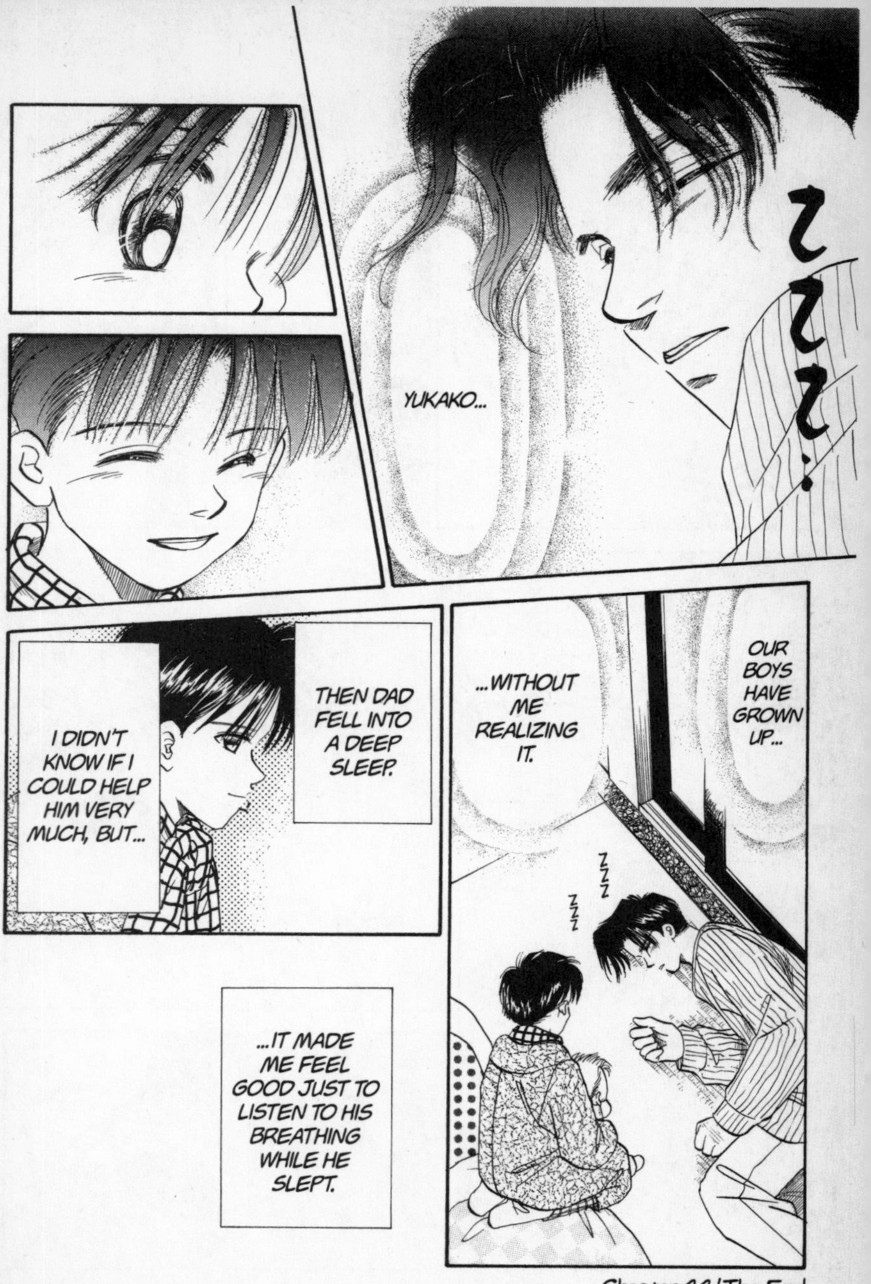
YUKAKO...
ててて
OUR BOYS HAVE GROWN UP...
...WITHOUT ME REALIZING IT.
THEN DAD FELL INTO A DEEP SLEEP.
I DIDN'T KNOW IF I COULD HELP HIM VERY MUCH, BUT...
ZZZ
ZZZ
...IT MADE ME FEEL GOOD JUST TO LISTEN TO HIS BREATHING WHILE HE SLEPT.

Chapter 44/The End

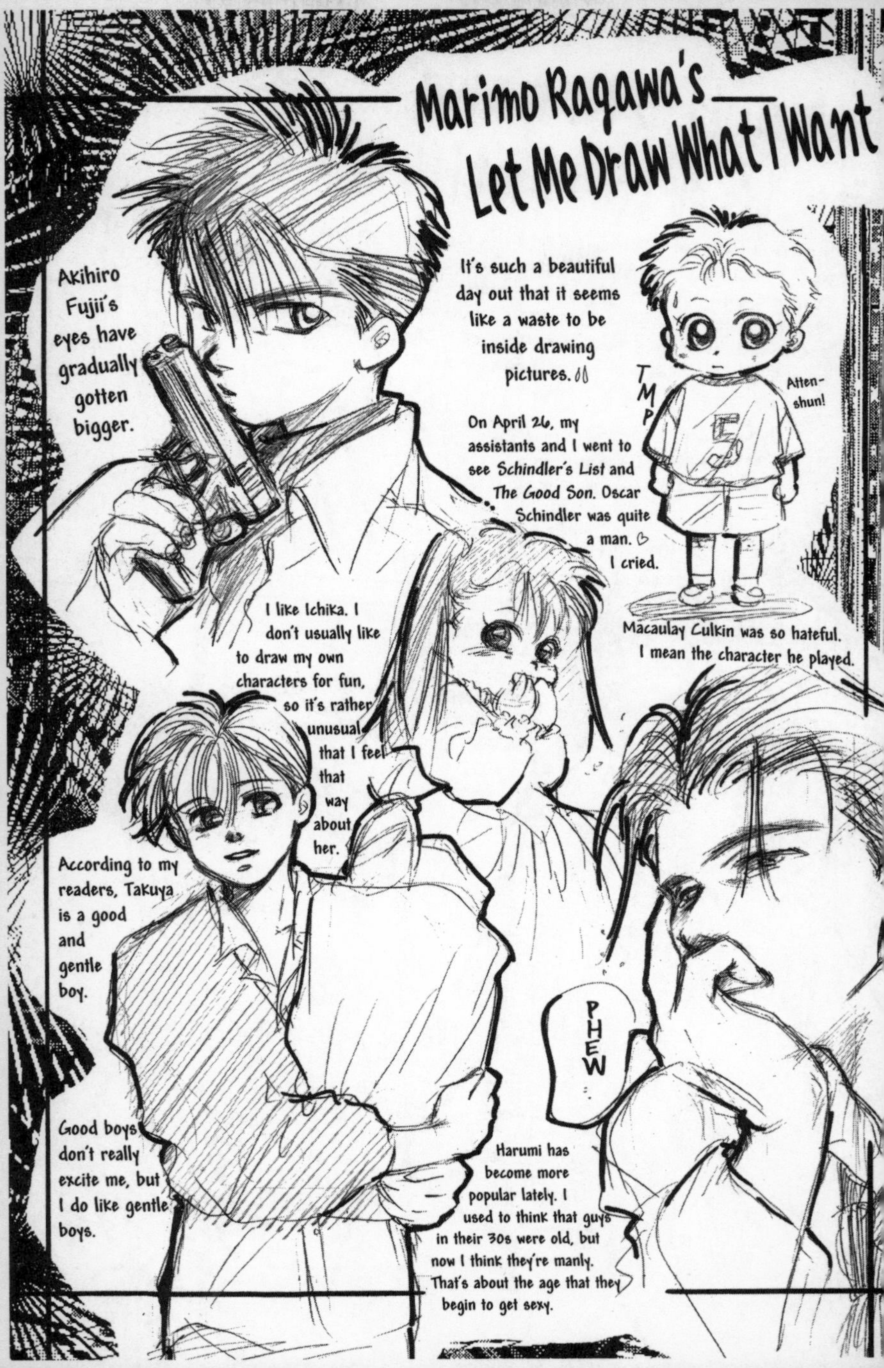
Marimo Ragawa's
Let Me Draw What I Want
It's such a beautiful day out that it seems like a waste to be inside drawing pictures.
TMP
Atten-shun!
On April 26, my assistants and I went to see Schindler's List and The Good Son. Oscar Schindler was quite a man. ♡ I cried.
Macaulay Culkin was so hateful. I mean the character he played.
Akihiro Fujii's eyes have gradually gotten bigger.
I like Ichika. I don't usually like to draw my own characters for fun, so it's rather unusual that I feel that way about her.
According to my readers, Takuya is a good and gentle boy.
PHEW
Harumi has become more popular lately. I used to think that guys in their 30s were old, but now I think they're manly. That's about the age that they begin to get sexy.
Good boys don't really excite me, but I do like gentle boys.

Marimo Ragawa's Let Me Draw What I Want

If you're wondering what this is, it's a postscript. (So was the previous page.) When I was in high school, I enjoyed classical literature and the Chinese classics. I never thought they were difficult. On the contrary, when it came to Chinese poetry, I could read a poem once and have it memorized. Sometimes I thought I must've lived in China in a past life!! But that's silly. Now I can't remember any of the Chinese poems I learned back then.

In those days, I attempted to read *The Tale of Genji*, but it was exhausting. I tossed the book aside very quickly.

All the characters I draw have round faces, don't they? I have a round face, too. Why don't you finish the drawings in pen, you ask? It's too much trouble. Anyway, aren't they more charming like this? Ha ha ha!

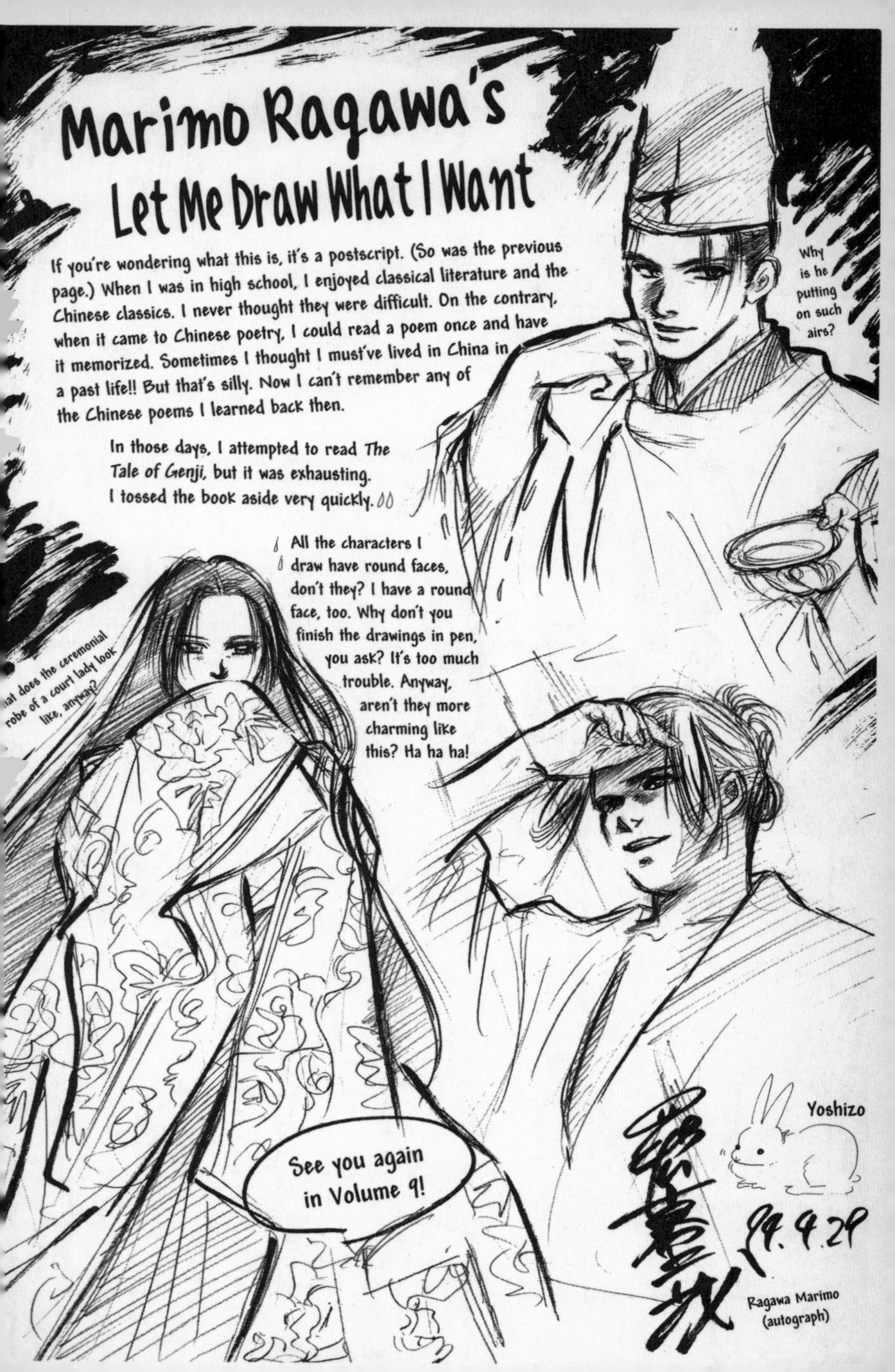
Why is he putting on such airs?
at does the ceremonial robe of a court lady look like, anyway?
See you again in Volume 9!
Yoshizo
97.4.29
Ragawa Marimo (autograph)

BABY & Me

Creator: Marimo Ragawa

SBM Title: *Baby & Me*

Date of Birth: September 21

Blood Type: B

Major Works: *Time Limit,
Baby & Me, N.Y. N.Y.,* and
Shanimuni-Go (Desperately—Go)

Marimo Ragawa first started submitting manga to a comic magazine when she was 12 years old. She kept up her submissions for four years, but to no avail. She decided to submit her work to the magazine *Hana to Yume*, where she received Top Prize in the Monthly Manga Contest as well as an honorable mention (Kasaku) in the magazine's Big Challenge contest. Her first manga was titled *Time Limit. Baby & Me* was honored with a Shogakukan Manga Award in 1995 and was spun off into an anime.

Ragawa's work showcases some very cute and expressive line work along with an incredible ability to depict complex emotions and relationships. Some of her other works include *N.Y. N.Y.* and the tennis manga *Shanimuni-Go*.

Ragawa has two brothers and two sisters.

BABY & ME, Vol. 8
The Shojo Beat Manga Edition

STORY & ART BY
MARIMO RAGAWA

English Adaptation/Lance Caselman
Translation/JN Productions
Touch-up Art & Lettering/Mark Griffin
Design/Yuki Ameda
Editors/Pancha Diaz and Shaenon K. Garrity

Editor in Chief, Books/Alvin Lu
Editor in Chief, Magazines/Marc Weidenbaum
VP of Publishing Licensing/Rika Inouye
VP of Sales/Gonzalo Ferreyra
Sr. VP of Marketing/Liza Coppola
Publisher/Hyoe Narita

Printed in Canada

Published by VIZ Media, LLC
P.O. Box 77010
San Francisco, CA 94107

Shojo Beat Manga Edition
10 9 8 7 6 5 4 3 2 1
First printing, June 2008

store.viz.com

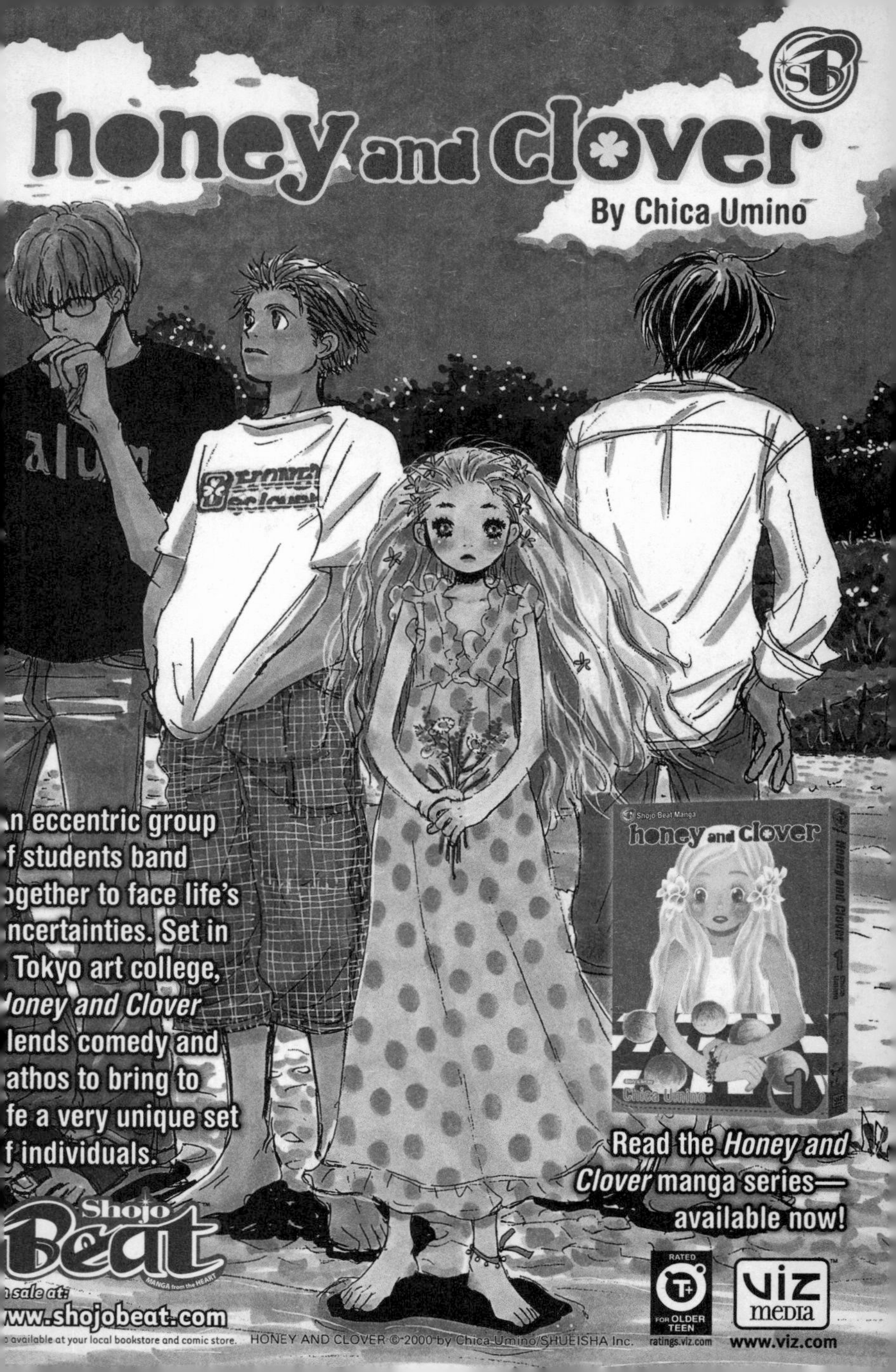

honey and clover
By Chica Umino
n eccentric group
f students band
ogether to face life's
ncertainties. Set in
Tokyo art college,
Honey and Clover
lends comedy and
athos to bring to
fe a very unique set
f individuals.
Shojo Beat Manga
honey and clover
Chica Umino
1
Read the Honey and Clover manga series—available now!
Shojo Beat
MANGA from the HEART
n sale at:
ww.shojobeat.com
available at your local bookstore and comic store.
HONEY AND CLOVER © 2000 by Chica Umino/SHUEISHA Inc.
RATED T+ FOR OLDER TEEN
ratings.viz.com
VIZ media
www.viz.com

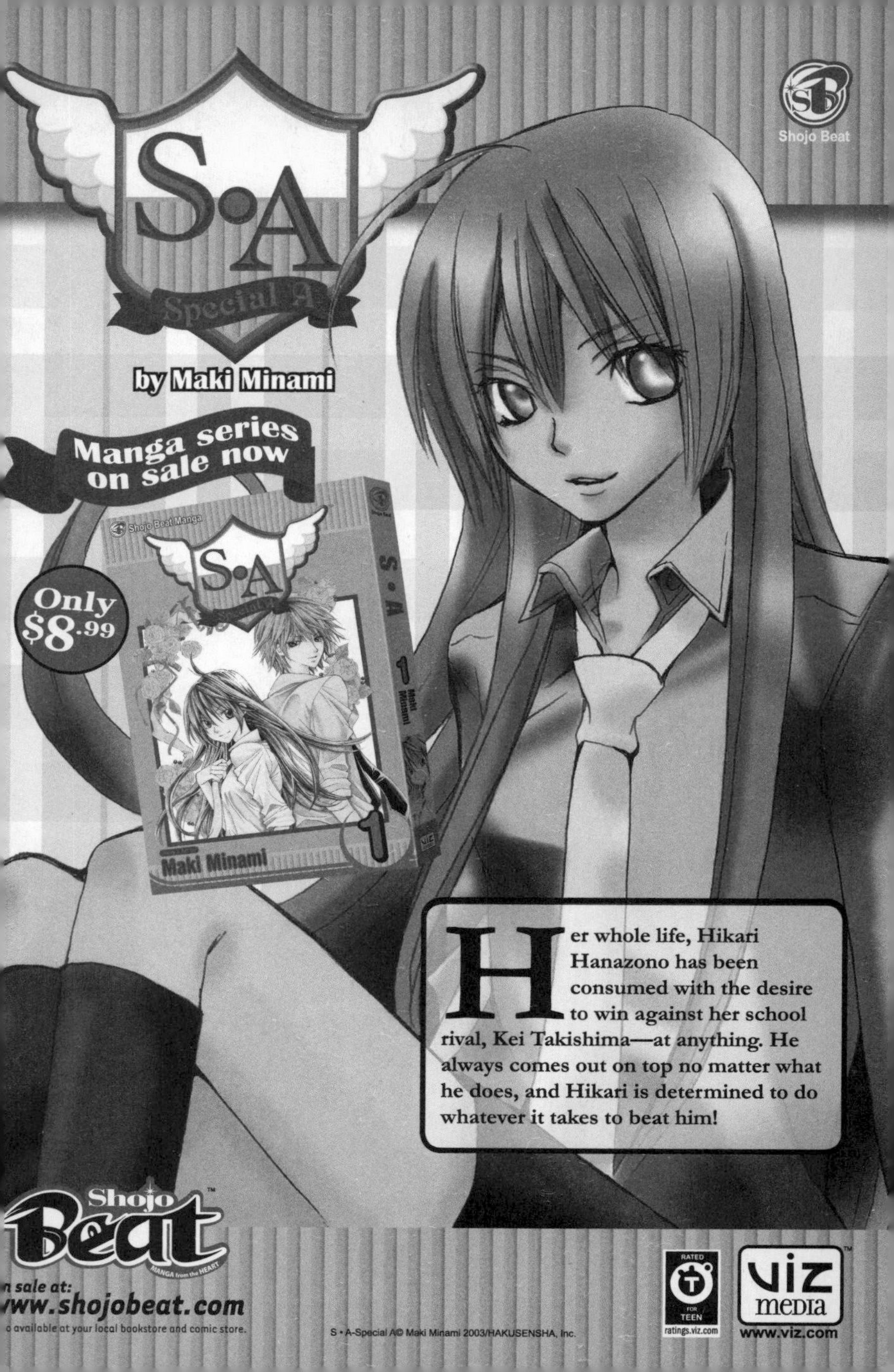
Shojo Beat
S·A
Special A
by Maki Minami
Manga series on sale now
Only $8.99
Shojo Beat Manga
S·A
1
Maki Minami
Her whole life, Hikari Hanazono has been consumed with the desire to win against her school rival, Kei Takishima—at anything. He always comes out on top no matter what he does, and Hikari is determined to do whatever it takes to beat him!
Shojo Beat
MANGA from the HEART
n sale at:
ww.shojobeat.com
o available at your local bookstore and comic store.
S • A-Special A© Maki Minami 2003/HAKUSENSHA, Inc.
RATED T FOR TEEN
ratings.viz.com
VIZ MEDIA
www.viz.com

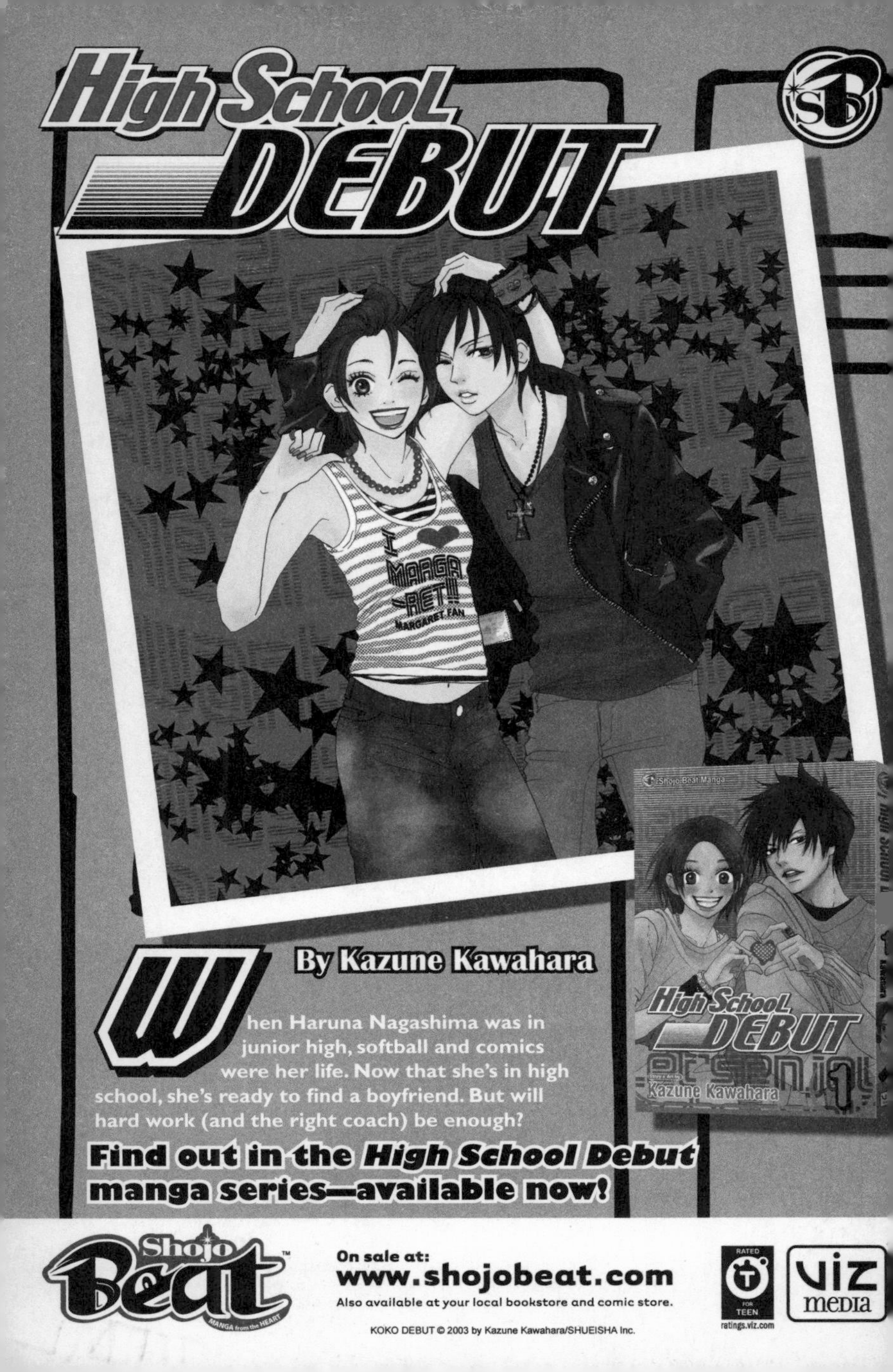

Tell us what ~~you think~~
about Shojo Beat Manga!

Our survey is now
available online. Go to:
shojobeat.com/mangasurvey

Help us make our
product offerings
better!